Myths and Symbols

MYTHS AND SYMBOLS

STUDIES IN HONOR OF MIRCEA ELIADE

EDITED BY

Joseph M. Kitagawa AND *Charles H. Long*

WITH THE COLLABORATION OF

Jerald C. Brauer AND *Marshall G. S. Hodgson*

THE UNIVERSITY OF CHICAGO PRESS

CHICAGO AND LONDON

International Standard Book Number: 0-226-43829-5
Library of Congress Catalog Card Number: 69-12132
The University of Chicago Press, Chicago 60637
The University of Chicago Press, Ltd., London
 Published 1969
Midway reprint 1982
Printed in the United States of America

PRE

To Mircea and Christinel Eliade

FOREWORD

Our colleague, Mircea Eliade, has led an active career for over four decades as a historian of religions, orientalist, and writer on both shores of the Atlantic. When we learned that he was celebrating his sixtieth birthday on March 9, 1967, we asked some of his friends to contribute essays on the subject of myths and symbols, which is a central motif of Professor Eliade's scholarly concern. We also invited a few literary figures to delineate the significance of his creative writing. It was admittedly no easy task for the Editorial Committee to limit the number of contributors because of his wide association among scholars and writers of various continents. If not for the limitation of space, we would have extended invitations to many others. Also, several among those who had intended to participate in this endeavor have been unable to do so owing to illness or other unavoidable reasons.

After full consideration of many factors, we have decided to publish this volume in English rather than in a multilingual edition, although we realize that any translation, however well done, does not convey the full meaning of the original text. The task of translation has also necessitated a delay in publication, but we trust that the present volume will reach a wider reading public than it would have otherwise.

It is our pleasant duty to thank all the contributors who have made this volume not only a meaningful tribute to Professor Eliade but also, it is hoped, a significant contribution to scholarship. It must be mentioned in this connection that we did not deem it necessary to provide biographical data on the contributors, who are well known in their respective fields. We are also grateful for the financial and moral support given by the Divinity School and the Committee on Social Thought of the University of Chicago. Professor Alan L. Miller and Mr. Lowell W. Bloss have carried out the painstaking editorial responsibility for the preparation of the manuscript. German articles were translated by Mrs. Benjamin C. Ray, Mr. Karl W. Luckert, Mr. and Mrs. Yasuharu Timothy Hosoi, and Professor Nancy E. Auer (now Mrs. Arthur E. Falk); French articles by Professor Harry B. Partin, Mr. Frederick Brown, and Mr. William Olmsted; Italian articles by Mr. Nicholas Pogany; and Spanish articles by Professor Charles S. J. White. We have also received various kinds of assistance from Professors Gösta W. Ahlström and George A. Weckman, and Messrs. Manabu Waida and Georges Tissot, as well as from the secretarial staff of the Divinity School of the University of Chicago.

We have included a brief curriculum vitae and bibliography of Mircea Eliade at the end of the book. A more complete bibliography, including his literary, critical, and journalistic writings in Romanian, Portuguese, and French (1932–67), his youthful production in Romanian (1921–28), and his reviews of writings of orientalists, historians of religions, and philosophers, will be published in the near future. For the present, the above may be sufficient to indicate the scope and depth of Professor Eliade's scholarly and literary contributions. Equally important, perhaps, is the fact that both he and Mrs. Eliade have touched the hearts of many with their genuine kindness and graciousness. We hope and trust that he will have many more years to continue his distinguished scholarly endeavor.

JERALD C. BRAUER
MARSHALL G. S. HODGSON†
JOSEPH M. KITAGAWA
CHARLES H. LONG
(Editorial Committee)

† We are indeed sorry that Marshall G. S. Hodgson, Chairman of the Committee on Social Thought and Professor of History at the University of Chicago, passed away on June 10, 1968.

CONTENTS

Foreword

I
PHENOMENOLOGICAL AND THEORETICAL . . .

II
HISTORICAL . . .

PHENOMENOLOGICAL AND THEORETICAL . . .

III

LITERARY . . .

I

PHENOMENOLOGICAL AND THEORETICAL . . .

NOMINA NUMINA

GIUSEPPE TUCCI

There is no doubt that a continuous growth of the pantheon has taken place in Buddhism. In the beginning gods were outsiders and Buddha himself was a master, a guide, a teacher—not a god. The gods of the people to whom the Buddhist preachers were addressing themselves were not admitted to worship, but survived as a concession to the belief of the masses; they were to be exorcised more than adored. They were *laukika*, belonging to the common world, and it was difficult even for the Buddhist masters to dispose of them abruptly. As *grāmadevatā*, as *bhūmi-pati*, as *yakṣa*, they still represented some ambiguous presences with which people had to deal in everyday life; in fact, they were supposed to be ambivalent: propitious when propitiated, dangerous when offended. Some belonged to the background of Indian religion like Indra and Brahmā, others to non-Aryan cultures or to the infinite world of local deities; the latter were therefore subject to unlimited variations. With the passage of time, the invasion of local cults, often representing very old heritages peculiar to the different parts of India, became wider and deeper until it reached its acme during the tantric period and entered the literature of Buddhism.

But there is another process which is worthy of notice, namely, the transformation into gods of *vidyā* or *dhāraṇī* formulas and moments of worship: names and abstractions became gods. The reason for this is to be found in the ever-increasing tendency in Buddhism to visualize in meditation the different aspects of the doctrine: it was not only necessary to master the teaching and to live up to it, but to transform it from a rational possession into an emotional one, to see its moments as distinct *ālambanas* (supports) of the complicated progress of the *excessus* from time to Timeless. The *ālambana* in such a process leads to a vision, as when the man initiated in a tantric school was supposed to see the god on whom he was meditating appearing from the phoneme representing the god's mystic essence visualized in the void or in the center of his heart; or, when evoking the Tathāgatas from infinite space, he imagined that they conferred the baptism upon him. The same happened when he was supposed to offer worship to them. The worship of these Tathāgatas, as well as the offering made to the infinite beings as mentioned by Sāntideva in his *Bodhicaryāvatāra*, was purely mental, but it had to be visualized—each of its parts had to be evoked in distinct forms.

This is clear in the cycle of the *pūjādevatā*, the worship deities, who are nothing but personifications of the different *upacāra* used in Hindu as well as in Buddhist worship. Acts or instruments of worship were given a form, an iconography: they wear their distinctive and appropriate symbols and only thus may they enter a very complex visualizing process which constitutes the ecstatic situation through which the meditating person is supposed to pass: he is not rationally reflecting on them, but he *sees* them. To give only one instance, in the cycle of Śaṃvara, according to Luipā, we have different *pūjādevatā* (Tibetan: *mc'od pai lha mo*), for example, flower, *puṣpā*; lamp, *dīpā*; incense, *dhūpā*; perfume, *gandhā*; offering of eatables, *naivedyā*.

But there are also other deities that correspond to instruments which are necessary complements of a *pūjā*, an act of worship: *viṇā*, *vaṃsā*, the flute; *mṛdangā*, drum; *murajā*, large drum. This of course has been necessitated by the fact that the *maṇḍala* in which a peculiar deity is meditated upon must be, as I said, visualized in its full complexity: the different aspects and moments of the *pūjā* as well as the worshiping process dilate themselves in an unending phantasmagoria in which the worshiper participates with a full experience of his entire being in the rapture of the meditative process. In such a situation the scheme of the worship is sublimized in a glory of divine forms.

When the meditating person wants to express the *ecstasis* of higher visions, he needs symbols to support it: the instruments or means or situations are changed into deities with a peculiar form because only that which is seen has the appearance of reality, relative as it may be, and is therefore able to act emotionally and psychologically upon us. The instruments of the *pūjā* are transformed into deities because in a divine world nothing but divine forms can appear: even emotional states are given a form and enter the fictitious pantheon which is composed of different choruses. Thus we have a goddess symbolizing the ecstatic smile, *hāsyā*; another the praise to the deity, *gītā*; and another the divine dance in honor of the same, *nṛtyā*. The ingredients of the *pūjā*, as *pūjā devatā* (*mc'od pai lha mo*), are given an adequate iconography and enter the scheme of the paradises; they are at the same time the emanation or projection of a peculiar state of concentration of the worshiper, who can himself gradually ascend to these paradises where everything must have a form to be visualized because visualization is consubstantiation.

The process of deification of peculiar aspects of meditation or even of certain moments of the life of Buddha can be easily extended: before becoming a god, Mahāshāmaprāpta was a moment of the process of meditation to which dogma (especially that of the *Prajñā*) often refers; Avalokiteśvara, who was to become one of the most important deities of the Buddhist pantheon, is nothing other than the divinization of the *avalokita* or *avalokana*, the inspection which the Bodhisattva made while in the Tuṣita-heaven to see where he could descend to earth.[1] This *avalokita* was then transformed into the merciful look of his eyes upon the miseries of the world and in the end assumed the aspect of the most compassionate god ready to listen to the entreaties and prayers of the devotees. The same may be said of Hevajra, one of the most famous tantric cycles in India and in Tibet, especially among the Sa skya pa. The deity is evidently a deification of a formula of invocation, *he vajra* (*oh vajra*); since the *vajra* is the symbol of nonexistentiality beyond time and space, it was easy to extol it and to transpose it into another symbol, a representation which could be taken as a support of concentration. The resulting name was again divided into its two component parts: *he* = compassion = *karuṇā* = *upāya*, and *vajra* = wisdom = *prajñā*. In this way the coherence of the coefficients of salvation (Tibetan: *zuṅ ạjug*) was again asserted.[2] The equivalence of Hevajra, Heruka, Śaṃ-

[1] See G. Tucci, "A propos the Avalokiteśvara in Buddhist Notes," *Mélanges Chinois et Bouddhiques*, 9 (1951): 174 ff.

[2] D. L. Snellgrove, *The Hevajra Tantra* (London and New York, 1959), part 2, p. 2; part 1, pp. 23–24.

vara, Akṣokhya, and Vajradhātu is evident; fundamentally they are all modulations of Akṣobhya.

The same can be said concerning the *vidyās*, or *dhāraṇi*, essentially formulas which by a slow process assumed an aspect (cf. *vidyāpurusa* of the *Guhyasamāja*) and were then given a place in the Mahāyāna pantheon; for example, *mahāmāyūrī vidyā*, the formula used during the exorcism against snakes and then transformed into a deity, came to have its own attributes. The same can be said of many other *vidyās* or *dhāraṇī* – for example, all those of the *pañcarakṣā*. Thus, in the *Mahāsannipātaratnaketusūtra*, a *dhāraṇī* is already said to be *sarva-maraviṣayabalapramardana*, and another one which has been equally revealed is called *aparājitā*; but they are at the same time a *rakṣā*, a protection to him who knows their inner meaning.[3] In all cases local deities belonging to the complex and age-old traditional religious world of the lower strata of population either lent them a shape or else contamination took place with other already iconographically defined entities.

In the same way, in the apotheosis which sublimates the *mystes*, when the Tathāgatas flock from the different quarters of space to confer the *abhiṣeka* (baptism) upon the meditating person, the components of the human illusory person (the five *skandhas*) are transformed into their adamantine types as feminine deities, and thus we have the cycle of *rūpa-vajrā* (form), *śabda-vajrā* (sound), *gandha-vajrā* (smell), *rasa-vajrā* (taste), and *sparśa-vajrā* (touch). In this case also concepts which had been elaborated by dogmatics and given no consistency, since they belong to the illusory appearance of time and space, assume a form and receive an iconographic precision and definition. I could multiply the examples, but the basis of this endless proliferation of gods and goddesses with their own peculiar forms and attributes is the need felt during the process of meditation, the *sādhana*, to have a precise support upon which one can concentrate so that a mere notion or situation, through the mediation of certain symbols, might evoke a vivid representation. The aim to be attained is a living experience of the apotheosis that can give the meditating person the certainty of his elevation; visualization is the testimony that he has ascended to a superior *kṣetra* (Buddhafield), and that in this very life he is enjoying, be it only for a short time, the blessing of the

[3] *Mahāsannipātaratnaketusūtra*, ed. N. Dutt (Calcutta, 1959), pp. 120, 135.

result or fruit to which his path is leading – not the ultimate fruit beyond any form, but the fruit of cofruition (*saṃbhoga*) as a preliminary necessary stage to the supreme unqualified identity.

On the other hand, when Mahāyāna introduced the idea of the infinity of *Buddhakṣetra* (Buddhafields or worlds), the texts imagined new names for the Tathāgatas preaching in each of them, and thus arose those litanies of the "thousand names of Buddhas" who are fictitious creations. The infinity of those Buddhaworlds allowed the possibility of imagining endless new Buddhas presiding in each of them, but they are mere creations of the authors of the different books which mention them. In spite of that, some of them acquired a certain consistency because, for example, they were introduced into the list of the thirty-five gods invoked during the confession.

Thus Buddhism is always open to a never-ceasing introduction of new gods who have no relation at all to any presences believed to exist in the actual experience of people, but are rather the transfiguration into supposed entities of mere names. In spite of this, some were introduced into the configuration of the actual worship because they became essential parts of the meditative process; others remained pure inventions in a religion which believed in the omnipresence of its preaching in a boundless and timeless universe.

THE SUPERHUMAN PERSONALITY OF BUDDHA AND ITS SYMBOLISM IN THE MAHĀPARINIRVĀṆASŪTRA *OF THE DHARMAGUPTAKA*

ANDRE BAREAU

In passing through the varied multitude of ancient canonical Buddhist texts constituting the *Tripitaka* of diverse schools, we shall see the evolution of the Buddha's personality as conceived by his followers in the first five centuries following the Parinirvāṇa. The *Mahāparinirvāṇasūtra* is certainly one of the most interesting works in this regard. It has been preserved for us in six different versions—one in Pali, that of the Theravādin; one in Sanskrit, that of the Mūlasarvāstivādin; and four in Chinese translation, of which one alone has disclosed the mystery of its origin: it is included in the Chinese *Dirghāgama* or *Tch'ang a-han king*,[1] which belongs, as does the collection itself, to the Dharmaguptaka.[2] This last version is particularly rich in all sorts of information on the conception of Buddha's personality, and it is therefore from this that we shall draw the elements of what concerns us here.

[1] *Taishō Shinshū Daizōkyō* (newly revised *Tripitaka* of the Taisho era), ed. Junjirō Takakusu *et al.*, 100 vols. (Tokyo, 1924–32), vol. 1, pp. 11a–30b.

[2] André Bareau, "L'origine du Dirgha-āgama traduit en chinois par Buddhayaśas," in *Essays Offered to G. H. Luce in Honour of His Seventy-fifth Birthday*, 2 vols. (Ascona, 1966), vol. 1, pp. 49–58.

If, in the greatest part of the tale, the Beatific is depicted as a real man, submitting to most of the vicissitudes inherent in the human condition and behaving as a human being, he appears in rather numerous and especially important passages as a superman, as a divine personage – or, better yet, as a being simultaneously superior to gods and men, endowed with extraordinary powers. It is this aspect alone which will here retain our attention; we shall study it while examining successively the superhuman character of Buddha, his character both divine and superdivine, the attributes which are loaned him, and, finally, the comparisons by means of which past devotees attempted to circumscribe his personality.

1. The Superhuman Character of Buddha

The Beatific is defined as the Supreme Man who "conquers the four castes," evidently an allusion to that spiritual sovereignty which makes him comparable to a holy universal king (*ārya cakravartirājan*), as we shall see further on. He is the Supreme Conquerer, his acquisition of the Way of Deliverance having been made possible by "immense victory" – victory over sadness and death personified by Māra. We shall see appearing here the myth of royalty.

The superiority of Buddha rests primarily on his sanctity, which is why he is held as Great Saint and Supreme Religious Being to whom no other religious being is superior. Similarly, he is celebrated under the name of Supreme Venerable and is defined as being "venerated by both gods and men." Perfectly pure, "lacking either blemish or stain," "immaculate," he is for that reason compared to pure and limpid water and to a sun without cloud or haze.

His principle virtue, that which his followers most often exalt, is unquestionably his wisdom. He is called the Great Sage, the Supreme Sage, the Divine Sage. His wisdom shines like a torch amid shadows; he possesses the Eye of Wisdom, which is infinite and without limitations. He thus possesses ten supernatural cognizances which are called the "ten forces" (*daśa balāni*) and which are perforce well known. His knowledge is superior to that of all the gods; his divine Eye allows him to see the divinities rushing in a crowd to Pāṭaliputra, then to Kuśinagara; he knows where the faithful who perished in a terrible epidemic during his trip to Nādaka are reborn; he can predict under what conditions each of them will obtain Deliverance in the near future; he foresees the future grandeur of Pāṭaliputra, where the king will have a fortress built.

Several times allusion is made to his veracity. The king Ajātaśatru knows that "what the Tathāgata says is never false" and Māra himself affirms that "the Buddha does not speak in vain." He himself opposes to the supplications of Ānanda the fact that "the Tathāgata cannot go back on his word." Viśvadāya is therefore right to bestow on him the fine title of Man of Truth.

His power of mental concentration is extraordinary, as he proved to Putkasa, and all those who see him are struck by the intensity with which he concentrates his faculties (*indriya*) and thus calms them.

His bounty is recognized because he is the great dispenser of plenty and peace both to gods and men, to whom he distributed a gift precious to all, the Eye of Science, owing to which his disciples can dissipate their doubts.

His superiority is brilliantly revealed in the prodigies which he accomplishes or which are produced under his influence. It was in such a way that in a wink of the eye he crossed the Ganges, so broad in front of Pāṭaliputra, with hundreds of disciples accompanying him, without using even a single skiff. His majestic puissance makes the three thousand worlds tremble, and frightening quakes announce to the universe the principal moments of his existence: his incarnation, his birth, his Awakening, his first sermon, the rejection of his vital structures, and his Parinirvāṇa.

To his spiritual superiority is added a physical superiority which is in some way the sensible manifestation of the former. All those who perceive him are struck by the perfection of his appearance, by the beauty of his visage and his body, which the thirty-two signs of the Great Man and the eighty secondary marks render yet more beautiful. By virtue of its brilliance and purity, his complexion is superior even to that of the gods, so agreeable is it to contemplate. As for his voice, it too is superior to those of the gods; the sounds which he voices are sweet and harmonious, while at the same time totally deep and grave like those of a great tamboura (*gabhīrikā*).

2. The Divine and Superdivine Characteristics of Buddha

The Buddha is not only superior to all humanity, but also to all groups of beings, divine or human, into which he penetrates while they wonder whether he is a man or a god. This problem is of course rapidly resolved when certain ones call him the Divine Sage. Furthermore, his followers like to recognize and even to celebrate his superiority over the gods themselves. He surpasses them in the beauty of his complexion, in the brightness of the light which sometimes emanates from his body, in the qualities of his voice, and in the extent of his awareness.

This explains why he is venerated by both gods and men. Our text gives some edifying examples of the devotion of the gods toward Buddha. When he, sick and thirsty, demanded in vain for Ānanda to give him drink, it was a divinity of the Himalayas who came full speed to bring him a mixture of eight kinds of pure waters. When the Beatific rested in the wood of *śāla* just before dying, the divinity who resided in the twin trees spread over him, in the guise of offerings, flowers blooming out of season. At the same moment, the gods flocked in a crowd to contemplate him one last time. A little later they participated in his funeral, and while making flowers and celestial perfumes rain down, while filling the spaces with divine music, and while singing their dithyrambs, each of the great gods and each group of divinities pronounced one or two stanzas of elegy. Like all the devotees, they lamented and wept over the disappearance of Tathāgata and they remained to accompany the funeral cortege. Finally, after the fire had consumed the remains of the Beatific, it was a divinity who extinguished the burning pyre by exercising his supernatural power.

Simultaneously superior to gods and to men, the Buddha is therefore considered the Supreme Being. He is thus called "he who lacks a companion in the world," "he who has no equal," "he who has no peer," "the Unique," "inestimable and difficult to conceive." This last expression is remarkable in that it reveals a novel aspect of the personality of the Tathāgata as it was conceived of by certain of his followers, namely, transcendance. By his own nature, the Buddha is foreign to this world where the gods and men live; he is supraworldly (*lokottara*), just as is his Law, and he tends to be identified with his Body of Law (*dharmakāya*).

We find here an echo of some docetic theses dear to certain schools of the Mahāsāṃghika group, in particular that of the Lokottaravādin, according to which the true Buddha would have remained unknown to the beings of this world, supraworldly in every sense of the term although the men and gods would have received among them a phantom, a personage magically created, emanating from the transcendant Tathāgata.

3. The Attributes of Buddha

The idea which the devotees formed of the Buddha is also expressed by the diverse attributes with which they invested him. The most extraordinary, if one may say so, are the thirty-two signs and eighty secondary marks which adorn his body and attest to his nature as the Great Man – that is to say, as universal sovereign either in the temporal domain as holy king (*cakravartin*) or in the spiritual domain as the perfectly Awakened.

One of these thirty-two signs is precisely the gilded color of his skin, which is celebrated several times in our text. Thus there is established a thin line between the sacred body of Buddha and gold, the unalterable, perfectly pure metal which nothing can sully, which has the color and brilliance of the sun, and which symbolizes this star. Shortly after the Parinirvāṇa, the Beatific placed his arms beneath his garment and raised it as a happy presage to his disciples, "a marvelous presage" says the *Sūtra*. Certainly, it was impossible to think that the body of the Tathāgata had been made of this precious metal, but this impossibility might have embarrassed the devotees. Also, after one dared to portray the Buddha, whether in painting, lapidary, or sculpture, one certainly did not hesitate to use gold to make statuettes of the Beatific or to refinish stone, metal, or wooden statues to represent the skin of his face and limbs on these images which are manufactured so frequently throughout the Buddhist world. One could even ask if the passages of our text where allusion is made to the marvelously gilded complexion of Buddha have not been added lately, with reference to already extant representations of the type defined above, which could scarcely have appeared before the beginning of our era. The diverse schools agree, however, on making a gold complexion figure among the thirty-two signs of the Great Man, and this unanimity obliges us to set this attribution back to a very ancient epoch, toward the time of Aśoka.

Our *Sūtra* mentions another marvelous physical characteristic of Buddha: the brilliance of his complexion, which was manifested with particular intensity shortly before the Parinirvāṇa and which was one of the precursors of that event. Ānanda perceived it with stupor, and, comparing the brilliance of his master's skin with that of the new pieces of material given by Putkasa, found the latter dull. Without doubt, one must understand that the complexion of the Beatific was extremely clear; in India, where skin color is a racial and social index, such a complexion is considered the sign of a lofty origin, of the purity of the line of one's origin and superiority of descent in the caste hierarchy.

But this lightness will certainly suggest another quality, assuredly supernatural, which is invested in the Beatific, namely, a luminous refulgence. In addition, devout authors attributed to Buddha a luminous aureole, for which rapports with the iconography are evident. It shines in such a fashion, we are told, that it eclipses the Great Community. Its radiant glow illuminates the entire world, making it similar to the rising sun or the moon which circles in cloudless space. It is likely that this conception owes its origin not only to the clarity of Buddha's complexion but also to the gilded color of his skin, which must have inspired the use of precious metal for reflecting light in a brilliant fashion.

At certain moments, judged more solemn than others, notably that of the Parinirvāṇa, the body of the Beatific is not content to shine but must emit a light so intense that it fills the universe, a light more powerful than that of the gods which penetrates those regions plunged in eternal shadows beyond the rays of sun or moon. Then, we are told, the beings who live there can mutually be seen and each of them can observe with astonishment that he is not alone in the world.

Finally, a stanza of dithyramb pronounced shortly after the Parinirvāṇa invests Buddha with a diamond body and sadly declares that even this is destroyed by impermanence. The author of this strophe probably had the idea that the body of the Beatific could not be constituted of the same flesh as men's, but that it was made of a substance if not truly precious at least more capable of resisting the forces of destruction and, in consequence, extraordinary.

4. The Comparisons

The beings to whom Buddha is compared also reveal the concept the faithful held of him. When he is called "Good Leader and Supreme Trainer," this only cites one of the ten titles conferred on Tathāgata over a long period of time, "Supreme Leader of men who should be trained" (*anuttara puruṣa-damya-sārathi*). This evokes the superiority of the Beatific through his relations to men.

It is especially admiration and veneration to which allusion is made by the epithet of Hero (*vīra*), or the occasional epithet of Supreme Hero. These sentiments are combined with the recognition of his superiority in the appellation Supreme Conqueror (*jina*), which is probably one of the oldest of Buddha's titles following the separation from Jina, the founder of Jainism, his contemporary and almost his compatriot. This title is explained by the description of the acquisition of the Way of Deliverance, the Awakening, as "immense victory." Perhaps there was already an allusion to the legend of the Beatific's triumph over Māra and his daughters and troops at the moment of the Bodhi, a legend which gives concrete expression to the complete spiritual victory which was the Awakening, a legend probably formed near the time our *Sūtra* was composed. Hero and Conqueror, Buddha is thereby identified with a man of noble caste, military, of the Kshatriya, which would be unbelievable in what concerns this champion of peace if one were to forget all the ancient sources which have him leave, not without reason, this social group.

From noble warrior, hero, and conqueror to that which can be regarded as the perfection of this ideal, the holy universal king (*cakravartirājan*), was only a step for the free play of the Indian devotees' ever alert imagination. This imagination had been gaily unleashed after a certain time, since the six parallel versions of our *Sūtra* underline in four places the close relation between the Beatific and the mythical sovereign, whom the emperors of the Maurya dynasty, Aśoka in particular, apparently tried to make identical. In effect, we are told, the rules for the funeral rites of a Buddha are similar to those for a holy universal king. This latter is, along with Tathāgata, the Pratyekabuddha and the Listener (that is, the Arhant), one of four men who are dignified by the construction of a funerary tumulus (*stūpa*) over their ashes, the only one of the four who is not a religious figure and, we should note, the last cited on the list. These four men are also the only ones to whom one should bear funerary offerings of perfumes, flowers, banners, parasols, and music. Finally, in the conclusion of a long recital of the life of king Mahāsudarśana which Buddha made to Ānanda to explain the choice of Kuśinagara as the place for the Parinirvāṇa, a recital which forms an integral part of the *Mahāparinirvāṇasūtra* except in the Pali version, Buddha declares that he has exercised six times the functions of holy king (*cakravartin*) in this same place.

Thus one observes that the devotees of the epoch were convinced that only a king who dominated the entire world could be compared to Buddha, yet they took care to show clearly, by means of several significant traits, that the temporal sovereign would remain inferior to the Beatific; cited after him in the lists where they both figured, he could not be any more than a Bodhisattva.

The Buddha is also compared to certain animals of a high symbolic value. One is the *nāga*, mentioned twice. In one case which speaks of the Bodhisattva in the breast of his mother, "similar to a *nāga* laid on its litter," it undoubtedly concerns an elephant more precisely a white elephant under whose aspect the future Śākyamuni will be reincarnated in the bosom of queen Māyā, according to a legend which was already manifestly famous in the epoch when this passage was composed. In the other case, Buddha is compared to a great *nāga* with neither blemish nor stain and at the same time to limpid and pure water, which allows one to think that the animal in question may be one of those semi-divine beings taking alternately the human aspect and the form of monstrous serpents, one of whose preferred habitats is the water. In the first passage Buddha is identified with one of the animals symbolizing sovereignty, the white elephant who is one of the seven jewels of the holy universal king and a mark of victory and prosperity. In the second, he takes on the perfect and superhuman purity of a mythical being whose rather poorly defined nature simultaneously partakes of that of man, of that of animals (among whom the *nāga* are generally counted), and of that of the gods.

But the animal with which Buddha is most often compared is the lion. Several times he is called the Lion of the Śākya; his gait is compared to the lion's and his voice to the roar of the lion who experiences no fear amid the forests. When he lies down at the place where he is soon to die, between the twin *śāla* trees, he reclines on his right flank "like a king of the lions." Not only rare in India but most likely unknown in the middle basin of the Ganges where Buddha spent all his life, this animal plays an important role in Indian symbolism, no doubt because of the Achaemenian influence manifested in Mauryan art. Like the elephant, the lion symbolizes royalty, and this is why it is so often found at the top of pillars raised by the emperor Aśoka. The frequent comparisons of the Beatific with the lion, in the diverse versions of our *Sūtra* and elsewhere in different Buddhist canons, indicate the authors' attempt to claim spiritual supremacy for the Buddha.

Certain comparisons, encountered somewhat rarely, underline other qualities attributed to Buddha: as limpid and pure water he lacks either blemish or stain; he is an infinite ocean of merits; his visage is similar to the Himalayas, as is his renown. The latter is further assimilated to a lotus flower which opens and exhales numerous extremely subtle perfumes. These diverse images are drawn from the ordinary stock of Indian poetry; they are clichés whose value should not be overestimated.

Most interesting are the comparisons with the eye and the rather numerous allusions to this organ. The Beatific possesses the divine Eye which permits him to view in diverse locations the divinities who remain invisible to other men. He possesses the Eye of Wisdom, which is infinite and unlimited. He gives to the masses the Eye of Knowledge, thanks to which his followers can dissipate their doubts. In the first instance the eye represents a proper means of vision but concerns a field forbidden to ordinary human beings. In the other two instances, the word "eye" designates a means of cognizance and is taken in a figurative sense, but it strongly suggests a direct, immediate cognizance which apprehends its object with perfect clarity, excluding any possibility of doubt as in ordinary vision. One must contrast this sense with that of another expression, so common in Buddhist texts, which has taken on a technical sense: *sākṣāt karoti*, which properly means "he sees with his own eyes," and serves to designate the whole physical or spiritual operation by which the Buddhist saint attains to perfect, self-evident knowledge of the Truth.

In most of the passages of our *Sūtra* which describe the lamentations of the faithful, religious or lay, at the announcement of the Parinirvāṇa or during Buddha's funeral rites, and in all six versions as well, the Beatific is called "Eye of the World," an expression whose original sense remains ambiguous. It can suggest that Tathāgata knows the reality of the world hidden beneath its illusory aspect with as much clarity as if he saw it directly, or it can suggest equally that he shows it to beings who live in the world, therefore acting as their servant by means of immediate and irrefutable knowledge. Here, in contrast to the three preceding expressions, the eye is not an attribute of Buddha, but Buddha himself, whose essence is precisely the knowledge of the Truth underlying the world, knowledge which is at the origin of the Way to Deliverance and the necessary condition for Salvation.

Another meaning, however, appears: in Indian mythology, as in the mythologies of many ancient peoples, the eye of the world is the sun, whose round shape and brilliance recall the shape of the pupil and the reflective power of various parts of the organ of vision. Moreover, it is not in the least unlikely that the Indian Buddhist authors had thought in this way about precedents and wished to suggest all three to their audience; this would be well within the habits dear to the passionate and stylish rhetoricians which the Indians have always been. The Buddhist canon itself will furnish us with innumerable analogous examples.

Thus we are led, by the examination of a somewhat ambiguous expression, to pass in review the richest series of terms of comparisons applied to Buddha, namely, those which concern light under various aspects. If his wisdom is only once compared to "a great torch seen in the shadows," it is almost always to radiant stars that appeal is made to describe the brilliance of the Beatific.

The moon is several times employed as a term of comparison. Among the least of his Community, Buddha is like the moon in the sky. The luminous aureole which emanates from his body shines like the autumn moon after the season of rains, when the sky is entirely clear. The luminous refulgence of the Beatific is similar to that of the moon circling in space without a single cloud covering it.

Buddha is also compared to the sun three times. In the stanzas of elegy pronounced after his Parinirvāṇa, he is called "Sun." His aureole shines like the sun in space during the springtime feasts when it is pure, without spots, and brightens by its vivid radiance the sky and earth. When it appears, his luminosity is comparable to that of the sun.

It is convenient to note that the comparisons with the moon are as numerous as those with the sun, that in either case the Beatific is only directly compared once to each of the respective bodies, and that, for the rest, his aureole and luminous refulgence are said to shine both like the sun and the moon. In the presence of such facts one would not suppose, as some formerly did, that the Buddha was only a solar myth.

The *Mahāparinirvāṇasūtra* of the Dharmaguptaka thus reveals a rather extensive conception of Buddha which all the first disciples could have formed of him. Let us state immediately that it does not differ essentially from those which one could draw from the study of the five other versions of the same work, so that this notion of the Beatific's nature corresponds to the very phase of devotion which was common to all the followers of the schools to which the six texts pertain, rather than only to the ideas proper to the sect of the Dharmaguptaka.

The Buddha is first defined as having attained perfection in all domains. His sanctity and his purity (that is, his morality) are perfect after he is completely stripped of the passions and vices which sully human nature. His wisdom is perfect, which permits him to perceive if not all (because our text contains no clear reference to his omniscience), at least more things than the knowledge of men and gods can grasp. Perfect also are his mental concentration and his bounty. Upon such spiritual qualities repose his physical qualities: his stamina, his poses, the beauty of his visage, of his body, of his complexion, and of his voice attain equally to perfection. The supernatural powers which he uses or which derive from his virtues and past acts attest, often with extraordinary grandeur, to the perfection of his qualities.

Not only is the Beatific perfect in all things, but he is without equal in the world; he is unique, the Supreme Being, superior to all the gods as to all men, both of whom are compelled to bring him their offerings, their services, and the testaments of their veneration. He is so superior to all beings that he is difficult for them to conceive, which seems to indicate that the devout authors of our *Sūtra* first began to conceive the transcendence of Buddha.

Perfect in all points, superior through distance from all beings, unique, the Beatific had evidently taken, in the thought of his followers, the place which the devotees of the great religions attributed to the great God whom they adored. The way was largely open to speculation on the Body of Law (*dharmakāya*) and on the nature of the Buddha (*buddhatā*), both identified with universal quiddity (*tathatā*) – that is, with the being of beings – speculations which were to make the Buddha Śākyamuni an emanation of the latter.

The elegiacal comparisons and the attributes loaned to Buddha express concretely diverse aspects of this conception, in a fashion more or less allusive, by means of symbols and myths. The myth of royalty, and more precisely of universal royalty (that of the holy king [*cakravartin*]), is frequently utilized. As this legendary sovereign, the Beatific dominates all men and alone enjoys this privilege. He is the Hero, the Conqueror; he is assimilated to the lion and to the elephant, animals which symbolize royalty. The latter allusions, however, simply concern rhetorical figures which one encounters almost exclusively in the different stanzas of elegies addressed to him. On the contrary, the comparison with the holy king (*cakravartin*) must be taken seriously since it serves to define the ritual of funerals and the funerary cult as well as the nature of the monument raised on the ashes of Tathāgata, and by that serves to define Buddha's social position, to acknowledge his absolute supremacy in the world of men.

Even as the holy king alone rules the world, even as the sun and moon reign alone in the sky, one during the day and the other at night, shedding their beneficial light on all the earth's inhabitants, just so does the *cakravartin* shed the benefits of his wise and pacific government upon all men. When the Beatific is compared to these shining bodies, their brilliance symbolizes the cognizance preached by Buddha to all beings which ought to allow them to attain that supreme good which is the Deliverance, cognizance which dissipates the shadows of ignorance as the light of sun and moon chase the obscurity of night. Furthermore, this brilliance, which makes them known and loans them to all humans, represents the glory of the Beatific which extends over all the earth. It is, however, always in the strophes of elegies that Buddha is thus compared to the sun and moon, in such a way that these assimilations do not leave the field of poetry. Therefore, these comparisons cannot be considered here as a veritable identification.

On the contrary, when our text mentions the clarity and the light which emanates from the Beatific's body, the glittering lightness of his complexion, the gilded and therefore shining color of his skin (gold being the same substance as the sun in the ancient imagination), the luminous aureole about his person, the jets of light which in diverse circumstances gushed from him and went to brighten the farthest reaches of the universe beyond the limits where the rays of sun and moon expire, it does not concern rhetorical figures but prodigies of Buddha's superhuman nature. One must see there a kind of realization, an actualization of symbols by means of the supernatural power loaned to the Beatific by his followers. These extraordinary phenomena have the same meaning as the light of the sun and moon which concerned us above; like it, they manifest simultaneously the glory of Buddha and the beneficial cognizance of the Way to Salvation which he dispenses among all men.

These great mythical themes of royalty, of the sun and moon, and of light are here only the means utilized to express and to make understood the true nature of Buddha while underlining his supremacy and his power and while illustrating these in elegiacal stanzas. One cannot, therefore, identify them with the nature of the Beatific, but only see in them the attributes, the symbols of certain aspects of the Buddha.

INDIAN VARIETIES OF ART RITUAL

STELLA KRAMRISCH

In the Vedic ritual of the sacrifice, the building of the altar was the necessary, pivotal performance. Without it, the myth of Prajāpati sacrificing himself into creation would have had no substance. Without this architectural rite, the sacrificer would have been unable to transcend the confines of his mortal body. The substance and form of the altar became, by the rites of architecture, the shape of transubstantiation of the sacrificer congruous with the substance of the creator.

By their performance, the rites of art create form. The function, form, and meaning of the Vedic altar continued, paradoxically, when Vedic altars were no longer built in the Hindu temple. Each building stone, or brick or log of wood, retains the name of Istakā, that is, "what belongs to the sacrifice," and the donor of the temple remains the Yajamāna, the sacrificer.

The Brahmanic, Hindu tradition of Indian architecture has set up large and lasting monuments. Other traditions in ever-renewed performance created works of art which, though neither monumental nor enduring, are the form of rites enacted and which could not have been performed and been effective without that form.

Here, three different spheres of rites performed through art will be considered: one tribal, as exemplified by the art of the Bhil; another, though complex in its components yet whole and compelling in its autochthony, the sphere of Aiyanar; and the third represented by the magic diagrams found throughout India and by certain corresponding textiles which are exclusively the rites of visualization performed by women.

The Spirit Rider

The Nukto rite of the Bhil is centered in a small, equestrian figure. The archetype of all the figurines of horsemen which give reality to the Nukto rite of the Bhil has vanished from the scene. Its meaning and function, however, come to life whenever the rite is performed, and the mystery of death in life is once more confirmed through the figurine of the rider on his horse. It plays the leading role in this essential tribal rite of the Bhil, although the Bhil today neither raise nor use horses. The equestrian figure in art and legend is associated with the feudal Hindu Rājputs, the northern neighbors of the Bhil.

The equestrian figure is one of the themes of art by which the tribal world and that of the feudal aristocracy are linked here on earth. Over and above this, its image is a magic link between heaven and earth. This is its purpose. In this respect, the function of the equestrian figurine is not different from that of the great temples which were erected in the cities. There the ascent to heaven was built up stone by stone, each stone carved with an image appropriate to its position in the entire edifice; the stones were piled high so that step by step the architectural ritual of the ascent became the monument, the temple. The architectural ritual is put into words in the ancient texts of that science. To this day, the oral tradition of the tribal Bhil verifies step by step the journey of the soul which has the spirit-rider for its acting support.

The liberating function of art is shared by the non-Hindu tribal, the Hindu peasant, and the Hindu elite in one tribal-village-urban continuum where the currents from the art of tribe and village to the elite, from the art of the elite to tribe and village, flow both ways.

The tribe of the Bhil, the "sons of the forest" (*vanaputra*), lives in Western India, from the Aravalli mountains in Rājasthan to the Vindhya range. It is in and near this region that in the course of the last two thousand years the Buddhist cave temples and monasteries of Ajanta were cut out of the rocks, the Jains built the marble temples at Mount Abu, and many Hindu shrines bear witness to the experience of the numinous. The Bhil are hunters, fishermen, and food gatherers; they have learned animal husbandry from their neighbors, the Gujar, and they are agriculturalists. Although centered in Rājasthan (Mewar), Gujarat, and Khandesh, they live in loosely connected groups in the mountains and less readily accessible parts of Sind (now in Pakistan), Kutch, and Rājasthan in the northwest, in the state of Āndhra in the southeast, and a small group of them is found as far to the northeast as Bengal.[1] Said to be of pre-Aryan origin, they are classified as proto-Australoid or as Veddid.[2] Their original language is lost; they form a psychological complex without linguistic, physiognomical, economical, or cultural unity.[3] Their spirituality is their own and holds them together. Formerly they ruled over their own country. This was prior to the arrival of the Rājputs. The Rājputs, "the sons of kings," invaded the country, subsequently Rājasthan, in about the sixth century A.D. They became the Kṣatriyas, the nobility *par excellence* of India. Some of these Rājput princes, including the most exalted of them, the Rana of Mewar, had their foreheads marked with the blood of a Bhil at the inception of their rule. This blood was drawn from a thumb or big toe.[4] This is an acknowledgment of the precedence of the Bhil as rulers of the country.

The Rājputs are horseowners and riders. The Bhil use the image of the horseman. It is that of a spirit-rider, "gothriz purvez," the ancestor of the clan. On it is focused the solidarity of the clan; it redeems the dead and liberates the living from the fear of death and the despair of loneliness. Moreover, the Bhil commemorate their fallen heroes, killed in a fight or cattle raid, by setting up stone memorial slabs carved in low relief with an equestrian figure, whereas on memorial stones set up for their dead, the Rājputs frequently have a standing figure in front view.[5] The Bhil confer on their ancestors the nobility of the horseman, whereas the Rājputs themselves do not particularly stress the equestrian status

[1] W. Koppers, "Die Bhil in Zentral Indien," in *Wiener Beiträge zur Kulturgeschichte und Linguistik* (Vienna, 1948), p. 17. P. H. Hendley, "An account of the Mewar Bhils," *Journal of the Asiatic Society of Bengal*, 44 (1875): 357, 358.

[2] W. Koppers, "Die Bhil," p. 20. C. von Fürer-Haimendorf, foreword to T. B. Naik, *The Bhils* (Delhi, 1956), p. x.

[3] Mathias Hermanns, *Die Religiös-Magische Weltanschauung der Primitiv Stamme Indiens*, 2 vols. (Wiesbaden, 1964), vol. 1, p. 13.

[4] W. Koppers, "Die Bhil," p. 14.

[5] W. Koppers, "Monuments to the Dead Erected by the Bhils and Their Neighbors," *Annali Lateranensi*, 6 (1942): 119–206 *passim*.

of their dead. From the hymns of the *Ṛg Veda* (second half of the second millennium B.C.), the group of horse and rider is vested with sacredness. Indra, the creator god, rode the horse for the first time.[6] Later tradition knows the sun god as rider[7] and the horse itself is fire, in all its aspects, on earth and in heaven, the sun on high and the spark of life.[8]

The Bhil ritual for the dead is celebrated in front of the entrance of the house of the deceased.[9] From above the lintel a twelve-runged bamboo ladder is suspended and subsequently also a long string with an arrow – the Bhil were primarily hunters – attached to it. This man-made setting and its paraphernalia contrast with the sacred grove, the central sanctuary of every Bhil settlement. There an unhewn stone or stones are the symbols of deity. In the cult of the dead, however, man is the symbol. The anthropomorphic image and representation – which here are those of the horseman – are linked with the cult of the dead. Another object required for the great Nukto rite, the rite of the dead, is the figurine of a cow. These figurines are made of the copper anklets of the widow of the deceased. The material of the figurines itself has magical virtue and takes part in the ritual, undergoing a spiritual alchemy.

The gothriz purvez is placed on an altar, the cow on a metal tray. The long string leads to the altar of the gothriz purvez and thence to the cow. Now the scene is set. The main actors are the Rawal, the master of ceremonies; the Barwo, the magician; and the Waha, the priest. The Waha, who acts as a Brahman or priest, is a male child from the clan of the dead person. The participants are the relatives of the dead person.

The preparation for the Nukto rite begins when the Rawal sings to the dying man at the first "ghanto," corresponding to the first rung of the ladder: "Alone go, brother to Bhagavān (the supreme God), through the seven depths." And at the third "ghanto" the Rawal speaks over the dead body: "Come, quite alone." And at the fifth "ghanto," it is the spirit (jīva) who speaks:

6 *Ṛg Veda* I.163.2.

7 *Agni Purāṇa* ch. 51.3.

8 Cf. *Ṛg Veda* IV.40.5.

9 See M. Hermanns, *Die Religiös-Magische Weltanschauung*, vol. 1, pp. 403–26, treating the Bhagoria Bhil, and W. Koppers, "Die Bhil," pp. 270 ff. The accounts differ in some respects according to variations of the Nukto rites in different clans and localities within the Bhil country.

"I am alone, brother, I am alone." The ghanto are the rungs of the bamboo ladder which the Rawal had hung from the doorframe. They represent the twelve stations of the mountain with their obstacles which the spirit (jīva) has to climb before it is purified and reaches Bhagavān.

The Bhil distinguish between the body, the psychic elements or the ghost (bhūt) and shadow, and the spirit (jīva) of man. They separate at death. The body is cremated; a heap of stones is piled up under a tree. There the bhūt is appeased in the first three days of the rites, after the death of the body. On the fourth day, the Nukto rites of three days begin. It is then that the Rawal ties the string on the wooden crossbar above the entrance. When the jīva has attained the seventh rung the stones are scattered; there is now no resting place on earth for any part of the man who died. The spirit rises from one rung of tests and judgment to the next, overcoming the obstacles of each rung. The spirit is purified during the ascent. In the night when the spirit has passed the tenth and eleventh rungs, it has been judged in the twelve courts and goes to Bhagavān. The Rawal has sprinkled the cow with milk to make the spirit pure and white. When the spirit has completed its ascent, during the first Nukto rite, on the fourth day after death, the twelve rungs of the ladder are destroyed and the spirit descends along the string into the arrow, the Rawal having poured water thrice over the metal horseman and thrice over the cow. By these rites the spirit is purified. The spirit now enters the equestrian figurine and the cow and overcomes the Barwo, who, having undergone in the meanwhile the necessary preparations, is in trance. The spirit makes the Barwo select the Waha, a young boy from the clan of the dead, who is now consecrated. The Waha is Gothriz Purvez; he is possessed by his spirit and is given the same name as the rider figurine on the horse who is also Gothriz Purvez, the ancestor of the clan, the liberated spirit of the man who had died. The Waha, trembling in his trance, holds the tablet with the figurine of the cow while the Rawal sings for the "Kṣatari," the hero, the spirit.

When the figurine of the cow held by the trembling Waha has itself ceased to tremble, it is taken in procession to the tree where the stones were collected and then scattered. The figurine of the cow is buried.

The Rawal tears the string on which the spirit has descended.

The Waha has ceased to be possessed by the spirit. The purified spirit (jīva) has been accepted in the clan of the ancestors. It dwells with Bhagavān, in the beyond. The Nukto rite has been completed. A meal and mask dance follow.

Without the Nukto rite, the spirit could not have been purified and could not have ascended. It would have remained alone, wandering between the two worlds, troubling the hearts and minds of the clansmen. The effigy of the spirit (jīva), Gothriz Purvez, the equestrian metal statuette, remains with them. It is not buried as is the figurine of the cow.

The embodiments of the purified spirit as ancestor of the clan in the living body of the entranced youth of the clan, the Waha, and in the equestrian metal statuette both prove to be its temporary abode. For this, the Waha was made fit by his trance and the equestrian statuette by its form. The figurine of the cow, too, is temporarily the place where the spirit dwells. But when this figurine ceases to tremble, the spirit has left it, and the little metal cow is buried, having served its purpose. Very few metal figurines of cows exist. The number of equestrian metal figurines is large. They vary considerably in shape, each variation having a formal consistency of its own. They are set up frequently in household shrines of Rājputs and other Hindus.

Without the figurine of the gothriz purvez, the spirit of the dead could not be purified and could not reach Bhagavān, the supreme God. The figurine, the work of art, is an essential means toward the attainment by the clan of a feeling of spiritual worth and earthly security, a feeling of peace and solidarity. The liberated spirit, the "Kṣatri," the hero, comes to dwell in the Nukto rite amid the clan, in the living, young body of the Waha and in the equestrian statuette.

The Waha discharged the function of a Brahman. For this purpose he was invested, like a Brahman, with a sacred thread. It is not only in this instance that the Bhil raise a child to the status of a Brahman or recognize in a child a special power.[10] It is the power of the assumed innocence of the child.[11]

The equestrian metal figurines, essential parts of rites and trance, were not, however, made during a trance experience. Invariably cast by the lost-wax process, they fall into different

[10] W. Koppers, "Die Bhil," pp. 147, 260.

[11] J. Abbot, *The Keys of Power* (London, 1932), p. 10.

stylistic groups. In one particularly spirited variety, a special technique of casting contributed to the tense alertness of its form. But to whatever style type of figurines horse and rider may belong, they seem to have come from a world of enchantment where innocence and trusting pride went into their conception. Their form lacks the tension and determination of similar ancient Iranian metal figurines,[12] as well as the cursive, fluid generalization of comparable animal figurines made of clay by Tallensi children of the African gold coast.[13] Essentially metallic in character, these pristine, though not primitive, figurines, assignable to the Bhil ambience whether made by Bhil or by hinduized metalsmiths, show rider and horse advancing, as it were, though the legs of the horse are always firmly planted on the ground. As a rule, the rider holds the reins with one hand and with the other a staff or weapon. His head is raised, his back is straight. With the four feet of the horse on the ground, the seemingly advancing movement of the group is effected by the position and spacing of the legs of the horse and by the position and spacing of the neck and head of the horse and the body of the rider, the latter frequently inclining back. Self-contained and static, the two appear to be drawn forward by an invisible pull. Though three-dimensional, the figurine is complete in its silhouette. Seen from various angles, rider and horse show themselves in ever-new responses of their masses and the connecting voids, which are left intact by the unobtrusiveness of the rider's legs. Like short, flattened ribbons, his legs adhere to the body of the horse and, as a rule, do not exceed the length of the saddle. It is the reins, arms, and weapon which enhance the airiness and onward pull. Whether of Don Quixotian elegance as in Rājasthan, or full-bodied as in Maharashtra, where the rider's face is planar and presents its features as ridges (according to the standards of tribal art), or has a three-dimensional face abstractly modelled like a lump of clay pinched into the peak of the nose, or is more naturalistically organized, with the horse's legs flexed and articulated (or made simply as sturdy cylinders), each group has a serenely harmonious balance of its own for the liberated spirit of the ancestor of the clan to dwell in. As this spirit in the Nukto rite takes possession of the Waha, a

[12] See, for example, *1000 Years of Iranian Art*, Smithsonian Institution Exhibition Catalogue, 1964–65, fig. 104.

[13] Leonhard Adam, *Primitive Art* (Penguin Books, 1954), pl. 11b.

child, so its image in turn embodies the immortal spirit of childhood as ancestor of the clan.

Cast solid by the lost-wax process, these figurines are distinct in style from the nervy zest of the thin-legged horses and frisky riders cast hollow in a special "wire" technique.[14] It is practiced by the quasi-hinduized metalworkers of the Kainkuya Mal caste, also called Dhokra, a migratory and partly settled caste of metalsmiths who came from Bihar to Bengal; by the Malar, who are said to have come to Bihar from Madhya Pradesh; and by the Kaser in Bastar, Madhya Pradesh. In their technique of hollow bronze casting, a ribbed surface results (often it is smoothed) from placing wax "wires" one-tenth of an inch thick, one against the other, and over them more wax wires, forming an ornamental relief pattern. By this technique an eerie elegance is obtained in the figurines from Bihar of which not only the horse but also the deer or antelope are chosen embodiments. Like the other small metal images here described, they too were kept on house altars. Warding off evil spirits, they are ritual animals of manifold meaning. Brahmanical tradition tells that Prajāpati, the Lord of Progeny, the creator "per generationem," committed incest with his daughter, an antelope.[15] Vivasvant, the sun, in the shape of a horse, mated with Samjñā, a mare. She was the daughter of Visivakarman, the Maker of the Universe, the creator "per artem."[16] Impetuous and fleet, horse and antelope are symbols of creativeness, full of secret, redeeming, and protestive power.[17] As such,

[14] The surface patterns of the "wire" technique in metal recall those produced by the coiled withes of Siki grass of which figurines and baskets are made to this day in North Bihar. See Ruth Reeves, *Cire Perdue Casting in India* (New Delhi, 1962), pp. 14, 17, and *passim*. In the equestrian figurines from western India, the body of the horse is sometimes cast hollow.

[15] *Aitareya Brahmana* III.33.

[16] J. Dowson, *A Classical Dictionary of Hindu Mythology and Religion* (London, 1914), p. 311.

[17] Brahmanical texts know not only the skin but also the horn of the black antelope to be full of secret powers. Cf. H. H. Oldenberg, *Vorwissenschaftliche Wissenschaft, Die Weltanschauung Der Brahmana Texte* (Göttingen, 1919), p. 42. During the Soma sacrifice, the priest wrapped a horn of the black antelope into his robe, saying, "Thou art the maternal lap of India." During initiation, the sacrificer is wrapped in the skin of a black antelope. H. H. Oldenberg, *Die Religion des Veda* (Berlin, 1917), p. 405.

A black antelope skin is also the seat of a Brahman during meditation. An early Chola relief shows the antelope as Vahana of Durga, the great Goddess (S. R. Balasubrahmanyam, *Early Chola Art* [Bombay, 1966], pt. I, pl. 1b). Horse and deer are also known as the vehicles of the luminaries (Abbot, *Keys of Power*, p. 142), the solar symbolism of the horse being pervasive.

they live in the art of the castes of the metalworkers in Bihar and West Bengal.

Related to their style and technique of work is that of the Kaser or Ghasia of Madhya Pradesh. It lacks the gracile fantasy of their work, and its wire criss-cross, spatial and parallel line texture, is more involved. The figurines are generally more ponderous.[18]

The figurine of the horseman as a spirit-rider is not always the focal point of a trance experience. As an image of the spirit freed from the human condition, it represents a state of perfection and fulfillment in which immortal heroes dwell. Representing a state of fulfillment, it is credited with the power of granting fulfillment of wishes and desires. When made of clay it is an offering to a god or hero like Kasumar Damor, a great magician, helper of the Barwo, and tutelary spirit of the people. At his mountain sanctuary such images, many on wheels, are deposited, along with clay horses, as part of vows and as votive gifts when a need is felt for having a child, regaining health, winning a court case, or for success as a robber.[19] Made of clay, the image is reduced to its minimal form and is part of the vast, timeless world of clay figurines into which history and legend may delve and give specific actuality and meaning to a perennial theme.[20] Images of seventy-two horsemen are installed on a platform somewhere in Kutch.[21]

In the small metal images the shapes of deer and antelope are assimilated the one to the other.

18 The "wire" technique is being practiced by itinerant or settled metal workers in West Bengal, South Bihar, Mayurbhani, Orissa, and in Madhya Pradesh as far south as Bastar. It is not always possible to assign on grounds of style alone each figurine to its place of origin. The Kader of Bastar, however, evolved a distinct style of the "wire" technique. The figurines made for the Kutiya Kond of Orissa are a style group by themselves. Other figurines from Orissa do not resemble them.

The work of Ruth Reeves (see n. 14), devoted to the hereditary metal craftsmen working for tribal and nontribal peoples in certain parts of central and eastern India, needs to be carried on wherever vestiges of traditional crafts survive.

19 Hermanns, *Die Religiös-Magische Weltanschauung*, vol. 1, p. 499, pl. XIII, fig. 24.

20 A. J. Patel, "Folk Terra-cottas of Gujarat," *Journal of M. S. University of Baroda*, 12 (1963): 63–70, discusses such "substitute" offerings donated in lieu of the actual animal. P. Jayakar, "Some Terra-cotta Figurines from Tribal Gujarat," *Marg*, 7 (1953): 27–32, states that the terra-cotta figures of the Rani Paraj areas of Surat are made by the potter women solely for the tribal people. The Rani Paraj terra-cottas have a fantastic, flamboyant style.

21 Their number is not accidental: 72 is 9 times 8, the sacred number of the "city of Ayodhyā," the "perfect dwelling," that is, the body of man. Cf. Stella Kramrisch, *The Hindu Temple*, 2 vols. (Calcutta, 1946), vol. I, p. 49.

They commemorate, legend tells, and keep as potent helpers, those white-skinned foreigners said to have come in the thirteenth century from Anatolia and Syria and to have killed the tyrant Punvaro. He had cut off the hands of the architect who had built the city of Patan so that he could not construct anything like it. The seventy-two horsemen took the fort and killed the chief.[22] Harking back to other, untold memories from Inner Asian horse-herding cultures, these apocalyptic horsemen transmute the fear generated by Muslim invasions into India into a liberating legend in which the evil power does not come from outside but is local, embodied in the tyrant Punvaro. His heinous crime and its punishment are in the Great Indian tradition. Capital punishment awaits the person who incapacitates a practicing artist and prevents creativeness from functioning.[23] The veneration of the creative act and the annihilation of the obstructor are mythologized in the battle of the creator-god Indra – the first to ride a horse – with the serpent dragon, Vṛtra, who had prevented the creative waters from flowing. The noble horseman – far more than the sacred cow – held the imagination of the Indian sculptor in tribe and village.

Autochthony

In South India, in almost every Tamil village, there is a shrine of Aiyanar.[24] Often a large, rough stone without any carving is set up under a tree. It stands for the presence of Aiyanar. Such a stone setting belongs to tribal tradition. But Aiyanar is a Brahman deity and his worshipers are Dravidian villagers. Generally his sanctuary is on the banks of a pond. Its waters fertilize the fields which he protects. In some of his sanctuaries, Aiyanar is represented in human shape; a kingly equestrian figure, he rides on a horse or an elephant. Horses are offered to him, large terra-cotta horses so that he does not lack a mount during the watches of the night when he rides around the village and looks after its safety. He rides with his retinue of heroes – and demons. Two horses at least must be offered to Aiyanar each year. The second

[22] A. Chandras, "Gujarat Fairs and Festivals," *Census of India*, 5 (New Delhi, 1961): pt. 7B, p. 228.

[23] A. K. Coomaraswamy, *The Indian Craftsman* (London, 1909), p. 21.

[24] Louis Dumont, "Definition structurale d'un dieu populaire tamoul: Aiyanar, le Maitre," *Journal Asiatique*, 246 (1953): 256–70.

is for Karuppan, the "dark god," the demon who accompanies him. Over the years, the horses accumulate in a sacred grove. Up to five hundred such large clay horses (twelve feet or more high) may be ready in one sanctuary for the nocturnal rides. New horses are set up while the old and broken ones are left to decay and return to the earth of which they were made. Under the image of Aiyanar a stone linga, the phallic symbol of Śiva's creativeness, is buried. The seed of Śiva, from which Aiyanar was born, it is said, fell near the bank of the waters.

The numinous lives integrally in Aiyanar's sanctuaries, in the nearby waters, in the soil, and in the trees which enshrine the multitude of clay horses in their upright splendor and in their decay. When the figures fall to the ground they are left to return to the earth, whose mystery emanates from the total setting and pervades the heterogeneous but utterly consistent legend of Aiyanar. Because these open-air South Indian village sanctuaries are replete with a living art and the living knowledge of the underlying myth whose components and ritual range from Brahmanical to tribal tradition, its salient points are here put down so that the majesty of form of these clay horses may be comprehended in its proper perspective.

Aiyanar, the Lord, is the son of the two great Hindu gods—Śiva, the Ascetic, Creator-Destroyer; and Viṣṇu, the Preserver. In order to arouse Śiva, Viṣṇu assumed the shape of a wonderfully beautiful girl called Mohini (Delusion). She excited Śiva, and he let his seed fall near the waters. From it, Aiyanar, the son of Śiva and Viṣṇu (Hariharaputra) was born. A king, while hunting, found the beautiful babe lying on the ground crying, but his face was radiant with a thousand suns.

The main sanctuary of Aiyanar, the Lord, is in the thickly wooded Shabari Hills in Kerala near the western coast of South India. There the Lord protects man from evil spirits and endows him with knowledge which leads to salvation. But in the sanctuary of Erumeli in Kerala, Aiyanar is worshiped in the form of a hunter.[25] His devotees dance wildly when they worship the Lord of this world of delusion, might, and fear.

Neither the wisdom aspect nor the orgiastic one are overtly part of the divinity of Aiyanar in the eastern Tamil part of South

25 Pyyappan, *Lord Ayyappan, Bharatiya Vidya Bhavan* (Bombay, 1962), p. 55.

India (he is not known north of the Godavari River), but the mystery of his birth from the two great Hindu gods is passed on to the potency of the waters and the earth of any particular locality where Aiyanar is worshiped. While he is the same everywhere, each time it is a different Aiyanar who is worshiped.[26]

The Lord, Aiyanar, the guardian of the land, has his generals and lieutenants. They are heroes (vīra), that is, the souls of those who died in battle. They are joined by the host of demons, of which the foremost is Karuppan, the dark god, who is all that Aiyanar is not. He is the adversary to whom blood sacrifices are due. Aiyanar is worshiped with flowers and fruits. The dark power within Aiyanar, the Hunter, has been hypostatized into Karuppan, his alter ego, the demon as protector. Together they are worshiped by the officiating priest, who also is the maker of their images. He is the village potter, a Kusavan by caste, son of a Brahman father and a low caste (Śūdra) mother. During worship he becomes possessed by Karuppan, the dark god, the alter ego of Aiyanar. Other names of Aiyanar are Bhūtanāth, Lord of Demons, and Dharma Śāsta, "in front of whom all laws (dharma) of society to which a person belongs must be abandoned" so that his presence may be realized.

The terra-cotta steeds are offered to Aiyanar by the village collectively or by individual devotees. Larger than real, the horses raise their fiercely noble heads ready to carry god or demon. The potter-priest gives them basic shapes which he knows how to modify in keeping with the ardent naturalism of South Indian sculpture. He has seen the rearing stone horses supporting the roofs of large halls of stone temples of the later phases of the Vijayanagar style of the sixteenth century.

Himself potter and priest, he molds the clay horses, impressing the clay with tensions experienced in shamanistic possession. The clay itself is taken from a ground of sacred fertility. It holds the linga of Śiva and the seed from which Aiyanar has sprung. Aiyanar, the Lord, scion of the two great Hindu gods, king of demons, synthesis of deity experienced on the many levels of India's religious structure, depends on the clay horses offered to him for his rides. Their power is vested in the soil from which they are made. It does not extend beyond the Tamil village and its autochthonous art.

[26] L. Dumont, "Definition structurale," p. 263.

Other South Indian open-air sanctuaries are consecrated to the goddess. In her sevenfold aspect, she is worshiped as the "seven virgins." Her sacred grove is a square enclosure. The image of the seven "heavenly virgins" is molded as one mass barely accentuated in its sevenfold undulating identity. The "seven virgins" form a sacred unit and are the tutelary deities of ponds. They go in procession with horses and torches. Whoever sees them dies.[27] These seven virgins, with their will-o'-the-wisp, wide-open, painted eyes, hold among themselves the message of death – and the power over birth. They too are offered horses.

The ancient Aryans sacrificed a horse to Varuṇa, the god of the fertilizing waters. In hymnic intoxication, they knew the horse as Varuṇa (*Ṛg Veda* I.163.4). They knew this because the horse had risen from the waters, from the primal fount of life (*R.V.* I.163.1). To the South Indian Dravida peasant of today, this hymnic realization of the fiery animal, the horse, of the fiery spark of life that is in the waters, of the fire that at daybreak seems to arise from the waters as glowing sun and sinks into their darkness and dies, becomes uncannily one with the power of Aiyanar and also with the eerie, fatal seven virgins. They have sprung from the soil, from swamp and pond, these autochthonous goddesses. They are ancient and local and have taken to them the steed that India had known long before the Aryans came to India with their horses. The Kusavan, the potter-priest, Aryan-Brahman and aboriginal by his blood, is competent to conceive and make the images and sanctuary of the seven virgins and their horses near the waters and to give it the sacred shape of the square, the symbol of cosmic order. The clear-cut symmetry of this sanctuary combines a mastery over the many levels of experience compressed in its extent. In the seven virgins, and also in many female votive images offered in the sacred groves, primary shapes are suffused with a visionary power. The content of tribal and rural art springs from primary concerns. They are those of life and death in man and in the cosmos of which he is part.

The form of the work of tribal and rural art of India is, in each of the two hitherto discussed instances, a product of heterogeneous provenance and actuality of purpose. Elsewhere in India, recent tribal art lacks the integrated strength of tribal art in

[27] H. Whitehead, *The Village Gods of South India* (London, 1921), p. 26.

Africa and is generally only an offshoot of what it might have been. Even where its character has not been diluted, its vigor has been sapped. But the loss of character of tribal art is the gain of the rural art of India. By a process of osmosis, the essence of tribal art flowed into rural art. There it has been shown that it is the priest who makes the clay horses and other images. While performing the rites, he becomes possessed by Karuppan, the dark god. Possession and trance of the priest as performer follow upon his work as maker or former of the sculptures which carry or contain the spirit that will possess him.

Among the tribal people of the Bhil, the work of art – an equestrian figurine – was an integral and focal point of a rite. Without it, the rite has no validity. The figurine is a locus of identification with the supernatural. Without it, this identification could not be established. It requires, however, the participation of a priest in trance to become effective. Here, artist and priest, though not combined in one person, are united as form and performer.

The spirit-riders of the Bhil, Aiyanar with his equestrian retinue of heroes and demons: both have their own locale, myths, and rites. The form of the sculptures is their visual equivalent and residue. Less rich in myth and rites are the traditions of the spirit-riders who guard the villages all over India and whose equestrian images and votive horses are made by the village potters in basic, primary shapes.[28] They all ride without stirrups, on saddled or unsaddled horses.[29] Where no rider is figured plastically, the living human medium in his frenzy may symbolically mount a clay horse by putting his toes on it.[30]

The horse is one of the main themes in the tribal and rural art of India. It rode deep into the interior of the country, carrying the liberated spirit and its own nobility, power, and fertility. It brings wish fulfillment to the poor and the suppressed; it is

[28] Alexandra Schmeckebier, ed., *Folk Arts of India* (Syracuse, N.Y., 1967), catalogue by Ruth Reeves, pp. 33–34.

[29] Stirrups on horses are shown in Indian stone sculptures from about the first century B.C. to the first century A.D. in Sanchi, Bhaja, Pitalkhora, and Mathura. This is their first occurrence anywhere in the world. See S. D. Singh, *Ancient Warfare with Special Reference to the Vedic Period* (Leiden, 1965), p. 63. Domesticated horses are represented among the terra-cottas found at Lothah, of Harappan age (*Indian Archeology, 1959–60 – A Review*, p. 18, pl. XV E).

[30] W. G. Archer, *The Vertical Man* (London, 1947), p. 44.

the "hobby horse" ridden by the followers of Śiva in Bengal at the Gambhira festival in the night of Śiva (Śivarātri), a wooden or bamboo stick decorated with colored paper and string; or it is a dancing horse which takes part in the dance in this festival[31] and in others also, in other seasons of the year and in other parts of the country (as in Tanjore, in the South).

The symbol, "horse," carries the hopes of every man in India. It has vivified the creative imagination of village potters and tribal craftsmen and is an outpost of their innumerable "styles." With its ancestral rider, it had entered India from on high, from the north, across the mountains and the social and ethnic strata of the country.

Horses are offered to any village god, male or female.[32] Deposits of clay horses abound not only in the sacred groves of South India and the western hills where Kasumar Dhamor protects his people, but also near the village shrines of Bengal, on the graves of Hindu Tantriks and Muslim saints. By an irony of creative justice, the village potter makes clay horses in their basic, timeless shapes not only for the lowly (the members of the "scheduled castes"), but also at the order of the high castes, the Brahmans and Kṣatriyas. These spirit horses and riders are massed for worship in a Brahmasthān.[33] The name means "Place of Brahmā" and is the traditional name, in ancient architectural treatises,[34] for the site of the innermost sanctuary of a stone temple of the great tradition. The spirit-rider here represents "the soul of a benevolent, unmarried Brahmin."[35]

The figure of the horse in the art of tribal and rural India retained its basic shape, particularly in the small terra-cotta images, alongside a form which had become more complex by assimilating to its own simplicity the naturalism which was part of the great tradition of Indian sculpture (as in the Tamil village horses), or by raising the little images of the spirit-rider to become expressive, sensitive, stylistically variegated emblems of the Bhil clans.

[31] B. K. Sarkar, *The Folk Element in Hindu Culture* (London, 1917), p. 111.

[32] A. Bhattacharya, "The Cult of the Village Gods of West Bengal," *Man in India*, 35 (1955): 19–30.

[33] Schmeckebier, *Folk Arts of India*, p. 33.

[34] Kramrisch, *The Hindu Temple*, p. 32.

[35] See n. 33.

The Art Ritual of Women

Magical diagrams are essentially nonfigurative; they are drawn or painted on the ground (dhuli-citra) with white rice paste or with colored powders. The magic function of art in India is vested in the diagrams, which are drawn primarily on the floor. Though not tribally restricted, the art of painting on the floor in rural India is, but for one significant exception, the prerogative of women. Its traditions are handed down from mother to daughter. A girl's training begins in her fifth or sixth year and she reaches competence in her twelfth year. A non-Brahman priest may be engaged at times. The art of painting on the floor is non-Brahman, although it may be practiced by Brahman women. The women learned it ultimately from traditions more ancient than those of the Aryan Brahmans, and they elaborated them in forms by which the floor is covered with magic potency in patterns peculiar to each part of India. The material used to make these magic diagrams, the rice powder, is felt to have magical powers in itself, like the copper which forms the substance of the Bhil spirit-riders. Rice powder acts magically. It scares away evil spirits.[36] The designs drawn with it on the floor have magical power. They are essentially diagrams. Within the confines of the more or less intricate geometrical lines of the diagram, an invoked presence finds its allotted place. Its power is confined and thereby held in its place and for the purpose for which the diagram was drawn. The magic diagram makes it possible for power to be present, and it brings this presence into the power of the magician who has made the diagram. This is a prerogative of women. Yantras, or magical diagrams, are also part of Tantrik practice.[37] A Mandala is such a magic diagram. Mandalas were widely used in Tantrik Buddhism. They determine the composition of one of the most characteristic and elaborate types of Buddhist paintings.[38] Tantriks who have made a Yantra have to avoid food prepared by women and even the sound of a woman's bangles.[39] Is this

[36] W. Crooke, *The Popular Religion and Folklore of Northern India*, 2 vols. (London, 1896), vol. 2, p. 191.

[37] Tantrik religion gives prominence to the female principle in divinity and to the union with it. Tantrik ritual uses complex diagrams as symbolic and magical contrivances (Yantras) in and by which deity is beheld in its cosmic manifestation and primordial unity.

[38] G. Tucci, *The Theory and Practice of the Mandala* (London, 1961), pp. 49–84.

[39] Abbot, *Keys of Power*, p. 14.

partly because they have to guard their art from those who had the power to evolve it?

The floor designs drawn freehand by women with white rice paste or powder on the earthen ground range from geometrical diagrams by themselves to their association with other symbols such as footprints—which are those of the great goddess. These spellbinding configurations are known under many names, such as Kolam, Mandana, Aripana, according to the style and region in which they were evolved.[40] Originally far removed from decoration, all these ritual magic designs are forms of a will directed to an end, which is to confine and control a supernatural power and to isolate it from the ground. The effect of these symbolic shapes is one with their efficacy. They do not form "abstract" patterns, for they are the shape of conceptions. They are intuited and functional diagrams transmitted by women.

Some of these designs are drawn every morning or evening; others are made at each sacrament of life (samskāra) and at the passage from one state of life to another. They are drawn at the birth of a child, at the boy's investiture with the sacred thread, and at the time of marriage. Others are drawn as acts of devotion when taking a vow (vrata) to achieve a desired result. These are drawn on certain days of the year of special significance in the course of the sun.

The Vrata Alpona[41] and Aripana are richest in design and connotation. The sun, the moon, the stars, the earth are integrated in them as well as the things desired by the young girl who draws them: ornaments, a mirror, and the like; and the whole cosmos is conjured up to bless and fulfill a young girl's wish—for even a simple wish is not to be fulfilled if no effort is made at the right time to communicate with the powers that work in heaven and on earth. Here it is the magic circle; in other designs it is the

[40] They are strictly geometrical in western and southern India and are called Mandana in Rājasthan, Rangoli in Maharashtra, Sathiya in Gujarat, and Kolam and Muggu in South India. They are richer in symbolical shapes in Benga, Bihar, and elsewhere in northern India where they are known as Alpona and Aripana; Apna is their name in the Western Himalaya, Cowka Purna and Sona Rakhna in Uttar Pradesh. The Paglya of Rājasthan include footprints in their design as do certain Alpona. See W. T. Elmore, *Dravidian Gods in Modern Hinduism* (1915), p. 27, pl. IV; J. Layard, "Labyrinth Ritual in South India," *Folklore*, 63–64 (1952–53):463–72.

[41] T. M. Chatterji, *Alpona* (Calcutta, 1948), p. 58, no. 32. Also, S. K. Ray, *The Ritual Art of the Bratas of Bengal* (New Delhi, 1961), pp. 41–48.

sacred square, a concatenation of curves, or an intersection of polygons that encloses the magic field. Into it the power of a god is invoked. It is assigned to its enclosure; it is spellbound. It cannot escape; it is controlled. It is held in its confinement, bound in the plane by the outline of the enclosure so that it cannot escape into the ground where, like lightning, it would be rendered impotent.[42]

The most ancient Sanskrit treatise on Indian painting prescribes the worship of the Sun God through an eight-petalled lotus flower drawn on the ground.[43] Several other Purāṇas[44] speak of the art of drawing the sun on the ground and say that the sun was worshiped in a circle in early days.[45] This practice, however, was not sanctioned by the Veda.[46] It belonged to those outside the Vedic pale; drawing on the ground is not associated with rites performed in temples.

The power of the supernatural is believed to be controlled magically and made effective at a given spot and time. The art of floor painting is a visual form of magic, a delineation of the presence of the numinous. Its diagrams avoid becoming stereotyped; they are enriched and evolve, whereas in the Vrata Alponas of eastern India the hopes and wishes of the artist are precipitated into the design on the floor.

Allied to the Vrata Alpona is the textile art of the Kanthā. The Kanthā,[47] a patched cloth, was made mainly in eastern Bengal (Pakistan), but also in Bihar, of worn-out and disused saris and

[42] C. G. Diehl, *Instrument and Purpose* (Lund, 1956), on the encircling of power; Abbot, *Keys of Power*, p. 83, on the function of the ground.

[43] *Viṣṇudharmottara Purāṇa*, chapter 2, verse 169. The text is of the sixth century but goes back to older sources. The "lotus flower" is a symbol, a "rose des vents" pointing to the eight directions. An actual lotus has a multiple of five petals.

[44] Purāṇas are encyclopedias of traditional knowledge dealing with everything from the creation of the cosmos onward.

[45] *Brahmā Purāṇa* 28.23–33; *Bhaviṣkya Purāṇa*, chaps. 48, 52, 205; *Śambha Purāṇa* 29.2–6.

[46] Haradatta commenting on *Gautama Sūtra* 11.20 says that when the sun stands in Aries young girls paint the sun and his retinue on the soil with colored dust and worship this in the morning and in the evening. This is to illustrate the meaning of the Sūtra which enjoins that customs, even though not expressly founded upon a passage of the Veda, are to be observed if they are not against the principles of the sacred writings. See Max Müller, *History of Ancient Sanskrit Literature* (London, 1859), p. 53.

[47] Stella Kramrisch, "Kanthā," *Journal of the Indian Society of Oriental Art*, 7 (1939): 141–67; "Kanthās of Bengal," *Marg*, 3 (1949): 18–29.

dhotis. The thin, white cotton cloth with colored borders was cut, patched, quilted, and embroidered. According to the thickness of the quilt and its size, it was used as a cover to be spread or as a wrap to be worn or folded as a bag. The white ground of the quilt was embroidered and reinforced with colored threads drawn from the colored borders. The colors of the Kanthās of the early part of the nineteenth century are mainly red and blue; in the later half, yellows and greens, particularly linden green, are also included. The materials of the Kanthā are rags and their threads. Joined afresh, these tatters are given a new wholeness. Their embroidered designs spring from this meaning. The Kanthā is a work which gives wholeness to things no longer of any use, to fragments without any significance. This rite of the restitution of wholeness is a domestic one, performed by women, though rarely by Brahman women. The more ornate Kanthās are the work of Kāyastha women, though women of all castes and classes of the rural population, including Muslim women, had and embroidered Kanthās. They were given as presents within the family or to friends.

Textile symbolism in India is hallowed by tradition. In the *Ṛg Veda* and the Upaniṣads, the universe is envisioned as a fabric woven by the gods. The cosmos, the ordered universe, is one continuous fabric with its warp and woof making a grid pattern.[48] Hence the importance of wholeness, not only of the uncut garment, like the sari or the dhoti, but also of the cloth woven all in one piece on which a sacred picture is to be painted.[49] Whether as cover for the body or as ground for a painting, the uncut fabric is a symbol of totality and integrity. It symbolizes the whole of manifestation. Inversely, rags are offered to the gods. Chindiyadeo, the Lord of Tatters, gives a new whole cloth if a rag is offered to him. There are rag shrines all over the country. Their goddess is Chithariya Bhavanī, "Our Lady of Tatters."[50] The Buddha wore a patchwork robe (saṇghāti); some of the reliefs of the Mathura school of the second century A.D. show him thus clad. Lord Caitanya (1485–1533), the apostle and visionary, draped in a Kanthā

[48] *Ṛg Veda* 6.9.3; 10.130.1; also *Bṛhadāraṇyaka Upaniṣad* III.8.7–8 and *Mundaka Upaniṣad* II.25.

[49] M. Lalou, *Iconographie des Etoffes Peintes dans le Mañjuśrīmūlakalpa* (Paris, 1930), p. 27.

[50] W. Crooke, *Popular Religion*, p. 161.

the ecstasies which overwhelmed his body.[51] The colorful patchwork of the robes of saints forms part of miniature paintings of the Mughal period. The patched robe of the Buddha or of a saint belongs to him in his nature of Savior. The rags are given a new wholeness. They clothe holiness.

Clothes worn near the body are part of its ambience and are personal. Should an enemy get hold of any bit of the cloth he might practice black magic against the former wearer.[52] The patchwork quilt as a collection of tatters guarantees immunity from black magic and offers protection and security, as do even the rags themselves when offered to the gods.

The symbolism inherent in the patchwork of the Kanthā is the ground which is embroidered with nearly equal perfection on both sides.[53] The act of making whole demands perfection throughout. The design is drawn by the embroiderer herself or by another woman. It is neither the work of a professional artist nor is it copied. No two Kanthās are ever alike; each is an original creation although Kanthās from the same district follow certain types and have more in common than those from villages at a greater distance.

The design of the square or rectangular field of the Kanthā relies in principle on a central circle occupied by a lotus flower. Four trees mark the four corners. The central, wide-open, many-petalled lotus is an ancient Indian symbol of universal manifestation and of this world in particular. The four trees are symbols of the four directions; they stem from Mesopotamia. The disk of the many-petalled lotus, when drawn as Alpona, on the floor, would support a vessel filled with water in the center. Deity is invoked and known to be present in a vessel filled with water. In the design of the Kanthā, the central lotus is inscribed in a square. The entire ground of the quilted cloth between the lotus and the directional trees is filled with figures, objects, symbolic devices, and scenes whose shapes and combinations are dictated by the imagination of the artist. Themes from ancient myths and legends are laid out next to scenes and figures commenting on contempo-

[51] B. K. Sarkar, *Folk Element in Hindu Culture*, p. 33.

[52] Cf. K. K. Ganguli, "Kantha, the Enchanted Wrap," *Indian Folklore*, 1 (1957): 3–10.

[53] Kanthās made by women of the weaver caste, however, imitate the effect of weaving and are meant to be seen on one side only. G. S. Dutt, "The Art of Kanthā," *Modern Review* (October, 1939).

rary life, and both are permeated with purely symbolic devices. The design of the Kanthā provides wide margins for showing the contents of the woman's mind. Their figures and symbols are freely associated and rhythmically assembled. In some Kanthās, the figures are those of animals only. A Muslim Kanthā, faithful to the precepts of a noniconic art, shows nothing but scrollwork. On the underlying order of the Kanthā as the framework is displayed the personality of the embroiderer. It shows not only in the planar composition but also in the selection of themes from the common reservoir of the tradition as it is lived by her at the moment of her needlework. The embroiderer's personality is especially clear in the selection and spacing of the stitches and the resulting texture and form of the embroidery.

The stitches are of the simplest kind, the running stitch being not only the main one but also the most ingeniously employed. According to length and spacing of the single stitches, they outline or, and this is their truly creative function, they organize the surface in a multitude of small squares and triangles so that the speckled texture of ground and embroidery is light or dense with colors. Closely parallel running stiches give a more gliding quality to the ground cover which they produce. Both of these modes and their combinations which fill a given surface are bounded by a continuous line which the back stitch yields. Within its firm contour, whether red or blue, the running stitches not only produce different color values, according to their density, but together with a particular texture of the surface, give an individual tonality to each Kanthā. Moreover, they are conducted so as to produce a unique effect of modeling on the textured surface. Modeling by means of running stitches appears to be an invention of the embroiderers of the Kanthās. It is a purely textile equivalent of modeling with brush and colors. In this, the "classical" tradition of Indian painting, as in Ajanta, excelled. Visualization in terms of the modeled form and an irrepressible sense of plasticity are essentially Indian. This age-old and "classical" Indian quality was given form in textiles in the art of the Kanthā of East Bengal in the nineteenth century. The effect of modeling is produced by the closely spaced rows of stitches running parallel to the outline of a figure. This produces an area of uniform texture and tone. Toward the interior of the outlined surface, the density and direction of the stitches change, producing another area set off from its neighbor zone. This, together with the speckled effect which leads the eye in more than one direction, also produces effects akin to op art but having representational intentions. The op art effect is bounded by the outline of the respective figure of elephant or horse.

The figures of the Kanthā, "modeled" by these colorful stitches allowing the white ground to shine through, are also foreshortened, and their limbs may overlap without, however, producing the effect of any spatial context. The figures are scattered rhythmically over the white ground and if limbs or figures overlap, their area is part of the embroidered ground, for though the figure may be "modeled" in terms of stitching, the modeling has no substance to it. It suggests volume by directional movement. Far from creating an illusion of the body, its embroidered form is dematerialized. Often the figures are shown in a contraction of front and profile. At other times, an X-ray view allows one to see across them. As a result of this, some Kanthās create their own figures, which have the shape of a man with or without a body, the number of limbs also being at the discretion of the artist. This, though, does not refer to their multiplicity, which iconography may postulate in the case of the figures of deities, but to their reduction to stumps instead of limbs, contraction of two limbs into one, or omission of one limb or another according to the needs of identification, rhythm, and compositional clarity.

By the middle of the century, the embroidery stitch is more frequently resorted to than it was earlier. It adds more compact areas and stronger hues to the Kanthā. But these stronger accents too sink into the ground of the Kanthā. The ground between figures, as often as not, is reinforced all over with stitches running in closely set parallels around each figure. For this, white thread is used and, less frequently, blue or red thread. These colors give a pointillistically muted tonality to the vibrant texture of the ground.

Thematically, the art of the Kanthā is an enriched textile version of the art of the Aripana or Alpona, the painting on the floor, its magic purpose being enhanced by the textile symbolism of its material and the way this is used. Stylistically, its form is entirely its own, adjusting an ancient propensity of India's classical art to its own textile sensibilities.

The art of the Kanthā is a rural art. While it is imbued with

Hindu myths, it is also perceptive of the life of India as it was lived in the nineteenth century, with some of its novelty absorbed by the stream of the tradition and integrated into its style. It is an art of leisure. Sophisticatedly primitive, the textile art of the Kanthā integrates many layers of the fabric of Indian life, tribal as well as urban, in its conception. The magic that underlies its purpose is that of love—not of coercion, as that of the diagrammatic floor drawings whose purpose is wish fulfillment. A Kanthā is given as a present, it is conceived with an outgoing mind, and it brings the entire personality of the maker to the person for whom it is made. Its composition is ritual, being laid out around the center of the lotus of manifestation. Its symbols have universal validity in the four directions. To their whirls and waves, to the lotus and the life trees, are assigned the innumerable figured scenes of the mythic, ever-present past together with episodes of the passing scene.

All of them are firmly stitched into a reconstituted, vibrant wholeness. The Kanthā is a form of a creative process of integration that took place within each woman who made a Kanthā. Succumbing to the effects of the industrial revolution, which were belated in India, the art of the Kanthā died within the first quarter of the twentieth century. It is not known when this art began. Its upsurge in a narrowly circumscribed area has not its like elsewhere. Kanthās from Bihar are without the wealth of associated content and textile imagination. Although made in the same technique, their widely spaced design is an adaptation, in terms of embroidery, of the staid, placid lines of a certain type of painting of Bihar. The Bengal Kanthās resemble a form of painting in Bengal only insofar as their overall character stems from the magic art of the Alpona. Like the South Indian sanctuaries teeming with their hundreds of clay horses, clay cattle, and clay human figures offered in sacred groves, which express in their form the mystery of autochthony, the Kanthās of East Bengal (East Pakistan) are saturated with numinous power, the "śakti" of this region, which, working through its women, is given form by innumerable disciplined stitches. Both these forms of art, that of the South Indian non-Brahman priest-potter and that of the Bengali Hindu matron (the older women, as a rule, made the Kanthās), represent traditional village art in fulfillment of rites of offering.

NO TIME, GREAT TIME, AND PROFANE TIME IN BUDDHISM

ALEX WAYMAN

This essay maintains that some important Buddhist texts contribute to a neat formulation of man's most treasured modes of thought: No Time as the source of religion, Great Time as the source of myth, and Profane Time as the source of reason. These three forms of Time are not so named in the Buddhist works. The limitation of data to Indo-Tibetan materials makes possible the addition of an expression "No Time" to the two categories "Great Time" and "Profane Time" utilized by Eliade for worldwide cultural materials, while he marshals the evidence and terminology that facilitate the integration of Eastern and Western spirit.[1] Eliade's ontological interpretation of such modes is well known. The present writer is not thereby released from the obligation to rework the available data according to his understanding of Buddhism. Then – to anticipate the development – without asserting any ontological status for such modes elsewhere in the world, it does appear that in the Buddhist case, in the Indian context, the three modes of thought allude to three modes of being.

There is no claim to involve all of Buddhism in this treatment, although the prevalent Buddhist genesis legend, already studied, will play a significant role.[2] The metaphysical discussion

[1] Among the works of Mircea Eliade, the following have been especially important to this paper: *Myths, Dreams and Mysteries* (London, 1960); *The Sacred and the Profane* (New York, 1961).

[2] Alex Wayman, "Buddhist Genesis and the Tantric Tradition," *Oriens Extremus*, 9 (1962): 127–31.

stems from one celebrated text of Mahāyāna Buddhism—the work called *Madhyānta-vibhāga* which Asaṅga (*ca.* 375–430 A.D.) is held by tradition to have received from the future Buddha Maitreya in the Tuṣitā (a heaven).[3] Asaṅga, a leading exponent of Yogācāra Buddhism, might be the author of the *Madhyānta-vibhāga*, upon which his younger brother (probably half-brother) Vasubandhu wrote a commentary.[4]

Religion, Myth, and Reason in Buddhism

Although the origins of Buddhism have not been fully explained in regard to such modes as "religion," "myth," and "reason," there is little doubt that in its subsequent development, well advanced in the early centuries B.C., Buddhism possessed all these categories of thought.

At the heart of its religion, Mahāyāna Buddhism places the Buddha himself with the body of omniscience called the Dharmakāya ("outside the three worlds"), and adds the two phenomenal bodies called Saṃbhoga-kāya ("at the top of the realm of form") and Nirmāṇa-kāya ("in the realm of desire"). Voidness (*śūnyatā*) means the annihilation of corrupting influences of man's nature, leaving unvoided the Buddha natures. The laws (*dharma*) stem from the void realm of nature(*dharmadhātu*).

Myth in Buddhism includes not only the important genesis legend and the mythical portion of the Buddha's legendary life, but also the extensive literature called the Jātakas ("birth stories"), explained as the illustrious births of the Buddha in his anterior incarnations as a *bodhisattva*, a being striving toward enlightenment while exhibiting exemplary conduct to assist other beings.

The reasoning side of Buddhism played an outstanding role, as the antagonist, in the development of the traditional Hindu schools of philosophy. So well developed is this side of Buddhism that some early Western Orientalists considered Buddhism to be preeminently rational.

3 Alex Wayman, *Analysis of the Śrāvakabhūmi Manuscript* (Berkeley and Los Angeles, 1961), pp. 33–34.

4 Gadjin M. Nagao, ed., *Madhyāntavibhāga-bhāṣya* (Tokyo, 1964). See also the salient work: Th. Stcherbatsky, *Madhyānta-Vibhanga* ("Discourse on Discrimination between Middle and Extremes"), ascribed to Bodhisattva Maitreya and commented on by Vasubandhu and Sthiramati, translated from the Sanskrit (*Bibliotheca Buddhica*, vol. 30 [Leningrad, 1936]; only the first chapter, with commentary and subcommentary, has been translated therein).

Creation according to the *Madhyānta-vibhāga*

Before setting forth the intended structure of three modes of thought, I shall separately treat the rather technical data of the *Madhyānta-vibhāga*, which not only contributes decisively to the present topic but also conveys a rather different picture of the Yogācāra from the way the latter is depicted in current surveys of Indian philosophy.

The *two realities* of the Yogācāra metaphysics are called *abhūta-parikalpa* and *śūnyatā*, here translated respectively as the "Imagination of Unreality" and "Voidness," compatible with Stcherbatsky's respective renditions, the "Universal Constructor of Phenomena" and the "Absolute." The *Madhyānta-vibhāga states* (I, 1):

> There was the Imagination of Unreality,
> And in it no duality (of subject and object).
> There was Voidness in it,
> And it was in that (Voidness).[5]

Of the reality called "Imagination of Unreality," what is the "Unreality" (*abhūta*) and what the "Imagination" (*parikalpa*)? The text states (I, 5): "What is imagined is explained as the 'objective thing' (*artha*); what is dependent, as the construction process of unreality; and what is perfect, as the unreality of both (subject and object)."[6] And from the text (I, 3) and Vasubandhu's commentary, we learn that the "Imagination" has its own four characters (*svalakṣaṇa*), called "objective thing" (*artha*), "personal organ" (*sattva*), "self" (*atman*), and "representation" (*vijñapti*):

> Perception was engendered as the projection of (six kinds of) objective things, (five) personal organs, self (= mind), and (six kinds of) representations. The objective thing does not belong to it (i.e., perception). Since the former (the objective thing) is unreal, the latter (perception) is also unreal.[7]

[5] abhūta-parikalpo 'sti dvayan tatra na vidyate /
śūnyatā vidyate tv atra tasyām api sa vidyate / /

[6] kalpitaḥ paratantraś ca pariniṣpanna eva ca /
arthād abhūtakalpāc ca dvayābhāvāc ca deśitaḥ / /

[7] artha-satvātma-vijñapti-pratibhāsaṃ prajāyate /
vijñānaṃ nāsti cāsyārthas tad-abhāvāt tad apy asat / /
Vasubandhu's commentary (Nagao, *Madhyāntavibhāga-bhāṣya*, pp. 18–19) clarifies the word "self" (*ātman*) as the "corrupted mind" (*kliṣṭamanas*) and the six things as objects grasped by the six sense organs (five by the word *sattva*), including mind as the sixth, in terms of six representations (*vijñapti*).

The implication is that when the Imagination of Unreality is not so imagining, its four characters are not grouped in subject-object relation, and that when it is so imagining, the "self" approaches the "personal organ," whereupon the "representation" falsely depicts the "objective thing." As with all such ultimate processes, the *modus operandi* of the primordial subject-object emergence is wrapped in mystery. However, it seems to involve an interaction of the "self" and the "personal organ" with Voidness as Dharmadhātu ("realm of Dharma"), which is the material cause.[8]

The reality called "Voidness" has this character (I, 13*a–b*): "the unreality of both (subject and object), and the reality (subjacent) of this unreality."[9] This translation, following Stcherbatsky, is consistent with Yogācāra definitions in other works as typified by two statements, one of which specifies what is voided and the other of which specifies what remains not voided. The following verse (I, 14) clarifies the sense of the "reality (subjacent) of this unreality" by names of Voidness, justified in the next verse (I, 15):

Thusness (*tathatā*) because not otherwise, True Limit (*bhūtakoṭi*) because not wrong, Attributeless (*animitta*) because the cessation of attributes, Ultimate State (*paramārthatā*) because the domain of the noble ones, the Realm of Dharma (*dharmadhātu*) because having the noble natures (*dharma*).

Verses I, 8–9 and Vasubandhu's commentary portray the Imagination of Unreality in a new role. Since its own characters (*svalakṣaṇa*) had projected the unreal perception, the younger Imagination of Unreality is now precisely that unreal perception of the unreal objective thing:

Now the Imagination of Unreality was consciousness (of) and mentals, composing the three realms (of desire, of form, and formless). Perception (= "consciousness of") sees the objective thing itself; its mentals

[8] Such an idea is found near the beginning of Asaṅga's *Śrāvakabhūmi*, in a passage for which original Sanskrit is lacking; here it is translated from Tibetan (Derge edition of Tanjur, *Sems tsam, Śrāvakabhūmi*, 2b): "However, that seed does not have the characteristics of difference so long as it stays apart from the six sense bases (*ṣaḍāyatana*). That seed has been handed down in lineage from beginningless time and has states obtained through the six sense bases which are attained by means of 'true nature' (*dharmatā*)."

[9] dvayābhāvo hy abhāvasya bhāvaḥ śūnyasya lakṣaṇam.

see modifications of the objective thing. The first one is the foundation-perception (= *ālayavijñāna*). The other ones pertain to experience. These are the mentals (namely, feelings, *vedanā*) which enjoy, (ideas, *saṃjñā*) which distinguish, and (motivations, *saṃskāra*) which activate (perception).[10]

That passage covers two stages of the process which the present essay intends to keep separate. They are "consciousness of," which sees the objective thing itself, and mentals, which see modifications of the thing. They are preceded by the atemporal state in which the Imagination of Unreality abides with Voidness deprived of the subject-object relationship.

No Time, the Source of Religion

No Time means the revelation of reality, everywhere, always. Man may or may not intuit the dazzling ultimate. It is *other* than Great Time when nature predicts by omens and man obeys. It is *other* than Profane Time when man predicts by reason and nature obeys.

The story of Buddhist genesis alludes to a mode of being prevailing as "men of the first eon" while the lower receptacle worlds are reevolving after the periodic destruction. These men have bodies made of mind, are self-luminous, feed on joy, and are wherever they wish to be. Their actions have immediate fruition, and so involve No Time.[11]

In the *Madhyānta-vibhāga*, No Time is the mysterious truth of a voidness reality subjacent to the unreality of subject and object—a reality neither joined to nor separate from the creative center called Imagination of Unreality. This Voidness is the goal to which the noble ones (the elect) aspire, because it has the noble natures, called in other Buddhist texts the "Buddha natures" (*buddhadharma*).

Generally, Buddhist texts referred to this state as Nirvāṇa, more properly "Nirvāṇa without remainder." "Nirvāṇa with remainder" is approximately Great Time. The Mahāyāna "Nirvāṇa without fixed abode" (*apratiṣṭhita-nirvāṇa*) is all three Times.

[10] abhūtaparikalpaś ca citta-caittās tridhātukāḥ /
tatrārtha-dṛṣṭir vijñānaṃ tad-viśeṣe tu caitasāḥ //
ekam pratyaya-vijñānaṃ dvitīyam aupabhogikaṃ /
upabhoga-pariccheda-prerakās tatra caitasāḥ //

[11] Wayman, "Buddhist Genesis."

Great Time, the Source of Myth

Great Time is the marvelous beginning of time in the sense of an interval not always progressing in a continuous line, as does Profane Time, which has an anterior past, a present moment, and a posterior future. The interval of time is colored by a glorious quality, because then is the contact with earth by the hero, walking with erect stature. His fabulous and exemplary adventures need only be recounted in myth to inspire the imagination, and possibly also the conduct of men in later Profane Time, especially men who are close to the soil. The myth of the Buddha's life also begins with this walking, as the child leaves his mother's womb by the right side, takes seven steps toward the north, and announces, "I am at the top of the world, . . ."[12] The future Buddha's seven steps are (No Time in) Great Time; his announcement is (No Time in) Profane Time (see below, pp. 53–54).

All those examples point to the touching of earth as constituting a symbolic moment which we could call Moment 1, as the preliminary moment to mundane life (in case of infant), to spiritual life (in case of Buddha), to the symbolization of the spiritual life (in case of main body of the rite), to acceptance in marriage (in case of the auspicious bride). At Moment 1, the being is not yet alive, but anticipates the whole future life. Astrologically, at the moment of birth the infant is at the center of the universe, in sympathetic communion with the planets and stars, which indelibly impress the being with a sort of centripetal force.[13]

This place where earth is touched is the Center, of which Eliade frequently speaks.

In the Buddhist story of genesis, on the surface of earth there appeared an earth essence—in the Tantric version called an ambrosia (*amṛta*)—which a greedy being tasted with his finger and then ate mouthfuls of. Other beings followed suit. Thus they became dependent on subtle morsel food and no longer fed on joy. They gradually lost the body made of mind as their bodies became heavier and more substantial. The ones who indulged least proudly retained their beautiful form. The sun, moon, and year became known. Hell beings, beings in the embryonic states, and the gods involved with desire (*kāmāvacāradeva*) still have

[12] Cf. Eliade, *Myths, Dreams and Mysteries*, pp. 110–15.

[13] Alex Wayman, "Climactic Times in Indian Mythology and Religion," *History of Religions*, 4 (1965): 310–11.

the subtle kind of food which does not give rise to excrement or urine.[14]

According to the *Madhyānta-vibhāga*, in the beginning the world became inner-outer, or subject-object. That is to say, what was always there in No Time continued just the same. But an imaginary relationship was introduced among the four characters, semi-divine beings as it were, of the Imagination of Unreality. Perhaps in a magic square they projected their own being through Voidness into an Imagination of Unreality the younger. This is first the foundation perception called "basic perception" (*ālaya-vijñāna*) which has as object the objective thing itself. Since as yet there are no modifications (*viśeṣa*) of the objective thing, there is no error (*bhrānti*) or specific illusion. Nevertheless, the objective thing is said to be unreal. The unreality here is the cosmic illusion, the beginning of downfall. The fascinating objective thing conceals in its very freshness the specific illusion that is sure to follow in a subsequent remove of Profane Time. From the beginning, the world was pervaded by delusion (*moha*). It is as the Buddha tells: all constructed things (*saṃskāra*) are suffering. In Great Time, the suffering is of transformation.

Profane Time, the Source of Reason

This is horizontality. Man has nature down where it can be handled. But he believes that his inner knowledge stems from outer happenings. Time now, according to Lévy-Bruhl, is what "our" minds—the minds of us, the "civilized"—take it to be. In his graphic words:

> extending indefinitely in imagination, something like a straight line, always homogeneous by nature, upon which events fall into position, a line on which foresight can arrange them in an unilinear and irreversible series, and on which they must of necessity occur one after the other.[15]

As long as man lives a profane life, his best guide is reason, which is limited and superficial, accompanied by the latest "laws of thought." The remarkable achievements of science fall here. Profane existence proves itself by accumulations such as merchandise

[14] Wayman, "Buddhist Genesis."
[15] Lucien Lévy-Bruhl, *Primitive Mentality* (Boston, 1966), p. 123.

and books (religious and secular), and also by desacralized leavings or residues. It is "the rest of life" after Moment 1.

In Buddhist genesis, the beings began to subsist on coarse morsel food, which gave rise to excrement and urine. The distinguishing characteristics of male and female arose, along with sexual desire and relevant acts. Then the idea of "private property" arose with individual rice plots, followed by stealing and consequent violence. Those beings elected a "great chosen one" (*mahāsammata*) to provide security.[16] This shows the emergence of lust and hatred, then private property and the status of ruler and ruled.

The *Madhyānta-vibhāga* alludes to this state of being by "mentals" seeing the modifications of the objective thing. These mentals pertain to experience, and are feelings, ideas, and motivations. They are also called the "evolving perceptions" (*pravṛtti-vijñāna*). This state is full-blown illusion.

Recapitulations

It is a basic feature of Eliade's writings that he denies a purely profane existence. The homogeneity of profane space is interrupted by certain "holy places" dear to the memory of even the profane nonreligious man.[17] While Eliade has not defined the profane life in the terms I have employed above, I see no conflict with his position on this matter. I can therefore go on to agree with him on this denial of the pure profane. There is no need to repeat here his well-presented justifications. My methods of demonstrating this conclusion are additional. Here there are two kinds of recapitulation – that of childhood and that of the daily life of man.

The Recapitulation in Childhood

In a brief communication[18] I called attention to the Indian theory of life stages, of which the first three are in point now. They are the first year of life under the Moon, the second and third years under Mars, and the fourth through twelfth under Mercury. In the first year – as modern child development study

[16] Wayman, "Buddhist Genesis."

[17] So in Eliade, *The Sacred and the Profane.*

[18] "The Stages of Life according to Varāhamihira," *Journal of the American Oriental Society*, 83 (1963): 360–61.

shows—the baby begins with no distinction between himself and his environment, and so is akin to the nondual state of No Time, from which he gradually emerges during the balance of the year. Recently emerged from the primeval waters called the amniotic fluid and still dependent on liquids, the infant is governed by the Moon. For purposes of our correspondences based on Indian classifications, the entire year will be taken conventionally as the "nondual state." About the beginning of the second year, the child starts to walk: this inaugurates the heroic stage of walking on earth. It is a kind of *anabasis*, "advance uphill" (classically used for "military advance"). Also in the next two years the child speaks magic syllables expressing his desires and commanding their fulfillment by parents. Morbid regressions to this state could be called *catabasis*, "retreat to the sea" (classically used for "military retreat"). So the child during those two years is governed by Mars, the commander-in-chief in Indian astrology. This is childhood's type of Great Time. Phylogenetic recapitulation in Profane Time is shown by the last period of childhood, the fourth through the twelfth year, when the lad or girl develops the power of reasoning while playfully dashing hither and yon under the dominion of Mercury. Modern studies show that the child is now a "socialized being" and his games increasingly have rules.[19] The ages assigned to these stages are of course stated with generality and are not meant to deny individual differences.

The Daily Recapitulation

Each day, man's life exhibits modes that disguise the three times. Properly speaking, the disguise is inaugurated by puberty, because the maturation of the sexually differentiated characteristics recalls what in the Buddhist genesis legend inaugurated the last period, corrupted by lust and hatred. In short, dreamless sleep corresponds to No Time, dream to Great Time, and the waking state to Profane Time.

I must stress—and in a similar vein, so does Eliade[20]—that the kind of correspondence referred to in the itemization of recapitulations does not imply identity with the three Times. Indeed, elements in correspondence are both related in some way

[19] Jean Piaget, *Play, Dreams and Imitation in Childhood* (New York, 1962), p. 142.

[20] Eliade, *Myths, Dreams and Mysteries*, p. 17.

and differ in some way. No Time, Great Time, and Profane Time each have a universal or shared character. The recapitulations are personal or private. Thus, Great Time is the source of myth as held by a certain society to work out public problems while a dream is a private matter to work out private problems. The dream is also like Great Time in its shortened psychological distance between subject and object, evidenced by the conversion of discursive thinking into nondiscursive imagery, especially in dramatic presentation, and also by its premonitory character (in the sense of showing trends). In contrast, dreaming is mostly inspired by experiences of the waking state, preeminently Profane Time, while Great Time is mostly inspired by No Time. Certain cases of unsuccessful ("unresolved") dreaming even parallel the successful "walking" of Great Time by the striking act of somnambulism. The recapitulations of childhood are more faithful to the three Times (hence the Biblical advice for entering the Kingdom of Heaven). That the third period (ages four through twelve), when the child is allowed to go out and play with other children, establishes Profane Time, is a matter to be justified. Buddhism generally explained that "discursive thought" (*vikalpa*) is the nescience (*avidyā*), or cause of it, that heads the Dependent Origination (*pratītya-samutpāda*) constituting Phenomenal Life (*saṃsāra*). This "discursive thought" is the basis of human reasoning with its rules. But a child playing by itself does not devise rules for games.[21] Therefore, I understand the third period of childhood to be involved in the parable of the Buddhist Mahāyāna scripture called *Sāgaramatiparipṛcchā*: "Now suppose this boy, being a child, would fall into a pit of night-soil while playing. . . . " It turns out that this "pit of night-soil" is a term for *saṃsāra*.[22]

While the recapitulations in both childhood and daily life are not identical with the three Times, they do share the universal character in a salient feature. That is to say, we can combine the childhood and daily recapitulations to observe that although the child, and then the child become an adult, are in aspects of Profane Time, they do indeed still recapitulate all three Times. They do so irrespective of the degree of religious feeling in particular persons, do so irrespective of such rites as baptism, and do so

[21] Piaget, *Play, Dreams and Imitation*, p. 142.

[22] The parable is quoted in Jikido Takasaki, *A Study on the Ratnagotravibhaga (Uttaratantra)* (Rome, 1966), pp. 246–47.

whether or not people indulge in food and sex sacramentally. In every life the "Moment 1" is Great Time, the rest of life Profane Time, but throughout life there are these recapitulations, echoes, and intimations of the Sacred. This is why no person in Profane Time can be utterly dissociated from No Time and Great Time. In this light, an irreligious as well as a religious person may use with sincerity such expressions as the "sanctity of the home."

Breakthroughs

By "breakthrough" I refer to the numinous experience as described by Otto (*Das Heilige*). It is an irrational revelation of overwhelming majesty or of mysterious power. The complete otherness of the revelation makes it appear as a breakthrough from a superior, nonhuman realm. According to the classification utilized above, this breakthrough would be from No Time into Great Time or from No Time into Profane Time. In the Indian context, the first case—overwhelming majesty of No Time in Great Time—is illustrated in the *Bhagavadgītā* by Krishna's revelation of his cosmic form to Arjuna. This is also the *saṃbhogakāya* of the Buddha preaching to the great *bodhisattvas* in the Akaniṣṭha Heaven. The second case—the mysterious power of No Time in Profane Time—is illustrated by the Hindu-Buddhist Act of Truth. This act is done by Sitā in the Hindu epic *Rāmāyana* and there are many examples in Buddhist scriptures. Here the performer declares the truth of his outstanding acts and commands the gods to produce the desired miracle. The miracle—an incredible event apparently violating "Nature's laws"—is the breakthrough. Ānandagarbha contains this ritual statement in his *Śrīparamādi-ṭīkā*: "He should recite, 'Oh Bhagavat Vajrasattva, just as it is true that all *dharmas* are like a dream, by virtue of that truth may I be allowed to see and be allowed to hear the such-and-such desired dream!'"[23]

Both kinds of breakthrough have been responsible in numerous cases for the striking religious phenomenon of "conversion." In the category of breakthrough I would also place some debatable

[23] / bcom ldan ḥdas rdo rje sems dpaḥ bden pa gaṅ gis chos thams cad rmi lam dan ḥdra bar mñam paḥi bden pa des bdag ḥdod paḥi rmi lam che ge mo mthoṅ bar mdzod cig / thos par mdzod cig ces brjod par byaḥo / (Kyoto-Tokyo Photographic reprint [1959–61] of *Kanjur-Tanjur*, vol. 72, pp. 305–3).

religious experiences, of more or less sullied character, all for "ego-defense": battlefield trauma, epilepsy, young man in the whorehouse, psychedelic drugs (as indicated by such images of "shattering" as walls breached by sea-water).

Participations

There is also the attempt to ascend to higher states of consciousness as though to live integrally in them, reified as modes of being—a sort of mystical immersion—or at least to be able to get into and out of those states whenever one wishes. Hence we speak of participation in Great Time or in No Time. Success here can be understood as either discovery or verification of spiritual truth, and also as the acquisition of supernormal powers. Eliade writes:

> Upon the plane of the archaic religions, participation in the condition of the "spirits" is what endows the mystics and the magicians with their highest prestige. It is during his ecstasy that the shaman undertakes, *in the spirit*, long and dangerous mystical journeys even up to the highest Heaven to meet the God, or up to the Moon or down into Hell, etc.[24]

Whatever be the truth in these cases, it is the human mind which so asserts it. It is a wonderful feature of Profane Time that it asserts the truth of religion. The higher Times have truth but do not assert it. Great Time should include the Buddhist search for or experience of suffering as a Noble Truth. For this it is necessary to reduce, even to abolish, psychological distance—man's advancing self-awareness in Profane Time that he is differentiated from the object (nature), which curtails a person's empathy with beings located mentally by that person in other groups. This factitious grouping—the castes of India and the world—is the prejudice engendered during the third period of childhood (see "Recapitulations," pp. 54–55).

Buddhism, in common with Hinduism, believed that by a regular course of conduct, such as restrictions on food and sex activity, and by finding the proper place and there a *guru*, a person (preferably male) could then undertake the somewhat arduous training for *samādhi* and thus ascend to various levels of consciousness, even the highest, the Incomparable Complete Enlightenment of

[24] Eliade, *Myths, Dreams and Mysteries*, p. 95.

the Buddha. This meditative ascension is usually stated in terms of sensory experience. The attainment of mental calm gradually brings out certain supernormal faculties, such as divine hearing. Eliade points out, "In short, throughout religious history, sensory activity has been used as a means of participating in the sacred and attaining to the divine."[25] In the *bodhisattva* doctrine of Mahāyāna Buddhism this is also stressed. Thus, in Atīśa's *Bodhipathapradīpa* (verses 35–36):

Just as a bird with unspread wings cannot fly up to the sky, in the same way the one without the power of the supernormal faculties cannot serve the aim of the sentient beings.

The merits of a single day that are due to the supernormal faculties would not occur in a hundred births for one lacking the supernormal faculties.[26]

In that way, those *bodhisattvas* who are called "great beings" (*mahāsattva*) are in Great Time, vastly able to serve the aim of sentient beings by dint of the supernormal faculties.

Extraordinary sensory experience is governed by the second instruction of the Buddhist path, which is arranged in three instructions: (1) morality (*adhiśīla-śikṣa*), (2) concentration (*adhisamādhi-śikṣa*), and (3) insight (*adhiprajñā-śikṣa*).[27] The implication of these instructions is that Buddhism is not seeking to attain Great Time or No Time just for the sake of doing so, or for the sake of gaining a striking experience. The old Buddhist aim was of liberation (No Time) and later came the Bodhisattva ideal (Great Time). Since Great Time had the seed of downfall into Profane Time, the Buddhist rationale of reaching that lofty state is to do it in circumstances whereby the concurrent hypnotic delusion is eliminated. And so it was taught that on top of the mental calming, the fruit of the second instruction, there should be the insight which sees things as they really are (what early Buddhism said) or which sees things arising as in a dream (what later Buddhism said).

The order of instructions places morality as the foundation for both mental calming and insight. This is borne out by the assign-

[25] *Ibid.*, p. 74.

[26] Manuscript translation from Tibetan by Alex Wayman.

[27] The famous Pāli text, Buddhaghosa's *Visuddhimagga*, is arranged in three parts in accordance with three instructions.

ment of certain rites to Great Time. Ritual action has this in common with the heroic conduct of Great Time: one has to give up all random action and do things with exactitude in the performance of a ritual, and one has to give up all mean and timid acts in order to have heroic conduct. That is to say, they both demand the abandonment of the usual human weaknesses exhibited in Profane Time. These rites have features in common with meditation procedures. I have in mind especially the *maṇḍala* rites of Tibetan Buddhism,[28] which are analogous to steps of meditation. Here one has to select the proper site, remove all the stones, potsherds, and other pains of the soil, and meditatively seize the site by vowing to perform the reviewed rite. In Buddhist meditation one must also find the right meditative object, eliminate gross corruptions from the mind, and seize the meditative object by leaving off the usual mental dashing hither and yon to a multitude of sensory objects.

These meditative procedures – the old ways or the "shortcuts" such as the *Tantras* claim to have – are meant to reach an otherworldly condition. It is here that the myth, especially the genesis legend, serves the function of reminding profane man of that mode of being he has lost and even suggesting how he may return. Then, what does Buddhism have to say about participating in Great Time and No Time as modes of being in the senses suggested by the genesis legend? It was believed in ancient Buddhism that by advanced meditative techniques one could draw from the physical body a duplicate of it called the "body made of mind" (*manomaya-kāya*), as recorded in the *Dīgha-nikāya*:

> Here a monk creates a body from this (his) body, having form mind-made, with all limbs and parts, not deprived of senses. Just as if a man were to pull out a reed from its sheath, he would know: "This is the sheath, this the reed. The sheath is one thing, the reed is another. It is from the sheath that the reed has been drawn forth."[29]

The *Laṅkāvatāra-sūtra* distinguishes three degrees in development of this "body made of mind": (1) its potential separation during stabilization in the pleasure of *samādhi*; (2) its separation due to

[28] See Ferdinand D. Lessing and Alex Wayman, trans., *Mkhas grub rje's* ("Fundamentals of the Buddhist Tantras"), (The Hague, 1968), pp. 279 ff.

[29] See Paravahera vajirañāṇa Mahāthera, *Buddhist Meditation in Theory and Practice* (Colombo, Ceylon, 1962), p. 440; and Mircea Eliade, *Yoga; Immortality and Freedom* (New York, 1958), p. 165.

reversal of the basis of the evolving perceptions and of the basic perception (*ālayavijñāna*), with a reorientation ("alteration of consciousness") toward *dharmas* (natures); and finally, (3) its becoming a body of the Buddha.[30] The second stage, pervaded by "forbearance of the unoriginated natures" (*anutpattikadharmakṣānti*), means living without terror in Great Time; while the third stage, when the "body made of mind" has been initiated as a Buddha, means living in No Time. These three stages of the "body made of mind" appear to reverse the three downward stages of the Buddhist genesis legend and, by mastering the three Times, to prove the myth.

In addition, there are ancient and modern claims that certain drugs, now called "consciousness expanding" (psychedelic), such as the current LSD – possibly the *soma* of the ancient Vedic cult is in the same category – bring one easily to the experience of Great Time. Drugs that arouse striking sensory images have precisely this *intense mindfulness* (*smṛti*) in common with *yoga*. In the case of drugs, however, the experience is of kaleidoscopic and somewhat distorted images rather than the "one pointedness of mind" (*ekāgratā-citta*) of *samādhi* and is uncontrolled by the subject except for some affective preconditioning ("expectancy"). Therefore, these drugs cannot supply the mental calm (*śamatha*) necessary for the supernormal faculties. They seem to amount to at least one of the two extremes rejected by the Buddha in favor of the Middle Path – the extreme of indulgence in a riot of sense images; possibly also they represent the extreme of mortification, of body chemistry.

Indeed, an artist of the visionary type is more likely to live in Great Time than any drug-taker. This is because when perception sees the bare objective thing, that object, as "nature," has the upper hand: being the only thing perceived, it has virtual hypnotic value. Notice the words of Picasso:

> There must be darkness everywhere except on the canvas, so that the painter becomes hypnotized by his own work and paints almost as though he were in a trance. . . . He must stay as close as possible to his own inner world if he wants to transcend the limitations his reason is always trying to impose on him.[31]

[30] See Alex Wayman, "Studies in Yama and Māra," *Indo-Iranian Journal*, 3 (1959): 119.

[31] Françoise Gilot and Carlton Lake, *Life with Picasso* (New York, 1965), pp. 110–11.

Jung writes consistently: "A great work of art is like a dream; for all its apparent obviousness it does not explain itself and is never unequivocal. A dream never says: 'You ought,' or: 'This is the truth.'"[32] The breakdown of formal profane structures through shortened psychological distance can bring types of religious experiences to artists and drug-takers as well as to *yogins*. However, there is no special distinction in reaching Great Time or No Time somehow or other, no matter in how disoriented a manner; for, after all, there are the recapitulations which all of us experience normally without risk.

Conclusion

If one accepts the terminology of three Times associated with three modes of thought and further accepts that these modes of thought allude to modes of being, he can easily grant that there are various ways of reaching or plunging into those modes of being as a veritable transfer or flight of consciousness to a different field or domain, one that is initially strange and possibly frightening. The three Times themselves, and the corresponding procedure used for dealing with them, are a kind of thinking well known from the ancient *Upaniṣads*, on the background of which Buddhism itself arose. The states of Waking, Dream, and Dreamless Sleep are encompassing categories and are themselves included in the Fourth State (Turiya), which seems to be the forerunner of the Mahāyāna "Nirvāṇa without fixed abode."

The use of the categories "No Time," "Great Time," and "Profane Time" for subsuming disparate features of man's development or states of consciousness is not surprising since the mind of man is structurally the same, though given to different "ways of thought"; and, after all, one can select from various sources the particular material that fits into a prearrangement. The formulation would be outstanding if it should prove to fit well with other salient features of man's thought and life which persons at large might cogently adduce as worthy of inclusion in such schema—that is, if it should turn out to be a more convenient description for worthy data than other schematic descriptions in use. This is for others to judge.

[32] C. G. Jung, *Modern Man in Search of a Soul* (New York, 1933), p. 171.

THE PROBLEM OF THE DOUBLE-SENSE AS HERMENEUTIC PROBLEM AND AS SEMANTIC PROBLEM

PAUL RICOEUR

My paper is of an interdisciplinary character: I propose to examine several treatments of the same problem of symbolism and to reflect on what the plurality of these treatments signifies. I accord to philosophy a task of arbitration, and on other occasions I have practiced arbitrating the conflict of several hermeneutics in modern culture:[1] a hermeneutic of the demystification and a hermeneutic of the recollection of meaning.[2] It is not this problem which I wish to take up here, but another problem set up by another genre of cleavage; the manners of treating symbolism which I propose to confront represent different *strategic levels*. I will consider two and even three strategic levels, taking the hermeneutic as a single strategic level, that of the texts. This level I will confront with that of semantics, but this semantics comprises two different strategic levels: that of lexical semantics, which is quite often called "very short semantics" (for example, by Stephen Ullmann or P. Guiraud), and that of structural semantics. The former is the level of the words, or rather, as Ullmann proposes to say, of the name, of the process of nomination or denomination. The latter, structural semantics, is characterized,

[1] *De l'interprétation; essai sur Freud* (Paris, 1965).

[2] I have alternately translated the word *sens* as "sense" or "meaning," according to my own judgment of the context. Other translators of Ricoeur have shown a propensity for "meaning" only [*translator's note*].

among other things, by a change of plan and a change of units, by the passage of molar units of communication, as are again the words and, a fortiori, the texts, to molecular units which will be, as we are going to see, certain elementary structures of signification.

I propose to examine what becomes of our problem of symbolism when it is transferred from one level of consideration to another. Certain problems which I have had the occasion to discuss under the title "Hermeneutics and Structuralism"[3] are going to reappear, but perhaps in some more favorable conditions, because the risk of conflict at the same level between a *philosophy* of interpretation and a structural *science* can be averted by a method which directly situates at different levels of realization the considered "effects of sense."

Broadly, this is what I would like to show: the change in scale of the problem causes a fine *constitution* to appear which alone permits a scientific treatment of the problem—the way of analysis, of the decomposition into the smallest units. This is the very path of science, as is seen in the use of this analysis in automatic translation. But in return I would like to show that the reduction to the simple authorizes the elimination of a fundamental function of symbolism which can only appear at a superior level of manifestation and which places symbolism in rapport with reality, with experience, with the world, with existence (I intentionally allow free choice among these terms). In brief, I would like to establish that the way of analysis and the way of synthesis do not coincide, nor are they equivalent: by way of analysis are discovered the elements of signification, which no longer have any relation to things said; by way of synthesis is revealed the function of signification, which is to *say* and finally to "*show*."

1. The Hermeneutic Level

In order to bring the inquiry to a successful conclusion, it is important to make sure that it is the same problem which is treated on three different planes. This problem I have called the problem of *multiple sense*. By that I designate a certain effect of sense according to which an expression of variable dimensions signifies one thing while at the same time signifying *another* thing, without

[3] "Herméneutique et structuralisme," *Esprit*, n.s. 35 (1963).

ceasing to signify the first. In the proper sense of the word, it is the allegorical function of language (*allé-gorie*: to say one thing while saying another thing).

What defines hermeneutics, at least in relation to other strategic levels which we are going to consider, is first the length of sequences with which it operates and which I call texts. It is first in the exegesis of biblical texts, and then profane ones, that the idea of a hermeneutics, conceived as a science of the rules of exegesis, is constituted; here the notion of text has a precise and limited meaning. Dilthey, in his great article, "Die Entstehung der Hermeneutik," said: "We call exegesis or interpretation such an art of comprehending the vital manifestations fixed in a durable fashion"; or again: "The art of comprehending gravitates around the interpretation of human testimonies preserved by writing"; or again: "We call exegesis, interpretation, the art of comprehending the written manifestations of life." Now the text comprises, other than a certain length in relation to the minimal sequences with which the linguist likes to work, the internal organization of a work, a *Zusammenhang*, an internal connection. The first acquisition of modern hermeneutics has been to propound the rule of proceeding from all to the part and to the details, to treat for example a biblical pericope as a linking, or, to employ the language of Schleiermacher, as the rapport between an interior form and an exterior form.

For the interpreter, it is the text which has a multiple sense; the problem of multiple sense is only posed for him if he takes into consideration such an ensemble, where events, personages, institutions, and natural or historic realities are articulated. It is all an "economy," all a signifying ensemble which lends itself to the overlay of the historic meaning upon the spiritual. Thus, in all the medieval tradition of the "multiple sense of the Scripture," it is by the great ensembles that the quadruple sense is articulated.[4]

Now this problem of the multiple sense is today no longer only the problem of exegesis in the biblical or even the profane sense of the word; it is itself an interdisciplinary problem. I wish to consider this problem first on a unique strategic level, on a homogeneous plane—that of the text. The phenomenology of religion,

[4] H. de Lubac, *L'exégèse médiévale; les quatre sens de l'Ecriture*, 4 vols. (Paris, 1953–65).

after the manner of Van der Leeuw and up to the point after the manner of Eliade, and Freudian and Jungian psychoanalysis (I do not distinguish sharply between them here), and literary criticism ("New" or not): these allow us to generalize the notion of text to ensembles signifying another degree of complexity besides the phrase. Here I will consider an example sufficiently distant from biblical exegesis simply to give an idea of the fullness of the hermeneutic field. The dream is treated by Freud as a *récit* which can be very brief but which always has an internal multiplicity; it is for this narration, unintelligible at first, that it is a matter, according to Freud, of substituting a more intelligent text which will be to the first as the latent is to the patent. There is thus a vast region of double-sense whose internal articulations design the diversity of the hermeneutics.

Now what causes the diversity of these hermeneutics? Partly, they reflect differences of technique: psychological decipherment is one thing, biblical exegesis is another. The difference here rests upon the internal rules of interpretation: it is an epistemological difference. But, in their turn, these differences of technique reflect some differences of project concerning the function of interpretation. It is one thing to use hermeneutics as a weapon of suspicion against the "mystifications" of the false consciousness; it is another to use it as a preparation for a better understanding of what once made sense, of what once was said.

Now the very possibility of divergent and rival hermeneutics—on the plane of technique and that of project—adheres to a fundamental condition which, to my mind, characterizes *en bloc* the strategic level of hermeneutics; it is this fundamental condition which now holds us back. It consists in this, that the symbolic is a milieu of expression for an extralinguistic reality. This is essential for the subsequent confrontation. Anticipating an expression which will make sense only on another strategic level, I will say: in hermeneutics there is no cloture of the universe of signs. Whereas the linguistic moves in the enclosure of a self-sufficient universe and never encounters anything but intrasignificant relations of mutual interpretation of signs (to employ the vocabulary of Charles Sanders Peirce), the hermeneutic is under the regime of the open state of the universe of signs.

My aim is to show that this regime of the open state adheres to the same scale where interpretation understood as exegesis operates, as exegesis of texts, and that the cloture of the linguistic universe is only complete with the change of scale and the consideration of significant small units.

What do we understand here by open state? In each hermeneutic discipline, interpretation is the hinge between linguistic and nonlinguistic, between language and actual experience (which supposes the latter). What makes the specificity of hermeneutics is precisely this *grip* of language on being and of being on language which is taken according to different modes. Thus the symbolism of the dream cannot be a pure game of signifying which switches from one thing to another; it is the milieu of expression where desire is going to be spoken. I have proposed the notion of a semantics of desire in order to designate the interlacing of two sorts of rapports: rapports of force, set forth in an energizing, and rapports of sense, set forth in an exegesis of sense. It includes symbolism because the symbolizable is first considered, in the nonlinguistic reality which Freud constantly called the Id, in its representative and affective drives. These drives and their offspring appear and hide in the effects of sense which we call symptoms, dreams, ideal myths, illusions. Far from our moving in a linguistic vicious circle, we are ceaselessly in the flux of an erotic and a semantic. The power of the symbol derives from this fact: the double-sense is the mode by which is conveyed the very ruse of desire.

So it is at the other extremity of the range of hermeneutics: if there is some sense in speaking of a hermeneutics of the sacred, it is where the double-sense of a text, which reminds me, for example, of Exodus, debouches on a certain wandering condition which is lived existentially as movement from a captivity to a deliverance. Under the summons of a word which gives what it orders, the double-sense aims here at deciphering an existential movement, a certain ontological condition of man, by the augmentation of meaning in relation to the event which, in its literalness, takes a place in the physical world or observable history. The double-sense is here the detector of a position in being.

Therefore symbolism, taken at its level of manifestation in the texts, marks the overture of language toward the other-than-itself. What I call its *overture*, this breakthrough to the open state, is *saying*; and saying is also showing. The rival hermeneutics break up, not upon the structure of the double-sense, but upon the mode of its open state (overture), upon the finality of showing. The strength and the weakness of hermeneutics is always there; the weakness because, taking language where it escapes from itself, hermeneutics also takes it when it escapes from a scientific treatment, which begins only with the postulate of the cloture of the signifying universe. All other weaknesses derive from it, and the weakness is first distinguished by the hermeneutics' surrender to the war of rival philosophic projects. But this weakness is its strength, because the place where language escapes from itself and us is also the place where language comes to itself: it is the place where language is *saying*. Though I understand the rapport of showing-hiding after the manner of the psychoanalyst or after that of the phenomenologist of religion (and I think that today one must assume these two possibilities together), it is each time like strength which *discovers*, which manifests, which brings to light, that language operates and becomes itself; then it becomes silent before what it *says*.

I will attempt a brief résumé: the sole philosophic interest in symbolism is that it reveals, by its structure of double-sense, the ambiguity of being: "Being speaks in many ways." It is the *raison d'être* of symbolism to disclose the multiplicity of meaning out of the ambiguity of being.

The remainder of this investigation has for its goal the discovery of why this grip on being adheres to the scale of discourse which we have called text and which is realized as dream or as hymn. That we do not know, but we will learn it precisely through comparison with other approaches to the problem of double-sense, where the change of scale will always be marked by progress toward scientific rigor and by the effacement of this ontological function of language which we are going to call the *saying*.

2. The Level of Lexical Semantics

The first change of scale is that which causes us to take into consideration the *lexical units*. A part of the Saussurian heritage is on this side, but one part only, since we will presently consider the works which depart from phonological analysis to the semantic and which will require for their development a change of scale much more radical, seeing that the lexemes, as one says, are still at the level of manifestations of discourse, as were the large units which we have just now considered. Nevertheless, a certain description and even a certain functioning of the polyseme can be managed at this level.

First, a certain description: the problem of multiple sense can be in effect circumscribed in the lexical semantic, as by the phenomenon of the polyseme or the possibility for a name (I adopt the terminology of S. Ullmann), to have more than one sense; it is still possible to describe this effect of sense in the Saussurian terms of signifying and signified (Ullmann had transcribed "name" and "sense"). Thus, the rapport to the thing is already excluded, although Ullmann did not choose absolutely between the transcription in the "basic triangle" of Ogden and Richards (symbol-referent-reference) and the Saussurian analysis on two levels. (We will presently see why; the cloture of the linguistic universe is not yet total at this level).

We will still continue the description in Saussurian terms while distinguishing a synchronic definition and a diachronic definition of the double-sense. Synchronic definition: in the state of speech, the same word has several senses—rigorously speaking, the polyseme is a synchronic concept. In diachrony, the multiple sense is called "change of sense," "transfer of sense." Doubtless one must combine the two approaches in order to take a collected view of the problem of the polyseme at the lexical level because there are changes of sense which have their synchronic projection in the phenomenon of the polyseme, namely, that the old and the new are contemporaries in the same system. Furthermore, there are changes of sense which should be taken as a guide in order to clear up the synchronic mess; in return, a semantic change always appears as an alteration in a preceding system: if one does not know the place of a meaning within a state of system, one has no idea of the nature of change which affects the value of the meaning.

We can finally push the description of the polyseme yet further in Saussurian ways by considering the sign no longer as an internal rapport of signifying and signified, of a name and a sense (it was necessary to formally define the polyseme), but in its rapport to other signs. One recalls the mastering idea of the *Course in General Linguistics*: treat the signs as the differences in a system. What does the polyseme become if we reclassify it in this perspective, which is already that of a structural linguistic? A first light is already shed on what might be called the functional character of the polyseme—a first light only, since we remain on the plane of speech and the symbol is a functioning of the word, that is to say, an expression in discourse. But, as Godel has shown in *Sources manuscrites du cours de linguistique générale*, as soon as one considers it the "mechanism of the speech," one is bound in an intermediate register between that of system and that of execution; it is at the level of the mechanism of speech that the regime of the regulated polyseme, which is that of ordinary philosophy, is discovered. This phenomenon of the regulated or limited polyseme is at the crossroads of the two processes. The first has its origin in the sign as "accumulated intention"; left to itself alone, it is a process of expansion which almost reaches a surcharge of sense (overload), as we see in certain words which, by dint of signifying too much, no longer signify anything, or in certain traditional symbols which have taken charge of such contradictory values that they are bent on neutralizing themselves (the fire which burns and which warms, the water which purifies and which drowns). On the other hand, we have a process of limitation exercised by the rest of the semantic field and first by the structuring of certain organized fields, like those which have been studied by Jost Trier, the author of the theory of semantic fields. Here we are still on Saussurian terrain, since a sign does not have, or is not, a fixed signification, but a value, in opposition to other values, which results from the relation of an identity and of a difference. This regulation issues from the conflict between the semantic expansion of signs and the limiting action of the field, which resembles, in its effects, the organization of a phonological system (although it differs profoundly in its mechanism). In effect, the difference between the organization of a semantic field and that of a phonological system remains considerable. Far from the values having only a differential, and therefore oppositive, function, they have also a cumulative value which makes the polyseme one of the key problems of semantics, perhaps even its pivot. We touch here on what is specific on the semantic plane, that which permits the phenomenon of the double-sense: Urban has already remarked that what makes language an instrument of knowledge is precisely that a sign can designate one thing without ceasing to designate another, and therefore, that in order to have an expressive value in regard to the second, it must be constituted in the sign from the first. He added this: "The cumulative intention of words is the fecund source of ambiguities, but it is also the source of analogical prediction, thanks to which the symbolic power of language is placed in a work."

This penetrating remark by Urban lets us perceive what could be called the functionality of the polyseme. That which we have perceived on the plane of texts as a particular sector of discourse, namely, the sector of plurivocality, we are now ready to ground in the general property of lexical units, namely, to function as an accumulator of sense, as an exchanger between the old and the new. It is thus that the double-sense can assume an expressive function with regard to realities signified in a mediate way. But how?

Here again Saussure can guide us with his distinction between the two axes of language function (actually, he no longer speaks here of language as a system of signs at a given moment, but really of the mechanism of language or discourse which is confined to the word). In the spoken chain, he remarked, the signs are in a double rapport: in a syntagmatic rapport which links opposed signs in a relation *in praesentia*, in an associative rapport which brings together similar signs susceptible of being substituted in the same place, but brings them together only in a relation *in absentia*. This distinction, one knows, has been revived by Roman Jakobson, who formulates it in similar terms: rapport of concatenation and rapport of selection. This distinction is considerable for the investigation of the problem of the semantic in general and of symbolism in particular. It is in effect in the combined play of these two axes of concatenation and selection which make up the rapport of syntax and semantic.[5]

Now, we have not only assured a linguistic status for the symbolic, but for symbolism. The axis of substitutions, in effect, is the axis of similitudes; the axis of concatenations is the axis of contiguities. There is thus a possibility of making correspond to the Saussurian distinction a distinction formerly confined to rhetoric, that of metaphor and metonymy; or, rather, it is possible to give to the polarity of metaphor and metonymy the more general

[5] Roman Jakobson, *Essais de linguistique générale* (Paris, 1963), chap. 2.

functional sense of a polarity between two processes and to speak of the metaphoric process and the metonymic process.

Here indeed we touch a root of the very process of symbolization which previously we had reached directly as an effect of the text. Here is what we know of the mechanism in that which we are now calling an effect of context. Let us take up the function of the regulated polyseme, which we have considered with the theory of fields in the plane of speech. Then it rather concerned a limited polyseme; the regulated polyseme is properly an effect of sense produced in discourse. When I speak I realize only a part of the signified potential; the rest is obliterated by the total signification of the phrase, which operates as uniformity of utterance. But the rest of the semantic virtualities is not abolished; it floats around the words as a possibility not completely abolished. Therefore, the context plays the role of filter: when a single dimension of sense occurs, thanks to a play of affinities and reinforcements of all analogous dimensions in the other lexical terms, an effect of meaning is created which can attain to perfect univocality, as in technical languages. Thus, we make univocal phrases from multivocal words, thanks to this action of sorting or screening by the context. But it happens that the phrase thus made does not succeed in reducing to a monosemic usage the potential of meaning; rather, it maintains or even creates a concurrence between several "places" of signification. By diverse procedures, discourse can realize the *ambiguity* which thus appears as the combination of a lexical fact—the polyseme—and a contextual fact—the permission allowed to several distinct or even opposed values of the same name to be realized in the same sequence.

Let us take bearings at the end of this second part. What have we gained by thus transposing to the lexical plane the problems encountered on the exegetical plane? What have we gained and what have we lost?

We have assuredly gained a most exact knowledge of symbolism: it appears to us now as an effect of sense (meaning), observable on the plane of discourse but erected on the base of a most elementary function of signs. It was possible to relate this function to the existence of an axis of speech, other than that of linearity, on which are placed only the successive and contiguous links relevant to syntax. The semantic and, more particularly, the problem of the polyseme and of the metaphor have thus received keys to the city in linguistics. In receiving a determined linguistic stature, the process considered receives a functional value; if the polyseme is not a pathological phenomenon in itself, neither is symbolism an ornament of language. The polyseme and symbolism belong to the constitution and function of *all* language.

There, then, is the acquisition on the order of description and function; however, the inscription of our problem in the linguistic plane has a reverse: the semantic is certainly included in the linguistic, but at what price? On the condition of holding analysis within the cloture of the linguistic universe. That we have not made apparent. But it is clearly seen if one restores certain of Jakobson's stages of analysis which we have omitted in the previous account. In order to justify the intrinsically linguistic character of the semantic, Jakobson brings together some views of Saussure on the associative relations (or, in his language, on the axis of substitution), and some views of Charles Sanders Peirce on the remarkable power of signs to interpret themselves mutually. There is a notion of interpretation which could not be foreseen with exegesis: every sign, according to Peirce, requires, beyond two protagonists, an interpretant. The function of the interpretant is filled by another sign or an ensemble of signs which develops the signification and which can be substituted for the considered sign. This notion of interpretant, in Peirce's sense, indeed recalls the Saussurian "group of substitution," but at the same time it actually reveals in it the place at the interior of a game of intralinguistic relations. Every sign, we are saying, can be translated by another sign in which it is more completely developed; that covers the definitions, the equational predictions, the circumlocutions, the predicative relations, and the symbols. But what have we thus done? We have resolved a problem of semantics with the resources of the metalinguistic function, which is to say, according to a study of Jakobson applied to the multiple functions enveloped in the act of cognition, with the resources of a function which places a sequence of discourse in rapport with the code and not with the referent. This is so true that, when Jakobson pushes the structural analysis of the metaphoric process (assimilated, one recalls, to a group of operations putting similitude in play on the axis of substitutions), it is in terms of metalinguistic operations that he develops his analysis of the metaphoric process. It is insofar as the signs intersignify among themselves that they enter into rapports of substitution and the metaphoric process becomes possible. In this way, semantics, with its problem of multiple sense, is held within the cloture of language. It is not by chance that the linguist here invokes the logician: "Symbolic logic," notes Jakobson, "has not stopped reminding us that the linguistic significations constituted by the system of analytic relations of one expression to others do not presuppose the presence of things."[6] One could not say more exactly that the more rigorous treatment of the problem of the double-sense had been paid for by the utter neglect of its aim toward the thing. We said at the end of the first part of this paper (pp. 67–68) that the philosophic import of symbolism is that in it the equivocality of being comes to be conveyed with the help of the multivocality of our signs. We now know that the science of this multivocality—the linguistic science—requires that we keep ourselves within the cloture of the universe of signs. Is this not the indication of a close rapport between *philosophy* of language and *science* of language and between hermeneutics as philosophy and semantics as science?

It is this articulation which we are going to specify while once again changing scale with structural semantics, such as it is practiced not only in applied linguistics (for example, in automatic translation), but also in theoretical linguistics—indeed, in all the disciplines which today bear the name of structural semantics.

3. Structural Semantics

Three methodological choices, according to Greimas, govern structural semantics.[7]

First, this discipline adopts from the very outset the axiom of the cloture of the linguistic universe; by virtue of this axiom semantics is governed by the metalinguistic operations of translation of one order of signs into another order of signs. With Jakobson, however, one does not see how the structures of the language-object and those constituted by the metalanguage, the ones in relation to the others, are situated. Here, on the other hand, the hierarchical levels of language are very clearly linked. First you have the language-object, the language in which you describe the elementary structures of the precedent; then there is that in

[6] *Ibid.*, p. 42.
[7] A. J. Greimas, *La sémantique structurale* (Paris, 1966).

which you elaborate the operant concepts of this description; and finally, there is that in which you define and make axiomatic the precedents. By this clear vision of the hierarchical levels of language at the interior of the linguistic cloture, the postulate of this science is better illuminated, namely, that the structures built on the metalinguistic level are the same as those which are immanent in language.

The second postulate or methodological choice is that of the changing of the strategic level of the analysis; one will take for reference not the word (lexemes) but the underlying structures entirely constructed for the needs of the analysis.

I can only give here a feeble idea of the enterprise; it concerns working with a new unit of reckoning, the seme, which is always found in a relation of binary opposition of the type long-short, breadth-depth, etc., but at a level more basic than the lexical. No seme or semic category, even if its denomination is borrowed from ordinary language, is identical to a lexeme manifested in discourse. Then one no longer has terms-objects, but rather relations of conjunction and disjunction: disjunction in two semes (e.g., masculine-feminine), and conjunction under a unique trait (e.g., the genus). Semic analysis consists in establishing, for a group of lexemes, the hierarchical tree of conjunctions and disjunctions which exhaust the constitution of the group. One sees the advantage for applied linguistics: the binary relations will lend themselves to calculation in a system of base 1 (0, 1) and the conjunctions-disjunctions to a treatment by machines of a cybernetic type (opened circuit, closed circuit).

But there is no less an advantage for theory, because the semes are the units of signification constructed from their relational structures alone. The ideal is to reconstruct the entire lexicon with the very least number of these elementary structures of signification. If one were to succeed there – and this is not an inhuman undertaking – the terms-objects would be entirely defined for an exhaustive analysis as a collection of semes containing only conjunctions-disjunctions and hierarchies of relations as brief as semic systems.

The third postulate is that the units which we recognize as lexemes, in descriptive linguistics, and of which we make use as words in discourse, belong on the plane of *manifestation of discourse* and not on the plane of *immanence*. The words – to employ ordinary language—have a mode of presence other than the mode of existence of these structures. This point is of the greatest importance for our research because what we have considered as multiple sense and as symbolic function is an "effect of sense" which is manifested in discourse but whose reason is situated on another plane.

All the effort of structural semantics will be devoted to reconstructing degree by degree the relations which permit the giving of an account of these effects of sense in growing complexity. I will retain here only two points of this reconstruction. First, it is possible to recover, with an unequalled degree of precision and rigor, the problem of multiple sense, considered as lexical property, and that of symbolic function, in some units superior to the word, such as the phrase. Structural semantics tries to account for the semantic richness of words by a method which consists of making the variants of sense correspond to some classes of contexts. The variants of sense can then be analyzed in a fixed nucleus (that which is common to all contexts), and in contextual variables. If one carries this analysis forward in the frame of operational language furnished by the reduction of the lexemes to a collection of semes, one succeeds in defining the effects of variable meanings of a word as derivatives of semes or sememes, born of the conjunction of a semic nucleus and of one or several contextual semes, which are themselves certain semic classes corresponding to certain contextual classes.

What we must have allowed in imprecision during the preceding analysis, namely, the notion of semantic virtuality, takes here a precise analytic character; one can transcribe in certain formulas involving only conjunctions, disjunctions, and hierarchical relations each of these effects of sense and thus localize exactly the contextual variable which leads to the effect of sense. In the same blow, one can account, with a very high degree of exactitude and rigor, for the role of the context which we described first, in still vague terms, as an action of screening or as a game of affinities between certain dimensions of sense from different words in a phrase. One can now speak of a sorting among contextual variables; for example (to recall the example of Greimas), in "the barking dog," the contextual variable "animal," common to "dog" and to "barking," permits the elimination of the sense of the word "dog" which would not be that of an animal, but of a thing; at the same time are eliminated the senses of the word "barking" which would belong for example to a man. The action of sorting from the context consists therefore in a reinforcement of the semes on the basis of reiteration.

As one sees in this analysis of contextual function, one retrieves the very problems which have been treated in the second part, but they are approached with a precision that only the use of an analytic instrument confers. The theory of the context is in this regard very striking; by causing the stabilization of the meaning in a phrase to rest upon the reiteration of the same semes, we can define with rigor what one can call the "isotopy of a discourse," that is to say, its establishment at a homogeneous level of sense; let us say that in "the barking dog" it concerns a beast's history.

It is from this concept of isotopy of discourse that the problem of symbolism can also be recovered with the same analytic means. What happens in the case of an equivocal or plurivocal discourse? No isotopy of discourse is assured by the context, but the latter, in place of filtering a series of isotope sememes, allows the unfolding of several semantic series belonging to discordant isotopies.

It seems to me that the conquest of this deliberately and radically analytic level allows us to better comprehend the rapport between the three strategic levels on which we have successively operated. We have first operated as exegetes with the large units of discourse, with the texts; then as lexical semanticians with the sense of the words, that is to say, with the names; and then as structural semanticians with the semic constellations. This change of plane has not been in vain; it marks a progress in rigor and, if I may say so, in scientific method. We have progressively brought ourselves nearer the Leibnizian ideal of a universal characteristic. It would be false to say that we have eliminated symbolism; it has rather ceased to be an enigma. It is in truth a fascinating reality and mystifying at its limit, where it invites explaining the obscure by the more obscure. It is now exactly situated and doubly so: it is first situated by rapport to multiple sense, which is a question of lexemes, and therefore of speech. In this regard symbolism has nothing in itself of the remarkable; all words of ordinary speech have more than one signification—the first of Bachelard is no more extraordinary in this regard than any word in our dictionary. Thus an illusion vanishes that the symbol would be an enigma on the plane of words. On the other hand, the possibility of symbolism is deep-rooted in a function common to all words in a universal function of language, namely, the aptitude of lexems for developing contextual variations. But symbolism is situated a second time by rapport to discourse; it is in discourse that there is equivocality and not elsewhere: this is where it constitutes an effect of particular meaning. The calculated ambiguity is the work of certain contexts and, we can now say, of texts which establish a certain isotopy in view of suggesting another in it. The transfer of sense, the metaphor (in the etymological sense of the word), resurges as change of isotopies, as play of multiple, concurrential, superposed isotopies. The notion of isotopy has thus allowed us to designate the place of the metaphor in language with more precision than would be allowed by the notion of the axis of substitutions borrowed by Jakobson from Saussure.

But then, does not philosophy regain its status at the end? Can it not legitimately demand why discourse, in certain cases, cultivates ambiguity? The philosopher will specify his question: ambiguity, why make it? Or rather: *in order to say what*? That brings us back to the essential: the cloture of the linguistic universe. In effect, the more we have been plunged into the thickness of language, the more we have been drawn out on its plane of manifestation, the more we have been sunk in the direction of sublexical units, the more we have realized the cloture of language. The structuralist sublexical units, properly speaking, signify nothing; there are some combinatory possibilities. They say nothing; they conjoin and disjoin.

There are, after all, two fashions of accounting for symbolism: by what constitutes it and by what it wishes to say. What constitutes it requires a structural analysis, and this structural analysis dissipates the "marvelous" in it. This is its function and, I will dare to say, its mission. Symbolism operates with the resources of all language, which are without mystery.

As for what symbolism wishes to say, this can no longer be informed by a structural linguistics. In the movement of coming and going between analysis and synthesis, the coming is not equivalent to the going. On the way back there emerged a problematic which analysis had progressively eliminated; Ruyer called it expressiveness, not in the sense of the expression of the emotions, that is to say in the sense where language expresses some thing, says something. The emergence of expressiveness is explained by the heterogeneity between the plane of discourse or the plane of manifestation and the plane of speech or the plane of immanence, only accessible to analysis; the lexemes are not only for the analysis of the semic constellations but they are for the synthesis of the units of communication.

It is perhaps the emergence of expressiveness which constitutes the marvel of language. Greimas puts it very well: "there is perhaps a mystery of language, and this is a question for philosophy, there is no mystery in language." I believe that we also can say that there is no mystery in language; the most poetic symbolism, the most sacred, operates with the same semic variables as does the most banal word in the dictionary. But there is a mystery of language: it is that language says, says something, says something about being. If there is an enigma of symbolism, it resides completely on the plane of manifestation, where the being's equivocality comes to be said in the equivocality of discourse.

After all, is this not the task of philosophy, to constantly reopen toward being said this discourse that linguistics, by necessity of method, constantly recloses toward the closed universe of signs and the purely internal game of their mutual relations?

ELIADE AND FOLKLORE

MIRCEA POPESCU

To treat with justice the relationship announced in the title of this article, which aims to be nothing more than an act of homage and gratitude to one of the most prestigious figures of contemporary Romanian culture and a spiritual member of my generation, is difficult for several reasons. First there is the impossibility of consulting an important part of the scientific, literary, and journalistic production of Mircea Eliade; I refer in particular to the publications done in Romania before and during World War II. These are all works which have direct or indirect relation to popular traditions.[1] Second there is the complexity of the problem itself. As a historian of religion—or rather, according to Altizer's definition, "the greatest living interpreter of the whole world of primitive and archaic religion"[2]—Eliade always had to rely very extensively on folklore material which carried evident traces of religious and archaic cosmogonies.

Therefore, to speak about "Eliade and folklore" would mean to review the whole of his scientific work and also to take into consideration his essays and his narratives, because as a cultural philosopher and novelist Eliade was also inspired by Romanian traditions. Remembering the reiterated warning of Eliade himself against the sterility of "perfectionism" by any means, I will therefore present only some aspects of the problem, documenting

[1] It is regrettable that I could not see some articles of *Vremea* and of *Cuvântul*, dedicated expressly to Romanian popular traditions, and also the precious collection of the review *Zalmoxis* (1938–43).

[2] Thomas J. J. Altizer, *Mircea Eliade and the Dialectic of the Sacred* (Philadelphia, 1963), p. 16.

some of these rather simple points with the material at my disposal, which, although incomplete, is yet fundamental.

In an article published in 1937,[3] Mircea Eliade confronted (I would say with a certain youthful enthusiasm and intentions perhaps a little too ambitious), an extremely fascinating but dangerous subject; proof of this is in the promise, still unfulfilled, of taking the argument up again with a deeper study of the problem in relation to the fundamental problems of death and the immortality of the soul.

The article in question, which follows his fruitful Indian experience (1928–32) and the disturbing novels *Isabel și Apele Diavolului* (1930), *Domnișoara Christina* (1936), and *Șarpele* (1937), in which ancient superstitions graft themselves perfectly onto modern existential dreams and anguishes, has a revealing title: "Folklore as a Means of Knowing." It begins with the indubitable statement that the "fantastic" and miraculous episodes of popular tales derive from real cases, scientifically documented, of "contagious magic" (according to Fraser's terminology) or "pragmatic Cryptestesia" (according to Charles Richet's usage) or levitation and incombustibility of the human body. It is possible to conclude that "at the basis of beliefs of peoples in the 'ethnographic' phase, and the folklore of civilized nations, we find *facts*, not fantastic creations."[4] In extremely remote times, experiences which today are so exceptional as to seem absurd must have been common, and the folklore remembers them — that same folklore which furnishes so many elements, in every part of the world, concerning the survival of the soul and immortality. Consequently, Eliade does not hestitate to affirm that "the folkloristic documents on death could be useful to us in the same way as we use geological documents for the comprehension of phenomena, which in the actual human condition, we can no longer control empirically (via experiments)."[5] And, more generally: "We maintain that problems directly pertaining to man, to the structure and limitation of his conscience, could be elaborated almost to the point of final solution, starting from folklore and ethnographic data."[6]

[3] "Folklorul ca instrument de cunoaștere" ("Folklore as a means of knowledge"), *Revista Fundațiilor Regale*, 4 (1937): 136–52.
[4] *Ibid.*, p. 149.
[5] *Ibid.*, p. 151.
[6] *Ibid.*, p. 138.

An audacious thesis, as we can see, and one that will certainly surprise those who know only Eliade the scientist; this aspect of his work is no doubt relevant to his complex personality, but it does not exhaust it, and, I would say, does not even determine it. His thesis should be discussed at length, and in a different context, and perhaps its author will clarify it later. I myself now return, for the purposes of this article, to the revaluation of folklore—which is not that inferior, "primitive," and rudimentary regressive manifestation of which there is such snobbish talk among the late-coming followers of illuminism and positivism. The apparently humblest popular traditions often hide very lofty metaphysical and religious significances. There is a nobility of origin in a great part of the folklore output which comprehends the survival of myths and archaic religious behavior.[7] The "popular theology" is not always to be disdained; when it is considered less superficially, it reveals concepts of the sacred and of God which are anything but vulgar or commonplace. Many beliefs are degraded myths or symbols, "hiérophanies déchues."[8] For the historian of religion, they usually present themselves as "living fossils,"[9] the study of which, always useful, becomes indispensable in the consideration of the ancient cultures which did not leave other testimonies.

Si, pour reconstituer l'histoire archaïque de la religion grecque, par exemple, nous devons nous contenter des textes peu nombreux qui nous ont été conservés, de quelques inscriptions, de quelques monuments mutilés et de quelques objets votifs, pour reconstituer les religions germaniques ou slaves, par exemple, nous sommes forcés de faire appel aux documents folkloriques, en acceptant les inévitables risques qu'en comportent le maniement et l'interprétation.[10]

It is an idea which will also return later, in *Myth and Reality* in 1963:

So we may conclude that Greek religion and mythology, radically secularized and demythicized, survived in European *culture*, for the very reason that they had been expressed by literary and artistic mas-

[7] Mircea Eliade, *Myth and Reality* (New York, 1963; London, 1964), p. 160.

[8] Mircea Eliade, *Traité d'histoire des religions* (Paris, 1949), p. 19.

[9] Mircea Eliade, "Preistoria unui motiv folkloric românesc," *Buletinul Bibliotecii Române*, 3 (1955–56): 47.

[10] Eliade, *Traité d'histoire des religions*, p. 18.

terpieces. Whereas the popular religions and mythologies, the only *living* pagan forms when Christianity triumphed (but about which we know almost nothing, since they were not expressed in writing), survived in Christianized form in the traditions of the rural populations.[11]

Therefore, these must be studied in order to know something of the ancient spiritual religiousness which still existed, in spite of its prehistoric roots, in the first centuries of our age.

But folklore is also valued by Mircea Eliade as a source of culture not subjected to the vicissitudes and risks of history: "Popular cultures, exactly because they maintain archaic spiritual universes, do not fall into the provincialism which fatally menaces historical cultures." And again:

> A popular culture is always "open"; its national genius, as peculiar as it may be, utilizes ecumenical expressions which go very far in space and rather deeply in time. For these reasons, we can also say that a popular culture is "beyond history": not in the sense that it lacks its own "history," but because this history consists above all in the re-evaluation of an extremely archaic heredity, coming from prehistoric times, in an unceasing rediscovery, altogether, and in a re-interpretation of the values of primordial spirituality.[12]

Compare here the motif, recurring in Eliade as philosopher of history, of antihistoricism, of the preference for the human soul's constants, for the apparently immobile cultures which "sabotage history." For him, "the passing of time, 'history,' does not necessarily constitute the substance of a belief or of an institution."[13]

The cultural historian cannot neglect folklore. For example, "Is it not sufficiently significant," Eliade asks himself rhetorically, "that a society accepts and assimilates exclusively certain legends and certain popular books, refusing or forgetting others? Should we not keep this in mind for the comprehension of the spiritual structure of such a society?"[14]

The religious historian considers folklore material with different intentions: he searches for "a mythical horizon," for evidence of human behavior toward the sacred, "cosmological significances,

[11] Eliade, *Myth and Reality*, p. 160.

[12] Eliade, "Preistoria," p. 54.

[13] Mircea Eliade, "Simbolismul arborelui sacru," *Revista Fundațiilor Regale*, 4 (1939): 136.

[14] Mircea Eliade, "Cărțile populare în literatura romãneasca," *Revista Fundațiilor Regale*, 6 (1939): 136.

traces of an anthropology or archaic cosmic-anthropology."[15] While the student of folklore studies the oral document or the "tradition" as the student of literature studies the written text, without excessively preoccupying himself with its "prehistory," the historian of religions pushes himself back deeply in search of that mythology and that religious conception which express themselves in such oral documents and in such "tradition."[16] A clear and masterly example of this type of research is Eliade's study "Mythologies asiatiques et folklore sud-est européen," published in 1961 in the *Revue de l'histoire des religions*.[17] The earth-diver motif, frequent in Romanian and Balkan popular traditions, is exhaustively researched in all its elements, compared, analyzed, and finally brought back to its very remotest prehistoric and Asian origins. The philosopher of history says justly, once again: "le fait que, continuellement réinterpreté et revalorisé, ce mythe archaïque a été conservé par les peuples sud-est européens prouve qu'il répondait à une nécessité profonde de l'âme populaire."[18]

Another masterful analysis is the one about the legend of Master Manole, a subject which Eliade had already amply considered in a book published in 1943,[19] which he mentioned again in some fundamental works on the history of religions,[20] and which he finally developed, perhaps conclusively, in the study "Manole et le Monastère d'Arges," published in 1957.[21] Starting from a celebrated Romanian *balada* and comparing it critically with many Oriental and Balkan variants, Eliade returns to the mythical, exemplary model of blood rites of construction, to a pre-Indo-European cosmogony, or, more precisely, to the spiritual world of paleocultivators, which explains the creation of the universe via the killing of a primordial giant.[22] In doing so, he attempts to reconstruct the various phases this religious conception passed through before it was crystallized in a popular artistic product. The ideology common to all epic-lyric songs of this type in south Eastern Europe is thus summarized:

15 *Ibid.*, p. 143.
16 Eliade, *Myth and Reality*, p. 200.
17 Vol. 160, pp. 157–212.
18 *Ibid.*, p. 210.
19 *Comentarii la legenda Meşterului Manole* (Bucharest, 1943).
20 See in particular *Traité d'histoire des religions*, pp. 377 ff., and *Le mythe de l'éternel retour* (Paris, 1949), 84–136.
21 *Revue des Etudes Roumaines*, vol. 3–4, pp. 7–28.
22 *Ibid.*, p. 23.

pour durer, une construction (maison, ourvrage technique, mais aussi oeuvre spirituelle) doit être animée, c'est-à-dire recevoir à la fois une vie et une âme. Le 'transfert' de l'âme n'est possible que par la voie d'un sacrifice; en d'autres termes, par une mort violente.[23]

In the initial part of the study, Eliade enumerates the various ways—"different but complementary"—in which one can approach a *balada* like the one by Master Manole. I cite here the entire passage because it furnishes precious indications for the study of folklore:

Le premier problème est d'esthétique: la valeur littéraire des différentes variantes enregistrées et leur éventuelle comparaison avec les créations populaires analogues de la Péninsule balkanique et de l'Europe danubienne; 2) vient ensuite le problème historique, avec ses divers aspects: a) la circulation du motif folklorique dans le Sud-Est européen et dans l'Europe danubienne; b) les éventuels emprunts et influences réciproques à l'intérieur de ces zones culturelles; c) l'identification du "centre d'origine," de la région où la ballade a pris naissance en tant qu'oeuvre poétique. En dehors de ces deux points de vue, qui intéressent surtout les stylistes et les folkloristes roumanisants et balkanologues, il faut tenir également compte: 3) de la perspective propre au folkloriste, qui s'applique à recueillir et à comparer des légendes et croyances analogues chez d'autres peuples européens, alors même qu'elles n'ont pas donné lieu à des créations poétiques autonomes; 4) de la perspective de l'ethnologue, qui considère l'ensemble des rites de construction, attestés un peu partout dans le monde, et s'efforce de les intégrer dans les différentes structures culturelles; 5) enfin, de la perspective de l'historien des religions qui, tout en utilisant les conclusions des folkloristes et des ethnologues, s'applique à retrouver la situation existentialle qui a suscité l'idéologie et les rites de construction, et s'efforce, surtout, de rendre intelligible l'univers théorique fondé par une telle situation.[24]

The tales present themselves to the student of folklore and to the religious historian in completely different perspectives. While the first preoccupies himself with the birth and diffusion of the various twists of the motif, the latter goes further and, for example, discovers that the marvelous story, which has by now become a literature of diversion and amusement, has in reality a very serious content of a religious nature: "les épreuves et les

[23] *Ibid.*, p. 22.
[24] *Ibid.*, pp. 7–8.

aventures des héros et des héroïnes sont presque toujours traduisibles en termes initiatiques."[25] At the end of the fable there is the "initiation, that is, passing, by way of a symbolic death and resurrection, from ignorance and immaturity to the spiritual age of the adult."[26]

If it [the tale] represents an amusement or an escape, it does so only for the banalized consciousness, and particularly for that of modern man; in the deep psyche initiation scenarios preserve their seriousness and continue to transmit their message, to produce mutations. All unwittingly, and indeed believing that he is merely amusing himself or escaping, the man of the modern societies still benefits from the imaginary initiation supplied by tales.[27]

The "desecration," or, better, the "degradation of the sacred" in folklore is a problem which Eliade often brings back to our attention. The process of "folklorization" usually consists in a "projection of concrete rituals, in the world of imagination."[28]

Everything that is "fantastic," everything that belongs to the extrarational — religion, magic, myth, legend — begins to degrade itself as soon as it enters "history," as soon as it participates in "becoming." . . . A myth, for example, or elements of a myth (produced, in its turn, by a ritual or by a primordial metaphysical conception) generate, at a certain moment, a legend. From the myth to the legend the process of laicization, of degradation, is evident. As soon as such a legend begins to circulate, to "live" while participating in "history," it also begins to transform itself, to move away more and more from its fantastic nucleus, to acquire an always increasing number of local, ethnic, and concrete elements.[29]

This process of folklorization can be pushed to its extreme limits. A classic case is given by the "sacred tree" or the "tree of life":

When it was no longer considered as a "vegetable" expression of absolute Reality, the sacred tree began to be appreciated from a decorative point of view. The symbol emptied of its original metaphorical content, maintained itself by its empirical and esthetic values. Besides, this is not the only case. The popular art of all countries stores entire series

[25] Mircea Eliade, *Naissances mystiques* (Paris, 1959), p. 259.
[26] Eliade, *Myth and Reality*, p. 201.
[27] *Ibid.*, p. 201.
[28] Mircea Eliade, "Les Daces et les loups," *Numen*, 6 (1959): 29.
[29] Eliade, "Cărţile populare," p. 137.

of cosmological symbols, which for a long time have been simply decorative "motifs."[30]

And elsewhere: "The collective memory stores under the form of 'ornament' or 'decorative' element, archaic symbols of purely metaphysical essence. The great part of popular ornamentation is of metaphysical origin."[31]

In a substantial review done in 1939 of a fundamental work by N. Cartojan, Eliade warns, however, that along with this phenomenon of "degradation of the fantastic, of transition from the mythical primordial nucleus to legends and tales in incessant development and alteration (local color, ethnicization)," there is another process: folklorization of historical data. Indeed, "the transformation of historical elements (peoples, happenings) into folklore categories, explains in great part the phenomena of popular literature." And, still further, a consideration which certainly would need further study:

> The popular creations — whether exclusively oral or exclusively written texts — are found somewhere between the level of pure principles (symbol, metaphysics, magic, which are at the origin of any popular product) and that of immediate historical reality (happenings and men, the memory of which is stored by popular memory and projected into mythical categories).[32]

The relationship between history and folklore will later be diluted. In tales, for example, the accurate memory of a certain stage of culture never appears; the cultural styles and the historical cycles are telescoped in them. Only the structures of an exemplary behavior survive, and these are being lived in a number of cultural cycles and historical moments.[33]

Another problem of methodology is the one concerning the "birth" of a popular tradition, which must not be confused with its simple "transmission":

> The age of a myth, of a belief or a custom, is no longer established according to the epoch in which a society transmitted it to the nearby people, but according to internal criteria. If the myth, the belief, or the custom respectively belongs to the neolithic period or to the bronze

[30] Eliade, "Simbolismul arborelui sacru," p. 680.
[31] Eliade, "Cărţile populare," pp. 146–47.
[32] *Ibid.*, pp. 137, 140.
[33] Eliade, *Myth and Reality*, pp. 196–97.

age, and since then has been transmitted, without essential alterations, we have the right to speak of a myth or belief of the neolithic period or of the bronze age, even if a society received it from a nearby society in the Middle Ages or in the nineteenth century.[34]

And, returning to Romania, Eliade deduces in such a way that many of the popular Romanian traditions, attributed until now to Slavic influence, actually go back infinitely further and are pregnant with archaic religious meanings.

Christianity "not only introduced a new perspective into the mystical and moral world, but it has also saved the mythical heritage of antiquity, integrating it into the great cosmic drama, and showering with spiritual values all the myths concerning 'creation,' 'birth,' and 'death.'" Archaic myths, such as the ones of the birth of a plant world from the body of a divinity, of certain plant species which therefore retained magic and curative power from the blood or seed of a divinity or from a killed mythical being, were assimilated and transformed by Christianity, acquired new metaphysical significances, or fell down to popular beliefs (as the faith in the healing power of certain "herbs," which would have grown under Christ's cross, or from his blood).[35] The nonbiblical cosmogonies, which disappeared long ago from the folklore of the West, maintain themselves alive in popular traditions in a conservative European circle: the Balkan and Oriental countries,[36] where, because of this, rural Christianity has a "cosmic dimension" of prehistoric origin.[37] The meager but sharp and genial considerations of Eliade on the "religious folklore of Oriental Christianity" open ample perspectives for the studies of popular traditions in Balkan countries and in southeastern Europe.

Obviously, these "ample perspectives" refer in the first place to Romanian folklore, which always remained at the center of Eliade's interest not only for an easily understandable and explainable sentimental reason, but also for its extremely remote primordiality. We have seen from what dizzying antiquity stem the mythologies and legends of cosmogonic immersion, of Master Manole, of the healing herbs. Certain variants of "Miorița," wherein we recognize

[34] Eliade, "Preistoria," pp. 50–52.

[35] Eliade, "Ierburile de sub cruce," *Revista Fundațiilor Regale*, 6 (1939): 369.

[36] Eliade, "Mythologies asiatiques et folklore sud-est européen," *Revue de l'histoire des religions*, 160 (1961): 210, n. 2.

[37] Eliade, *Myth and Reality*, p. 160.

traces of the archaic magico-religious ties between the hunter and his prey, take us back to cultural paleolithic forms, while numerous Romanian agricultural customs are typical of neolithic times. "When," observes Eliade, "a history of popular Romanian culture is written, on the basis of discoveries and methods of modern ethnology and paleontology, we will see how deep the roots of our spirituality are."[38]

For this "history of the Romanian popular culture," which would be more than a simple introduction to the history of Romanian culture *tout court*, Mircea Eliade, as we have seen, has already written several fundamental chapters. Others, like the preannounced[39] "Folklore roumain et mythologies asiatiques" are in preparation. The religious history of Dacia, of which Eliade has already given us a magnificent essay in "Les Daces et les loups,"[40] will certainly be a revelation, putting to profit, as usual, the folkloristic data. This folkloristic data constitutes also the background of great parts of his narrative, up to that saga of the Romania of yesterday and today which is the novel *Noaptea de Sânziene*, published for the first time in French in 1955 under the title *Forêt Interdite*.[41] But the presence and incidence of folklore in the literature of Mircea Eliade would require another, differently planned, discussion. Here it is sufficient to mention it.

[38] Eliade, "Preistoria," p. 50.
[39] In *Buletinul Bibliotecii Române*, 3 (1955–56): 42.
[40] *Numen*, 6 (1959): 15–31.
[41] Mircea Eliade, *Forêt Interdite* ("*Noaptea de Sânziene*"), (Paris, 1955).

THE WEIGHING OF THE SOUL

S. G. F. BRANDON

In the comparative study of religion there is a motif which, though of minor significance, has both a great intrinsic interest and a fascinating iconography. It is the *psychostasia*, or weighing of the soul. Although the term *psychostasia* will frequently be used in this essay as a convenient designation, it will quickly be seen that it is not an exact one. In the idea, as it occurs in many religions, of a fateful assessment by weighing made immediately before or after death, what is then weighed varies greatly – often, as we shall see, it is not the soul. What is weighed, however, is always an entity regarded as being peculiarly representative of an individual human being.

The idea of a postmortem assessment of a person's life by weighing first occurs in ancient Egypt.[1] Its best known form of expression, frequently illustrated in books on Egyptology, dates from the New Kingdom period (1580–1090 B.C.) and is found in vignettes that illustrate the superior copies of the so-called *Book of the Dead*. Such depictions in these mortuary papyri, which were designed to assist the newly dead through the terrible ordeals that faced them, are full of a recondite imagery and clearly represent the elaboration of a long tradition. They show the heart of the dead person being weighed in the scalepan of a great pair of balances against the feather symbol of *Maāt*, which stands in the other scalepan. *Maāt* designates the Egyptian conception of

1 The subject of a postmortem judgment has been treated at length by the present writer in a work entitled *The Judgment of the Dead: A Historical and Comparative Study* (New York, 1968). The reader is referred to this work for fuller documentation and bibliographies than can be given here.

the law of cosmic order, which was embodied in the sun-god Rē, the supreme deity of the Egyptian state.[2] In mythological imagery *Maāt* was represented as a goddess wearing a feather on her head, who was related to Rē as his daughter; sometimes, by a transference of imagery well known in the comparative study of religion, *Maāt* was also regarded as the food on which Rē was nourished.[3] The concept of *Maāt*, whatever the imagery used in representing it, is of fundamental significance for the evaluation of ancient Egyptian culture. The concept first occurs in texts of the Old Kingdom (*circa* 2400 B.C.), where it connotes not only cosmic order but social order also, so that the term can be legitimately translated as "truth," or "justice," or even "righteousness." In its social extension, accordingly, *Maāt* represented a criterion or standard for personal character and conduct.[4]

In the depictions of the judgment scene in the *Book of the Dead*, it is usually the heart of the deceased that is weighed against the symbol of *Maāt*. The heart, which was represented by the hieroglyph *ib*, was regarded by the Egyptians not only as a vital organ of the individual person but also as a conscious entity that could act independently of, and sometimes against, its owner. It was referred to as the "god in a man," and it was hypostatized as a moral censor of the individual in a manner far more realistic than that which informs the Christian concept of the "voice of conscience."[5] The *Book of the Dead* actually contained a special prayer, which was also engraved on the scarab amulet laid on the embalmed body, for the deceased to address to his heart at the moment of the fateful weighing, beseeching it not to witness against him.[6]

These representations of the Weighing of the Heart generally include other figures than that of the deceased and have accompanying texts relating to various moments of the transaction. The

[2] Cf. H. Bonnet, *Reallexikon der ägyptischen Religionsgeschichte* (Berlin, 1952), pp. 430–34; H. Frankfort, *Kingship and the Gods* (Chicago, 1948), pp. 51–52, 149.

[3] Cf. Bonnet, *Reallexikon*, pp. 432b–33b; S. Morenz, *Aegyptische Religion* (Stuttgart, 1960), pp. 120–23.

[4] Cf. Brandon, *Judgment of the Dead*, chap. 1.

[5] Cf. A. Piankoff, *Le "coeur" dans les textes égyptiennes* (Paris, 1930); Brandon, *Man and His Destiny in the Great Religions* (Manchester, 1962), p. 45.

[6] Cf. E. A. W. Budge, *The Mummy* (Cambridge, 1925), pp. 289–98; Brandon, *Judgment of the Dead*, chap. 1.

fine *Papyrus of Ani*, now in the British Museum, provides the most elaborate presentation of the scene, and it will be convenient to follow its pattern here.[7] The great black scales, weighing the heart of the scribe Ani against the feather of *Maāt*, dominate the center of the scene. The fateful assessment is watched in obvious anxiety and trepidation by Ani and his wife. The plummet of the scales is carefully attended by the jackal-headed mortuary god Anubis, and the verdict is recorded by the scribe-god Thoth. To the right of the scene a fearsome hybrid monster *Am-mut* ("she who devours the dead") waits in anticipation of an adverse verdict. The transaction is also watched by the two goddesses of birth and by Shai, the god of destiny, while the *ba* of Ani is depicted on the portal of his tomb. Above the scene sit the figures of the divine Ennead of Heliopolis, to whom the verdict of the scales is reported by Thoth.[8] In many other versions, Osiris, the god of the dead, is represented as watching the judgment from the eminence of his throne. The *Papyrus of Ani* is distinctive in the omission of this feature and in the depiction of the justified Ani as being conducted, after his vindication as one who is *maā kheru* ("true of voice"), into the august presence of Osiris.[9]

This postmortem Weighing of the Heart, as presented in the *Book of the Dead*, is an impressive conception, once its bizarre imagery is understood. On analysis, however, it contains many problems, the solution of which has to be sought in the earlier history of the Egyptian mortuary cultus. These problems cannot be pursued here,[10] and it must suffice for our present purpose to note that the *Book of the Dead* contains another conception of the judgment after death which appears to be unrelated to that of the Weighing of the Heart. In chapter 125 the deceased is represented as having to make two so-called Negative Confessions: one addressed to Osiris and the other to forty-two demonic beings, each of whom was connected with some particular place in Egypt. These "Confessions" are not really confessions, but as-

[7] Cf. E. A. W. Budge, *The Book of the Dead: The Papyrus of Ani*, 3 vols. (London and New York, 1913), vol. 1, pp. 219–20 (Budge dated it for 1450–2400 B.C.); J. Yoyotte, "Le jugement des morts dans l'Égypte ancienne," *Sources orientales*, 4 (1961): 44. It probably dates from about 1250 B.C.

[8] An analytical description of this scene is given by the present writer in his *Judgment of the Dead*, chap. 1.

[9] On the meaning of *maā kheru*, see below, p. 95.

[10] They are dealt with in the writer's *Judgment of the Dead*, chap. 1.

severations of innocence concerning various specified offenses. The purpose of these asseverations is clearly stated in the rubric that introduces chapter 125: "Words spoken when one enters the Hall of the Two Truths. To separate N. from his sins, and to see the face of all the gods."[11] Accordingly, the deceased is equipped with formulas designed to give him clearance on this crucial occasion. The situation thereby envisaged is quite different from that of the Weighing of the Heart, and it suggests derivation from a different conception of the postmortem judgment.

The investigation of this other conception helps to illuminate the significance of the idea of the weighing of the heart in the context of Egyptian ethical insight. The earliest mortuary documents, namely, the *Pyramid Texts* (*circa* 2425–2300 B.C.),[12] indicate that already two distinctive lines of thought existed concerning a judgment after death. One was clearly of a primitive kind, and was doubtless colored by current juridical custom. The following passage is representative: "There is no accuser (representing) a living person against N. (i.e., the deceased); there is no accuser (representing) a dead person against N. . . ."[13] The postmortem situation envisaged here is that, as accusations might be brought against a person in this life, putting him in danger unless he could clear himself, so in the next world the deceased might find himself in jeopardy by some posthumous accusation. Such a threat is anticipated and countered by asserting the fact of one's innocence. The attitude involved is ethically negative, for it was deemed sufficient for the achieving of eternal felicity that one's actions should not be challenged after death. The other view of the postmortem judgment in the *Pyramid Texts* is more positive. It finds expression in the following statements: "He desires that he may be justified (*maā kheru*) through that which he has done. For *Tfn*, with Tefnut, has judged N.; for the Two Truths (*Maāty*) have heard; for Shu was witness; for the Two Truths have pronounced the verdict."[14] A definite process of judgment is clearly

[11] For example, see the *Papyrus of Nu* (British Museum), chap. 125, in Budge, *Book of the Dead*, vol. 2, p. 572. Cf. T. G. Allen, *The Egyptian Book of the Dead* (Chicago, 1960), p. 196; Yoyotte, "Le jugement des morts," p. 51; cf. Maystre, *Les déclarations d'innocence* (Cairo, 1937).

[12] Cf. Bonnet, *Reallexikon*, pp. 620b–23a.

[13] *Pyr.* 386a-b (in K. H. Sethe, *Die altägyptischen Pyramidentexte*, 2d ed. [Hildesheim, 1960], vol. 1, p. 201). Cf. H. Kees, *Totenglauben und Jenseitsvorstellungen der alten Aegypter* (2 Aufl., Berlin, 1956), p. 106.

[14] *Pyr.* 316d–317a-b (in Sethe, *Die Pyramidentexte*, vol. 1, p. 172). The

envisaged in this text, and, since the "Two Truths" connote a conception current in the solar theology of Heliopolis, there is some suggestion that Rē, the sun god, was concerned with this postmortem tribunal.[15] For us, however, the significance of the passage lies in the expression *maā kheru* (*mʒʿ ḫrw*). The two words mean, literally, "true of voice," and in the implied context they can be translated "justified." The context relates to the legend of Osiris and its use in the royal mortuary ritual.[16] According to the legend, Osiris appeared before the tribunal of the gods of Heliopolis after his resurrection, and his case against his murderer Set was tried. Set was condemned, and Osiris was pronounced *maā kheru*, being thus justified and vindicated.[17] Since the dead pharaoh was ritually identified with Osiris in the mortuary ritual, it would appear that the Osirian title *maā kheru* was also ascribed to him.[18] However, it is important to note that the royal desire is expressed that this postmortem justification will be deserved "through that which he has done."

In the *Pyramid Texts* no reference is made to a weighing of the heart of the deceased, nor does it appear in the so-called biographical inscriptions on the tombs of nobles dating from the

crucial statement reads *ỉmr.f mʒʿ ḫrw.f m.ỉrt.f* (316d). For other translations see: K. H. Sethe, *Übersetzung und Kommentar zuden altägyptischen pyramidentexten*, 6 vols. (Hamburg, 1935–62), vol. 1, p. 391; Yoyotte, "Le jugement des morts," p. 25; L. Speleers, *Les textes des pyramides égyptiennes*, 2 vols. (Brussels, 1923), vol. 1, p. 26; S. A. B. Mercer, *The Pyramid Texts*, 2 vols. (New York, 1952), vol. 1, p. 83, vol. 2, p. 149.

[15] Cf. Brandon, *Judgment of the Dead*, chap. 1.

[16] Cf. Brandon, "The Ritual Technique of Salvation in the Ancient Near East," in *The Savior God*, ed. S. G. F. Brandon (Manchester, 1963), pp. 19 ff.

[17] See *Pyr.* 1556a: *ʿbš stš mʒʿ wsỉr.*

[18] This interpretation would be disputed by R. Anthes, who, in his important article "The Original Meaning of *mʒʿ ḫrw*" (*The Journal of Near Eastern Studies*, 13 [1954]: 21–51), maintains that *mʒʿ ḫrw* was "applied to the deceased king when he was transfigured; they who praise him relate in fact that he is acclaimed as right or (in their quality of the celestial counterpart of the Court of Heliopolis) repeat this acclamation; this idea is certainly not influenced by a reminiscence of the justified Osiris" (p. 50). He concludes, "There is, to my knowledge, no primary connection between Osiris and *mʒʿt, mʒʿ ḫrw* recognizable, . . ." (p. 51). It is strange that, though he asserts that this contention cannot be refuted by reference to *Pyr.* 1556a (cited in n. 17 above), Dr. Anthes omits giving his reasons why this should be so. Cf. J. Spiegel, *Die Idee vom Totengericht in der aegyptischen Religion* (Glückstadt, 1935), p. 43; H. Junker, *Pyramidenzeit: Das Wesen der altägyptischen Religion* (Zurich, 1949), pp. 83–85; Kees, *Totenglauben*, p. 105; S. G. F. Brandon, "A Problem of the Osirian Judgment of the Dead," *Numen*, 5 (1958): 115 ff.

latter part of the Old Kingdom period, of which that of Herkhuf, an Assuan noble, is a notable example.[19] But these inscriptions do indicate that the more positive moral approach of one of the two *Pyramid Texts* traditions cited, concerning the postmortem judgment, was in the process of being developed. It is in the so-called *Instruction for King Merikarē*, a writing of the First Intermediate Period (2200–2050 B.C.), that the first suggestion of a form of postmortem assessment inspired by the practice of the marketplace rather than that of the law court occurs.[20] The old king is represented as warning his son about the judgment after death: "The council which judges the deficient, thou knowest that they are not lenient on that day of judging the miserable. . . . A man remains after death, and his deeds are placed beside him in heaps. . . ."[21] Although a tribunal, with judges and an accuser, is envisaged, the criterion will be a man's deeds—they are apparently to be set out in two obvious and contrasting heaps of the good and the bad. How the Egyptians imagined a man's past deeds could thus be presented for this postmortem scrutiny is not known, but the important factor involved in this conception would seem to be that the individual's eternal destiny would be decided by his own past actions and not by the prosecuting counsel or the judges. In other words, the verdict on a man's life would be automatically determined, and, therefore, impartial and objective. By invoking such a notion, it is possible that the author of the document, mindful of the perversion of justice in this world, sought to show that the judgment after death would be immune from external interference.[22]

The concept of weighing first appears in the *Coffin Texts*, which

[19] Cf. Brandon, *Judgment of the Dead*, chap. 1.

[20] The imagery might also derive from the practice of assessing the products of the labor of various peasants. For market scenes during the Old Kingdom see A. Erman, *Aegypten und aegyptisches Leben im Altertum* (Tübingen, 1885), vol. 1, pp. 655–56.

[21] J. Wilson, trans., in *Ancient Near Eastern Texts*, ed. J. B. Pritchard, 2d ed. (Princeton, 1955), p. 415b. Cf. A. Erman, *The Literature of the Ancient Egyptians* (London, 1927), pp. 77–78; Yoyotte, "Le jugement des morts," p. 34.

[22] The Middle Kingdom literary text known as the *Complaints of the Peasant* eloquently attests both the perversion or delay of justice by magistrates and belief in the impartiality of the postmortem weighing: cf. Brandon, *Judgment of the Dead*, chap. 1. One of the asseverations made by the deceased in the Declarations of Innocence in the *Book of the Dead* indicates that tampering with scales was known in Egypt: "I have not *weakened* the plummet of the scales."

document Egyptian mortuary belief during the Middle Kingdom (2160–1580 B.C.).[23] References to the idea are imprecise and suggest that the notion was still at a formative stage, as, for example, in the following passages: "O Osiris N., this is the balance of Rē, in which he weighs *Maāt*"; "The offence of which thou art accused is eliminated, thy fault is wiped out, by the weighing on the balance, in the day of the evaluation of qualities."[24] In another passage, which was subsequently incorporated into the *Book of the Dead*, the balance or scales is actually hypostatized as an awful deity from which the dead seek protection.[25]

Accordingly, it would appear that from the Old Kingdom period Egyptian eschatology had incorporated two different conceptions of the judgment after death. One conceived of it as taking the form, familiar in current practice, of defending oneself against accusations; the other saw the judgment as an assessment of a man's moral worth, and it was imagined as being a process of weighing. Hence these two conceptions find expression in the *Book of the Dead*, and, by their juxtaposition in that corpus of funerary texts, pose the problem of their relationship.

The manner in which the Egyptians seem to have related the two conceptions appears to be indicated in the arrangement of the *Papyrus of Ani*. The Weighing of the Heart is presented as a single dramatic episode at the beginning of the document; its accompanying hieroglyphic libretto makes no reference to the contents of chapter 125, which contains the two Declarations of Innocence.[26] Therefore, it seems reasonable to infer that those responsible for the composition of this *Papyrus* intended to present the Weighing of the Heart as the crucial transaction that awaited the deceased Ani in the next world. In the vignettes which illustrate chapter 125, the weighing is again represented in abbreviated form at what appears to be the end of the Hall of the Two Truths, in which the deceased has to make his double Declarations of Innocence.[27] This arrangement, accordingly, suggests a sequential process whereby the weighing followed the

[23] Cf. Bonnet, *Reallexikon*, pp. 669a–70a.

[24] A. de Buck, ed., *The Egyptian Coffin Texts*, 7 vols. to date (Chicago, 1935–), vol. 5, p. 321c-d (Spell 452); vol. 1, p. 181c-e (Spell 44).

[25] *Ibid.*, vol. 4, pp. 298–302 (Spell 335 = *Book of the Dead*, XVII. 23). Cf. Spiegel, *Totengericht*, p. 48; Kees, *Totenglauben*, p. 303.

[26] See *The Book of the Dead: Facsimile of the Papyrus of Ani*, ed. E. A. W. Budge, 2d ed. (British Museum, 1894), plate 3.

[27] *Ibid.*, plates 31 and 32. Cf. Brandon, *Judgment of the Dead*, chap. 1.

Declarations. If this order is intentional, it would appear that the Weighing of the Heart was regarded as constituting a test of the truth of the Declarations. Such an interpretation would be powerfully confirmed by the signal emphasis laid upon the weighing by its special presentation at the beginning of the *Papyrus*.

It would seem legitimate to conclude, therefore, that by the New Kingdom period the Egyptians, while still retaining the ancient idea of the postmortem judgment as a juridical process of accusation and counter-asseveration of innocence, were more concerned with the judgment after death as an automatic and impartial assessment of their moral worth. Those scholars who have interpreted the Osirian judgment in the *Book of the Dead* as a declension from a higher moral tradition of the Old Kingdom have concentrated their attention on chapter 125 and have rightly stressed the magical factors involved, such as knowing the identities of the forty-two demonic beings addressed in the second Declaration of Innocence.[28] But they have overlooked the fact that the Egyptians saw the Weighing of the Heart as an automatic process of moral assessment, immune from the interference of magic or other devices that might deflect the impartiality of its verdict.[29] Moreover, this conclusion is confirmed by the long continuance of belief in the weighing as the decisive transaction of the judgment of the dead. This belief continued when the other conception faded. A catena of passages can be given to attest the reality of this belief from the middle of the second millennium B.C. down to the second century A.D.[30] In other words, the idea of the Weighting of the Heart surely reflected a deeply rooted conviction of the people of Egypt that, after death, man was faced with an assessment of his moral worth which was wholly

[28] For this view, see J. H. Breasted, *The Development of Religion and Thought in Ancient Egypt* (London, 1912), pp. 307–9, and *The Dawn of Conscience* (New York, 1935), pp. 262–65; Kees, *Totengericht*, pp. 274–75; J. Černý, *Ancient Egyptian Religions* (London, 1952), pp. 90–91; Budge, *The Mummy*, p. 293; H. Frankfort, *Ancient Egyptian Religions* (New York, 1948), p. 118; Yoyotte, "Le jugement des morts," p. 50.

[29] The Egyptian artists usually represented the deceased in a posture of humility and apprehension during the weighing of his or her heart. If a favorable verdict could have been obtained by magical means, it is difficult to understand how the consequent charade of the Weighing of the Heart could have persisted for so many centuries, as it obviously did. See Brandon, *Judgment of the Dead*, chap. 1.

[30] *Ibid.*

searching and impartial, and that on its issue his eternal future depended.

Phenomenologically this Egyptian conception of the judgment of the dead is unique both in chronological precedence and in the elaborate form of its presentation. The idea subsequently found expression in many other religions, most notably in medieval Christianity. In some instances Egyptian influence can be traced, or reasonably assumed, but in none did the notion acquire so dominant a significance as it did in Egypt.

Before considering the form which the idea took in Christianity, we may briefly note its manifestations in ancient Greek and Hebrew religion. The classic instance in Greek literature is in the *Iliad* XXII.179, where Zeus is described as weighing, on his golden scales, the fates of Achilles and Hector as the two heroes engage in their fateful combat under the walls of Troy. In the strict sense, this transaction is not a *psychostasia*, but a *kerostasia*, for it is the *kēres* of the heroes that are weighed against each other, not their souls (*psychai*).[31] The weighing is also done before their deaths, and it is intended to decide their fates and not their moral worth. Other occurrences of the so-called *psychostasia* in classical literature and art are generally of the same character, in that they concern decisions on the destiny of the living and not on the reward or punishment of the dead.[32] It would seem, however, that the essence of the idea of such weighing was that of the impartiality of the assessment—even Zeus uses the scales instead of decreeing according to his own insight or will.

Belief in a postmortem judgment came comparatively late in Israel. It is in the second century B.C. that the idea first finds expression in Hebrew literature, and it is then, as it continued to be, essentially connected with the destiny of Israel according to the traditional *Heilsgeschichte*. Thus, while the personal aspect of this judgment is not neglected, it is rather as a signal act of retribution enacted on the nations for their oppression of Israel

[31] J. Harrison, *Prolegomena to the Study of Greek Religion*, 3d ed. (New York, 1955), p. 183.

[32] Cf. L. Kretzenbacher, *Die Seelenwaage: Zur religiösen Idee vom Jenseitsgericht auf der Schicksalswaage in Hochreligion, Bildkunst, und Volksglaube* (Klagenfurt, 1958), pp. 29–36; E. Wüst, "Psychostasie (Seelenwägung)," in Pauly-Wissowa, *Realencyclopädie der Klasseschen Altertumswissenschaft*, XXIII. 2 (1957), 1442–44.

that Yahweh's Day of Judgment was conceived.[33] However that may be, the idea of assessing a person's worth by weighing was already current in Hebrew thought. Job is represented as exclaiming: "Let me be weighed in a just balance, and let God know my integrity!"[34] And in Daniel 5:27 there is the famous judgment on Belshazzar: "TEKEL, you have been weighed in the balances (*b*ᵉ *mô z*ᵉ *nayyâ*) and found wanting." Such passages concern a premortem evaluation of moral worth; the latter passage relates to Belshazzar's destiny and is thus similar to the Greek image of the determining of an individual's fate. Neither passage appears to have an eschatological reference, and it would seem that the idea of weighing is just an imaginative concept borrowed from current commercial usage. The idea does, however, occur in an eschatological context in the *Similitudes of Enoch*, which date perhaps from about 100–80 B.C.,[35] in the following verse: "And the Lord of Spirits placed the Elect One on a throne of glory. And he shall judge all the works of the holy above, / And in the balances shall their deeds be weighed."[36] Whether Egyptian influence is to be seen here cannot be determined. Other sources of derivation could be suggested; but whatever the origin of the concept, it is evident that it was an image of no special significance and that it never acquired in Hebrew eschatology the dominance that it had in the Osirian mortuary faith.

The great currency which the idea of a *psychostasia* acquired in medieval Christianity is attended by many problems, the elucidation of which is both fascinating and instructive. What appears to be the earliest extant example of the concept occurs on the great sculptured cross of Muiredach at Monasterboice, County Louth, Ireland, which dates from 923.[37] Among the various sacred epi-

[33] Cf. Brandon, *Man and His Destiny*, pp. 137–40; Brandon, *Judgment of the Dead*, chap. 3.

[34] Job 31:6.

[35] Cf. R. H. Pfeiffer, *History of New Testament Times: With an Introduction to the Apocrypha* (New York, 1949), pp. 75, 76.

[36] LXI. 8; R. H. Charles, trans., *The Book of Enoch* (London, 1921), p. 80. Cf. F. Martin, *Le livre d'Hénoch* (Paris, 1906), pp. 127–28.

[37] On the cross of Muiredach and its date see M. de Paor and L. de Paor, *Early Christian Ireland* (London, 1958), pp. 147–49; L. Stone, *Sculpture in Britain: The Middle Ages* (Harmondsworth, 1955), p. 27. For main Byzantine example of about the same time, cf. Beat Brenk: *Tradition und Neuerung in der Christlichen Kunst des ersten Jahrtausends: Studien zur Geschichte des Weltgerichtsbildes* (Vienna, 1966) p. 81, Fig. 4.

sodes carved thereon in a primitive Celtic idiom is one which depicts a huge pair of scales, in one pan of which sits a small human figure. To the left, another human figure of vast proportions dominates the scene: in its right hand, it holds a curiously shaped staff, the butt of which rests on the head of a recumbent human form that appears to be pulling down the other scalepan, which is empty. The carving has been very eroded by centuries of exposure to the weather, and details are hard to discern. The scene, which has no explanatory inscription, can be identified and interpreted only by reference to later and better preserved examples of the episode concerned. The large figure undoubtedly represents the Archangel Michael presiding over the weighing of a human soul. The recumbent figure, which the Archangel is striking with his staff, must, accordingly, be that of the Devil or one of his demonic minions who is attempting to interfere with the verdict of the scales.

This scene on the Muiredach Cross, as we have just noted, appears to be the precursor of a scene which becomes the crucial episode in medieval depictions of the Last Judgment. Such representations, which are conveniently designated "Dooms," appear suddenly in Christian art during the twelfth century. Previously, the Last Judgment had been represented symbolically in terms of the separation of the sheep from the goats by Christ, according to Matthew 25:31 ff.: the Church of St. Apollinare Nuova, Ravenna, provides a sixth century example of this presentation and the Hypogeum of the Aurelii, Rome, probably preserves one of the third century.[38] The sudden appearance in the twelfth century of what might fairly be described as realistic depictions of the Last Judgment constitutes an interesting problem of Christian iconography which does not, however, directly concern our subject. It will, accordingly, be sufficient for our purpose if we briefly describe the relation of the episode of Weighing the Soul to the other episodes in two of the earliest and most notable of the Dooms.

On the western wall of the basilical church at Torcello, near Venice, the Last Judgment is most impressively portrayed in a

[38] See F. van der Meer and C. Mohrmann, *Atlas of the Early Christian World* (London and Edinburgh, 1958), pp. iii, 236; M. Gough, *The Early Christians* (London, 1961), plate 73 and p. 262. On the presentation in the Hypogeum of the Aurelii see J. Carcopino, *De Pythagore aux Apôtres* (Paris, 1956), pp. 154–55.

mosaic of Byzantine inspiration.[39] The drama is set forth in five registers of scenes. In the top register Christ descends into Hades to rescue the righteous who had lived before his first coming. The next register shows Christ seated within a mandorla, attended by the Virgin and John the Baptist and the Twelve Apostles. In the register below the resurrection of the dead takes place. Beneath this scene the saved and the damned of mankind are represented as divided into two groups, with the latter being thrust by angels into Hell. The bottom register shows their respective fates: the blessed pass into Paradise, represented symbolically as "Abraham's bosom,"[40] while the lost appear naked in the flames of Hell. The *psychostasia* is placed in the fourth register, namely, that in which the division between the saved and the damned is portrayed. Its location is significant: it constitutes an episode that separates the two groups into which mankind is divided at the Last Judgment. In other words, the Weighing of Souls is clearly regarded as the crucial transaction that effects that fateful division. This Torcello *psychostasia* consists of the figure of the Archangel Michael holding a pair of scales, the balance of which two awful black demons try to disturb with claw-like tridents. No objects can be discerned in the scalepans, but there can be no doubt that the scene is meant to indicate that the fate of individual men and women will be decided at the Last Judgment by a process of weighing, performed by the Archangel Michael against the menace of demonic interference.

Before we examine the origin and significance of this Christian *psychostasia*, it is necessary also to look at another early Doom to get a complete picture of the conception. A most notable example is carved on the tympanum of the main western portal of the Romanesque cathedral of St. Lazare at Autun, in eastern France. Like the Torcello "Last Judgment," that of Autun also dates from the twelfth century.[41]

39 The work dates from about the twelfth century. Cf. D. Talbot Rice, *Art of the Byzantine Era* (London, 1963), pp. 180–81, and *The Beginnings of Christian Art* (London, 1957), pp. 170–72; J. Fournée, *Le jugement dernier* (Paris, 1964), pp. 65–67, 135, plates 2, 47, and 55; Kretzenbacher, *Die Seelenwaage*, pp. 72–74, Abb. 18, 19. An eleventh-century prototype without a *psychostasia* is provided by the Panagra Chalteon in Salonika: cf. Brenk, *Tradition und Neuerung*, pp. 82–84.

40 On the concept of Abraham's bosom see Brandon, *Judgment of the Dead*, chap. 5.

41 On the Autun Doom see the superb study of D. Grivot and G. Zarneki, *Gislebertus, sculpteur d'Autun*, 2d ed. (Paris, 1965).

The Autun Doom is divided into three registers of scenes, and the whole composition is dominated by the huge seated figure of Christ within a mandorla. The *psychostasia* is featured in the middle register: the figures in the top register generally denote Christ's appearing at the Last Day, while the bottom register shows the resurrection of the dead. The *psychostasia* itself is a remarkable depiction in a composition unparalleled for its religious and iconographic interest. A huge pair of scales is suspended from the floor of the top register. In the left scalepan is a small nude human figure, obviously representing the soul; the right scalepan is occupied by a toad-like demon. The Archangel Michael, a strange elongated figure typical of the sculpture of Gislebertus, carefully tends the scalepan containing the soul, while two diminutive souls cling for protection about the knees of the Archangel.[42] A frightful demon with a long emaciated body, about the legs of which a three-headed snake entwines itself, is represented as attempting to pull down the right-hand scalepan, with its demonic occupant—since this pan is higher than the other, acquittal is evidently denoted by the soul's outweighing the toad-like fiend.[43]

This form of presentation of the *psychostasia* in Western medieval art is typical. It causes the Weighing of the Soul to appear not so much as an assessment of the character or moral worth of the individual person but rather as a contest between Michael and the Devil. Before we attempt to analyze the motives that lie behind such a presentation, however, we must consider the origin of the concept itself.

First, we have to note that the idea of a postmortem Weighing of the Soul by Michael at either the Immediate or Last Judgment had no warranty in the sacred scriptures of Christianity.[44] The few references or allusions to moral assessment by weighing in the Old Testament provide some slight suggestion for such a postmortem test, but their influence must have been feeble compared with that of the description of the Last Judgment in the *Apocalypse of John* (20:12 ff.). There "the dead were judged by what was written in the books, by what they had done." This idea of judgment from a written record of one's deeds is both an obvious and impressive one, and it finds notable expression in the *Dies Irae*,

[42] *Ibid.*, plates J and K.

[43] Michael seems to be pressing down the scalepan containing the soul, against the pull of the demon on the opposite arm of the balance.

[44] Cf. Brandon, *Judgment of the Dead*, chap. 5.

the great penitential hymn of the mortuary liturgy of the Western Church.[45] In view of the existence of such an authoritative image of the process of judgment, it is strange that the *psychostasia* supervised by Michael, which had no scriptural sanction, should have figured as the crucial transaction in the medieval Dooms.

The idea of a postmortem weighing of deeds had found expression in Patristic literature long before it appeared in iconography. Thus St. John Chrysostom had written: "In that day our actions, our words, and our thoughts will be placed in the scales, and the dip of the balance on either side will carry with it the irrevocable sentence."[46] But such passages may be adjudged to be only general, figurative statements of a postmortem reckoning of human deeds and, as such, are not to be taken as evidence of belief in a *psychostasia*. However that may be, the idea of a weighing of souls after death can be traced in Christian apocryphal literature back to the second century. Its earliest extant occurrence is in the *Testament of Abraham*, which seems to have been composed in Egypt by a Jewish Christian.[47] The book gives a description of the next world as seen by the patriarch Abraham, who is conducted there by Michael in order to alleviate his fears about dying. Abraham sees an angel, resplendent in light, "who held the balances (and) weighed (ἐζυγίαζεν) the souls." Another angel, a "fiery angel, who had the fire, proved (ἐδοκίμαζεν) the souls." Michael explained to Abraham: "These things which you see, holy Abraham, are the judgment (*krisis*) and the retribution (*antapodosis*)."[48] The angel that holds the balances is identified as "Dokiel, the archangel, the just weigher (ζωγοστάτης), and he weighs the just deeds and the sins according (ἐν) to the justice of God."[49] The fact that the concept appears in a work composed

[45] In the frontispiece of the *Liber Vitae* of New Minster, Winchester, a demon threatens a soul with a written record, probably of its life. An open book appears on the throne in the third register of the Torcello Doom, but it probably represents the witness of the Holy Scriptures.

[46] It is significant that this statement of John Chrysostom is quoted by Vincent de Beauvais (*Speculum historiale*, Epil. 118), whose work greatly influenced medieval iconography. Cf. E. Mâle, *Religious Art from the Twelfth to the Eighteenth Century* (New York, 1958), pp. 62–77.

[47] On the date and provenance of the writing see M. R. James, *The Testament of Abraham* (Cambridge, 1892), pp. 7–29, 76. Cf. Wüst in Pauly-Wissowa, *Realencyclopädie der Klassischen Allertumswissenschaft*, XXIII. 2, 1454.

[48] James, *Testament of Abraham*, p. 91.

[49] *Ibid.*, p. 93. J. Michl, in *Reallexikon für Antike und Christentum*, 5

in Egypt is surely significant, for there, in the second century A.D. as we have seen, the idea of a postmortem assessment by weighing was even current in popular literature, besides being familiar through its widespread depiction in the funerary papyri and in temples.

If the antiquity and probable derivation of the idea of the *psychostasia* in Christian thought are thus well attested, the same cannot be said of Michael's role in the transaction as it is depicted in the iconography of medieval Catholicism. In the *Testament of Abraham*, it is not Michael who is the ζωγοστάτης, but Dokiel, an otherwise unknown angelic being; Michael's role is rather that of *psychopompos*.[50] It would seem that it was from this role that Michael eventually graduated to the crucial office of ζωγοστάτης. The way in which this transformation was effected is probably to be seen in the importance that Michael acquired, in popular Christian thought, in connection with death. The moment of death came to be regarded as the most crucial, as well as the most awful, of human destiny. As the soul of the dying person issued forth with the last breath, demons waited to seize it, unless they were prevented by angels.[51] In the curious Coptic writing known as *The History of Joseph the Carpenter*, which dates from the fourth century but incorporates earlier traditions, Michael, with Gabriel, receives the soul of Joseph and conveys it, safe from demonic menace, to God.[52] Michael was naturally cast for this role by his reputation in the Johannine Apocalypse as the captain of the heavenly host that had overthrown the Devil and his evil angels.[53]

It is not clear how Michael actually acquired his office of guard-

(1962): 210, explains the otherwise unknown archangel Dokiel as "göttliche Feinheit, göttlicher Scharfsinn."

50 In the fourth century *Apocalypse of Paul*, chap. 43 (in M. R. James, *The Apocryphal New Testament* [Oxford, 1926], pp. 547–48), Michael is represented as continually praying for men in the presence of God; he also promises to intercede at the judgment: "and I say that if any man doeth but a little good I will strive for him and protect him until he escape the judgment of torment." Cf. Michl, *Reallexion für Antike und Christentum*, 5 (1962): 250–51.

51 Cf. Brandon, *Judgment of the Dead*, chap. 5.

52 XXIII:4, in S. Morenz, *Die Geschichte vom Joseph dem Zimmermann* (Berlin, 1951), pp. 66, 69. This writing also contains a reference to "just balances" as a postmortem concept requiring no explanation (I: 6); in *ibid.*, pp. 2, 35, 126.

53 *Apoc. Joh.*, XII: 7–8. Cf. R. H. Charles, *The Revelation of St. John*, 2 vols. (Edinburgh, 1920), vol. 1, pp. 323–24.

ian of the *psychostasia* at the Last Judgment.[54] Probably it was through his increasing significance as the champion of man, at the fateful moment of death, against demonic attack. For the *psychostasia*, as we have already noticed from the Torcello and Autun Dooms, was conceived not so much as an assessment of the soul than as a contest between Michael and the Devil for the soul's salvation or damnation. Indeed, in almost every other example of the *psychostasia*, the Archangel is represented as concerned not with the actual weighing but with repelling or thwarting demonic attempts to obtain an adverse verdict.[55] In popular devotion, this protective theme seems to have become one of deliverance from the consequences of an adverse verdict. Thus, in a fourteenth century French poem the devils are recognized as being entitled to their proper prey:

> très haultement crioient tous:
> Provost Michael délivrez-nous
> Et nous adjugez notre proye![56]

The contest motif, which is thus very apparent in the medieval *psychostasia*, inevitably prompts the inquiry of whether this was the cause of the introduction of the *psychostasia* as the crucial episode in the depictions of the Last Judgment. And here we may note in passing that there is abundant evidence from many countries of medieval Europe that the *psychostasia* was often represented independently of the Last Judgment as a whole, thus attesting to its key significance in eschatological thought.[57]

The fact that the *psychostasia* appears in the second-century *Testament of Abraham* without any suggestion of demonic interference, and that Michael was not associated with it, would indicate that originally the conception was concerned only with the postmortem assessment of the soul. The contest motif was probably introduced when Michael, as man's champion against the

[54] See n. 50 above.

[55] See the valuable collection of illustrations given by Kretzenbacher in his *Die Seelenwaage*.

[56] Cf. Fournée, *Le jugement dernier*, pp. 99–100.

[57] Cf. E. Mâle, *L'Art religieux du XIIIe siècle*, 6th ed. (Paris, 1953), pp. 413–14; Kretzenbacher, *Die Seelenwaage*, *passim*. It is to be noted that the *psychostasia* does not appear in all medieval Dooms; e.g., it is absent from the Dooms at Poitiers, Reims, St. Denis, Beaulieu, Laon, and (in England) at St. Thomas, Salisbury.

Devil, acquired the office of supervisor of the fateful balances. But, if the *psychostasia* was at first conceived essentially as a post-mortem ordeal experienced by the individual soul, as it had been in ancient Egypt, what was its exact function in the medieval conception of the Last Judgment? This question has to be asked, since the *psychostasia* in the *Testament of Abraham* is clearly an assessment of the soul immediately after death, and not of the resurrected dead at the Second Coming of Christ. The subsequent importation of the *psychostasia* into the Last Judgment was most probably effected without conscious reference to its original place in the Immediate Judgment. And the consequent sense of dislocation or confusion of motif is doubtless to be seen as part of that greater dislocation that inheres in Christian eschatology through the inclusion of both an Immediate and a Final Judgment in its scheme of retribution, owing to the nonfulfillment of the original *Parousia*-hope.[58] A similar reduplication of theme occurs, for example, in the presentation of the sufferings of Purgatory and Hell.[59]

In a series of related episodes portrayed in the medieval Doom, the *psychostasia* does, in fact, constitute the only definite means whereby the resurrected dead are divided between the saved and the damned. It is possible, therefore, that its introduction was due to the need for finding some transaction that could be graphically presented as the crucial act of discrimination between the just and the unjust.[60] However that may be, the centrality of the *psychostasia* in the composition of the Doom had the effect, obviously unintended, of making the fate of men depend on Michael, and not on Christ, who appears seated in majesty above and outside the central drama.[61]

Although the *psychostasia* was thus the central episode of the

[58] Cf. Brandon, *Judgment of the Dead*, chap. 5, and *History, Time and Deity* (Manchester, 1965), pp. 183 ff.

[59] See references in n. 58 above.

[60] Where the *psychostasia* does not appear, the division between the saved and the damned is sometimes represented as being made by an angel armed with a sword, an idea possibly inspired by the expulsion of Adam and Eve from the Garden of Eden, according to Genesis 3:24.

[61] "On peut se demander ici quel est le juge véritable: le Christ ou saint Michel? Dans bien des oeuvres, en effet, le Christ est plus un témoin qu'un juge. Il devient une sorte de président honoraire qui a délégué tous pouvoirs à son archange et se contente de confirmer son choix" (Fournée, *Le jugement dernier*, p. 98). Cf. Brandon, *Judgment of the Dead*, chap. 5.

Doom and could also be represented separately as the essential means of judgment, there was an obvious uncertainty about what was weighed in this fateful transaction. Generally, in the scalepan at Michael's right hand a small nude human figure is shown, which traditionally represented the soul, while in the other scalepan a demon appears. The variations from this norm are interesting. In the splendid Doom on the west portal of the cathedral at Bourges, a chalice, possibly a symbol of the saving blood of Christ, replaces the figure of the soul.[62] At Amiens it is the Agnus Dei, again a symbol of the redeeming Savior.[63] Often, as for example in Roger Van der Weyden's polyptych at Beaune, two nude figures are weighed against each other. The symbolism here can surely only denote an assessing of the good and evil selves of the deceased, since it would be illogical to weigh two different souls against each other.[64] Occasionally the soul is tested against some kind of weight, such as stones, in the other scalepan.[65] Such variety must indicate a certain fluidity of both conception and tradition, although, as we have noted, the depiction of a soul in one scalepan is the more usual custom, as it is, of course, the more intelligible. From the fact that demons are often represented as trying to drag down the scalepan opposite the soul, it would appear that virtue should outweigh vice to secure acquittal.[66]

The depiction of the *psychostasia* disappeared with the cessation of the making of Dooms in those countries affected by the Protestant Reformation. The practice also gradually died out in Catholic lands, though baroque examples are known and the memory of the weighing of souls was preserved in folkdrama

[62] Cf. J. Bony, *French Cathedrals* (London, 1961), plates 72, 74; Fournée, *Le jugement dernier*, p. 101, plate 31.

[63] Cf. Bony, *French Cathedrals*, plate 101; Fournée, *Le jugement dernier*, p. 101; M. P. Perry, "On the Psychostasis in Christian Art," *The Burlington Magazine*, 22 (1912–13): 209, 210, 215; Kretzenbacher, *Die Seelenwaage*, p. 151, illustration 43.

[64] Cf. Perry, "On the Psychostasis," p. 104; Kretzenbacher, *Die Seelenwaage*, pp. 39, 155–56, 157–60. Fournée, *Le jugement dernier*, p. 101, asks: "Mais on ne voit pas comment la balance pourrait pencher en même temps du côté des élus et du côté des réprouvés" (see also p. 98). In the *psychostasia* depicted in the glass of the cathedral of Coutances, the two nude figures in either scalepan seem to be differentiated by the fact that one (who is saved) wears a mitre (cf. *ibid.*, plate 28).

[65] See, for example, illustrations 40 and 41 in Kretzenbacher, *Die Seelenwaage*.

[66] See n. 43 above.

into modern times.[67] The widespread custom of representing it in the Middle Ages doubtless attests to some deeply rooted need to portray visually a crucial ordeal which was to be faced by all men at the Last Judgment. As we have also seen, however, another motif operated in the depiction: instead of being an assessment of the moral worth of the soul, which was its natural significance, the Christian *psychostasia* tended to become a contest between God, in the person of Michael, and the Devil for possession of the soul of man.

It is in the mortuary faith of ancient Egypt and in medieval Christianity that the idea of postmortem assessment by weighing found its most notable forms of expression. The idea does appear in other religions, but generally it does not figure as a primary concept. One of the references in the *Qur'ān* may, however, be particularly noted, since weighing seems to be invoked as an assurance of a completely impartial judgment: "We shall place the balances (of) justice on the day of resurrection and no soul shall be wronged, even to the extent of the weight of a grain of mustard seed. We shall make the assessments. We shall know how to cast the account."[68] In Zoroastrianism the concept is also clearly employed to emphasize the exactitude of the postmortem judgment:

> just Rashnu will weigh (its deeds). He lets his spiritual scales incline to neither side, neither for the saved nor yet for the damned, nor yet for kings and princes. Not for a hair's breadth will he diverge, for he is no respecter (of persons). He deals out impartial justice both to kings and princes and to the meanest of men.[69]

As in Islam, however, the *psychostasia* is only one among several eschatological ordeals. The same may be said of its role in Hinduism. Yama, the god of the dead, is presented also as their judge, and reference is made to weighing:

[67] Cf. Kretzenbacher, *Die Seelenwaage*, pp. 184–222. See also Brandon, *Judgment of the Dead*, chap. 5.

[68] Surah 21:48; see also Surah 101:5–8. D. Sourdel, in *Sources orientales*, 4 (1961): 184, thinks that the idea of the *psychostasia* in the *Qur'ān* is more likely to have derived from Mazdean than Christian tradition; but cf. Brandon, *Judgment of the Dead*, chap. 6.

[69] Translated from the *Dâstân-i Mēnōk-i Krat* by R. C. Zaehner, *The Dawn and Twilight of Zoroastrianism* (London, 1961), p. 303. Cf. M. Molé in *Sources orientales*, 4 (1961): 162. On the identification of Rashnu with the *Činvant* ("Separator"), see Zaehner in the *Bulletin of the School of Oriental and African Studies*, 17 (1955): 247.

In that world they lay (good and bad deeds) on a balance. What of either – whether good or bad – draws (down), the consequences are in accordance therewith. But he who knows, he already ascends the balance in this world, (and) renders unnecessary a weighing in that world. His good works prevail, not his bad works.[70]

The balances of Yama appear also in Tibetan iconography. In the remarkable painting of the Judgment reproduced by W. Y. Evans-Wentz in his edition of *The Tibetan Book of the Dead*, white and black pebbles, symbolizing respectively the good and bad deeds of the deceased, are being weighed.[71] In the popular art of Japanese Buddhism, Emma-Ô, who is the Japanese version of the Indian Yama-rāja, is depicted at his tribunal with various equipment for judging the dead, among which a huge pair of balances appears, but no emphasis seems to have been laid upon its function or significance.[72]

Although the *psychostasia* plays only a minor role in these other religions, it is surely significant that in all the eschatologies concerned, a motif, taken from the marketplace, appears in the conception of the postmortem judgment, which should by nature evoke the imagery of the law court. As we have seen in dealing with the earliest and the most carefully developed use of the notion, that of ancient Egypt, it was doubtless introduced originally into eschatological imagery to satisfy the aspiration for an impartial verdict. It is possibly significant also that in the Christian presentation demons are often represented as trying to interfere with the true balance of the scales. In other words, the inherent conviction is that such a form of assessment is impartial and objective, and that it could be deflected only by the forcible interference of an evil agency. It is an idea that has also been preserved, very notably, in modern mythology by the blindfolded figure of Justice holding the scales and a drawn sword.[73]

[70] *S'atapathabrāmaṇa*, 11, 2, 7, 33, in *Religionsgeschichtliches Lesebuch* (Tübingen, 1908), p. 145. Cf. P. Deussen, *The Philosophy of the Upanishads* (Edinburgh, 1919), p. 325.

[71] W. Y. Evans-Wentz, *The Tibetan Book of the Dead*, 3d ed. (London, 1957), pp. xxx–xxxiii, 37–39, 166, 240.

[72] See S. Eliséev, "The Mythology of Japan," in *Asiatic Mythology* (London, 1932), plate facing p. 416.

[73] Cf. E. Panofsky, *Studies in Iconology* (New York and Evanston, Ill., 1962), p. 109.

GOD IN AFRICAN MYTHOLOGY

E. G. PARRINDER

In a footnote in his great work *Shamanism*, Mircea Eliade remarks that Africa is omitted from his study because it "would lead us too far."[1] He indicates several works on African cults, but it is true that the mass of books on Africa is so immense that even one who ranges freely over Asia, Oceania, and America may feel that there is a limit to what one man can read. From being regarded as the Dark Continent, about whose societies little was known and about whose religion virtually nothing, Africa has become almost a wearisome subject of literature. Thirty years ago a bibliography of only French West Africa filled a large volume, and today limited collections of "Africana" fill whole rooms of specialized libraries. There are journals on all kinds of African subjects, including religion, and a library of African religion alone is planned in London. Africa is easy of access and, with the sole exception of the Congo, white people are still welcomed and wander unarmed and untouched to the most remote places. Countless students in search of a Ph.D. have spent months or years on some small detail of African life and then buried their findings in typescript in a university library.

Even the Africanist feels daunted by the vast amount of material now available, and one effect of this is often to limit interests and writing to a very small area. Anthropologists are some of the chief students of African society, and the older ones included religion and myth in their researches. But several tendencies are now observable. One is to limit religion to a small part of the study or to omit it altogether. Another is to restrict oneself to a

[1] M. Eliade, *Shamanism* (London, 1964), p. 374 n.

small language group, the more "untouched" the better. A third, affecting all African studies, is the failure to look beyond Africa, an unwillingness to make comparisons, which results in a cultural isolation expressed in terms like "fetishist," used of Africa alone. African anthropologists often unconsciously hold attitudes which falsify conclusions reached about African religion. The "fetish" may be regarded as a mere idol and the myth as foolish romance because it is assumed that idol and myth are out-of-date and unscientific, and if in fact they do exist in the "higher" religions, then these too are mere superstitions.

Here some aspects of African mythology are selected in the light of themes that have been the concern of thinkers in other countries. That nearly all African peoples believe in a Supreme Being is now generally recognized. The few possible exceptions in South Africa may be so because their ancient beliefs changed under the influence of Christianity, which supplied a doctrine of God but whose apologists may have misrepresented the older faith. Yet, that this universally acknowledged Supreme Being apparently has no worship has often been noted. This is not peculiar to Africa, and Eliade remarks in *Patterns in Comparative Religion* that absence of cult "is characteristic of most of the sky gods."[2] But if the High God is, in some myths, a *deus absconditus*, does that necessarily make him a *deus otiosus*? Even if he has little cult worship today he may preserve something of his position by acknowledgment as sovereign God, or as principle of creation and sustentation, or as both transcendent and immanent. The myths show his concerns with men today as well as in the past.

African myth deals with questions of cosmology, of the divine and human natures and relationships, and as such it is likely to be influential for a long time, despite the arrival of Islam and Christianity, both of which are little more than a hundred years old in the tropical and southern regions of Africa. That God is creator or origin of all things appears in many myths, some examples of which can be given.

The Yoruba of Nigeria, whose religion and art are well known, speak of God as Ol-orun, owner of the sky, or Ol-odu-mare, the infinite or almighty Lord. He lived in heaven with other gods and

[2] M. Eliade, *Patterns in Comparative Religion* (New York, 1958), pp. 46–47.

down below was the earth, then only a marshy waste, where lesser gods would sometimes come down on spiders' webs to play or hunt in the marsh. There were no men yet because there was no solid ground. Finally, the Supreme Being called another divinity to go as a demiurge to form the earth. The demiurge was Great-divinity, Orisha-nla or Oba-tala (the Supreme Being is never called an *orisha*, a divinity). He was given a bag which, according to one version, lay between the thighs of the Almighty; in the bag was a snail shell, a pigeon, and a hen. Great-divinity came down to the marsh, poured out earth from the shell, and the pigeon and the hen scattered it about till dry land was made. Then Ol-orun sent a chameleon, a reptile which often appears in African story, to report on the condition of the world. At first he said it was wide but not dry enough; the second time he said it was both wide and dry. The place of creation was Ilé-Ifé, the "house of that which is wide," which to this day is the sacred city of the Yoruba, the home of all things.[3]

The Fon of Dahomey are neighbors of the Yoruba, but their mythology differs in many ways, though there are some borrowings. The Supreme Being (Mawu) is predominant in the myths and is usually male, though in some versions Mawu is female, paired with a male Lisa. More rarely, these twins are spoken of as children of a primordial female. Generally Mawu is called creator, the one who formed the world with the help of a snake in whose mouth Mawu was carried; wherever they stopped, mountains appeared. When creation was finished there were too many mountains and the earth was in danger of sinking into the sea that surrounded it. So Mawu asked the snake to coil itself round, with its tail in its mouth, to support the earth. The circular snake is a common African symbol of eternity, life, and continuity, as it is in other continents. Some versions say that there are thousands of snake coils above and below the earth, others that the snake twisted itself around four pillars that uphold the earth, and yet others that the snake is fed with iron by monkeys and if they stop this it will eat its own tail and the earth will slip into the ocean.[4]

The Dogon of Mali have become well known through the re-

[3] E. B. Idowu, *Olódùmarè, God in Yoruba Belief* (New York, 1962), pp. 19 ff.

[4] P. Mercier, in *African Worlds*, ed. D. Forde (New York, 1954), pp. 220 ff.

searches of Marcel Griaule and his school, and their myths are very complex. It is not known how many neighbors of the Dogon share their views, but they show that African mythology can be intricate and subtle. Here the Supreme Being (Amma) created the sun and moon first, like pots surrounded by copper rings. The earth and stars were made of clay pellets flung into space. The earth spread out flat like a body lying face upward; it was female, and in his loneliness Amma had union with it, from which spiritual beings were born. However, there was disorder first; the jackal was born before some twin spirits and violated the earth. Therefore Amma decided to create men without the help of the earth. But when he had formed them, the twin spirits (Nummo) saw that there was a danger of twin births disappearing, and they drew on the ground an outline of male and female on top of each other, and ever since human beings have been bisexual, having in childhood the soul of the opposite sex as well as their own, which is removed at circumcision or excision. In later myths of the Dogon, Amma does not appear very much, and the dominant roles are played by the twin Nummo spirits, green and sinuous principles of vitality, and eight ancestors. But the Dogon have retained the worship of Amma and his altar is prominent in every village.[5]

Across the other side of Africa a sophisticated version of the relationships of God to the world is given for the Gikuyu of Kenya by President Kenyatta.[6] Ngai, the Divider of the Universe, created a great mountain as a sign of wonders and a resting place. This is the Mountain of Brightness, known in English as Mount Kenya. From this place Ngai showed the world to the ancestors of the races of men and offered them different tools. Some chose spears or bows and took to hunting and herding. Gikuyu, the ancestor of the people of that name, chose a digging stick and Ngai taught him agriculture. Ngai took him to the top of the mountain and showed him all the lands, with forests and plains; in the middle was a cluster of fig trees and Gikuyu was told to make his home there. A wife was provided for him called Moombi, Molder or Creator, and she bore him nine daughters. When they had no sons, Gikuyu went to the mountain to ask the help of Ngai, and was told to sacrifice a lamb and a kid near a fig tree by his house.

[5] M. Griaule, *Conversations with Ogotemmêli* (New York, 1965), pp. 16 ff.
[6] J. Kenyatta, *Facing Mount Kenya* (New York, 1953), pp. 3–4.

The meat was offered to Ngai by all the family, and when they went home there were nine young men who married the girls. The story helps to explain why the Gikuyu formerly had a matriarchal society. But the cult of Ngai has continued in groves of trees reserved for his worship.

Such stories could be multiplied many times, and they show some of the first principles of African mythology. It is concerned to answer the questions of the origins of the world and mankind. It generally postulates a Supreme Being who is both transcendent and creator. The creating functions may be shared with lesser beings, or exercised by God alone. The precedence of the Creator is in line with religious thought in other parts of the world, but it does not imply an "original monotheism," as proposed by Wilhelm Schmidt and others, for there are many more spiritual beings and beatified ancestors who figure in African religious cults, though in theory they are subordinate to the Supreme Being.

The belief that the Supreme Being retired from the world after creation is widespread in Africa. In some of the most popular West African stories it is difficult to distinguish God from the sky in this withdrawal, and this suggests that the myths refer as much to the distance of the vault of the firmament as to God. In primordial times, it is said, the sky was low and hung just above men's heads. This led to undue familiarity; children wiped greasy hands on the sky after meals, and women tore bits off the sky for cooking. Particularly annoying were thumps given to the sky by long pestles with which women pounded meal. The sky was annoyed and moved away bit by bit. The final removal is blamed on a woman who had a long pestle and hit the sky so hard that it went away in anger to the far distance.[7]

It is remarkable that similar stories are told thousands of miles away by people of the upper Nile regions. The Nuba of the Sudan say that at first the sky was so close to the earth that it touched men. Women found that it pressed on them and they could not lift their spoons high enough to stir millet porridge and their fingers were burned on the pots. Finally, a woman was angry with the heavenly pressure and forced her spoon against it to make a hole. The sky was offended and moved away to its present distance. Another Nuba version says that the clouds were formerly so near

[7] E. G. Parrinder, *African Mythology* (London, 1968).

that people tore pieces off them to eat, and so they went off. Their neighbors, the Dinka, say that when the sky was low God gave the first man and woman one grain of millet for each day. But the woman was greedy and pounded more grain with a large pestle which hit the sky. The theme of death is added to this, because death had not been there formerly but came with the divine removal.

In many African tales a rope is said to have hung from heaven to earth either in primordial times or sometime later. The Dinka say there was such a rope originally and man could climb up it to reach God, but after the woman had offended God he sent a blue bird to cut the rope. The Nuer of the Sudan relate the rope to death, for in former times when men grew old they climbed up to the sky, became young again, and returned to earth. But animals, who often figure in myths of death (in this case the hyena and the weaver-bird), climbed the rope to heaven but cut it on their return, and it was drawn up to the sky so that men have died ever since.

Many peoples of central and southern Africa speak more personally of God (Mulungu) living on earth at first, but retiring to heaven after men had offended him by killing some of his people. Some say that God could not climb a tree, which was the normal way to the sky, so he asked the spider to help him and went up by the spider's thread. The notion of a heavenly rope may have been helped on by the sight of long spiders' webs hanging from trees, or apparently from the sky, on misty mornings.

There are possible links between these myths and those of ancient Egypt and elsewhere which tell of the separation of heaven and earth, sometimes by their children, and others which speak of a former Golden Age, or the expulsion of the first parents from Eden. Yet in African myth it is usually God and the sky which go away, and not man who is driven off from God. In Burundi it is said that God formerly lived on earth and created children, but when he once made a crippled baby its parents were so angry that they plotted to stab God with a knife, and he went off to heaven. And the Lozi (Barotse) of Zambia have a story of a man, Kamonu, who was so clever that when God lived on earth he imitated all his works. God was troubled by this, especially when Kamonu learned from him the art of working in iron and turned his skill to fashioning a spear with which he killed some of the animals God had made. God rebuked Kamonu and sent misfortune to him, and then moved away with his family to a river island. But Kamonu followed him there and later to the top of a high mountain. Then God asked the birds where he could go, and finally climbed up to the sky by a spider's web.

Some of these myths appear to be simple Just So Stories having little relation to life or worship. They have an explanatory purpose, but sometimes they go beyond this and deal with the problems of death and suffering, as in the Burundi story quoted above. Occasionally the problem of suffering is taken up in stories of later times. A well-known Ila story of Zambia tells of a woman who had suffered many troubles, for all her family had been smitten by God (Leza), "the One who besets." When her husband, children, and grandchildren had died the woman thought she would die too, but strangely she became younger. Then she resolved to find God to get an explanation for her sorrows. Since God was in heaven she tried to make a ladder of trees to reach it, a sort of Tower of Babel. But when the highest trees in her ladder were near the sky the bottom ones gave way and the structure collapsed. Then the woman set out to find the horizon where earth and heaven meet, and she traveled from one country to another. In each place she visited, people asked the purpose of her journey and she said she was seeking God to find the reason for her troubles. But they replied that this is the common lot of mankind and everybody suffers bereavements, for Leza, the Besetting One, sits on all our backs. So in the end the woman gave up her search and died in due time.[8]

The Chaga of Kenya have a similar story with a happier ending. A father, angry with God because his sons had all died, took some arrows to shoot him, setting out for the place of sunrise. When the sun was rising, a great host of shining ones appeared, but as they advanced they complained of a bad smell, as if a man were there. They found the Chaga man and took him to God, who knew what he wanted and told him to shoot his arrows; if the man wanted his sons they were behind him and could return to earth, but they were so radiant that the man told God

[8] E. W. Smith and A. M. Dale, *The Ila-speaking Peoples of Northern Rhodesia* (London, 1920), vol. 2, pp. 197–98.

he must keep them. Then God promised the man more sons and good fortune, and his last state was better than the first.

There are many other stories of visits paid by human beings to the world beyond, sometimes under the ground and at other times to the sky. There men and women can obtain good fortune if they observe instructions given to them, but if they do not then disaster comes.

That death is unnatural is held by most, if not all, African peoples, and it is believed that men did not die in the olden days. God is connected with the coming of death, though its happening is blamed on one of his messengers. The commonest theme is that God sent two messengers to tell men about death. The Mende of Sierra Leone say that the dog was sent to inform men that they would not die, and the toad to say they would die. The dog could have arrived first but he stopped to eat on the way and was passed by the toad, who announced that death had come. Although the dog then called out that life had come it was too late, and death has been with men ever since. This adapts the theme of the race of the hare and tortoise, which is popular in African fables. But it is remarkable that an almost identical story is told by the Zulu of South Africa. Here God sent the chameleon to take the message of life, but since this reptile walks slowly it was quickly passed by the lizard, who was sent later to say that men would die and got there first.[9]

A variant on the theme of death is a Pandora's box kind of story. The Lamba of Zambia say that the first man was a nomad, but when he wanted to settle down he had no seeds and sent to God for some. God gave the messengers small bundles, with instructions that one in particular must not be opened. But the messengers were curious and on the way they opened the forbidden bundle and death came out to spread throughout the world. A different version is recorded of the Kono of Sierra Leone, who say that God had told the first couple they would not die, and when they got old he would give them new skins. He gave a bundle of new skins for men to the dog, but on the way to man the dog joined other animals in a feast and revealed what was in his bundle. The snake heard this and slipped out to steal the

[9] E. W. Smith and E. G. Parrinder, eds., *African Ideas of God*, 3d ed. (New York, 1966), pp. 108, 286, and *passim.*

skins. Since then men have died but the snake is immortal because it sheds its skin.

After such myths of the creating and destroying powers of God, it is important to note that some African peoples have stories of the first men in which God apparently plays no part. Both the Zulu and the Thonga say that the first man and woman came out of a reed which exploded. The Herero of southwest Africa say that their ancestors and cattle came out of a tree which is still supposed to exist in the veld, though sheep and Bushmen emerged from a hole in the ground. And there is a story of the Congo Pygmies which says that the chameleon heard some whispering in a tree and cut it open with an axe, whereupon a man and woman came out. However, another Pygmy story says that the first people were made by God, who lived with them on earth for a while.[10]

Most remarkable are stories told by the Ashanti of Ghana, who have clear beliefs in a Supreme Being, a day set aside for his worship, and some altars and temples for his priests. The first men and women came out of the ground, accompanied by a dog and a leopard. This was on a Monday, and the names of the seven men and several women who emerged are still related at times on Monday or Tuesday. The men and women were afraid of the world, but their leader calmed their fears on Tuesday by laying hands on them. On Wednesday they began to build houses, but their leader was killed by a falling tree. Next, the dog went to find fire and they cooked food. The God of Creation then appeared and he took one of these men as helper. There are still annual ceremonies held in the forest at which libations are poured for these first people.[11]

Many other African peoples do connect God with the creation of the first men: the Dogon of Mali, the Yoruba of Nigeria, and the Shilluk and Dinka of the Sudan are among these. The famous Kintu, ancestor of the Baganda, came from the gods and a woman, Nambi, fell in love with him. She was the daughter of Gulu, king of heaven. Nambi's relatives despised Kintu because he was a herdsman, and to test him Gulu took away his sole cow so that he had to live on herbs. But Nambi told Kintu that the cow was

10 P. Schebesta, *Les Pygmées du Congo Belge* (Brussels, 1952), pp. 302, 316–17.

11 R. S. Rattray, *Ashanti* (Oxford, 1923), pp. 123–24.

in heaven and he went there to fetch it. Gulu imposed a number of tests on him, but Kintu passed them all and at last was given Nambi as wife. When they were leaving the sky, Gulu told them to hurry and not turn back, as Nambi's brother, Death, would want to go with them. But Nambi had forgotten grain for her fowls and insisted on returning, whereupon Death came with her to earth. Kintu fought Death and drove him into the ground, but he still comes out at times and kills people.

Enough has been said to indicate that God has vital roles to play in African mythology and that he is not merely a manifestation or personalization of the sky. He is a creator, a providence, and has relationships with men. God is primordial and old, but by virtue of this he is the founder of things and the guardian of law. It is generally believed that God is just, even if his ways are mysterious and may bring suffering to men. The ancestors also are concerned with the laws and customs of the tribe and visit offenders with their displeasure by sickness and trouble. But God has a kind of remote control. He is ultimately responsible; he is a final court of appeal if ancestors and gods fail; and he is the judge of men after death.

Yet the Supreme Being seems to have little role in the everyday cultus. Some people do have kinds of worship of God—the Dogon and Ashanti, the Gikuyu and Shona—but these are exceptions. For most of Africa it is true that the Supreme Being has no temples, no images, no priests, and no sacrifices. There may be occasional libations or simple gifts of nuts, and prayers may be made to God without any intermediary. This is a "spiritual" worship, but in point of time and energy it is less important than the many attentions paid to ancestors and gods.

Mention can be made of some of these gods, whose cultus is most elaborate in West Africa. It is remarkable that there are very few traces of veneration of sun or moon in tropical Africa. This may be due to the fact that the sun is always oppressively present in the tropics and no action is needed to ensure its power as among northern peoples. The dangerous storms are more significant than sun or moon; they are dynamic, fertile, and awesome. Sometimes the Supreme Being has attributes of the storm, and among the Ashanti the thunderbolt is called "God's axe" and the rainbow "God's arch."

One of the most interesting storm gods is Shango of the Yoruba; he is doubly important because he combines regal, ancestral features with natural ones. He has a "history." Shango was the fourth king of the Yoruba, ruling over the now ruined city of Old Oyo. He was a strong ruler and medicine man as well as a tyrant who could kill men with fire from his mouth. His people revolted and Shango withdrew to the forest with three wives. After wandering about he finally hanged himself at a place called Koso. Some of the followers of Shango deny this and say that he did "not hang" (*ko-so*). He had the power of bringing down fire from heaven on the houses of his enemies, they say, and finally climbed up to the sky by a chain, from where he still rules with the aid of thunder. Despite, or with the help of, these stories, the priests of Shango became powerful, and to this day his temples are in every important Yoruba village. The priests claim to have the same power of invoking fire from heaven, and when there is a storm they profess to find "thunder axes" which fall from the sky. Symbolic "thunder axes" with double blades are carried by them in procession. When the Yoruba empire stretched from Benin to Dahomey, the cult of Shango as national ancestor went with it, and became linked with cults of the storm under other names.

It may be that the cult of the Supreme Being was pushed into the background by the virile Shango, and in practice this seems to be so. In a count of the temples in the modern city of Ibadan there were seven temples of Shango and none of the Supreme Being Ol-orun. But Ol-orun is not an *orisha*, a divinity in the same class as others. Shango is an *orisha*, and only one among many, for the same count found forty-seven temples of all the gods, and nine of these were for the god of earth and agriculture.

In other parts of Africa it seems that the ancestors hold the center of the field in religious practice. Cults of gods, including temples and priesthood, are most highly developed in West Africa, but they are not entirely absent in other parts of the continent. Storms and earth, mountains and river, smallpox and snakes, may not have the elaborate cultus in many places that they have in Dahomey and Nigeria, but there are more traces of their importance than is sometimes recognized. Many a mountain or river has no obvious temple or regular ritual, but on special occasions it is invoked to help man or divert evil.

Rites designed to propitiate the ancestors are common in West

Africa, since survival after death is believed in everywhere. Nevertheless, in much of East and South Africa ancestral cults are the most obvious marks of religious life. The dead are concerned with their proper interests – the continuity of family, birth of children, health and prosperity. The land too is their property, not merely the possession of individuals. Thence they are interested in the crops and by extension are besought for rain as if they controlled the weather. The ancestors are all-powerful, just like gods. Whether ancestral "cults" are really religious worship has often been debated, but it may be noted that where careful records and comparisons have been made between requests offered to gods and to the dead there seem to be few differences between the prayers and rituals.

Some writers have concluded that since the ancestors are so important, and God is acknowledged as the originator and ruler of all, therefore God must be the great ancestor. Sometimes it seems as if he is regarded in that way, yet the main trend of myth and cultus seems to be against it. The Supreme Being is neither a "divinity" like other gods nor a man of any kind, past or present. Although he is spoken about in anthropomorphic fashion, this does not equate him in any way with any man, however powerful or beatified.

Others, on the contrary, have maintained that the Supreme Being is so little like a man that he is a mere force, an impersonal energy if not a hypothesis. This is too extreme. It is increasingly accepted that many African religious beliefs express the idea of a universal power which both causes and pervades all life, but that does not mean that this abstract idea is not clothed in anthropomorphic terms. It happens in many other religious systems, and it would be surprising if such expression were lacking in Africa, which, as shown by its art, has never been afraid of physical imagery.

The universal energy, cosmic *mana*, is believed to proceed from God. The French scholars have shown this for the Dogon and kindred peoples. The Dogon believe in Amma, the Supreme Being, who created all men and animals. He endowed them all with a vital force, an impersonal energy which is distributed in living beings and things of nature. With a subtlety not uncommon in African thought about the soul, the Dogon distinguish between personal souls that pass from this life to the world of the ancestors and the vital force which remains in the world of men and has a kind of immortality, being passed from one generation to another.

The belief in a vital force, energy, or dynamism has been expounded most clearly by Placide Tempels in his *Bantu Philosophy*. The vital force, he says, is in all men and creatures and forms the bond between them. For Bantu psychology it is impossible to conceive of man existing in and by himself, without any close relationship to the forces all around him, both animate and inanimate. Man is not just an individual, or even merely a social being; he is a vital force which is in close and continuing contact with other forces. He influences them, but they constantly influence him. Yet this system of forces is not a simple democracy. The notion of a magical power that pervades all existence uniformly is a Western misunderstanding. In African thought there is a potent life in all beings but there are basic differences between beings, for there are different forces. It is important to man to discover and respect the proper relationships between persons and things. This involves the discovery of one's own proper place in life and the need to approach higher forces with due respect, not as an equal.[12]

There is a hierarchy of powers. Above all others is God himself, the Spirit and Creator. He has power in himself and is by his nature the "Strong One." He gives existence, force, increase, and survival to other beings, all of whom are dependent on him. So God is "the One who increases power." After the Supreme Being, the fount of all life, come the next ones in the hierarchy, the gods and the first fathers, founders of different families. The later dead follow these, and then the chiefs and old people now alive. At the lowest level are magical and inanimate forces, with which man has also to live at peace.

It is clear that the belief in vital forces is not an abstract system without a living God. God himself is often given attributes and "praise-names" which emphasize his vitality and omnipotence; these are used as freely in modern African Christian prayer and in the Islamic Beautiful Names as they are in the traditional invocations. For even where there are no temples or priests for the Supreme Being, his name is often invoked at the beginning of prayers addressed to other deities. The name of God comes in proverbs which make up much of the language; it is basic in

[12] P. Tempels, *Bantu Philosophy* (Paris, 1959), pp. 41 ff.

many salutations at morning and evening and other times; and it is the principal element in the protective texts inscribed on houses and motor lorries.

The Supreme Being in African thought is not an "it" but a "he," and this makes his personality distinct from that of other beings. In the myths God has life and consciousness like men, and he often has a wife or wives and children. He is clearly anthropomorphic, yet it is remarkable that no images are made of the Supreme Being. Despite the abundance of African sculpture, and its frequent sensuality, Africans have expressed surprise or shock upon seeing paintings of God done by William Blake or medieval artists. They say that no temples are built for God because a temple could not contain the omnipresent and widespreading, "whose circular headdress is the horizon."

Although God is spoken of as living in a celestial village like a chief with wives and servants, he is not human. Generally there are no stories of God as a human being, an ancestor. Though he once lived on earth, he was not a man. Equally, he is not tribal or national. If this question is put, reference is then made to the creation, when God made all tribes, black and white. As in other mythologies, the place of creation may be localized as the central or best place on earth. To the Yoruba Ilé-Ifé is the home of all mankind; to the Gikuyu it is Mount Kenya. But though God once acted there, he is not localized there; his power extends to all men.

God is the creator of all, either directly or indirectly through his servants. He is the final power behind all life and the ultimate court of appeal if justice fails everywhere else. He is the judge of all, either in this life or after death, and this means that the moral laws are finally dependent upon him. "No man will escape the judgment of God," says a Yoruba proverb, meaning that if an evildoer prospers in this life he will be punished in the next, in "the heaven of potsherds," a sort of celestial rubbish dump. A favorite proverb says "sea never dry," meaning that as the sea never dries up so the mercy of God is unfailing. "God is God" and "No King as God" are favorite proverbs illustrating the supremacy and omnipotence of God. The sky is "the face of God" from where he sees all men, and he is both all-seeing and allwise. Even if there is no elaborate cult there are many references to God in daily life.

Some writers have suggested that God in African thought is

only the creation of lonely philosophers whose observation and desire for explanation led them to postulate a first cause or a providence. This is too foreign and does not fit in at all with the concept of vital forces which inspire all life and which depend upon and are constantly related to God. God is much closer to ordinary people than is suggested by the picture of an African Descartes. On the other hand, the universe is so rich, so teeming with life, that Africans postulate not just a solitary God, but God in relationship to countless beings both divine and human.

This raises the problem of polytheism. Clearly, African religion is far more than "fetishism" or "animism." Personal spiritual beings are believed in, led by a Supreme Being. But is this polytheism or monotheism, or, as one writer suggests, is it "diffused monotheism"? Although lesser gods are worshiped, they are regarded as servants of the Supreme Being, and in theory the essence of all sacrifices belongs to him.[13]

Evans-Pritchard, in his monumental *Nuer Religion*, constantly emphasizes belief in God as Spirit. God is the Spirit in the sky, but he is not the sky; he is the Spirit that is everywhere and invisible, but he is a living person who created and sustains man and all things. Nuer religion is clearly pneumatic and theistic, but is it monotheistic? Evans-Pritchard says that

> a theistic religion need not be either monotheistic or polytheistic. It may be both. . . . On one level Nuer religion may be regarded as monotheistic, at another level as polytheistic; and it can also be regarded at other levels as totemistic or fetishistic. These conceptions of spiritual activity are not incompatible. They are rather different ways of thinking of the numinous at different levels of experience.

Nevertheless, the spirit that is manifested at these different levels is not thought to be independent of God; it appears in many ways and symbols, but there is a unity that is monotheistic, if it is also "modalistic."[14] This unity is dynamic, the personal, vital force that creates and sustains, directs, governs, and judges all things. God in African thought is not just a "sky deity," a personified firmament, but the personal essence and power inspiring all life and the universe.

[13] E. B. Idowu, *Olódùmarè*, p. 204.
[14] E. E. Evans-Pritchard, *Nuer Religion* (New York, 1956), p. 316.

SPEAKING OF A PLACE

KEES W. BOLLE

A city like Madras is not really a city. It is much more conspicuously a collection of villages. Each one has its own central temple – one devoted to Viṣṇu, one to Śiva, or one to Devī (the goddess *par excellence*). If the temple is not the residence of any one of these principal deities, it is dedicated to a manifestation of one of them or to a deity related to them. In each case, it is essential to come to terms with the idea of the local presence of the deity. Countless town and village plans in India demonstrate what was said long ago by the great Tamil poetess Avvaiyār: "One should not live in a place which does not possess a temple,"[1] or by the *Tēvāram*: "A place without a temple is an arid waste."[2] Orderly human life presupposes a specific, local, sacred presence.

The distinctions that are most important in India are very different from the confessional and historical distinctions that we have grown used to in the West. They become most transparent in terms of "location" and "locale" and only secondarily in terms of doctrine, politics, and even social division. I am not suggesting that political and social factors are insignificant, but I believe that their significance can best be grasped when the symbolic nature of specific locations is understood. Understanding such symbolism is a desideratum for the general student of Indian civilization who is inclined to think of mere "primitive survivals" if he thinks of sacred places. It is a desideratum also for the general historian of religions. For the structure of this symbolism – found

[1] C. P. Venkatarama Ayyar, *Town Planning in Ancient Dekkan* (Madras, 1916), p. 2.
[2] *Ibid.*, p. 155.

in many places of the world—is peculiar, and for the sake of a clear understanding must be distinguished from other symbolisms. Not every central symbolism is local in nature, and the fading significance of a local sacred place does not necessarily imply a "secularization." If it fades, it is usually replaced by a central symbolism of a different order, perhaps more dynamic, often more confusing, but always more difficult to label in our religio-historical terms. But whatever the results of the inquiry are, it remains essential to understand the religious symbolism of locations. It is not merely "primitive," but shows an astounding flexibility, and for that reason alone may have come to be regarded—mistakenly—as the cornerstone of *all* traditional religion.

Only examples can show the peculiar nature of symbolisms. The type of symbolism the outsider senses, rather than grasps, in the temple-oriented town plans in India has a long history and can perhaps best be called "the symbolism of being there." It is not my intention here to trace this history but to select some examples that to me seem eloquent.

Traditionally, every Hindu family is devoted to some local deity. The family continues their respect to the god of their original hometown. The generic name of such a deity is *kuladevatā* (deity of the family or race). Every family has a worship room (*pūjāśālā*) where the image of the *kuladevatā*, to whom they pay their respects every day, is kept.

It would be a mistake to equate these things with very widespread customs that even in antiquity gave the impression of ceremonial survivals—as the household gods that Rachel smuggled with her from her native place (Genesis 31), or the worship of the *penates* in ancient Rome. Without going into the problem of Western conceptions of "universality," I would suggest that they form the major hindrance for us in appreciating the Indian customs and, especially, their tenacity through the ages. The family deity is what he is because he is local. This simple point is the most difficult to understand. He is *essentially* a local deity, but at the same time universal. When a family moves, they take their god along, or, more accurately, they take God along. God too moves. One god has many shrines, different shrines in different places, and sometimes great temples, but the principal domicile of the deity remains the same. Naturally, some of the temples are more famous than others; one might say that they are more tangibly the real residence of God. But unless one understands the primacy of the *place*, the nature of the sacred in most of Hinduism remains incomprehensible, and the plurality and variety of gods continues to form an unsolvable puzzle. *God is universal because he is there.*

The central symbolism of "being there" explains why Indian history knows much more of pilgrimages than we do. A man may decide, for whatever reason, to go on a pilgrimage from one important temple to the next. It is well known that in each place the devotee will, among other things, walk around the sanctum *pradakṣiṇam*, keeping the sacred center to his right. It is less well known that the route of his whole journey, if done well, follows the same plan. It is advisable to travel from Madras to Benares to Calcutta and back to Madras, rather than the other way round. Thus, also on a large scale — where it would be difficult to point to *the* sacred center — the (structurally) local symbolism is decisive.

No wonder that through the centuries so many efforts have been made to form scrupulous plans for the building of towns and villages. Before the square temple complex — such a conspicuous feature of the great South Indian temples — the so-called *agrahāra* is found, usually a wide street where the "aristocratic" Brahmin families live. Ideally, the whole village is ordered accordingly, around the dwelling place of God.

To say that each group is thus assigned its proper place is bound to raise offensive associations in the modern Western world. One might even feel inclined to associate it with the proverbial dictum of the cartoon-like Southern segregationist: "I like them in their own place." But such associations are not in order here; they merely hint at a problem I should like to bring up later, the fact that central symbolisms differ fundamentally from culture to culture. For the moment it is sufficient to say that the symbolic orderliness of the Indian village has nothing to do with anyone's likes or dislikes or an ideological endeavor to preserve an anachronism that had no semblance of a religio-symbolic basis from the beginning. The Indian caste system is not an easy target for modern world improvers but a fact of life that for hundreds of years has been established around a central symbolism. Of course, many changes came about. Some castes and tribes grew in importance while others declined, but no change put an end to the central symbolism of the orderly presence. The fact that *tribes* must be mentioned in one breath with castes only underlines the pervasive significance of the *place* of ethnic groups. Intellectually, in the course of the Brahmanizing process, the existing state of affairs seemed to relate perfectly to the Vedic view according to which man as such was not created at the beginning of time, but rather *society* with its major divisions (as expressed most directly in the *Puruṣasūkta*). From the point of view of the modern historian of Indian religion, the application of Vedic texts may seem dubious – the Aryan classes are not the same as the innumerable tribes and castes of later Indian history – but the indisputable symbolism of the place made the joining of the two seem self-evident.

There may be countless shrines, but every village has its *grāmadevatā, the* village deity. It is significant that the term *grāmadevatā* (like *kuladevatā*) is commonly known and used to refer to the god or goddess who is central to the village, whatever the "personal" name is. One shrine is as essential as it is traditional. In many instances, the deity may not be personally conceived at all, and, as we shall see, in many cases is definitely not. The certainty of the place is apparently much more important than the identity of the deity. The majority of these deities – most of whom are goddesses – are represented without an anthropomorphic image. This is not surprising if one recalls that in most cases the same thing is true for the great god Śiva. He is usually represented by the *liṅga*. This is not a "personal" image, not a picture of what the god looks like, but is in most cases a slab of stone of a particular shape and in an upright position. Because of its form, most scholars since Frazer have been satisfied by explaining it as a phallic symbol.

The long-lived popularity of phallic interpretation for everything upright – such as spears, tridents, or Egyptian obelisks – is particularly interesting as a Western cultural phenomenon. It is striking because it betrays an ideological obsession or a dogmatic assertiveness that has little to do with the object it pretends to explain. Explanations of this sort generally disregard the setting in which the symbol occurs. It is like saying that the host in the Christian communion celebration represents bread, or that it represents foodstuff in general. Once one has said that one has said absolutely nothing. The notion of fertility and everything it entails should not be used except with the greatest caution.

The nonpersonal representations in Indian sanctuaries can best be seen in relation to the "symbolism of being there." Admittedly, this expression neither defines nor explains things sweepingly, but at least it does some justice to the phenomena—not all are stones in an upright position. At village sanctuaries we sometimes find just an enclosure to mark the presence of a deity. It seems to me that the use of a mere enclosure is the most eloquent example of the symbolism of being there. It is as if all questions that come to the enlightened "secularized" mind are declared to be absolutely nonsensical. You do not ask for a creed concerning theological or sociological certitudes or agricultural effectiveness when you see a mere enclosure. You do not even ask about the sex of the deity thus represented; the only thing you can say is "presence."

Henry Whitehead reports that in Irungalur (Trichinopoly District) he found "a small enclosure sacred to Kurumbaiamma, outside the village, without any image or sacred stones in it at all. . . ."[3] Only at the annual festival of the goddess is a small earthen pot, "curiously decorated,"[4] placed in it, in a booth erected for the occasion, to represent the goddess. The pot is not prepared at the enclosure, but at the chief local shrine of the goddess about a mile outside the village "and during the festival it is treated exactly like the goddess."[5] Offerings and sacrifices are made to it and it is carried on the head of the *pūjārī* in processions.

The representation of a *grāmadevatā* by an earthen pot is a common feature in celebrations. It is worth noting, however, that in this instance the small enclosure does not hold a permanent symbol. There is nothing to indicate its sacredness but the enclosure itself.

A point worth mentioning and already indicated in this last example is the liturgical *function* of sacred places, for the "symbolism of being there" is not merely a static imagery. It is alive with what could well be called a "topographical religiosity." The festivities of the village gods are a series of sacred events.

Nowhere is the "topographical religiosity" clearer than in the happenings around the boundary stones in many local cults. These

[3] Henry Whitehead, *The Village Gods of South India* (Calcutta, 1921), p. 37.

[4] *Ibid.*, p. 37.

[5] *Ibid.*, p. 38.

boundary stones are upright stones that, as indicated by the name, mark the limits of the village. These limits do not necessarily coincide with the administrative boundary of the community, at least not anymore. The name for these stones in the Tamil country is *ellai-kal.* Whitehead describes one of those annual festivities at Irungalur in which the *ellai-kal* has a significant part, perhaps as seat of a divine being. The celebrations, lasting ten days, are in honor of the goddess Kurumbai. Here too a decorated pot (the *karagam*) is taken round in procession morning and evening on the eighth, ninth, and tenth days. On the eighth day, after having been properly decorated at the shrine of Kurumbai, it is carried to the center of the village and deposited there in a booth to which it is returned at the end of each procession through the village.

On the tenth day, at about seven a.m. before the procession starts, a lamb is killed in front of the karagam. The throat is first cut, and then the head cut off and the blood collected in a new earthen pot filled with boiled rice. The pot is put in a frame of ropes and taken by a pūjārī to a stone, about four feet high, called ellai-kal (*i.e.* boundary-stone), planted in the ground some three hundred yards off. A crowd of villagers run after him with wild yells, but no tom-tom or pipes are played [as in the other processions]. When he comes to the boundary-stone, he runs round it thrice, and the third time throws the pot over his shoulder behind him on to another smaller stone, about two feet high and some five or six feet in circumference, which stands at the foot of the ellai-kal. The earthen pot is dashed to pieces and the rice and blood scatter over the two stones and all around them. The pūjārī then runs quickly back to the booth, where the karagam stands, without looking behind him, followed by the crowd in dead silence. The man who carries the pot is supposed to be possessed by Kurumbai, and is in a frantic state as he runs to the boundary stone and has to be held up by some of the crowd, to prevent his falling to the ground. The pouring out of the rice and blood is regarded as a propitiation of an evil spirit residing in the boundary-stone called Ellai-Karuppu, and of all the evil and malignant spirits of the neighbourhood, who are his attendants.[6]

After the episode of the boundary stone the people, headed by the *pūjārī,* return to the central booth and prostrate themselves before the *karagam.* The festivities continue with a purification ceremony, another lamb sacrifice, and a procession.[7]

[6] *Ibid.,* pp. 100–101.
[7] *Ibid.*

Whitehead shows an acute power of observation, and as a rule his explanatory remarks, and other remarks inspired by his very British common sense, can easily be separated from his very precise descriptions. It is only with some reservation that he touches on the meaning of these cultic matters around the *ellai-kal*: "the blood of the victim seems to be regarded as the food of malignant spirits."[8] And indeed, it seems but natural to think first and foremost of some propitiation ceremony for a rather demonic being. However, if the popular beliefs are summed up accurately in the end of the quotation above, and an evil spirit is thought to reside in the boundary stone, it is worth observing that the propitiation of this spirit propitiates as well all his attendants dominating the neighborhood.

It seems rather clear that a general animistic theory does not suffice to explain the proceedings. Of course spirits play a role, but not enough of a role to interpret the relationship in the cult between the center (the booth in the middle of the village) and the boundary stone.

No religion is ever free from more or less "superstitious" concomitants, but if in this instance we look for the *locus* of the sacred, it can best be understood in terms of the "symbolism of being there." Only then does the role of the boundary stone make sense. The divine presence is literally extended to the limits in the cultic process. The role of "malignant spirits" is no doubt important, but it is secondary. The same thing can be said about the universal fear of the world outside, which has often been exaggerated to explain the magical and religious significance attributed to boundaries in many civilizations. Fears alone are never enough to create a symbolism people live by, and they are certainly not enough to account for the tenacity of such celebrations as those of Irungalur.

Another example of "topographical religiosity" comes from a village in the South Arcot District nine miles northwest of Vriddhachalam. Its name is Mangalam, but it is commonly known as Maduvetti Mangalam – "buffalo-sacrificing Mangalam" – because of the great traditional sacrifices held from May to June each year in honor of a village goddess. Eight men – all Paraiyans – are chosen from eight adjoining villages. One of them is selected as leader.

[8] *Ibid.*, p. 100.

His wife must not be with child at the time and she is made to prove that she is above all suspicion by undergoing the ordeal of thrusting her hand into boiling gingelly oil. On each of the ten days for which the festival lasts this Paraiyan has to go round some part of the boundaries of the eight villages and he is fed gratis by the villagers during this time. On the day of the sacrifice itself he marches in front of the priest as the latter kills the buffaloes. The Paraiyans of the eight villages have a right to the carcasses of the slaughtered animals.[9]

The share a low caste has in the ceremony is intriguing, but most important for the present discussion is the integral part the surrounding villages have in the cult. That is where the eight officiating Paraiyans come from, and their leader is "to go round some part of the boundaries" of them. The number eight is somewhat too neat to correspond to empirical reality. In all likelihood it reveals rather an "ideal-typical" topography of a sort that has guided many town planners in various parts of the world.[10] The number eight coincides with the number of cardinal points and intermediate directions of the compass.

All examples given so far, in spite of their variety, show the strength of the local symbolism. The variety in articulation – the devotional unity of the family; an orientation in the world at large; the orderly arrangement of society; the consolidation of the village; the expulsion of fears; a general, topographical religiosity – is made possible by the structure of the central symbolism itself.

Finally, I should like to make a few remarks about the gods Hariharaputra and Harihara. The two do not have very much in common perhaps, except that "syncretistic" tendencies seem striking in both. And it must be admitted that at first sight their imageries and myths seem to point to certain endeavors of integration of the cults of Śiva and Viṣṇu. Nevertheless, "syncretism" suggests the harmonization of disparate religious ideas, or even a doctrinal concoction made up of different creeds, while the figures of Hariharaputra and of Harihara can each be understood without artificiality in the unity of *local* symbolism.

Hariharaputra, worshiped in South India, is best known by his older name, Aiyanar. He is one of the few important village deities of a pronounced masculine type. Last but not least, his relation

[9] W. Francis, *Gazetteer of the South Arcot District* (Madras, 1906), pp. 392–94.

[10] See the very informative work by Werner Müller, *Die heilige Stadt* (Stuttgart, 1961).

to the great Hindu gods has been "systematized" in South Indian tradition more clearly than that of most other village deities. This means that his "personality" is better known to us than those of the majority of *grāmadevatās*, although it is difficult to tell when the major features of his mythology of integration were created. It is certain that Aiyanar himself is an ancient deity—witness his occurrence in ancient Tamil literature.

The myth which relates Aiyanar to Hinduism is briefly as follows. At one time the world and the gods were threatened by a powerful demon. The demon was particularly hard to defeat since everything he put his hands on turned to ashes. It was Viṣṇu who succeeded in destroying the demon by assuming the form of a beautiful woman, Mohinī ("the deluding one"). The demon, infatuated, was asked by Mohinī to anoint himself before coming to her. In anointing himself, he could not but touch himself, and thus he himself became ashes. While all this was taking place, Mohinī made a great impression on Śiva. When the episode was over and calamity warded off, Śiva asked Viṣṇu to assume the same beautiful form. Aiyanar was born as the child of Śiva and Viṣṇu. The name Hariharaputra indicates this origin: "son of Hari (Viṣṇu) and Hara (Śiva)." The Sanskrit name is clear evidence that this myth of his origin cannot be the "original myth." But what myth is ever truly "original"?

It would be too hasty to make a generalization about syncretism. It is most significant that the birth of Aiyanar was related to two universal gods, and, especially, to the victory over a world-disrupting demonic power. These outstanding features of the myth are in perfect harmony with Aiyanar's character as a village god. On his vehicle, a white elephant, he rides around and protects the community and the fields, watches over the gardens, and chases thieves. One of his names is Purattavan, "the policeman."

Descriptions such as those of Aiyanar may appear to be somewhat too down-to-earth to a modern student—whether consciously secularized or not—to be regarded as a very profound symbolism. But there is no reason to look down on the seemingly naïve portrayals of an Aiyanar. Not only have many of such cults been of great size and importance in the history of India, but it would be an error in our understanding if we thought of the village cults in isolation, apart from the "great" achievements of Hinduism. Aiyanar's relation to Viṣṇu and Śiva is a relationship of the same sort as exists between the "ideal-typical" conceptions in the local symbolisms of the villages and the equally "ideal-typical" descriptions of man's world in famous Hindu scriptures. The latter are highly sophisticated and have their crown in the cosmographic treatises of the Purāṇas. To the dwelling place of man corresponds a sacred geography. The two are inseparable. In the "naïve" mythology of Aiyanar an immediate experience of divine presence is expressed. In each of the great Purāṇas we find the glorification of one supreme deity. Aiyanar guarding the village and the fields is no primitive abstraction; it is rather a concrete picture complementing and forming the presupposition of the puranic imagery of the cosmos.

If the village symbolism is regarded as merely "naïve" or "primitive," the cosmic visions of the Purāṇas must be regarded likewise. Of course, this is the easiest way out of the problem: both can be relegated to the status of oddities. But this means that we are not willing or able to understand the function of sacred places except in terms of primitive survivals, whether on a microcosmic or on a macrocosmic level. It would also mean that we close our eyes to one of the most available areas in which the unity of Hinduism can be understood. The "symbolism of being there" links the most elementary devotion of the villages to the great *bhakti* theologies.

The concluding example of a structurally local symbolism, the figure of Harihara, is linked to royalty in various places. Hence this figure can give us a glimpse of the viability of the symbolism in the course of worldly history. He is of little importance at present, but was held in great respect in medieval times.

The name Harihara combines the names of Viṣṇu and Śiva, and in his temples he is plastically portrayed as a combination of the two. As in the case of Hariharaputra, however, we should not immediately think of an artificial syncretism. The question of where such supposed artificiality began and who began it is unanswerable. If one insists on this question, no myth can have any meaning in the end; the god's relationship to the throne could only help to explain the origin of the god as the clever design of some people with a socio-political aim in mind. Historically, this is a very unlikely course of events. It is equally improbable that the figure of Harihara represents an attempt at harmonization of two sects, to wit, of certain Śiva and Viṣṇu worshipers. The thought that such an attempt—religious syncretism proper—would explain Harihara is common currency in scholarly circles, especially among art historians. It neglects the very simple fact that you cannot very sensibly posit harmonizations of two sects if neither of the two have anything that can properly be called a creed. In other words, the explanation is the result of an inadequate knowledge concerning the limitations of Christian religious ideas. In fact, the word "sect" is misleading.

Harihara had many temples devoted to him in the Vijayanagar empire and was the deity who appeared most closely related to the throne. From the Indian subcontinent his image and cult were also transplanted to Southeast Asia. Evidently, the religious symbolism was powerful enough to make the transplantation succeed, as it did, for example, in the Javanese kingdom of Majapahit. After his death, the first ruler of Majapahit, king Kṛtarājasa, was represented in a temple image after the likeness of Harihara.[11] A clearer demonstration of a god's relationship to the throne is unthinkable. The unity of the two supreme deities in Harihara's symbolism makes the association understandable. Comparable to Aiyanar in relation to the Indian village, the "symbolism of being there" could be powerfully expressed through an additional identity with the king. Whatever the precise political powers were, they could be joined without undue artificiality to the urge to conceive a oneness at the center of the "topographical religiosity."

In short, the "symbolism of being there" can be seen as the mainstay of Hinduism in the vicissitudes of its history. More tangible than any other element, it accounts for the proverbial yet puzzling conservation of Indian culture. At the same time, it explains much of India's spiritual impact beyond its borders. Many names changed in the process or were linked in various manners: those of Viṣṇu and Śiva, many seemingly subordinate gods, the Buddha, and sometimes royal rulers. A certain structure remains. The symbolism grows, decays, and varies in the course of history, but it does not grow into a symbolism of a fundamentally different type.

The "symbolism of being there" is of crucial importance for our understanding. I realize quite well that it is not easy to "apply." I should like to see the phrase used to go beyond partial and more or less evolutionary interpretations (such as animism or

[11] N. J. Krom, *Hindoe-Javaansche Geschiedenis* (The Hague, 1931), p. 370.

fertility symbolism), whose adequacy is contestable. The symbolism is evident. The fact that it has not been given the attention it deserves is due to various circumstances. The tenacity of seemingly "scientific" anthropological notions is only one of them. A second is that the important work done by a scholar like Willibald Kirfel, who dealt exhaustively with puranic cosmographic descriptions, could not embrace at the same time the multitude of village cults. The study of the latter has been principally the domain of anthropologists who do not feel at ease with the major Hindu writings.

Perhaps one more possible reason may be mentioned. It is an unconscious unwillingness to abandon outdated ideas. For such abandonment would at once make it necessary to come out into the open with fundamental uncertainties. It is much easier to look down on crude village symbolisms than to be placed before the question: what makes the place from which you look down so superior? It is as if the study of Hinduism is purposely kept divided between fieldworkers and Sanskritists; it gives both an occasion to point to some area which is "obviously" something out of a dim past or something primitive. This situation is truly like a survival—a survival of a divide-and-rule policy, a preservation of one's own prestige, if only in a small area.

The fundamental uncertainties concern the point of view from which religious phenomena are viewed and assigned their place. It seems to me that the historian of religions might have a useful function here. Not that he will be able to manufacture points of view, but at least to him the recognition of the "symbolism of being there" should have consequences. He should be able to see the distinctive character of this symbolism and at the same time perceive the major reason for its neglect. The "symbolism of being there," with its polarity of local, concrete imagery and transcendental geography of the world, is not absent in the West, but it cannot be said to be the central symbolism of the Jewish and Christian tradition. Instead of this polarity, another polarity is more conspicuous in the West, especially since the time of the Renaissance; this polarity is not the local orientation of man vis-à-vis a transcendental arrangement of the universe, but the puzzle of man's freedom vis-à-vis the mysterious freedom of God. The will of God and his decisions have been elaborately discussed, and, apart from some mystical circles, the presence of God got the worst of it. It is not by chance that Western scholars have debated at length whether or not Hinduism was concerned with ethics, and if it was decided that it was not, it was counted as evidence of its primitiveness or inferiority. It is peculiar to notice that in Western tradition, when people like to think of themselves as totally secularized, they still show an extraordinary concern for the element of volition. The cliché argument against synagogues and churches is precisely that they are as unwilling to change life as they are incapable of changing it.

SILENCE AND SIGNIFICATION

A Note on Religion and Modernity

CHARLES H. LONG

"The eternal silence of these infinite spaces terrifies me." This statement comes at the end of that section of Pascal's *Pensées* entitled "From a Knowledge of Man to a Knowledge of God." It is the culmination of a somber meditation on the fragility and finite nature of man when compared to the infinity of the world and nature. It is somewhat strange to find such a poignant statement in the midst of that most creative and optimistic period in western cultural history that we refer to as the age of the Enlightenment. And this strangeness is increased when we are reminded that Pascal is not a scholastic theologian of the Protestant or Roman variety protesting the reduction of the world to a new rationalism or mathematization; he is a more complex person than this. He is in fact very much a part of his age; he knows its language, being one of the greatest mathematicians of his time, and is, for all intents and purposes, a product—a distinguished product—of his age. The complexity of his character is revealed when we learn that he is not only a great mathematician and scientist but is also an ardent advocate of Jansenism, that ethical-moralistic orientation which reminds us most in Catholicism of a kind of puritanical Protestantism.

Before we jump to conclusions, however, and place Pascal in the category of so many of those contemporary scientists whose understanding of religious and humanistic matters is still at the Sunday School level or worse, and whose knowledge in these areas is not at all commensurate with their sophistication in the areas of scientific knowledge, we must take note of the fact that since the publication of the *Pensées* and his work on conic circles, these works have become basic documents for a proper understanding of the respective histories of theology and science. In other words, in confronting Pascal we are dealing not with a schizophrenic personality but with one of those rare human souls who struggles simultaneously with the fundamental problem of man's creativity and his fundamental nature.

Pascal expresses in this statement and throughout the *Pensées* the fundamental crisis of his historical period. The precision with which he delineated the problem of theodicy for his time is attested to by the fact that Voltaire turned again and again to a refutation of his arguments, for Voltaire knew that in Pascal he was confronting a thinker who struggled with the problem of God and man with the same diligence, intelligence, and wholeness that he devoted to his scientific investigations. The importance of the problem is attested to again by the other systematic genius of the Enlightenment, Immanuel Kant, who was the only thinker of this period to address himself to this problem with equal acuteness.

But Pascal is more than simply an expression of his age. He is, to be sure, especially in his *Pensées*, writing a kind of existential treatise, a treatise and meditation on the state of the human heart in his time, and it is just because he is a man so engaged with the fundamental problems of *his time* that he expresses meanings which are valid for the human problematic of the entire modern period. His orientation in the *Pensées* bears resemblances to a pattern and logic of human thought which is present in all religious orientations, a pattern of thought which has become crucial for our contemporary period. In the face of the creativity which has come into being through the new understanding of nature, God as a structure of intimacy has disappeared and a new world latent with creative possibilities and terrifying dread appears. Let us listen to his words, for they express the freshness of this problem; they give us a chance to see how this issue was stated *at the beginnings*:

> for who will not marvel to find our body, which a moment ago was not visible in the universe, which was itself imperceptible in the bosom of the whole, is at present a colossus, a world, or rather, a whole when compared with the world which lies beyond our ken? . . . Anyone who regards himself in this way will be terrified at himself, and seeing himself sustained in the body that nature has given him, between two

abysses of the infinite and the void, will tremble at the sight of these wonders, and I think that, as curiosity changes to wonder, he will be more disposed to contemplate them in silence than to presume to question them.[1]

In this passage Pascal traces a pattern of experiences which is a response to this new form of scientific nature. There is first the experience of the marvelously new, the sheer fabulous character of it; then there is awe and fear, a trembling at the sight of these wonders; and finally, Pascal says, "as curiosity changes to wonder, he will be more disposed to contemplate them in silence than to presume to question them." I shall return to this pattern later, but first let me say something about this pattern as it expresses itself in the history of religions.

We know from the studies of such historians of religions as Wilhelm Schmidt, Raffaele Pettazzoni, and Mircea Eliade that one of the central problems in recent study of history of religions is the problem of the High God. It was Mircea Eliade who observed that the problem of the High God among primitives became a central issue for historians of religions in the same generation that Nietzsche proclaimed the "death of God." And, Eliade continues in his observation, one of the most important elements in the structure of the High God symbol is the tendency of the High God, who is always the creator-deity, to become a *deus otiosus* after the world has been created. He describes this tendency explicitly in his *Patterns in Comparative Religion.*

What is clear is that the supreme sky god everywhere gives place to other religious forms. The morphology of this substitution may vary; but its meaning in each case is partly the same: it is the movement away from the transcendence and passivity of sky beings towards more dynamic, active, and easily accessible forms. One might say that we are observing a "progressive descent of the sacred into the concrete"; man's life and his immediate surroundings come more and more to have the value of sacred things. . . . Every substitution marks a victory for the dynamic, dramatic forms so rich in mythological meaning over the Supreme Being of the sky who is exalted, but passive and remote . . . the supreme divinities of the sky are constantly pushed to the periphery of religious life where they are almost ignored; other sacred forces, nearer to man, fill the leading role.[2]

[1] Blaise Pascal, *Pensées*, trans. Martin Turnell (New York, 1962), p. 216.
[2] Mircea Eliade, *Patterns in Comparative Religion* (New York, 1958), pp. 43–52.

And then there is this final statement which I should like to use from Eliade's work:

> this slipping of the omnipotence, transcendence, and impassiveness into the dynamism, intensity, and drama of the new atmospheric fertilizing vegetation figures, is not without significance. It makes clear that one of the main factors in the lowering of people's conception of God . . . is the more all-embracing importance of vital values and of "Life" in the outlook of economic man.[3]

Eliade's description of the history and structure of the High God may be summarized as follows: (1) he is a being who created the world; (2) his symbolism is related to the sky and thus he always represents transcendence, power, and wisdom; (3) after the creation of the world, the High God becomes *deus otiosus*, removed from the world he has created; (4) in his place are substituted the dramatic deities of fertility and creativity; (5) the High God is not completely forgotten, but he is no longer a part of the life of man and the world; he has no cult and worship is not addressed to him; (6) he is called upon or remembered in moments of strife or catastrophe when the basic structure of the world is threatened and when no help can be gained from the deities of fertility and creativity.

This pattern of elements and experiences in the structure of the High God bears a similarity to the structure of experience of the marvelously new. Subsequently there is the experience of awe and trembling fear before the wonder of the world, and finally, for Pascal there is the movement to silence. Now, I said there is a similarity, not a one-to-one relationship between the two structures, but the similarity is so marked that it might give us some insight into the religious experience of modern man; it might show us how, within the context of modernity, some basic patterns of man's religiousness may be discerned.

Pascal, unlike the enthusiasts of the Enlightenment, possesses that insight of double vision. He is able to see the infinite world of possibility which the new science makes possible, but he discerns at the same time that God has departed from this world and he is terrified by the infinite spaces, the void. In his meditations on God and the Biblical tradition he keeps alive the memory of

[3] *Ibid.*, p. 127.

a God who has disappeared, but even here there is the remembrance of a kind of skeletal structure of the Divine Creator. While his insights are penetrating and precise, the structure of the Supreme Being in the very moment of his most ardent advocacy is still detached and abstract. It is the Supreme Being as a giver of laws and the guarantor of the moral life; there is little of the joy of intimacy and relatedness in the *Pensées*.

Nevertheless, it is at this point that he has almost predicted the course of modern western cultural life since the Enlightenment. Can any of us deny that western culture moved from the enthusiastic euphoria of the marvelously new world of the new science to a contemplation of this wonder with trembling fear and awe, and finally, as I shall argue, to a spirit of contemplation with silence. We have only to remember the enthusiasm of Voltaire, Auguste Comte, and the leaders of the French and American revolutions to understand this response to the marvelously new world and its possibilities. But already, before the great wars, Goethe and several others knew that this world contained evil and terrifying implications. The wars, the instability of these centuries, the enormity of Buchenwald and Auschwitz, of Hiroshima and Nagasaki, seem to be summed up in the statement made by Robert Oppenheimer when he saw the first atomic explosion—"thou hast become the destroyer of all worlds."

Creativity and Silence

The results of the new world and the new creativity have not been unambiguously good. From a religious point of view one might say that man has lost his religiousness—that God is dead and that man no longer has any model or guide for the conduct of his life. This way out is too easy, for such a position reduces the religious imagination to ethics and fails to understand that religion is the continual quest for the meaning of human existence. In addition, this easy position overlooks two major facts, one of which is a product of the modern period itself; the other is of more ancient vintage. The modern fact is that humankind must be understood as one species, and any assessment of the meaning of mankind in any ultimate sense cannot be limited to the meanings of one culture or one historical period. The ancient fact is its correlate: religious man senses that he participates in a reality which is more than historical and cultural—religiously, man is an ontological being.

While the western world became the dominant cultural area of the world during the modern period, its meanings and understanding must be seen against the cultures and histories of the world. This means that the language of western cultural creativity is not the complete language of mankind during this period. I have used the term "language" metaphorically here, for this metaphor enables me to relate aspects of the modern world which are too often overlooked. The new language of reason modeled on the mathematical symbols of Newton expressed a universal intention. As over against the language of transcendence of the Abrahamic tradition, with its exclusivistic pretensions, it was a language which included all mankind.

It would have been difficult for the enthusiasts of the Enlightenment to foresee that the technicalism resulting from the new science would become the vehicle of extreme nationalism, devisiveness, colonialism, conquest, etc. This is not, however, the whole story of this creativity; one must also take account of those peoples who had to undergo the "creativity" of the western world—those peoples and cultures who became during this period the "pawns" of western cultural creativity. They were present not as voices speaking but as the silence which is necessary to all speech. They exist as the pauses between the words—those pauses which are necessary if speech is to be possible—and in their silence they speak. As opposed to the existential and historical presumptions of man making his world, those who lived as the *materia prima* (raw material, I think, is the economic way of expressing this) kept the ontological dimension open through their silence. This silence is as necessary as it is forced. It is not strange that in the nineteenth century, when the western world admitted the death of its God, that at just this moment western man sought him not in his own traditions and cultures but in the cultures of primitive and archaic peoples. It was from this silence that he tried to evoke once again a sign of intimacy and relatedness to ontological meaning.

There is another place where this voice of silence may be heard. It is internal to western culture itself. I am speaking of the exhaustive pursuit of all forms of human expression in the western world. With the removal of the traditional restraints, western man began an exhaustive pursuit of the infinitely large and the infinitely minute and subtle structures of life and the world. This conquest of the new world led to both beneficial and monstrous results. Every aspect of geographical, social, sexual, artistic, psychological, and intellectual life has been almost exhaustively explored. Modern abstract art as well as *musique concrète*, the era of colonialism and human and economic exploitation, the creation and the destruction of the novel as a literary genre—all of these meanings and events are products of this period. Its monstrosities are Buchenwald, Hiroshima, Nagasaki, the evils of racism in America, and the political enslavement of peoples in every nation on the planet. In the very pursuit of his authentic selfhood, western man has come face to face with silence, with the exhaustion of the forms of the world. What more is there to be said after Buchenwald or after a flight to the moon or after one has said that God is dead?

Modern western man in the midst of his tremendous creativity and noisiness finds himself confronting an awesome silence—a silence which cannot be banished by the clamor of his activities. It is the wonder and monstrosity of his deeds which has evoked this mood of silence. The great language of creativity which he used to subdue and exploit his world has been placed in jeopardy; its mighty words are overwhelmed by the silence of the pauses between the words. This language has been prostituted by the very techniques which brought it into being; after having been used and misused for so long by so many, this language has come to be distrusted by western man himself.

Now, this silence which has come about in the modern period may well be a sign of a kind of cultural catastrophe, for when a culture is unable to trust its own language and the names which it has assigned to things it is indeed in trouble. As in the myths of creation of the High God, in a period of catastrophe man is unable to gain help from the lesser gods of cultural creativity, and he must turn again to the creator of the beginning. This is a characteristic religious orientation. It is the "*be still* and *know* that I am God"; it is the Hindu *muni* whose silence is a testimony to God's holiness; it is the silence of Meister Eckhart who, after ascending to the Godhead, found an unspeaking and unspeakable void; and again, it is the Delphic oracle of Socrates which does not speak but signifies.

The Irony of Silence

It is difficult to get at the meaning of silence, for, though a kind of power is signified through its quality, the power of silence is so unlike the power of words that we have no words to express it. Or, to put it another way, the power of silence can only be expressed through the words, words which are able to move beyond and break through their own creative intent to the intentionality of silence. Silence is thus radically ironic. It brings us up short in the same manner as the prime minister who, upon being asked for advice from his king, told the king that the best advice he could give him was that he should not accept advice from anyone.

The fact that silence presupposes words is what gives it this ironic twist. Without words there can be no silence, and yet the sheer absence of words is not silence. Silence forces us to realize that our words, the units of our naming and recognition in the world, presuppose a reality which is prior to our naming and doing. This attentiveness reminds us, in the words of Merleau-Ponty, that

> we must consider speech before it is spoken, the background of silence which does not cease to surround it, and without which it would say nothing.[4]

Something of this same irony is present in Ludwig Wittgenstein's *Tractatus*. It is doubly ironic that a philosophical work which brought about the major orientation in philosophy to linguistic analysis speaks also of the limits and impotence of language. In a philosophical work devoted to language, we find one of the clearest expressions of silence. One of the most profound statements in the *Tractatus*, and, indeed, in all recent philosophy, is Wittgenstein's aphorism, "What can be shown cannot be said." Max Black, author of one of the commentaries on the *Tractatus*, explains Wittgenstein's aphorism in this manner:

> Showing, however we understand it, has to be conceived as quite unlike assertions by means of configurations of objects standing as proxies for objects . . . it is we the users of language who "say things," make assertions by means of arbitrary co-ordinations we have assigned to words; but whatever shows itself, independently of any arbitrary con-

[4] Maurice Merleau-Ponty, *Signs*, trans. Richard McCleary (Evanston, Ill., 1968), p. 46.

ventions we may have adopted – *what is shown is not something we express.*[5]

In other words, what shows itself is prior to speech and language and the basis for speech and language; furthermore, because it shows itself, it cannot be said – it is silent. But it is not only in the notion of showing that Wittgenstein places limits on language, for he places all value outside the world of language. Finally, at the end of the *Tractatus*, he makes the following surprising statements.

> 6.522. There are indeed things that cannot be put into words. *They make themselves manifest*. They are what is mystical.
>
> 6.54. My propositions serve as elucidations in the following way: anyone who understands me eventually recognizes them as non-sensical, when he has used them as steps to climb beyond them. (He must, so to speak, throw away the ladder after he has climbed up it. He must transcend the propositions, and he will see the world aright.)
>
> What we cannot speak about we must pass over into silence.[6]

The strangely ironical use of language as a testimony to silence may very well be a sign that the possibility of moving from Pascal's trembling and terrifying awesomeness to a contemplation in silence is at least a possibility, and if a possibility, the basis for a new ontology.

What is distinctly new in this position is that we are given a philosophical orientation which sees all language as enveloped in silence. In other words, the interrelation of language and silence gives us a new understanding of the totality of man's language and range of experience. The value of the new position is that it is possible to include within it that which goes by the name of rationality and that which is historical.

The old distinction between existence *in intellectu* and existence *in re* which lies behind the discussion of Anselm's ontological argument could be radically transformed. Could not existence *in intellectu* be transformed into the silence of Being, a mode of being that does not make itself known through the demonstrations of a language which stands for objects but through that kind of showing in silence which is necessary for speech and all

[5] Max Black, *A Commentary to Wittgenstein's Tractatus* (Ithaca, N.Y., 1964), p. 190.

[6] Ludwig Wittgenstein, *Tractatus Logico-Philosophicus*, trans. D. F. Pears and B. F. McGuinness (London and New York, 1963), p. 151.

the objects to which speech refers. Existence *in re* could from this point of view refer to the denotative nature of language and its propositions. As I have tried to show in my previous remarks, silence does not mean absence; it rather refers to the manner in which a reality has its existence. The silence of the nonwestern world during the period of colonialism did not mean that these cultures did not exist; it only pointed to the mode of their existence and — as we have learned in our study of the history of religions — indicated that the expression of their existence through symbols and myths was at the same time the expression of an ontological position. It means that silence is a fundamentally ontological position, a position which though involved in language and speech exposes us to a new kind of reality and existence.

Now, if any of these hints are correct, it means that that being than which nothing greater can be conceived is in fact not simply a concept of the intellect but in fact refers to the signification of silence, the world of symbols, values, and meanings which throughout the history of mankind man has deciphered from the silence which shows itself, which manifests itself, and which forms the basis of our worlds of making sense. It means that any new ontology must take account of the historical expressions of all cultures — those prehistoric, archaic, colonial, western, and eastern cultures whose silence expresses a fundamental ontology of both objectivity and intimacy. It is a silence which may no longer terrify us, and it is a silence which in its showing might give us an understanding of the human mode of being which moves us beyond conquest, enslavement, and exploitation. In acquiring this understanding, we may recover that patience and sensibility which lie at the heart of a religious attitude: "Be still and know that I am God."

II

HISTORICAL . . .

THE THREE LAST VOYAGES OF IL'JA OF MUROM

G. DUMÉZIL

The imprudent choice of Trojan Paris, the somewhat hierarchized choices of the three sons of Ferīdūn in the Iranian epic and of the three sons of William the Conqueror in our medieval *exempla*, and the judicious choice of the Tyrolean shepherd, thanks to which his confreres of today still know how to yodel whether or not, like him, they make the cows dance, have been successively recognized as so many vivacious expressions of the Indo-European ideology of the three functions. All, in one manner or another, claim to demonstrate the superiority of the first two functions, or, more generally, that of the first under one of its aspects: royal majesty, virtue and religion, wisdom, magic gifts.[1] Thus, it may be that a *bylina* (Russian folktale) has retained this lesson, with traits proper to the Russian ideology about the beginnings of modern times.

A type of tale abundantly attested in the Slavic group and on

1 Paris: G. Dumézil, "Les trois fonctions dans quelques traditions grecques," *Eventail de l'Histoire Vivante* (= *Mélanges Lucien Fabvre*), 2 (1954): 27–28; the sons of Ferīdūn: Marijan Molé, "Le partage du monde dans la tradition iranienne," *Journal Asiatique*, 240 (1952): 455–63, with a "Note complémentaire," *ibid.*, 241 (1953): 271–73 (rectifying p. 457, n. 1 of the article of 1952); the sons of William the Conqueror: Archer Taylor, "'What bird would you choose to be?' A Medieval Tale," *Fabula*, 7 (1965): 97–114; the *ranz-des-vaches* (Swiss pastoral melody): Lucien Gerschel, "Sur un schème trifonctionnel dans une famille de légendes germaniques," *Revue de l'Histoire des Religions*, 150 (1956): 73–92. The problem is taken up as a group in G. Dumézil, *Mythe et Epopée*, vol. 1, *Les trois fonctions dans les épopées des peuples indo-européens*, part 4, chap. 1 ("Le choix"), (in press).

the Caucasian and Siberian confines, as well as in Germany, all of Europe, and even in the Thousand and One Nights, has resulted after almost one hundred years in a good monograph by Reinhold Kohler (reprinted in *Kleinere Schriften*, 1 [1898]: 537–40).[2] It may be summarized as follows:

Three brothers are going to seek a marvelous animal which their father has demanded. They arrive at a trifurcation, near which is found an inscribed stone announcing, in a more or less clear fashion (with some ambiguity for one of them at least), the destiny of him who will travel on each of the three roads. Only he who chooses the apparently, or really, most dangerous road attains the object of the quest. When he rejoins his brothers, who have sometimes fallen into misery, they, being jealous, throw him into a well or pit and bring the animal back to their father. But the animal saves him who conquered it.

Certain variants articulate the motifs in other ways. For example, in A. Dieterich, *Russische Volksmärchen* (Leipzig, 1831), and in J. N. Vogl, *Die Altesten Volksmärchen der Russen* (Vienna, 1841), vol. 2, the two elder brothers have gone to seek a woman, and it is because they do not return that the youngest leaves to search for them. He arrives at a trifurcation. The inscription relating to the three ways announces, among other things, that the traveler who takes the road on the left "will be killed by the winged wolf." The youth takes to the road and joins battle with the winged wolf who, conquered, helps him to acquire simultaneously the water which gives life to the dead and a lovely princess. Then he finds the cadavers of his brothers and revives them. Jealous, they tear him to pieces, but the wolf revives him in turn.

The triple inscription at the intersection is variable but conforms to a uniform type. Here are some examples.

He who will go to the right or to the left will encounter no danger; he who will go straight ahead will surely perish or will surely return with happiness. (Avars of the Daghestan, Caucasus)

[2] Johannes Bolte and George Polívka, in their notes to Jakob Ludwig Karl Grimm, *Kinder- und Hausmärchen* (Leipzig, 1913), which they edited, have added no variant containing the motif of the inscribed stones (No. 57, "Der goldene Vogel," pp. 503–15). Stith Thompson, *Motif-Index of Folk Literature*, under the rubric N 122, only reflects P. Köhler. I have published a Laze story in *Documents anatoliens sur les langues et les traditions du Caucase*, 4 (1967), where there is (p. 41, secs. 290–95) the motif of the three roads without inscription (two roads are "broad and good," the third "narrow and thorny," and it is this last which the hero chooses).

If you go straight ahead, you will not return; if you go to the right, you will drown; if you go to the left, you will kill your horse, but you will find happiness. (Imeretians of Transcaucasia)

He who will take this road here, he will return; he who will take this other, he will die; he who will take the third, it is completely certain that he will not return. (Greece)

He who will take this road here, he will return; he who will take this other, he will perhaps return and perhaps not return; he who will take the third, he will not return. (Greece)

He who will go to the right, he will be satisfied, but his horse famished; he who will go straight ahead, he will be hungry, but his horse will be satisfied; he who will go to the left, he will be killed by the winged wolf. (Russia)

He who will go straight ahead will be hungry and cold; he who will go to the right will come back safe and sound, but his horse will die; he who will go to the left will be killed, but his horse will survive. (Russia)

He who will go straight ahead will encounter the lash for the sin which he will commit; he who will go to the right will cry great tears because he will commit a sin against his brother; he who will go to the left will not fall into any unhappiness and "will bend his brothers under his hands." (Poland)

He who will go to the right will become very rich; he who will take the middle road will become rather rich; he who will go to the left will not return. (Turkestan)

The first road is that of happiness, the second that of regret; he who will take the third will undoubtedly never return. (Thousand and One Nights)

There is nothing in this which is arranged according to the structure of the three functions. But the motif of the three roads furnished with inscriptions has been utilized in a completely different way in a *bylina* of the cycle of Il'ja of Murom, where it seems to have been adjusted to a trifunctional theme. It is the *bylina* generally entitled "The Three Last Voyages of Il'ja." The great collections contain twenty-five variants of it, of which eleven are incomplete, lacking either the last voyage (six variants) or the last two voyages (five variants).[3] Only the fourteen complete variants will be considered here, almost all of which originate in the government of Olonets. From the point of view of the "third road," which is particularly important because it controls the denouement, one can distinguish three groups.

The first group includes A. F. Gil'ferding, nos. 266, 287, and P. V. Kireevskij, vol. 1, pp. 86–89. Here is a résumé of the first variant of Gil'ferding (vol. 3, pp. 361–65; noted in 1871):

Il'ja of Murom, an old man, plods along on his good horse and arrives at a trifurcation. On a stone, he reads the inscription: "To go by this road is to be killed; to go by the second is to be married; to go by the third is to be enriched." He decides to take the first: at his age what good is wealth, which he has in abundance? And why run the risks of marriage?

Traversing a forest, he encounters an army of forty thousand brigands, who make ready to strip him. After a bantering discourse in which he describes his rich vestments and the handsome trappings of his mount, he massacres the brigands and goes back to the inscription, whose first line he corrects: "Mendacious was the inscription written; by this road I went and was not killed!" And he starts out upon the second road, which ought to lead him to marriage.

He arrives at a palace where a very lovely young woman welcomes him, "kisses him with lips of sugar," serves him a feast, and offers him more. When they have entered the chamber, she invites him to sleep first, at the bottom of the bed near the wall. He excuses himself ironically – old fellows should rest near the outside of the bed because it is necessary for them to be able to go into the courtyard during the night. At the same time he grabs the beautiful princess and throws her to the bottom of the bed. Now, the bed is faked and the young woman topples over into a subterranean cavern, the door of which he only had to be shown. He breaks it down, delivers forty tsars and forty kings who had been less prudent than he, and puts the enchantress cruelly to death. Then he returns to the intersection and corrects the

[3] Texts cited here and on the following pages may be found in: P. N. Rybnikov, ed., *Pesni sobrannyja P. N. Rybnikovym*, 3 vols., 2d ed. (Moscow, 1909–10), vol. 2 (1909); P. V. Kireevskij, comp., and P. Bezsonov, ed., *Pesni sobrannyja P. N. Rybnikovym*, 10 vols. (Moscow, 1863–79), vol. 1 (1863); A. F. Gil'ferding, *Onežskija byliny*, 3 vols., 2d ed. (Moscow, 1894–1900), vols. 2 (1896) and 3 (1900); N. S. Tikhonravov and V. F. Miller, *Byliny staroj i novoj zapisi* (Moscow, 1894); V. F. Miller, *Byliny novoj i nedavnej zapisi* (Moscow, 1908).

second line of the inscription: "Mendacious was the inscription; by this road I went and was not married." And he sets out along the third road, which should lead to wealth.

He traverses a somber forest and arrives at a cavern signaled by a new inscription:

> Treasure for extracting by Il′ja of Murom!
> Let him engage skilled and able carpenters!
> Let him construct a cathedral church
> for the pontiff Nicolas of Možaisk,
> in the illustrious city of Kiev!
> And then Il′ja of Murom will die.

Il′ja conforms to the prescription. Once the cathedral church is built, he passes before a deep cavern, enters it and dies.

The other stories of this group are similar. Here is the third part of Gil′ferding, no. 287 (*ibid.*, pp. 424–29; also noted in 1871):

> And he goes, the old fellow, by route and by road,
> And he finds on the way a burning gray rock,
> And on the rock there is an inscription:
> "Silver and gold are dumped here,
> Let Il′ja of Murom remove them,
> Let him take away the gold and silver,
> Let him found three cathedral churches,
> The first church for the Savior so pure,
> And the second for Mikula Možanskij,
> And the third for George the brave."

Here is the same voyage in Kireevskij:

> He goes, the old fellow, by the route, by the road,
> And there on the ground an enormous stone,
> And on the stone still a new inscription:
> "Under this stone
> Is a great forged coffer
> And in the coffer an incalculable sum."
> The old fellow made the stone roll aside,
> He drew up, the old fellow, the great coffer,
> And on the coffer there was yet another inscription:
> "To whomever the contents fall,
> Let him construct the church of India,
> Let him construct the church of the cavern."
> Then the old fellow constructed the church of India,
> And as he commenced to construct the church of the cavern,
> Then the old fellow was petrified.

The second group is distinguished from the first in that the construction of the churches or other foundations is not commanded by an inscription accompanying the treasure, but is freely decided upon by Il'ja after the discovery of the treasure.

A variant (P. N. Rybnikov, no. 176 [vol. 2, pp. 508–12], almost identical to A. F. Gil'ferding, no. 221 [vol. 3, pp. 145–50]), replacing the inscription by a cross, makes the transition from the first group:

> He went by the great route,
> He found on the way a most marvelous cross.
> The old guy stopped near the cross, he shook his head,
> He shook his head and pronounced:
> "This cross should not rise here for nothing.
> It rises upon a deep cavern,
> There is surely gold and silver without measure."
> He dismounts, the old guy, from his good horse,
> He takes the cross in his white hands,
> And he takes it away from the deep cavern,
> And he hauls out the guts of the cavern — a treasure of gold,
> And he carries it off to the illustrious city of Kiev,
> And he constructs a cathedral church.
> Then also Il'ja was petrified,
> And even today his remains are not corrupted.

This group is composed of Rybnikov, nos. 110, 128, 154, and Gil'ferding, nos. 58, 271. The treasure is employed everywhere in pious works: construction of a church, support of orphans and the ill (Rybnikov, no. 110); construction of monastery and church, establishment of "church songs and bell chimes" (Rybnikov, no. 128); construction of three cathedral churches (Gil'ferding, no. 287), (Rybnikov, no. 154); construction of cathedral churches, establishment of bell chimes (Gil'ferding, no. 58); construction of monasteries (Gil'ferding, no. 271).

In Rybnikov, no. 142 (vol. 2, pp. 311–14), where the third voyage has become the second, the road which should lead to wealth leads in fact to "a king, a pagan monster" and the religious merit takes another form:

> He killed the pagan monster
> And he brought all the land of holy Russia to
> The Christian faith.

In the third group some variants are diversely aberrant. In A. F. Gil'ferding, no. 190 (vol. 2, pp. 691–94), Il'ja refuses to go look for the treasure:

> "I will not go by the route where you become rich,
> I have at home incalculable treasures of gold."

In N. S. Tikhonravov and V. F. Miller, no. 6 (pp. 14–17), Il'ja simply takes the treasure without saying what use he will make of it. The same is true in P. N. Rybnikov, no. 16 (vol. 2, pp. 632–35), which concludes, at the very end of the third voyage, with these words:

> And he went on the side where he should become rich,
> And he went on the third side,
> And he killed the pagan monster,
> And he carried off a measureless treasure of gold,
> And he returned to the city of Kiev.

In V. F. Miller, no. 11, pp. 24–26, Il'ja takes the roads in the order three, one, two. By the road which should lead to wealth, he arrives at the lair of a monster whose head he cuts off; from his victim's treasures, he withdraws only a magnificent harness for his horse. The episode of the brigands is of the ordinary type, but that of the princess ends well, in an idyll. She is a good girl, without trick bed or cavern; hardly has she kissed the old fellow on the mouth than she demands him to lead her to Kiev, into the church of God, and to marry her in good and proper form:

> They went to the church of God,
> They exchange the rings,
> They go to their little palace,
> There they make feasting and drinking,
> In the palace of white stone,
> Throughout exactly twelve weeks.

Let us leave aside this third group, which, speaking truly, is only a collection of divergent deformations. In the first two groups, the place and the intention of the third episode are the same. By the discovery, exterior or interior, that the old hero makes of what is true wealth, the conclusion, his happy death, is found assured. Put simply, the pious foundations are more strongly motivated in the first group than in the second.

The meaning of the tale is simple. In the last three voyages, Il'ja touches the "bottom of things." Indeed, he has implicitly recognized it all his life, interesting himself only in the good battle. At life's end, however, thanks to the ultimate examination in three tests which has been prepared for him by Providence, he grasps it explicitly, in full consciousness. He receives, and we along with him, three lessons; the first barely confirms him in what he knows best, the second brings a strong, useful counsel, and the third is a veritable revelation.

The *tests* oblige the old hero to choose successively between courage and cowardice, between abandon and resistance to the allurements of voluptuousness, and between cupidity and the scorn of material goods. This is to say, in my jargon, that the tests confront him successively with one problem of the second function and two problems of the third, to which belong sexuality and wealth. But the *lessons*, through the revelation occasioned by the third test, are distributed over a complete gradient of the three functions, in the three zones of *valor* and *force*, of *voluptuousness*, and of *sanctity*: "strongly confront the enemy, defy sexual temptations, bring back all to God."

The inscription of the first road is not truly mendacious; the announced risk is real and for anyone but Il'ja would surely be realized. The choice which the hero makes and the result of the test are also what one expects: he goes straight to the risk, he gives preference to the road whose inscription seems to defy him in the kind of action in which he excels, he seeks the unknown but signaled enemy, and he is the conqueror. Thus, neither on his side nor on ours is there any surprise; as far as we know, here he could wish only for the combat and the conquest. Finally, this episode in itself, parallel to some others in his career, teaches nothing he does not know already.

Unlike the first, the other two inscriptions are deceptive; they announce no peril, but rather promise what most men consider natural pleasures. These, however, are pleasures in which Il'ja has never felt an interest: he has arrived at old age without experiencing the need to be married, and, if his exploits have brought him wealth, he has always disdained it. Nevertheless, between these two matters of indifference there is a hierarchy: when he returns to the intersection, it is not wealth but marriage which he chooses, although not without retaining enough suspicion to allow him to perceive the peril in time (this conforms well to the ordinary misogyny of folklore so abundantly illustrated in the literature of the *byliny*). And his conduct in the circumstance, for him and for us, brings in a judgment, a counsel: the beauty of women, the first fruits of pleasure which they willingly accord, and the promises which they afterwards make are just so many traps against which there is no other remedy than refusal—as Napoleon has said, flight—and, when one can, chastisement.

The third inscription which Il'ja has twice mistaken because he understands it in a literal sense, the third road which he takes to the end seemingly only in order to be complete and to have explored all, is found on the contrary, either by virtue of the gloss which Providence had drawn up for its use (first group of variants), or thanks to his own instinct (second group), to lead to the most meritorious action, to the succession of "good works" which God uses to call to himself, under the best conditions, this old man whose services until then had profited only men.

Therefore, one can say that the subject of the *bylina* is a belated but complete extension of Il'ja's knowledge of the world: after having made a last positive demonstration of his characteristic advantage—force and bravura—on its ordinary level, he triumphs in the only manner possible, that is to say negatively, in the zone of sexual pleasures of which he has scarcely any experience. Finally, through a veritable transformation of the notion of wealth, he abruptly becomes a holy man, ready to present himself before God.

The tableau of lessons is nonetheless asymmetric because if force and true wealth (that is to say the wealth consecrated for God and for men of God) are indeed desirable, voluptuousness and all things which condition it are, in the epic context, fundamentally bad, not recoupable, beyond a conceivable turning to other account.

As for the theme of the three roads and the three inscriptions, it had to undergo, to serve as frame for the three lessons, a triple alteration: (1) it is one and only one person, not three, who successively attempts the three roads, in such a way that it concerns more a setting in hierarchy than a choice; (2) the inscriptions, or several among them, are either mendacious or of double meaning; (3) the ordinary type of wording has been modified to adapt it as much as possible to the contents of the tests and the lessons.

Moreover, in this last operation the author has imposed on himself a constraint which adds further to the asymmetry of the ensemble: he has visibly chosen three participles not only for their suitability to the context but also for their consonant forms (for example, Gil′ferding, no. 266, *ubítu* ["killed], *ženátu* ["married"], *bogátu* ["enriched"]).

One cannnot specify, of course, whether these transformations have been made by the author of the *bylina* himself for the *bylina* – that is, whether he imagined the story of the three voyages such as we read it in order to close with dignity the heroic life of Il′ja of Murom, or whether this author restricted himself to applying to Il′ja an apologue already constituted, preserving an old "pre-Russian" philosophy set to the taste of Christian Russia. The fact that no literary source – apocrypha, life of an oriental saint, etc. – has been recognized for this *bylina* recommends the second hypothesis.[4]

[4] Jan Máchal, *O bohatýrském epose slovanském* (Praze, 1894), pp. 155–56, and Reinhold Trautmann, *Die Volksdichtung der Grossrussen: Das Heldenlied* (Heidelberg, 1935), pp. 400–402, indicate that only the motif of the three roads provided with inscriptions and the motif of the perfidious and chastised woman come from Russian tales. Trautmann's conclusion: "Aber dies Schicksalmotiv, in Anwendung gebracht auf den alten und weisen Recken, der allen Verlockungen der Welt, aber auch allen ihren Hindernissen überlegen ist, hat doch ein erfreuliches Lied geschaffen."

ON SIN AND PUNISHMENT

Some Remarks concerning Biblical and Rabbinical Ethics

GERSHOM SCHOLEM

The remarks I want to make on sin and punishment as they became apparent in Judaism will concern three different levels which correspond to the three dimensions of the Judaic religious world: (1) the Hebraic Bible, (2) the sources of Rabbinical Judaism in the Talmud and Midrash, and (3) the Judaic esoteric teachings or secret doctrine, regardless of whether we want to call it Jewish Gnosis or Mysticism, as it is expressed in the literature of the Kabbalists. In this study I shall stress a few points which are significant for the phenomenology of Judaism as a historical manifestation. Historical reflections upon the development of these separate notions, important as they obviously are in other perspectives, are out of place in this context. In particular I would not like to become involved here in discussions concerning the relations between the concept of sin and punishment in the Old Testament and definite phases of development of Biblical Judaism, or even with certain literary sources of Biblical literature. The historical significance of such analyses, which always have a more or less hypothetical character, is undisputed. But within the scope of the considerations which are to be discussed here, we may treat the Hebrew Bible as a document in which definite and extremely effective ideas about this subject have been advanced for the first time or given their final form. Even though these ideas originate in different parts of the Bible, and also, certainly, in very different periods, they have had the effect of a homogeneous complex of ideas in religious history and in the theology of Judaism and also in Christianity, paradoxical as it may seem in some respects. But precisely where the Bible was considered as a document of religious revelation, such paradoxes could be considered resolved by a higher unity which contained in itself at once different models and paradigms, examples of possible attitudes.

In broad outline, one may perhaps say that the Old Testament notion of punishment, which might be called the "myth of punishment," fluctuates between two poles which are set up in the first chapters of Genesis and the Book of Job. Since one would expect the Old Testament to be full of concentrated presentations and consistently thought-out formulations of the question of sin and its consequences, it is indeed remarkable that in a complex of writings the size of the Old Testament there are very few of them. Nevertheless, a unified conception underlies the great majority of Biblical writings, insofar as a direct, unbroken relationship is established between sin or offense on the one hand and punishment on the other. They appear in an inseparable relation, whether as cause and effect or even as two sides of a unified, self-contained process. For it is precisely the undoubted and dramatically emphasized unity and "unbrokenness" of the events which has made them into mythical paradigm cases. In writings which call themselves "Theology of the Old Testament," opposition to labeling such paradigm cases as mythical has not been absent, and understandably so. The break with the world of polytheistic mythology was of such great significance in the Biblical religion that talk of monotheistic myths struck theologians with mild terror. I believe, however, that we can pass over this objection, which stands on poor philosophical grounds and assumes that the rational and clear spirituality of these myths, to use the words of an important author, is evidence against their mythical character.

The most significant and immensely effective presentation of this subject in the Bible is of course chapters 2 to 11 of Genesis. Nothing else in Biblical writing corresponds to the detail and penetrating power of these chapters. To this day it has remained the most significant "myth of punishment," if I may use this term, which Judaic and Christian theologians have tried to understand.

These chapters present a primordial history of mankind in which there is a completely unified view, a unified theology of history. All hardship that befalls mankind is punishment for falling away from God, for disobedience and insurrection. This punishment affects all levels of natural and historical events. In a series of great images this primordial history is, as it were, dramatically developed. Every offense is flanked or followed by its own kind of punishment. Adam and Eve disregard God's prohibition and enjoy the fruit of the Tree of the Knowledge of Good and Evil. This is the first and, at the same time, most profound myth in which the Bible has made the relationship between God and man problematic. The Bible does not explicitly say what the knowledge of good and evil really is, or why it is not suitable for man in his blissful, paradisiacal condition. The consequence of gaining this knowledge is the annihilation of the paradisiacal condition. One could probably also ask whether, in the narrator's view, this knowledge is not identical with the punishment, because this knowledge of good and evil is a knowledge which destroys the paradisiacal condition from within. This knowledge cannot sustain itself in the realm of Paradise, the realm of the uninhibited and blissful relation between Creator and creature, because the knowledge of good and evil, moral reflection, undermines and destroys this state of integrity. From the point of view of the punishment, the results which follow upon the snake's advice to Eve are very remarkable, not to say questionable. For if the threat of death seems at once reasonable punishment, then the same cannot be said of the moral knowledge nor of the sexual shame which, according to the narrator, are positive values. Moreover, Adam and Eve's awareness of their nakedness is the only aspect in which the story makes the possession of the newly acquired knowledge of good and evil become at all acute. But we may probably say that it is not really part of the punishment which is threatened here. This knowledge is attained at the price of punishment, namely, death, work, pain of childbearing, and the cursing of the earth. But that which is bought at this price is itself a possession which from now on remains a part of man. Man, who before in Paradise had an unproblematical relationship with God, now stands opposed to him, and the newly acquired knowledge of good and evil, the differentiation and the choice between them, coincides with responsibility toward God. It is this responsibility which, on a higher plane than the natural and biological effects, is the consequence of Adam's deed. This myth knows nothing of original sin in the sense of the humanly irresolvable corruption of man's moral nature which Christian dogma read into this story. But the continuation of the Genesis story does recognize a progressive alienation of man from God, as it is shown here for the first time in broad outline. This alienation is a corollary of punishment which leads into a new framework of sacred history after dramatic climaxes and only with the summoning of Abraham and the Patriarchs.

Further actions in which sin and punishment are intertwined follow upon Adam and Eve's Fall. There is the first murder, no longer resulting from disobedience, as Adam's sin did, but rather from envy. But astonishingly enough, this first murder is not punished by death but rather by excluding the murderer from all permanent human relationships. A divine sign even *protects* Cain from being killed. In a remarkably dialectical sense, the sword is invented as a fatal instrument of murder and of revenge only by the descendants of the first murderer! This is followed by the myth of the perversion, the moral decay of mankind, which again certainly does not begin within man, but rather with an intervention from a higher sphere. As the Bible says, it is the union of the "sons of the *Elohim*," beings of a higher order, with the daughters of men which introduces further degeneration of the human race. People scheme and plot nothing but evil; the earth becomes corrupted, full of oppression and acts of violence. As punishment, God brings the Flood over the earth. And, as the last punishment myth in this series, there appears the story of the Tower of Babel and the confusion of language. Here, in a very remarkable preventive action, God himself destroys the unity of human language and thus also the possibility of communication among men to prevent the completion of the Tower. The Biblical report does not give reasons why it is sinful to build a tower up to the heavens instead of spreading out across the earth. Thus, the Bible has opened the door to the most profound and paradoxical speculations, as it has in the case of Adam's sin and its significance. There is something extremely suggestive about these first punishment myths as the Bible tells them: each is charged with an element of the impenetrable, the unfinished, and the questionable. In a very different way from all the other Biblical stories of sin, punishment, and guilt, they invite the reader's wonder and his own reflection. The fact that they lend themselves very poorly to any rationalization, that they strongly resist, so to speak, any demythologizing, to use a popular expression, has not lessened their imaginative power and their symbolic force. Quite the contrary is true.

In the Bible there are only two other punishment myths having the same great power. One of these concerns the relation between the Sinai revelation and the story of the golden calf and its consequences; the other concerns the disobedience of Israel which is punished by the forty years of wandering in the desert. In these myths, if we may call them such, the relation between the revelation, the falling away from God, and the punishment is almost completely rationalized; the relation is direct, even where the punishment is spread out over a long period of time. Later this becomes still more pronounced in the view of history which understands every historical hardship of the people of Israel, up to the destruction of the first temple and to the exile, as a consequence of their reversion to idolatry. Here the punishment has become almost diffused and enters into a long, drawn-out historical process, but it is always revived by the constantly renewed relapse.

While the primordial history expressed itself in those suggestive myths which could be endlessly interpreted, in the history of the people of Israel the relationship between sin and punishment is depicted with much greater precision – I would almost have said with a certain amount of rhetoric. Its most important documents are the two great proclamations of punishment in Leviticus 26 and Deuteronomy 28, where the consequences are developed. These consequences arise from Israel's failure in the face of God's word, the commandment demanding obedience; indeed, they arise from the covenant with Israel. The authors of these very impressive invectives, which have also played an important role in the consciousness of later Judaism, do not shrink from any radicalism. The catastrophes of history and the rebellion of nature, which were just as much *vaticinia ex eventu* – subsequent, back-dated prophecies – as prophetical visions, are represented in these speeches as one great infliction of punishment called forth by the disobedience and the fall of the people. But the punishment here is not regarded as an automatic consequence which occurs immediately; it appears to be rather incongruous in comparison to the original transgression. It is a punishment myth which has already been extended into the cosmic-historical. It is probably one of the most amazing phenomena of religious history: a people has incorporated a long speech such as that in Deuteronomy 28:15–34 into its scriptures, reads it aloud every year in the synagogue, and, for thousands of years, has recognized itself and its fate as depicted in it. I quote here only a few verses from this dreadful tirade (Deut. 28:15–34, Revised Standard Version):

> But if you will not obey the voice of the Lord your God or be careful to do all his commandments and his statutes which I command you this day, then all these curses shall come upon you and overtake you. Cursed shall you be in the city, and cursed shall you be in the field. . . . Cursed shall you be when you come in, and cursed shall you be when you go out. The Lord will send upon you curses, confusion, and frustration, in all that you undertake to do, until you are destroyed and perish quickly, on account of the evil of your doings, because you have forsaken me. . . . And the heavens over your head shall be brass, and the earth under you shall be iron. The Lord will make the rain of your land powder and dust; from heaven it shall come down upon you until you are destroyed. . . . And your dead body shall be food for all birds of the air, and for the beasts of the earth; and there shall be no one to frighten them away. . . . Your sons and your daughters shall be given to another people, while your eyes look on and fail with longing for them all the day; and it shall not be in the power of your hand to prevent it. A nation which you have not known shall eat up the fruit of your ground and of all your labors: and you shall be only oppressed and crushed continually; so that you shall be driven mad by the sight which your eyes shall see. . . .

In place of the simple relation between disobedience to God and a specific punishment, as in those earlier myths and stories of Genesis, there appears here a genuine paroxysm of punishments. Nothing is left out, nothing from the whole field of ancient man's experience. Everything rebels against him, and the paroxysm of punishment becomes a paroxysm of hopelessness. In a religious world which has not yet developed the idea of the Last Judgment and in which the relation between sin and punishment is this-worldly and immanent in the events, the utmost has been attained here in approaching the eschatology which will soon burst forth. What was formerly only punishment has now in a strange way become the discharging of God's "wrath," in which punitive justice is expressed as an aspect of divine nature itself and thus has crystallized itself into a monotheistic anthropomorphism which is exceedingly rich in consequences. God's wrath, of which Amos speaks with unheard-of urgency, is itself the punishment in which he displays and manifests himself. That this instance of punishment in which God's wrath flares up is really an instance in the upbringing of Israel by God, and is thus an instance of divine pedagogy, as theologians sometimes assert, seems to me somewhat doubtful. In any case, it would constitute a rather desperate pedagogy.

Moreover, it has been rightly said that perhaps not the whole multitude of earthly evils has been brought forth only for the punishment of human sin. The destructive forces of the natural elements were already contained in the original organization of nature. But it also remains an open question of how far these forces have been realized through human sin, as it is understood in the Old Testament. Much has been projected backward by later theology from the Messianic state of a redeemed world into the paradisiacal state, and it remains very uncertain how many of such ideas were already implicit in the Biblical stories themselves. The continuously active mythical imagination was given infinite material by paralleling primordial time and final time and by contrasting them with everything lying between. Thus, for example, Isaiah's prophecy (Isaiah 25:8) of the swallowing up of death in a redeemed world has had great consequences in post-Biblical Judaism when confronted with the myth of the Fall and of death. But such paralleling was extremely foreign to the Biblical religion, even on the prophetic level. The redemption of which the prophets speak in no way excludes, a priori, sin and punishment as lasting phenomena. But now punishment and cursing are indeed no longer correlated; punishment will no longer be a curse as it obviously is in very important passages of the Torah such as those I have discussed above.

In summary, then, one can say that suffering in all its forms is understood by Biblical religion as punishment. It can also be assumed that the decisive factor of the lost innocence of man – indeed, perhaps of nature also – plays a role in this. It seems a hypothetical assumption to me, although much can be said for it, that the condition of purity or impurity is identical with that of innocence and of being untouched (Hebrew: *temimuth*), guilt or impurity. The Biblical way of speaking about the consequences of sin makes extensive use of metaphorical technique which is associated with the condition of impurity. Here less intention is given to ritual impurity in the real sense than to the impurity produced by the disruption of the original innocence and the untouched state of man and land. This metaphorical technique, associated with the condition of impurity, points to something in the sinner which represents a degraded, profaned condition in contrast to the earlier condition. Thus there are often repeated prophetic speeches concerning the necessity of purification of sinners as well as speeches in many portions of the Torah concerning the desecration and impurity of the land as a consequence of the sinning of the people of Israel. Also, the talk about the restitution of the lost, or reconciliation as a restoration of lost purity, gains from this point on the great importance which such talk has in the Bible. Perhaps this too is still a mythical discourse about punishment, but it is indeed a discourse which has been very strongly modified and transformed into a metaphorical one.

The great counterthrust against these ideas about a straight and direct relationship between sin and punishment, whatever forms it might have assumed, is found in the Book of Job. Therefore, the Book of Job is not without reason the most provocative Biblical text; it is still extremely relevant today, and without it Judaism would not be what it is in the history of religion. Here the undialectical element in the relation between sin and punishment is radically put into question. Job raises a question which, once asked, is unanswerable. Job knows himself to be innocent; in addition, no one is able to disprove to Job his innocence. By asking the reason for his suffering, which he takes to be punishment, and unjust punishment at that, Job explodes the undialectical connection between sin and atonement. To make things worse, God ironically acknowledges the justification of Job's complaint by not answering Job on the level on which the question was asked, namely, that of the suffering of the innocent and the just. Instead, God answers him with—to be precise—the entirely meaningless question of whether Job had been present at the Creation. This meaningless answer to something that Job had not maintained at all is really only bearable, it seems to me, if one assumes that its intention is to show ironically that Job's question had also been meaningless. But this remains completely hidden. Instead, Job's question and the inadequacy of the answers given by his friends, who speak like professors of theology, is strongly underscored. The most ironic thing in a book so rich in ironies is that Job, more put down by God's question about cosmogony than given a pertinent answer, declares himself satisfied with it. It is as though Job, after destroying and annihilating the familiar punishment myth, accepts it again, as it were indifferently. Only now it is pushed out of the realm of history and primordial history and back into a completely impenetrable realm of cosmogony, about which there will also be no appropriate or fruitful answer in this context. I would also make a further remark. The story of the Book of Job, the major speeches between Job, his friends, and God, is built into the framework of that famous story of God's wager with Satan concerning Job's behavior when confronted with innocent suffering. *This rational explanation for the suffering of the innocent Job is never given as the answer in the book itself.* It seems as if this framework for the story, formed by the first two and the last chapters, is there only to make the existence of the Book of Job just tolerable in the canon of the Bible. I would say that without this framework for the story the Book of Job would not have been handed down to us. It would have been destroyed. The asking of the question which explodes everything that preceded was tolerable in its endless thunder only when it was built into a quasi-optimistic context like that of the story of the wager, which is never again touched upon in the rest of the story. Thus, the Book of Job leaves us with that unanswered question which echoes down through the millennia into our own time.

In Rabbinical Judaism, but also to a great extent in Judaism as represented in the Apocrypha and Apocalypses, the formulations of notions of sin and punishment whose chief characteristics I have tried to stress have remained of unbroken vividness and have frequently come into sharper focus. Moreover, new instances also appear. A particularly penetrating formulation, and thus also partly a transformation of the Biblical notions of sin and punishment, can be demonstrated, it seems to me, primarily by three points. But I would not like to maintain that I have thereby penetrated all the important aspects of this problem in Judaism.

First of all, the development of the idea of God's power to judge and punish (Hebrew: *middath ha-din*) is important here as one of the two main aspects of divine nature, which is conceived as complementary to divine grace and mercy (Hebrew: *middath ha-rahamim*). This notion must have been very old in Palestinian Judaism since it is already taken up by Philo, who must have heard about it from Palestinian teachers. These two qualities (Hebrew: *middoth*) are decisive for the Rabbinical conception of God. In the sometimes mythically dramatized conflicts between divine judgment and mercy or in the equilibrium between them, we have one of the most clearly defined representations of the religion of the Jewish Aggadah, in which the religion of the synagogue and of the people of Palestine intermingle and unite. God's power of judgment is at the same time a punitive one (Hebrew: *middath pur'anŭth*). Man's transgression calls forth God's punitive power. To be sure, after man has been warned by the great questions of the Book of Job, this relation of sin to punishment is no longer necessarily unbroken. The effect of the punitive power is postponed in certain cases; it remains suspended and discharges itself perhaps only after the death of the sinner. Frequently this *middath ha-din*, this punitive power, is thought to be personified in a mythical manner, and divine severity is almost equivalent to a punishing or avenging angel who afflicts the guilty one or takes revenge on him. All of man's moral actions evoke one of these two sides in God, and the Jewish theologians read the Bible as a story about their constant interaction. In passing, it may perhaps be mentioned that the classical documents of Rabbinical theology know of no quasi-hypostatized characteristic of God's love which in the true sense would be the exact parallel to the two already mentioned. It is not that these texts do not speak of God's love, but the significance of love is minor in comparison with God's mercy and grace (Hebrew: *rahamim* and *hesed*). Only later generations, in referring back to the Bible, have again made it a central point in God's teachings.

In the second place one should stress the conception of sin as a destruction of the communion with God, as, for example, E. Sjöberg has pointed out in his book *Gott und die Sünder im palästinischen Judentum* (Stuttgart and Berlin, 1938). Sin drives out God's presence, sending it farther and farther away, back into inaccessibility. And where sin does not completely abolish God's presence, it makes it into a particularly dangerous manifestation of the power of judgment. The actual separation of God and man is effected only by sin. A famous passage of the Midrash states that it is actually sin which progressively effects the withdrawal of divine immanence from the world and makes God completely transcendental and removed. Of course, such thoughts are always presented with reference to verses from the Holy Scriptures, but the particular, frequently extravagant type of exegesis and emphasis employed here lends weight and a particular physiognomy to the Rabbinical pronouncements. I would like to cite at least one example of such mythical exegesis, one which concerns the subject with which we are dealing. Genesis 3:21 speaks of garments of fur or skin which God made for the first couple after their expulsion from Paradise. An old Jewish exegesis, taken up by Church Fathers and Gnostics, has explained that originally man was provided with a body of light and with garments of light (Hebrew: *kutnoth 'or*); through sin, however, he acquired a material body made of skin (Hebrew: *kutnoth 'or*). In his body of light he obviously still existed in unbroken communion with God. The "garments of skin" which were produced after the sin separate him quite obviously from this communion with the divine. Light is no longer reflected back to God, but a skin, a material body, stands between man's essential nature and God.

Third, the Talmudic exegesis itself loves to stress in great detail the this-worldly relation between sin and punishment, although it already knows another such relation, namely, the punishments in the other world and those of the Last Judgment. This "atomization" of the relation between guilt and atonement is a very apparent tendency, at least in some strata of Rabbinical literature. This tendency is exemplified, for instance, in a very detailed exposition in the Talmud, in which a rather large number of very important Rabbinical authorities took part, about specific punishments for violation of a long list of very specific commandments (Tractate Sabbath 32b–33b of the Babylonian Talmud). To each transgression or sin, there corresponds a precisely determined evil, and vice versa: where there is an evil, it indicates a particular deed of the person who has been afflicted with this evil. In this context, the principle "measure for measure," as it is formulated in the Talmud, attained great significance. Certainly, such a measure of punishment which could correspond to the measure of the sin is not at once recognizable even by man, and thus the reservations toward casuistry, which is carried out in such a radical manner, still remain very effective. Here too the two great basic motifs of the religious conception of punishment are conflicting, as could hardly be avoided. One conception of punishment is that of a predictable and defined consequence of the sin. This is contrary to the other conception, which stresses as a moral motif the very unpredictability and incalculability of the consequences of sin. But that death has come into the world through sin and until the full realization of redemption is repeatedly called forth by sin—about this fact Rabbinical theology has hardly any doubt. This can be seen from the interpretations of the story of the Fall. An expansion of the myth of the Fall into the cosmic, and thus a mythical amplification of the punishment for Adam's sin, is not foreign to the popular homiletic exegesis of the Midrash. We hear, for example, that six things were withdrawn from Adam: his original luminosity, the original tremendous size of his figure, life, the fertility of the earth, the fertility of the trees, and the brightness of the heavenly lights, which, since then, have been dimmed. One formulation which has played a significant part in Jewish tradition and which speaks of a general cosmic consequence of Adam's sin goes still farther. It says: Although all things in the world were created in an original profusion in which their natures were completely revealed, after Adam's sin they have nevertheless been diminished and distorted. Moreover, they will not return to their former state until the coming of the Messiah. Thus here, too, there is a fallen state of nature in Judaic religious thought, a conception which could inspire no particular sympathy in the later apologists who had to defend Judaism rationally against the claims and assertions of Christian dogma. Therefore, outside of the Kabbalistic-mystical range of ideas, this notion of the fallen state of nature was readily interpreted away or twisted into something harmless or metaphorical.

In this world all punishments are terminal, no matter how horrible and comprehensive they may be. A saying which is repeatedly stressed in Jewish tradition asserts that the unfounded hate of the inhabitants of Jerusalem for each other entailed the destruction of Jerusalem as a consequence. In addition to such an immanent connection between sin and punishment there also appears in post-Biblical Judaism, probably from Iran, the conception of an other-worldly reward after death and of a Last Judgment. This conception then leads directly to the elaboration of the myths of Paradise and Hell. That the two completely different conceptions thus started to compete with each other is quite obvious. The delineation of this-worldly and other-worldly punishments has indeed always been difficult for the theologians and has always had something of the character of a desperate solution. With the acceptance of other-worldly punishments, and especially the Last Judgment, a religious feeling was satisfied for which the measure of this-worldly punishments seemed insufficient for the enormity of some crimes. Thus, a question was raised about the possibility or even absolute certainty of eternal damnation and eternal punishments which has assumed bitter forms both in Judaism and Christianity, even if in Judaism the forms have not been so dogmatically fixed and hardened as in the Catholic church. The utterances of the Jewish authorities always leave room here for completely contradictory answers among the Jews, and this question has remained open as long as the notion of Hell and everything associated with it possessed any vitality for the religious consciousness of the Jews. The eschatological ideas in Judaism were generally much more fluid than in Christianity and were capable of greater variation. This was advantageous even for the conceptions of the nature of the punishments in the other world and for the limited or unlimited duration of the punishments doled out at the Last Judgment. It is understandable that within the framework of these ideas Job's question about the prosperity of the wicked in this world and about the suffering of the just could also find a kind of answer, but hardly an answer which would have been acceptable to the author of the Book of Job. The just man suffers in this world in order to be rewarded in the next.

Finally, I would like to devote a few words to the ideas of the Jewish Kabbalists, the esoterics of Rabbinical Judaism. There are primarily two tendencies in which the originality of the Kabbalists has expressed itself in answering the question with which we are concerned here. For one thing, we are dealing here with a broadening of the significance of sin and its consequences which completely disregards that which the exoteric sources of historical Judaism advance about it. The essence of sin is seen here in the disruption of the cosmic harmony, in the destruction of an original unity in which not only God's severity and grace were in a harmonious balance but in which all areas of creation itself were also permeated with this harmony and man stood in unbroken communion with the Godhead. This communion consisted in the contemplation of the divine and its mysteries, of the unity of the living God which manifests itself in God's creative power. Adam's disobedience of the divine commandment was a decision which destroyed this communion and which was disastrous in its effect upon all creation. Sin produced separation where harmony and unity should reign; this is precisely its mysterious nature. "Punishment" in the usage of the Kabbalists is the isolation of things and of man from God. Man, who assimilated such isolation into his being and into his actions, creates a false, inauthentic view of reality. All the consequences of Adam's Fall and of man's sins are included in this basic understanding of the nature of sin as isolation. This is developed in the Kabbalists' mystical exegeses of Adam's sin. The Tree of Life and the Tree of the Knowledge of Good and Evil are, according to the Kabbalists, fundamentally one; they stem from a common root in that they represent the polarity of divine creative power whose tension is overcome in a higher unity. The Creative and the Reflective, the Giving and the Receiving, grow out of the same ground. Adam's task was to comprehend their unity, for life and knowledge must not be torn from one another; they must be recognized and realized in their unity. According to the Kabbalists, however, Adam separated the trees from one another. He thus isolated the power, namely, the principle of divine severity, which is operative in the Tree of the Knowledge of Good and Evil, and let it work upon him in isolation. The "punishment" in which the isolated knowledge now appears as an evil is nothing other than the consequence of this isolation. The taking away of the fruit, its separation from the Tree of Knowledge, is the symbol of this action which destroys unity. God's severity, his punitive justice, is now no longer restricted by the unbroken union with divine grace; it has almost been made autonomous and operates as an autonomous force of evil. To abolish this separation and disruption of the original state, apparent in the hardship of human entanglements in life, is the true mystical task of Israel. It can be realized only in redemption. The abolition of the separation, the myth of the Fall of man and the consequences brought about by all this has been completely interiorized here.

The later Kabbala, however, goes one step farther. Here the myth of Adam's Fall, which called forth disorder in the world, has been transferred to a still earlier event. In the development of divine creative power itself there is something which brought forth disharmony and disorder and the reign of divine severity long before the creation of the earthly Adam. In these theosophic speculations of the Kabbalists about the "breaking of the vessels" which God wanted to use during the Creation and which broke in his hands, there is of course not yet that which we would call a myth of punishment. But there is a myth of the origin of the isolated operation of punitive justice or punitive severity. This is a process which, as the Kabbalists say, occurred in the primordial man, in Adam Kadmon, the spiritual Adam. It did not occur in the first-created Adam, but in an emanation, an outpouring of divine potencies which exhibits a configuration of all these original powers in the figure of a spiritual primordial man in whose image the earthly Adam was created. Here we are dealing with a myth of the Fall, but really no longer with a myth of punishment. For in the sense of the Kabbalists this Fall itself was a deep necessity of a divine action which left the original infinity of God in order to act and to become effective in the finite. According to the Kabbalists, the infinite can operate unbroken and without conflicts only in the infinite itself. It is the nature of the decision to create which makes such a conflict-free action impossible; it must call forth an entanglement and disharmony in everything finite just because it is finite. But with this, I fear, we are already far away from the original point of departure of our Biblical consideration.

Another, more naïve, answer to the question about guilt and atonement was accepted by the Kabbalists when they took over the doctrine of transmigration of souls. In this doctrine there is, of course, an immanent theory of punishment and its application to the events of the world. The acceptance of the doctrine of reincarnation makes the acceptance of a Last Judgment or otherworldly reward basically superfluous. Actually, it is not an originally Jewish contribution to our problem, as significant as this notion has been in Kabbalistic Judaism. The transmigrations of the soul were understood here as the exile of the soul from its own human realm. Just as the exile of the body, which is most strikingly symbolized in the history of Israel, was punishment for sins, it is no less so for the exile of souls, which must purify themselves in long wanderings through human or even nonhuman realms because of sins which they have accumulated in their former human existences. These are a few of the most important ideas which I wanted to discuss here.

THE DEATH OF GAYŌMART

GEO WIDENGREN

I

In two previous articles I have tried to reconstruct some parts of the now lost *Sassanid Avesta* which belonged to the *Dāmdāt Nask*, one section (*nask*) of the *Avesta* which gave a relation of cosmology and anthropology as they appeared to Zoroastrians of Zervanite belief.[1] We call Zervanite that special type of Iranian religion in which Zervan, the God of Time and Destiny, was worshiped as the highest deity. Originally at home among the Magians of Media,[2] that very type of western Iranian religion was blended with the religion once preached by Zoroaster and in this syncretic form was propagated by the Parthian and Sassanian Mobads, the heirs of the old Magians.[3]

In the Sassanian canon of holy writings, the *Avesta*, the story of whose establishment as the Scriptures of the Sassanian Zoro-

[1] Geo Widengren, "Zervantische Texte aus dem 'Avesta' in der Pahlavi-Überlieferung: Eine Untersuchung zu Zātspram und Bundahišn," in *Festschrift W. Eilers* (1967); "Primordial Man and Prostitute," in *Studies in Mysticism and Religion*, a Festschrift for G. Scholem, ed. R. J. Zwi Werblowsky (Jerusalem, 1967). For *Dāmdāt Nask*, see W. Geiger and E. Kuhn, eds., *Grundriss der iranischen Philologie*, 2 vols. (Strassburg, 1895–1904), vol. 2, pp. 18, 20; R. Reitzenstein and H. H. Schaeder, *Studien zum antiken Synkretismus aus Iran und Griechenland* (Studien der Bibliothek Warburg VII), (Leipzig and Berlin, 1926), pp. 6–7, 11–12, 18–19; as early as E. W. West, trans., in F. Max Müller, ed., *Sacred Books of the East*, 50 vols. (Oxford, 1880), vol. 5, p. xxiv, with reference to *Zātspram*, IX 1, 16, *Bundahišn* is quoted as being from *Dāmdāt Nask*.

[2] Geo Widengren, *Die Religionen Irans* (Stuttgart, 1965), pp. 149–50 (French edition in preparation).

[3] For the Achemenid, Parthian, and Sassanian Magians, see Widengren, *Die Religionen Irans*, pp. 149–51, 214–16, 222, 255–56, 288–90.

astrian Church modern scholarship has tried to reconstruct,[4] it is a priori probable that Zervanite teachings once occupied a prominent place, for Christian polemics on the side of the Persian martyrs demonstrate sufficiently clearly that Zervanism was the dominant aspect of Sassanian Zoroastrianism against which the most violent attacks were launched by the Christians.[5] But in the now extant *Avesta* we seek in vain for Zervanite texts; even the name of Zervan himself is found only in a few passages, characteristically enough in a part of the *Avesta*, the *Vendidad*, which we can ascribe to the Median Magians. This fact must be due to an epuration of the *Avesta* carried out to remove such doctrines, which a later, more strictly orthodox Zoroastrian epoch considered heterodox. In my history of the religions of ancient Iran, I have tried to associate this epuration with the last redaction of the *Sassanid Avesta*, brought about during the reign of the great Xosrau Anōšurvān (531–79 A.D.).[6]

While we accordingly search in vain for Zervanite doctrines in the present *Avesta*, which is the fourth part of the original *Avesta* of Sassanian times, Pahlavi literature is full of Zervanite texts, though more or less tinged with Zoroastrianism. In his epochmaking investigations "Questions de cosmogonie et de cosmologie mazdéennes," H. S. Nyberg was the first scholar to edit and comment on an important series of Zervanite texts, chiefly the *Bundahišn*, chapters 1 and 3, and several chapters from the *Mēnōk i Xrat*, both valuable Pahlavi treatises containing much ancient material.[7] In pursuing this line of research Nyberg was following up a pioneer effort of Junker, who had convincingly shown the importance of Zervanite religion and speculation for the Hellenistic ideas of Aion,[8] and Schaeder, who in some particular points had investigated Mani's dependence on Zervanite beliefs.[9] I carried

4 Here the researches of Bailey, Nyberg, and Wikander have been of fundamental importance; see the essay of synthesis in Widengren, *Die Religionen Irans*, pp. 245–59.

5 Widengren, *Die Religion Irans*, pp. 255–56, 283–84.

6 *Ibid.*, pp. 256–68.

7 F. H. S. Nyberg, "Questions de cosmogonie et de cosmologie mazdéennes," *Journal Asiatique*, 214 (1929): 193–316; 219 (1931): 1–134, 193–244.

8 H. Junker, "Über iranische Quellen der hellenistischen Aion-Vorstellung," *Vorträge der Bibliothek Warburg*, 1 (1923).

9 H. H. Schaeder, *Urform und Fortbildungen des manichäischen Systems* (Leipzig, 1927), (originally in *Vorträge der Bibliothek Warburg*, 4 [1924–25]).

on this last line of research in my small book *Mani and Manichaeism*, and above all in a special article already alluded to in the introduction.[10]

In that article I was above all interested in the Zervanite passages of texts relating how the evil principle Ahriman (Ahra Mainyu in the *Avesta*) made an assault on the highest realms of light where the good principle, Ōhrmazd (Ahura Mazdā) had his residence, but was repulsed and hurled back into the lowest regions of darkness, his own abode. This story of the attack of the Evil Principle before the creation of the actual world constitutes the background of the corresponding Manichaean description of the battle of the Two Principles.[11]

The Manichaean relation puts Primordial Man, in the texts in Middle Iranian languages called Gēhmurd (Gaya Marta in the *Avesta*), in the very center of actions directed against the onslaught of the Evil Principle, in Manichaean Iranian tradition called Ahriman. The Pahlavi texts have many things to relate about his Zoroastrian counterpart Gayōmart (Gaya Marta),[12] but the fight he once waged against Ahriman is alluded to only cursorily. Nevertheless, it is obvious that Gayōmart fought intensely and heavily, for it is mentioned that Primordial Man had caused immense damage to the host of Ahriman and its leader.[13]

[10] Geo Widengren, *Mani and Manichaeism* (London, 1965), pp. 44 ff., 56 ff. (German edition, *Mani und der Manichäismus* [Stuttgart, 1961], pp. 51 ff., 60 ff., 70); and "Zervanitische Texte."

[11] Widengren, "Zervanitische Texte."

[12] On Gayōmart see the valuable collection of translated passages (the *Avesta* and Pahlavi texts especially are now somewhat antiquated in places as far as the philological treatment is concerned) in A. Christensen, *Les types du premier homme et du premier roi*, 2 vols. in one (Stockholm, 1917), vol. 1, pp. 11–101, and S. S. Hartman, *Gayōmart* (Uppsala, 1953), where an attempt was made to distinguish between various layers in the traditions. This attempt has not been received by the critics in a very positive way, although the collection of texts was warmly welcomed. I am convinced, however, that the approach of Hartman was sound in principle, even if I cannot follow him in his rather mathematical methods. The research work I devote to the same object is intended to supplement Hartman's pioneer efforts. Of course, I am not in a position to say for the present what the ultimate result will be.

[13] See *Bundahišn*, ed. and trans. Behramgore Tehmuras Anklesaria (Bombay, 1936), p. 17, verses 11–13; p. 70, verses 5–6; and for this problem see Hartman, *Gayōmart*, p. 33, as well as Widengren, "Primordial Man and Prostitute," and the short hint in my contribution, "Les origines du gnosticisme et l'histoire des religions," in *Studies in the History of Religions* (Supplement to *Numen*, 12 [1967]), pp. 18, 21.

The story of Gayōmart comprises the following episodes: his creation; his battle against Ahriman; his dealings with J̌ēh, the Demon-Whore; and his death. Of these episodes, the third was analyzed by me in an earlier article.[14] In the following pages I shall try to treat some aspects of the story of how Gayōmart met his fate, being killed by Ahriman. As in my two previous articles, my primary interest is in the possibility of reconstructing the Avestic background of this part of the story of Gayōmart. This approach is conditioned by the fact that, to ascertain the influence exercised in the ancient Near East by the Iranian idea of a Primordial Man, we must be sure of the date when this idea first appears in literature. This question of method is the more important as it has often been alleged that all the Iranian religious ideas of real importance for the history of religion as found in Pahlavi writings are of a very late date, definitely post-Sassanian.[15] That such allegations were never put forward by any scholar possessed of a first-hand knowledge of Pahlavi literature need not be emphasized.[16] Actually, we are in possession of very definite linguistic and stylistic criteria by means of which we are able to trace at least some of these Pahlavi passages back to now lost Avestic texts; this had already been pointed out by West, the great pioneer of Pahlavi studies, more than seventy years ago.[17] As I have mentioned most of these criteria in my earlier articles (which to some extent supplement each other in this regard), I shall not repeat them here but shall only say a few words about these criteria when actually using them in the following discussion.[18]

The texts relating the death of Gayōmart were edited and translated by Schaeder, and after him by Zaehner, who, in his well-

[14] Widengren, "Primordial Man and Prostitute."

[15] I have criticized this attitude in my contribution to the Messina colloquium on the origins of Gnosticism ("Les origines du gnosticisme et l'histoire des religions"), and, especially, in my "Zervanitische Texte."

[16] But in the publications of F. Duchesne-Guillemin, for example, we miss a clear statement that the Pahlavi texts are of fundamental importance for a historical understanding of Iranian religion. As early as the twenties, F. H. S. Nyberg saw the problem, as indicated by his words in the preface of his *Hilfsbuch des Pehlevi* (Uppsala, 1928), p. 3, where he says: "Fallen doch die brennendsten und wichtigsten Probleme nicht nur der iranischen Philologie und Linguistik, sondern der Orientalistik überhaupt zur Zeit in das mitteliranische Gebiet."

[17] E. W. West, trans., in E. F. Max Müller, *Sacred Books of the East*, vol. 37, pp. 31 ff., 469 n. 1.

[18] I refer to my contributions to the volumes presented to E. Eilers and G. Scholem (see note 1).

known book *Zervān*, collected, edited, translated, and analyzed all relevant texts of some importance to Zervanite religion. The reason that these texts are taken up again for a fresh study here and in not less than three earlier articles is due to the fact that I think it possible to analyze these texts from both linguistic and historical points of view in other ways than Zaehner has done. This difference of method has also led to different translations at several points, of which the more considerable ones are to be found in my previous articles. In the present article, where I have found it necessary, I have made observations on text and translation when I have differed from the reconstruction and translation of the text offered by Zaehner, whose presentation of the texts is presupposed everywhere.

II

Ahriman effects the death of Gayōmart by sending out the deity or demon of death, Astovihāt, against Gayōmart. This action of Ahriman is described in both the *Zātspram* and in the *Bundahišn*. We quote in the first instance the relevant passage in the *Zātspram* (IV 4–10 = K 35 237 r 8 – 237 r 12):

u-š apar frēstīt Astovihāt apāk 3,000 uzvārtān yaskān i xvat hēnd vīmārīh i gōnak gōnak ku-š vīmārēnēnd ut margēnēnd Gayōmart u-šān nē vindāt čārak, čē vičīr būt i brīnkar Zurvān pat bun andar āmatan i Ahriman ku apar ō 30 damistān Gayōmart i t<ak>īk hān i ǰān bōžišn frāč brihēnam.

And he sent out Astovihāt with 3,000 discernible diseases which are illnesses of different kinds, so that they could make Gayōmart ill and kill him, but they could find no means (of doing it), for it was the decision of the decree-deciding Zurvan in the beginning at the coming of Ahriman: "For 30 winters I decree for the valiant Gayōmart the salvation of life."

Observations on the Text:

The word *uzvārt* cannot possibly mean "chosen" as Zaehner translated it in *Zurvān* (p. 247). The root *var-* + *uz* is found in Middle Parthian.

To understand the construction of the sentence *čē vičīr būt*, etc., it is necessary to keep in mind that the following *ku* is dependent on *vičīr būt*. Therefore, *pat bun andar āmatan* gives the qualification of the time when this decision was taken. There is a slight discrepancy here from what is said in the *Bundahišn* passage. We shall revert to this problem later.

The short passage from the *Zātspram* just quoted betrays its Avestic origin in various ways: in the construction *u-š apar frēstīt Astovihāt*, the verb precedes the object; in the construction *ku-š vīmārēnēnd ut margēnēnd Gayōmart*, the verb again precedes the object; the place of the verb is also irregular in the construction *i xvat hēnd vīmārīh i gōnak gōnak*; the construction *Gayōmart i takīk hān i ǰān bōžišn frāč brihēnam* presupposes that *Gayōmart* is a virtual dative (cf. the Avestic construction with *baxš-* [+ *vi*], [cf. Chr. Bartholomae, *Altiranische Worterbüch* (Strassburg, 1904), p. 924; hereafter referred to as *AirWb*]). The syntactic construction is so forced that it cannot be taken as a normal Pahlavi alternative of the regular construction *hān i ǰān bōžišn i Gayōmart i takīk* or *hān i Gayōmart i takīk ǰān božišn*. The epithet *brīnkar* renders Avestic *θwarəštar-* (*AirWb* 798, cf. *Y*.57:2) with the verb *θwarəs-* (AirWb 795–96), rendered in the Pahlavi translation by means of *brītan* or *brihēnītan*. We meet with the correspondence *θwarəštar* ~ *brinkār* not only in *Y*.57:2, but also, for example, in *Y*.42:2. Here *AirWb* 798 is wrong, giving as the Pahlavi translation *āfrīnkar*.

For *frāč brihēnīt* in the Pahlavi Yasna the original Avestic text (*Y*.71:6) has *fraθwaršta*, and therefore we may assume that behind *frāč brihēnam* there was such an Avestic form as the verb *fra-θwars-*, which is constructed with the dative (cf. *AirWb* s.v.). This verb is used in Yt13:56 in the sentence *fraθwarštəm paiti zrvānəm*. It is important to observe that Zervan accordingly is given this verb as an expression of his activity. Behind the Pahlavi expressions *Zurvān*, respectively *zamān* with *brihēnītan* or *brīnkar*, we have therefore to surmise the Avestic *Zrvan* with *fraθwars-* or *θwarəštar*. Our conclusion, then, will be that behind this passage in the *Zātspram* there was originally a Pahlavi translation of an Avestic text, now lost.

The second passage is as follows (*Bundahišn*, ed. Anklesaria, pp. 44:12–45:1):

u-š Gannāk Mēnōk mēnd ku-m dāmān i Ōhrmazd hamāk akārēnīt hēnd yut hač Gayōmart,
u-š Astovihāt apāk 1,000 dēv i margīh-kartārān pat Gayōmart frāč hišt u-šān zamān tāi brīn nē <mat ēstāt>, ōžatan čārak nē ayāft, čiγōn

gōβēt ku pat bun i dahišn kaδ Gannāk Mēnōk ō patyārakīh mat zamān hān i Gayōmart zīvandakīh ut xvatāyīh ō 30 sāl brihēnīt.

And the Evil Spirit thought: "All the creatures of Ōhrmazd have I made of no effect save (only) Gayōmart."

And he let loose upon Gayōmart Astovihāt with 1,000 death-bringing demons, but for them the time had not yet come to decision and they found no means of slaying (him), as it is said that in the beginning of the creation, when the Evil Spirit came to attack, Time decreed for 30 years the life and rulership of Gayōmart.

Observations on the Text:

If we now compare the sentence in *Bundahišn* 44::12–13, *u-š Āstovihāt apāk 1,000 dēv i margīh-kartārān pat Gayōmart frāč hišt*, with the corresponding passage in *Zātspram* K 35 237 r 8–9, *u-š apar frēstīt Astovihāt apak 3,000 uzvārtān yaskān . . . ku-š vīmārēnēnd ut margēnēnd Gayōmart*, we note, besides the general agreement, *one* characteristic detail: the syntactic construction in *Bundahišn* is absolutely normal, the verb *frāč hišt* being placed at the end of the sentence; in *Zātspram*, on the other hand, the verb *apar frēstīt* (as already observed) has its place before the object, *Astovihāt*, thus revealing its Avestic origin. Therefore, it is obvious that the relation in *Zātspram* is the older and more original one, as was the case also in the passages treated by me in previous articles, although traces of Avestic constructions were found in the *Bundahišn* texts.

The comparison also demonstrates that from the syntactic point of view we should translate as I have done and not as Zaehner did (*Zervān*, p. 247): "Astovihāt was sent against him," etc., in the *Zātspram* passages. Of course, this is a mere trifle, but syntactic questions in this case are of importance for our method of reconstructing possible Avestic passages, and for this reason they cannot be left out of consideration.

The duration of Gayōmart's life is mentioned in another passage of *Bundahišn* where we read the following notice (*Bundahišn*, ed. Anklesaria, pp. 68:13–69:6 [= Paris Suppl. Pers. 2043, p. 73: 6–10]):

šašom artīk Gayōmart kart hač hān čiγōn pat spihr i Gayōmart paitāk būt ku andar aβigatīh pat kōxšišn i axtarān ut apāxtarān 30 sāl zīvast *čiγōn guft Zamān pēš hač aβigat<īh>ku Gayōmart i takīk ō 30 damistān zīvandakīh ut xvatāyīh brihēnīt.*

The sixth battle Gayōmart fought because of the reason that in the horoscope of Gayōmart it was revealed that he would live for 30 years during the period of assault when the stars and planets are involved in strife as Time said before the assault: "For the valiant Gayōmart for 30 winters life and rulership is decreed."

If we compare the two essential passages concerning the duration of Gayōmart's life the following table is presented:

Zātspram	*Bundahišn*
apar ō 30 damistan Gayōmart i takīk hān i ǰān božišn frāč brihēnam.	*Gayōmart i takīk ō 30 damistān zīvandakīh ut xvatāyīh brihēnīt.*

There can hardly be any doubt that the common source of *Zātspram* and *Bundahišn*, utilized by both writings, reads in this passage:

apar ō 30 damistān Gayōmart i takīk frāč brihēnam,

which was followed by some expression for "life." That this sentence was expressed in the first person singular, as is the case in *Zātspram*, would seem to be obvious because this decree is put in the mouth of Zurvān in the relation given in *Zātspram*; therefore, in this case too, *Zātspram* has preserved more or less the original Pahlavi wording. This saying *Bundahišn* has rendered in the third person singular, still using, however, the verb *brihēnītan.* The expression employed in *Zātspram, hān i ǰān bōzišn*, would seem to be slightly more poetic than the more prosaic *zīvandakīh* in *Bundahišn* and therefore might reflect the original expression. On the other hand, it is rather tempting to assume that *xvatāyīh* in *Bundahišn* represents a supplementary notion, since Gayōmart was not only Primordial Man but also Primordial King according to the traditions left to us.[19]

The comparison between the two texts also demonstrates that

[19] See the texts in Christensen, *Les types du premier homme*, pp. 66 ff., and the discussion on pp. 88–91. It is certainly important to observe that already in the *Mandaean Ginza*, in that section of Iranian legendary history which was taken over by the Mandaeans, Gayōmart is conceived of as a ruler of Iran (see M. Lidzbarski, *Ginzā* [Göttingen and Leipzig, 1925], p. 411). The enumeration of Iranian legendary and historical kings given in *Ginzā* is the oldest extant list of such rulers.

we have to understand the syntactic construction as given in my translation above (which agrees with that of Schaeder and not that of Zaehner), for *ku* clearly introduces the direct speech. This further implies a Pahlavi translation preserved in *Bundahišn* as in *Zātspram* because of the verb's position.

III

Gayōmart's death is described in *Bundahišn* in two passages of similar content. They are found in *Bundahišn*, ed. Anklesaria, pp. 69:12–70:2 (= Paris Suppl. Pers. 2043, p. 74:7–12) and *ibid.*, p. 100:7–15 (= Paris Suppl. Pers. 2043, pp. 113:11–224:7). If we compare these two passages we must change the place of two sentences in the second passage to facilitate the comparison. In the table given below this adjustment is pointed out in the text.

Bundahišn 69:12–70:2	*Bundahišn* 100:7–15
(kaδ) Gayōmart margīh apar mat pat hōy dast ōpast. andar bē vitīrišnīh tōxm andar +*ō damīk šut, čiγōn, nūnič andar vitīrišnīh hamāk martōm tōxm bē rēčēnd. hač hān čiγōn tan i Gayōmart hač ayōkšust kart ēstāt, hač tan i Gayōmart 7 aδvēnak ayōkšust ō paitākīh mat.*	*kaδ Gayōmart vīmārīh apar mat pat hōy dast ōpast. 2. kaδ Gayōmart andar vitīrišnīh tōxm bē dāt, hān tōxm pat rōšnīh i xvaršēt bē pālūt hēnd u-š 2 bāhr Nēryōsang nikās dāšt ut bāhr-ē Spandarmat patiγraft. 1. hač sar sruβ ut hač xōn arčīč ut hač mazgəsēm ut hač pāy asēn ut hač astak rōy ut hač pīh āpagēnak ut hač gōšt pōlāt ut hač ǰānbē-šavišn zarr ō paitākīh āmat.*
(When) . . . death came upon Gayōmart, he fell on his left side. At his passing away (his) seed went into the earth – as even now all men at (their) passing away emit (their) seed. Because of the fact that the body of Gayōmart was made out of metal, from the body of Gayōmart came forth seven kinds of metal.	When sickness came upon Gayōmart, he fell on his left side. 2. When Gayōmart at his passing away gave away (his) seed, that seed was purified in the light of the sun: two parts of it Nēryōsang took care of and one part Spandarmat received. 1. From his head lead came forth, from his blood zinc, from his marrow silver, from his feet iron, from his bones brass, from his fat, crystal, from his flesh steel, and from his soul at its departing gold was visible.

Observations on the Text:

At the beginning of these two passages we meet with a remarkable syntactic construction: (*kaδ*) *Gayōmart margīh apar mat* or *kaδ Gayōmart vīmārīh apar mat*, in both cases followed by *pat hōy dast ōpast*. This fact demonstrates a very fixed tradition, for it is of no great importance whether *margīh* or *vīmārīh* belongs to the original and authentic tradition – arguments could be invoked in favor of either variant and it could be argued that both expressions had their place in the Avestic tradition. What is really significant is that this tradition is preserved in both passages in almost exactly the same wording and that the first part of the tradition exhibits a syntactic construction which at once attracts our interest. We should compare the construction found here, *apar matan* with the virtual dative, to two different types of syntactic construction in the Pahlavi language, one with the same structure as this example and another provided with prepositional expressions. I give below some illustrative examples of both constructions.[20]

I. With virtual dative
  A. With *apar matan*
    1. *hān čiγōn-aš patyārak apar mat, pat gyāk murt*, said of Gayōmart (*AZ* IV 4).
    2. *ut vas hān i drōγdātastān i-š apar mat ēstēt* (Bahman Yt. II 44).
    3. *hakar-at hač kas muštōmandih apar mat* (*PT*, p. 70: 1–2).
  B. With *apar rasītan*
    1. *čē-t aβdom margīh rasēt* (*MX* II 111).
    2. *ut hakar dēn bē nē hilēt . . . -aδak-tān apar rasēm* (Abyātkar i Z. 12).
    3. *ku-š im astvandy tany husravīhy ut āpatīhy rasāt u-š avē astvandy ruvān artāyīhy apar rasāt* (Karter, *KZ* 19; not correctly rendered in Sprengling's publication[21]), which means: "in order that good reputation and fortune may come to this corporeal body and that righteousness may come to this corporeal soul" (cf. *Karter NiR* 20–21, where the same expression is found).
  C. With *apar nihātan*
    či-m dast apar nihāt (*PN* 18:10–11).

[20] Because of the scope of the present volume I have restricted myself to what seemed to me absolutely necessary, but I hope to return to the subject in a wider context.

[21] M. Sprengling, *Third Century Iran, Sapor and Kartir* (Chicago, 1953), p. 53, where he translates rather freely: "in order that he may attain. . . ."

In all these cases the enclitic pronoun *-t*, *-tān*, and *-š* represents the oblique case and therefore also the dative, as pointed out by Nyberg (*Hilfsbuch des Pehlevi*, vol. 2, p. 210), with some references to the texts given in his chrestomathy, of which *MX* II 111 and *PN* 18:10–11 have been quoted here.

D. With *apar nišāstan*
ēvak xvat ut ēvak kanīčak apar nišāst (*KN* II 15, cf. *mā arvandān apar nišast*, Y. 11, 2, 8). In this case *ēvak* is the representative of the oblique case, corresponding to a construction **pat ēvak apar nišāst*.

II. With preposition

A. With *apar āmatan* in Middle Parthian
Gwrtnyws Kysr . . . apar Aryan xšatr u amāh āmat (*Šāhpuhr KZ* 3), *apar amāh āmat* (*KZ* 9).

B. With *ō matan*
kaδ patyārak ō dām mat nazdist ō gāv<mat>. kaδ ō Gayōmart mat, murt pat gyāk (*Abyātkar* i Z. III 15–16; the position of *murt* at the beginning of the apodosis shows the sentence to come from a Pahlavi translation of an Avestic text). It is interesting to compare the sentence quoted above (I. A. 1.), *čiγōn-aš patyārak apar mat*, with *kaδ (patyārak) ō Gayōmart mat*. This comparison would seem to show that even in a passage coming from a Pahlavi translation of an Avestic text one was rather inclined to prefer a construction with preposition, when there would be another oblique case, to an enclitic pronoun, as even the proper name Gayōmart. Hence we may conclude that, in the two passages quoted above, *Gayōmart margīh apar mat* and *kaδ Gayōmart vīmārīh apar mat*, when the construction without preposition is employed, it means that an Avestic text was used on which the translator felt dependent. To the sentence *pat hōy dast ōpast* we may add from *Abyātkar* i Z. III 16, *murt pat gyāk*, because it comes from an Avestic text.

The expression *apar āmat* (*mat*) obviously renders Avestic *upā.ǰasaṯ*, as we can see, for example, from the following passage (*Y*. 30:6), where we read:

hyaṯ īš ādəbaomā pərəsmānəng upā, ǰasaṯ
Upon whom, taking counsel together there came delusion,

which is rendered in the Pahlavi translation in the following way:

kē-č avēšān frēft ō pursišn apar mat hēnd
who even deceived came to questioning.

We may also compare such passages as *Y.* 45:5 and *Vd.* 6:27.

IV

In the traditions about Gayōmart's death only fragmentary remnants of a once much richer mythic story have been preserved. Above all, his fight against Ahriman and the demons has been alluded to only in a short passage in the now extant texts, as was stated in our introductory remarks. On the other hand, as we have seen, his passing from life is described in some detail. Among these details, one of the most interesting is surely that he is said to have possessed a body made of metal, so that at his death eight metals came forth from his body. These metals are lead, zinc, silver, iron, brass, crystal, steel, and gold. Accordingly, both in *Bundahišn and Zātspram*, not seven, but eight metals are mentioned, the eighth being gold, the most noble metal, which incarnates the Ego of Primordial Man, as Schaeder very aptly observed. This is quite in agreement with a well-known Iranian way of counting.[22] As early as 1907 Bousset had a clear understanding of the implications of this relation of Gayōmart's death, associating the metals with the planets.[23] Reitzenstein later followed up this conclusion.[24] What is perhaps still more important is the fact that Gayōmart, as the possessor of the seven metals, is also possessed of the metals which represent the seven ages of the world, according to a tradition preserved in *Bahm. Yt.* II. This is because of his macrocosmic character, duly noted by Bousset. Therefore, it can be said (as it is in both *MX* XXVII 18 and *Dāt. i Dēn* LXIV 7) that the metals exist from the body of Gayōmart.[25] Gayōmart is a counterpart of the macrocosmos and from him mankind has inherited the character of being a microcosmos. This immensely important speculation will not be considered here.

I shall only take up for consideration the date of this idea of

[22] H. H. Schaeder, *Studien zum antiken Synkretismus aus Iran und Griechenland*, pp. 228–29.

[23] See W. Bousset, *Hauptproblems der Gnosis* (Göttingen, 1907), pp. 206–7, where he pointed out that the metals represent the seven planets.

[24] R. Reitzenstein, *Studien zum antiken Synkretismus*, pp. 18–19, 45.

[25] This was noted already by Bousset, *Hauptproblems der Gnosis*, p. 206, where he emphasized Gayōmart's cosmic nature.

the metals as contained within the body of Gayōmart. The problem here is our usual one: can Pahlavi tradition in this case too be traced back to an Avestic text, now lost? In order to answer this question we shall compare the two relevant passages from *Bundahišn* and *Zātspram*:

Bundahišn 100:8–10
hač sar sruβ ut hač xōn arčīč ut
hač mazg asēm ut hač pāy āsen ut
hač astak rōy ut hač pīh āpagēnak
ut hač gōst pōlāvat ut hač ǰān-bē-
šavišn zarr ō paitākīh amāt.

Zātspram X 2 = K 35 243 v. 5–8
kaδ viturt ayōkšust-čihr 8 aδvenak
ayōkšust hač handām handām bē
būt hēnd i hast zarr ut asēm ut
āsen ut rōy ut arčīč ut sruβ ut
āpagēnak ut almās. pahrōmih i
zarr rāδ hač gyān ut tōxm dātīhēt.
viturt Gayōmart, zarr Spa<n>dar-
mat frāč patiγraft.

Observations on the Text:

The two lists (as has been duly observed in previous research on these lists) are arranged according to two different principles: *Bundahišn* starts with the head and ends with the soul, whereas *Zātspram* enumerates the metals in an order corresponding to their values. Both texts are obviously fragmentary, and, for this reason, supplementary. *Bundahišn* tells us from what parts of the body the metals come while *Zātspram*, which in this case is shorter, gives details about the most precious metal, gold – where and by whom it was received after the death of Gayōmart.

Schaeder's translation of the first sentence in the *Zātspram* passage is impossible for philological reasons. He translates it as "Als er verschied, entstanden (wegen seiner) Matallnatur acht Arten Metalle aus seinen einzelnen Gliedern, das sind Gold," etc., putting a stop after *viturt* (read by him *viδard*) and misreading in *i hast zarr* the ideogram *'YT* as *ē* (which of course is a mere trifle). Here Schaeder has been forced to put in brackets in his translation what ought to be expressed in the Pahlavi text in some way or another, for example, by means of the postposition *rāδ*, actually employed a bit farther on in the same text.

Another way has therefore been tried. Starting from the observation that the verb *viturt* is placed after the conjunction *kāδ* at the very beginning of the sentence, it may be possible to assume that this passage, like so many others in *Zātspram*, is based on an Avestic "Vorlage." In that case *ayōkšust-čihr* would reflect an

Avestic composite noun *ayoxšusta . čiθra-*, "he whose seed (origin) is metal." We find in the language of the *Avesta* many composite nouns where *čiθra-* enters as the second part of the noun; these are registered in *AirWb* 1946, middle col. *s.v. čiθra-*. We have no noun composed with *ayōxšusta-*, but two with "fire," *ātar-*: *ātrə . čiθra-* and *ātars . cirθra-*. From the Avestic point of view, then, the idea in itself is quite acceptable. Accordingly, we may solve the difficulty by assuming that the translator has mechanically rendered *ayōxšusta . ciθra-* by *ayōkšust-čihr*, an epithet well fitted for Gayōmart, whose origin, *ciθra-*, as we learn from the texts, is metal, *ayōxšusta-* (*AirWb* 162), or, properly speaking, "molten metal," which is quite natural if metal was assumed to be the liquid of Gayōmart's body. It may be added here that composite nouns where *čihr* is the second element are produced in New Persian.[26] It is generally assumed after Christensen that the series of seven metals represents a Babylonian influence.[27] This is most probable because of its association with the seven planets, but this does not speak against an Iranian origin of the idea itself, that is, that Primordial Man had metals as his corporeal liquids. Eliade, who has quoted the *Zātspram* passage, has a good reference to *Śatapatha Brāhmana* XII 7, 1, 7.[28] Here it is said about Indra (*SBE* XLIV, p. 215):

> From the navel his life-breath flowed, and became lead – not iron, nor silver; from his seed his form flowed, and became gold.

It is evident that the same type of archaic speculation underlies both the Indian and the Iranian conceptions, and we have therefore to do with a very ancient Indo-Iranian idea which, however,

[26] See F. Wolff, *Glossar* (Berlin, 1935), p. 894, col. *s.v. čihr.*

[27] Christensen, *Les types du premier homme*, pp. 52–53. Therefore, he assumed the eighth metal, which he put as diamond (so he translated *almās*, but see note 28 below), to have been added afterwards, finding support in the fact that *Bundahišn* gives a list of *seven* metals in the passage (p. 70; 1 f). But Schraeder obviously found that correct explanation; see note 21 above.

[28] M. Eliade, *Forgerons et Alchimistes* (Paris, 1956), p. 73 (where I suppose *Śatapatha Brahmana* XXI is a misprint for *ŚB* XII where the relevant passage actually is found as indicated above in the text). The names of the metals in the Pahlavi texts need some comments. For *āpagēnak* see H. W. Bailey, *Zoroastrian Problems in Ninth-Century Books* (Oxford, 1943), pp. 131–32; for *almās* see *ibid.*, p. 134 (steel, as indeed Schaeder already saw); for *āsen* this reading has been accepted following Bailey; the term *pōlāvat* is a NW word, one of the few sure NW words in the group of Pahlavi texts treated in this article.

has undergone the influence of Babylonian astrological speculation according to which the metals were associated with the planets.

V

The death of Gayōmart, the episode whose literary prehistory we have tried to analyze, had already received its literary fixation in the *Sassanid Avesta*. But it did not leave as many traces of its Avestic origin as the other text groups dealing with cosmological and anthropological ideas, which I dealt with in my preceding articles. As I have noted, this is due to the fact that only very fragmentary remains are left of a once much richer tradition. Nevertheless, there are unmistakable traces of the *Avesta* tradition both in ideas and in the linguistic heritage of Avestic syntactic constructions. This Avestic tradition is clearly Zervanite in its tendency, showing typical syncretic traits (Babylonian influences). Moreover, the present Pahlavi tradition does not derive from a single source, as is shown by the different lists of metals, which differ in the numbers seven or eight and the names of the various metals.[29] It is highly instructive to observe further that the name of Zervan is still preserved in the *Zātspram* but not in the *Bundahišn*. Contrary to what I have done in former articles, it has not been possible here to reconstruct the original story of Gayōmart's death as it was found in the Zervanite book *Dāmdāt Nask* in the *Sassanid Avesta*.

[29] The list in *Bahman-Yašt* II, 44 has only seven metals, among which *brinj* is included instead of *sruβ*, whereas *āpagēnak* is lacking. *Zātspram* has *almās* where *Bundahišn* has *pōlāvat*. Presumably we have to do with at least three different lines of tradition.

SYMBOL OF A SYMBOL

ANGELO BRELICH

In spite of its title, the present study is not intended as a contribution to the discussion of theoretical questions relating to symbols. Rather, as we shall see, it is connected with observations which the scholar whom we are celebrating in this book has dedicated, on several occasions, to the symbolism of initiation. The subject, of which we shall try to show a peculiar historical application, allows the author to express his gratitude to Mircea Eliade, whose work has continuously stimulated and enriched him.

It is known that while human sacrifices were very rare in ancient Greece, they recur in an enormous number of Greek myths. This singular discrepancy between ritual praxis and myth is generally interpreted in the sense that myths would retain the memories of a more ancient epoch wherein human sacrifices were conducted more frequently.[1] On the basis of extant documents, however, one would have difficulties in exactly identifying this epoch: certainly, it was not the Mycenaean, for which neither texts,[2] representations, nor results of excavations[3] furnish any documentary

[1] See, for example, L. Ziehen under *Opfer*, col. 588 in Pauly-Wissowa, *Realencyklopädie der klassischen Alterumswissenschaft*, 16 vols. (Stuttgart, 1894 to date); M. P. Nilsson, *Geschichte der griechischen Religion*, 2 vols., 2d ed. (Munich, 1955–61), vol. 1, p. 23.

[2] The tablets which record the offering of a man or a woman to a divinity (for example, Tn 316, from Pylos) certainly do not allude to human sacrifices: the offer is put on the same plane and is mentioned in the same context with the offering of precious objects which, obviously, are not "sacrificed." Since the Mycenaean tablets know the institution of the "slaves of the divinity," it is plausible to think that the persons offered were destined to this function, or, in any case, to occupations pertaining to the service of the gods.

[3] Findings of human bones (besides the ones of the buried) in tombs of the Mycenaean epoch were interpreted as traces of human funerary sacrifices. But as early as 1955, after synthesizing the results of the most recent studies,

evidence. To claim that we may refer to an even older epoch would be gratuitous and also unlikely; the Greek myths, which speak of human sacrifices, reflect religious and cultural conditions quite different from those of the Middle or Early Helladic Period.

Certainly it is probable that a myth of human sacrifice would not develop in a culture which would totally ignore such a practice. Nevertheless, it is arbitrary to deduce the frequency—in any epoch—of a practice from the quantity of the related myths. There is an alternative solution: the Greeks were parsimonious in sacrificing human victims even though they had the experience of human sacrifice and utilized it on the mythical plane. The Greek myths are not relics of remote cultural epochs: they are *significant* myths for the historical epoch which retains them in function.

There are several ways in which a myth can function in a society. Here, however, we shall limit ourselves to just one case type which will not require too many comments or discussions because it is generally known: that of myths connected with cults. These myths are often defined as "aetiological." We do not want to exclude here the possibility that there are pseudo-myths too (the argument is more complicated than it may seem), but it will suffice to say for now that several Greek myths connected with cults are "aetiological" only in that sense in which every myth is aetiological: in other words, they are myths which "found" a reality by telling its origin, that is, the *aition* of the very cultural institution to which they refer themselves. Foundation-myths of cults and rituals exist in the most various religions and there is no cogent reason why just the Greek myths should always be pseudo-myths.

A myth of human sacrifice can relate itself to a cult in various ways. Even among these we shall make a choice. For example, we shall omit those cases where the myth directly concerns the recipient of the cult: a certain hero or heroine must have a cult because, in mythical times, he or she was sacrificed (e.g., the daughters of Leos, the Hyakinthides, Marathon, etc.). Let us now say briefly and without argument that in this case the cult of

Nilsson (*Geschichte*, pp. 178, 376 and n. 3) affirms that the only case in which there are "sure traces" of that institution is represented by the royal tombs of Dendra, excavated by A. Persson. Today, however, not even these traces are considered sure or probable; see G. Mylonas, *Mycenae and the Mycenaean Age* (Princeton, 1966), pp. 116–17, 128–29.

a person conceived as a sacrificial victim (killed, in mythical times, to overcome a crisis situation) wants to perpetuate the benefits which the killing of a human victim brings to the community; one does not kill human victims, one worships—with regular cultual acts—a particular hero, and it is the myth which, presenting the hero himself as a sacrificial victim, specifies the meaning and function of the cult.

We shall instead dwell on another case, one in which the myth of human sacrifice does not involve the recipient of the cult, but rather the forms of the ritual. According to some myths, the cults to which they refer demanded human victims "in the beginning" or now "commemorate" a killing which took place in a remote past (actually, in mythical times). Several scholars believe—as did also the Greeks—that in these cases one really deals with the "substitution" of ancient human sacrifices; therefore, the "aetiological" account would, in these cases, have a historical value and conversely it would have no mythical, that is, religious, value.

Pausanias (9, 8, 2) tells that at Potniai, in Boeotia, there was a temple dedicated to Dionysos Aigobolos ("the one who strikes goats"):

> Once upon a time, while sacrificing to Dionysos, the people, under the influence of wine, became so violent that they killed the priest of the god. Immediately after, an epidemic struck the murderers and from Delphi came the cure, which consisted in sacrificing an adolescent to Dionysos. Not many years later, they say, the god substituted a goat, as a victim, for the youth.

The basic scheme of the story—transgression, calamity, consultation of the oracle, foundation of a cult—which is common to numerous cultual myths of Greece, would suffice by itself to tell us that we are not dealing with a historical happening.[4] The cult of a god—a god who with his epithet qualifies himself as the recipient of goat sacrifices, including the sacrifice of a goat, is a historical reality. But the myth affirms that the sacrifice of goats is the substitution for a human sacrifice, an extreme remedy for a crisis provoked by a misdeed. The real cult, like any cult, is a means to maintain order, to prevent it from falling back into chaos (which the myth concretizes in the catastrophe—the plague—

[4] I examined a particular category of these myths in *Studi e materiali di-soria delle religioni*, 30 (1959): 247–48.

against which the cult itself is said to have been instituted). The cult culminates in the immolation of a goat which the myth presents as a substitution for the human sacrifice; this means that the myth – organically belonging to the cult – has the function of rendering the sacrifice of a goat *equivalent* to a human sacrifice (fully equivalent, because the god himself institutes it as such). Starting from the myth, the sacrifice of a goat appears as a "symbol" of the human sacrifice, but in this case the myth does not have an existence independent from the cult: the myth is the origin-myth of the cult (which implies the sacrifice of a goat); it is therefore the (mythical) human sacrifice that constitutes an equivalent of the (real) sacrifice of goats, thus defining its very significance.

Let us move to a different case, which, however, will refer us to an analogous function of the idea (rather than the praxis) of human sacrifice. At Tegea they used to say (Paus. 8, 53, 2 sq.) that Leimon, son of the eponymous hero Tegeates, killed his brother Skephros, whom he suspected of slandering him to Apollon, who, in Artemis' company, was visiting the city; as a punishment, Artemis would have killed Leimon with an arrow. In spite of the sacrifices that Tegeates and his wife offered to the two gods, a great sterility struck the country; the oracle of Delphi ordered funeral rites for Skephros, which were included in the festivities of Apollon Agyieus. During the rites of this festivity, the priestess runs after a man. This action is understood as a *mimesis* of the chase of Leimon by Artemis. Although a human sacrifice as such does not even appear in the myth – at least in the form in which the myth has been recorded by Pausanias – and we are told instead of a killing done as a punishment, the case is not without analogy to the one previously recorded: a catastrophe is avoided by the institution of a rite conceived as the equivalent of a killing. In other words, a myth of "killing" originates the rite of pursuit.

There are several rites of pursuit in Greece, but we will mention here only one other which has an explicit link – this time not purely mythical – with the killing of human victims. In the Agrionia of Orchomenos, Dionysos' priest would chase with a sword a group of women labeled with a collective name and conceived as descendants of the Minyades (Minyas' daughters, who, struck by Dionysian frenzy, would have killed one of their sons). It was provided, according to Plutarch (*Quaestoines Graecae*,

38 = 299F) that the priest would really kill that woman whom he would have been able to catch during the pursuit. Plutarch also mentions that during his own times a priest named Zoilos actually killed one of the women during the rite. The consequences of his act, however, turned out to be negative: Zoilos himself died after long suffering of a wound he had received and the citizens of Orchomenos, severely judged for this institution, deprived Zoilos' family of the hereditary priestly dignity. We may ask ourselves why the fulfillment of his duty as required by the rite would bring catastrophic consequences for the priest, contempt for the community, and dismissal of the priest's entire family from the cult. Above all, one will ask, why did the entire episode assume such exceptional importance if it was provided by the norms of the cult: was it perhaps so difficult for a man to catch one of the women in flight that – although it was a yearly rite – this almost never occurred? Everything leads us to think that even the chase in the Agrionia was only "symbolic," as was the one in the feast of Tegea. This norm of the cult perhaps existed only to be regularly evaded because its *significance* was sufficient: it was the "equivalent" of a human sacrifice.[5] In some cases this significance was rendered concrete by a cultual myth; in others it was suggested and introduced by a fictitious cultual norm. Again, in other cases this significance was realized in a different manner: at Tenedos they worshiped Dionysos Anthroporrhaistes ("the one who tears men to pieces"); his sacrificial victim, however, was not a human being but a young calf.[6] Also, its mother, the cow, was treated *as a human being*, a newly delivered mother, and the young calf was made to wear buskins. The killer of the calf would become a fugitive, chased by a shower of stones tossed by the people *as if* he had in reality killed a human

[5] As in the case of the so-called sophism of the Thessalians (Zenob. 4, 29) which consisted of a human hecatomb dedicated to Apollon Katabaisios and was regularly postponed from year to year. Also, a case like the one already mentioned by Herodotus (7, 197) and later quoted in the pseudo-Platonic *Minos* (315 C), together with the sacrifices to Zeus Lykaios, exactly as an example that Greeks used human sacrifices, raises doubts: the oldest of the descendants of the mythical Athamas had to be sacrificed *if* he entered the prytaneion. It is easy to guess that he never entered it; the cultic norm thus retained its value even if it was never put into practice.

[6] This is independent of the question of whether at Chios, Dionysos, with the epithet Omadios, would actually receive human sacrifices through quartering, as stated (but perhaps through deduction from the name or a myth, as frequently happens in later authors) in Porphyr. *Abst.* 2, 55.

being (Aelianus, *De natura animalium*, 12, 34). In this case the epithet of the god and the double ritual simulation (treating the victim as a human and the sacrificator's flight) concur in establishing that the significance of the rite is that of a human sacrifice.

We establish then that the Greeks knew human sacrifice[7] and that, as their myths show, they knew on which occasions it was necessary to resort to it.[8] In most cases, however, they would find a way to "realize" it without really executing it: it sufficed that an expedient would render some ritual action *equivalent* to the human sacrifice. Such an expedient could also be a *myth* presenting the ritual action as a "substitution" of the killing of a human victim. In many cases myth and ritual action constitute an organic whole, the value of which is that of human sacrifice and which, therefore, could be defined as a "symbol" of human sacrifice. Up to this point the facts are peculiar, but clear. There exist, however, cases only apparently belonging to the types mentioned above, which I wish to consider now.

At Sparta, the flagellation of the adolescents[9] in front of the altar of Artemis Orthia had its own foundation-myth (Paus. 3, 16, 9, ff.): On one occasion, while sacrificing to the goddess, the men of the four "quarters" of Sparta started a brawl; many of them died by the same altar while the remainder fell victim to an epidemic. This scourge, if we keep in mind numerous analogous myths, must be considered as the punishment of the goddess, of-

[7] Or other forms of "ritual killings": we retain here the distinction, already proposed by several authors (Crawley, Schwenn, Henninger, etc.) between properly called human sacrifices — those offered to some superhuman recipient — and other rites which may require the killing of human beings without belonging to the cult of superhuman beings. The value of this distinction goes well beyond the purely terminological plane. In Greece, besides the few cases (and none beyond doubt) of periodic human sacrifices and some other occasional ones (such as the one of the three Persian prisoners sacrificed by Themistocles to Dionysos Omestes), nonsacrificial killings existed, like the one of the *pharmakoi* in some Greek cities.

[8] In those cultural areas where ritual killings are practiced, they are usually connected with the same occasions: funeral rites, foundation and purification rites, agricultural rites, rites for the rain, rites celebrated on occasion of calamities of various sorts, wars, etc. Now, almost all of these occasions are mentioned in the Greek myths of human sacrifice.

[9] I have studied the cases briefly illustrated in the following pages and have provided a detailed discussion of the entire documentation in a volume which is now in preparation. I am limiting myself here to the mention of those details which are relevant to the subject at hand.

fended by the sacrilegious behavior of the brawlers (that is, of the city itself, which they represented in its totality—the four quarters). Indeed, as in analogous cases, the city consults the oracle to find out how to expiate the crime. The oracle orders it to "wet the altar with human blood" and hence a sacrifice is instituted, with a human victim drawn by lots. But then Lykurgos ("culture-hero" of Sparta, the founder of the constitution) "reforms" the cult: instead of the human sacrifice, he finds another way of "wetting the altar with human blood"—by having the "ephēbes" flogged to bleeding.

On the basis of our reasoning so far, we might say that the myth integrates the ritual act of the *diamastigosis*, emphasizing its equivalence with the human sacrifice.

At Brauron, near Athens, the Athenian girls, before marrying, had to comply with what was called *arkteia*, which we can now define as a period of seclusion in the sacred place of the local Artemis (called precisely Brauronia).[10] The girls also played a role in the penteteric feast of the goddess (Aristoph., *Lysistr.* 643) when they appeared as *arktoi* ("she-bears"), and wore a particular costume called *krokoton*. A sacrifice of a goat is the only known sacrificial act of these festivities (Hesychius, *Brauroniois*). Now, this cult also has its own foundation-myth (apparently in common with the cult of Artemis Munichia at the Peiraeus, where an *arkteia* is also documented).[11] Once, a she-bear was killed in the *temenos* of the goddess; immediately after, an epidemic—or a famine—struck the city. The oracle was consulted for a remedy. According to a group of texts, the *responsum* ordered the institution of the *arkteia*, but, according to another group of texts, the remedy could be nothing but the sacrifice of a young girl. Some lexicographers, paroemiographers, and scholiasts tell us on the subject that a man named Embaros volunteered then (although on condition that he obtain the ministry of the cult for himself and his descendants) to sacrifice his own daughter. Instead of do-

[10] The excavations of the late J. Papadimitriu at Brauron brought to light even the little rooms where the *arktoi* lived (*To Ergon Archaiologikie Hetairia to 1961* [Athens, 1962], p. 24). Compare the inscription which mentions these cells (*Bulletin de Correspondance Hellénique*, 86 [1962]: 671).

[11] Some texts localize the institution in "Munichia or Brauron" (Harpocr.), others in "Munichia and Brauron" (schol. Aristoph. *Lysistr.* 645); a gloss of Suid. (*arktos*) stages the myth in the *demos* Philaidai, to which belonged Brauron, another gloss (*Embaros*) and other texts in Munichia or, more generically, at the Peiraeus.

ing so, however, he hid his daughter in the *adyton* of the sanctuary, dressed a goat like his daughter (or: called this goat his daughter) and sacrificed it to the goddess. What is important is that the goddess – whom we would rather think of as having been deceived – accepted this goat sacrifice in place of the requested young girl sacrifice. As a matter of fact, not only did the catastrophe cease – according to the myth – but also they continued in the cult, as we have seen, to sacrifice a goat, while all the young girls (the one of the myth, the unique girl, Embaros' daughter, was their mythical prototype) would "hide" themselves in the temple, performing the *arkteia* (that is, identifying themselves, at the same time, with the she-bear, the *arktos*, killed in the myth).

This case is more complex than the preceding one, and not only because of the manifold variants of the myth: also, and in the first place, the human sacrifice ordered by the oracle is "replaced" not by one, but by two rituals, the goat sacrifice and the *arkteia* of the young girls. Moreover, the *arkteia* of *all* the girls substitutes for the killing of *that* particular girl singled out as victim. At the same time, it is not just the substitution carried out by the mythical Embaros which indicates how the *arkteia* was an equivalent to the killing: the equivalence is also expressed by the name of *arktoi* given to the secluded girls with reference to the mythical she-bear which was killed. Perhaps one would also wish to add another difference: here the substitution of the human sacrifice takes place *in the myth itself*; but, actually, in the Spartan case too the substitution takes place in the myth itself. Independently of the question of Lykurgos' historical existence (still affirmed by some historians), everybody concurs in admitting that this figure is characterized by attributes and deeds which are certainly mythical rather than historical: his "reform" of the cult of Artemis Orthia is a foundation-myth. The difference, if any, is that the Spartan myth divides into two acts (realization and abolition of the human sacrifice) what the Brauronian-Munichian (actually Athenian) myth condenses into just one – the demand for human sacrifice *immediately* evaded through the substitution.

On the whole, in the case of this Artemis cult also, it would seem that a particular rite (the *arkteia*) should be conceived – in the light of the myth that organically belongs to it – as an equivalent of human sacrifice.

But in these two cases—which, by the way, are not isolated, but must now suffice—we are dealing with something else.

We all know that the Spartan institutions concerning boys represent what comes closest in Greece to the initiatic institutions of the so-called primitive peoples.[12] Indeed, we are not confronted by a mere resemblance, because both types of institutions have the same identical function to the extent that compliance with their rules is mandatory for all boys and constitutes the indispensable condition for the boys' admission into the society of adults. Besides various formal aspects of those institutions, which show surprisingly precise correspondences with the initiatic rituals of several so-called primitive populations, there are other aspects which point at an organic insertion of the initiations of a primitive type into the higher civilization and into the polytheistic religion. To these latter aspects we may ascribe the grouping of certain rituals around the sanctuary of a goddess, Artemis Orthia. It is true that no author directly relates the *diamastigosis* to the *agoge*, to the age-sets, to the typically initiatic discipline of the boys; nonetheless, direct (epigraphic) documents concerning the Spartan age-sets come exactly from the temple of the Orthia, the goddess to whom the winners of the singular *agones*, separately fought by the different age-sets, dedicated the prize received. Almost all the documentation about the ritual flogging comes to us from the Roman period: these data—compared with the only description that is more ancient (Xenophon, *De constitutione Lacaedemonorum*, 2, 9)—show what transformation the rite had suffered. Nevertheless, they reveal the essential facts: the subjects of the ritual were the adolescents (the "*ephēbes*"), and the ritual was a "proof of endurance"—so tough that, as in some initiation trials among "primitive" populations, several boys would die.

In Athens, at least in "historical" times, no institutions similar to the Spartan ones, or definable as pertaining to initiations, existed. Nevertheless, some institutions regarding girls show peculiar formal affinities with female initiations. Thus it is sufficient for the *arkteia* to note that—if not in practice, in any case in

[12] Even before the innovating studies of H. Jeanmaire (*Couroï et Courètes* [Lille, 1939]) and of G. Thompson (*Aeschylus and Athens* [London, 1946]), M. P. Nilsson, in an article entitled "Die Grundlagen des spartanischen Lebens" (*Kilo*, 12 [1912]: 308 ff. = *Opuscula selecta*, 2 [1952]: 826 ff.), had already pointed out significant facts about the subject in question.

theory—it was obligatory for girls of a certain age-set (according to later sources, those between five and ten) as a condition for marriage. It implied a seclusion outside the city; during this period of segregation the girls were denoted by a categorical term defining them as animals (she-bears). In a longer discussion it would be possible to demonstrate that these (and other) formal similarities are not casual:[13] the *arkteia*, together with other Attic female institutions, is the outcome of the transformation undergone by an ancient female initiation rite at the level of the superior polytheistic civilization.

In the two cases considered here, thanks to their sufficient clarity, we are faced by rituals in which youngsters of either sex undergo a treatment similar—within the frame of changed cultural and social conditions—to the treatment to which boys as novices are subjected in "primitive" societies. Now, the myth of the origin of each of these two rites mentions a human sacrifice for which the rite would be a substitution.

It is a well-known fact that during the initiatic process, among almost all the peoples who practice initiation, the "novices" must (ritually) die, before the (ritual) birth of the initiated. The initiatic death is realized in different ways which range from a very realistic dramatization to light symbolic allusions. In addition, several frequent elements of the procedure can be "interpreted" (not only by scholars, but also by the very societies which are actively involved) as the realization of ritual death: at times, the segregation itself (during which, for example, the novices paint themselves white, make themselves invisible, or observe silence—*as if* they were dead); in other places the torture to which novices are subjected; in other cases some particular sign which is impressed on their bodies, or simply the suppression of the use of their personal names, etc., are pervaded by the symbolism of death.[14] The initiatic death often expresses itself as the *killing* of the novice; this because the true protagonist of the initiations is the community itself, which, in its own interest, transforms the young boys into socially responsible individuals.[15] Therefore, it is the society which acts and causes the death of the "initiandi"—

[13] The argumentation will be found in the volume mentioned in note 9.

[14] Regarding the initiatic death and the significance of the initiatic trials, see M. Eliade, *Birth and Rebirth* (New York, 1958), pp. 13 ff.

[15] On this aspect of initiations see my contribution in the volume *Initiation*, ed. C. J. Bleeker (Leiden, 1965), pp. 227 ff.

that is, *kills* them. These deaths and killings are for us acts of ritual fiction, but for the societies involved it is their very ritual character which makes them *equivalent* to a real death or killing.

"Primitive" peoples also have myths connected with the initiatic procedure (or, better: myths which are *integral parts* of it). These myths often tell of "real" killings antecedent to the institution. Let one example here suffice for all: According to the Wiradjuris, Daramulun – who also has the role of the mythical initiator among other populations of southeastern Australia, but with different myths [16] – was supposed to catch, "kill," bring back to life, and return (except for an extracted tooth) the boys. Instead of doing so, however, he would actually kill and eat some of them. When the supreme being Baiame discovered this fact, he destroyed Daramulun and imprisoned his voice inside those trees whose wood was then used for bull-roarers (the sound of the instrument corresponding to the voice of the initiator).[17] Since then the bull-roarers have been the initiatic instruments which transform the boys into adults, killing them "ritually" rather than "actually." Here, however, the de facto opposition is not between real and symbolic killing, but between mythical and ritual killing, both symbolic and equivalent.

Going back to the two Greek cases illustrated above, we may observe that in the Spartan rite the boys suffer one of the typical tortures of initiation, flagellation, which has the value of a "test" – indeed, not everybody passes it – but which here as elsewhere has also the value of a symbolic killing. In the myth, this action actually "substitutes" for the human sacrifice, that is, it defines itself as the equivalent of such a sacrifice. In the Attic rite, the girls are secluded, like the "initiandi" of both sexes in "primitive" societies. As we have said above, seclusion as such can have the significance of a state of death, but the Attic institution also emphasizes the specific implication of seclusion by calling the girls secluded in the temple "she-bears," with reference to the *killed* mythical she-bear: as the she-bear lived in the temple and then was killed, so the girls must live in the temple and suffer a "killing." Moreover, the seclusion of the girls, according to the

[16] Some of these myths are mentioned in Eliade, *Birth and Rebirth*, pp. 11 ff.

[17] R. H. Mathews, "The Burbung of the Wiradthuri Tribes," *Journal of the Royal Anthropological Institute*, 25 (1896): 297.

myth, substitutes for the sacrifice of a girl (the prototype) ordered by the oracle but evaded by the priest, whose deceit (exactly as in Sparta the "interpretation" of the oracle given by Lykurgos) finds the consent of the gods. In both cases, the symbolic killing ritual — which has initiatic value — is related to a mythical killing; the first is destined to substitute for the latter.

The Greek cases, though, present a peculiarity which it would be a pity to ignore: the mythical killing presents itself in the form of a *human sacrifice* (destined in both cases — but not in all analogous cases in Greece — to Artemis). At first it would seem sufficient to explain that the idea of sacrifice occupied such a central place in Greek religion that it attracted into its orbit any killing of nonprofane character. But if we look more carefully, we shall note that even in this detail a perfect parallel exists between rite and myth. It was said that the Spartan *agoge*, even though retaining the function of tribal initiations in primitive societies, was inserted into the superior Greek civilization and into the polytheistic religion. In fact, the flagellation of the boys is an act of the cult and takes place in front of the altar of the goddess Artemis Orthia in the presence of her priestess. Correspondingly, the mythical killing too assumes the aspect of a cultic act, and precisely that of a sacrifice offered to the goddess herself. The same is true for the Attic institution which in historical times no longer was, but only "represented" an initiation: seclusion would indeed take place outside the city (Athens), but in a temple, not in the woods or in the wilderness, and would culminate (probably with the release of the girls and the seclusion of the next age-set or its representatives) in the great feast of the goddess Artemis Brauronia. To the cultual character of the rite corresponds the quality of the mythical human sacrifice, ordered, according to the myth, by the oracle.

Besides this coherent transposition on a polytheistic religious plane, the terms of the relation between symbolic killing in the rite and mythical killing remain unchanged.

We started from some cases where a myth concerning killing, a cultic epithet, a fictitious cultic norm, etc., had the function of making a ritual action equivalent to a human sacrifice, an institution which Greek civilization greatly limited in practice, but of which it wanted to save the value through myths and symbolic rituals. At first it seemed that even the flagellation of Spartan adolescents and the seclusion of the Athenian girls, with their foundation-myths based on a human sacrifice, had the same function. But under a more careful examination it appeared that this supposition was erroneous. In these last cases (and in several other similar cases which we could not consider here) the complex of myth and ritual did not aim to give a symbolic equivalent of the human sacrifice, but rather of that *symbolic* killing which is characteristic of the procedures of initiation. It is exactly the peculiarity of the cases we have considered that suggested the bizarre title of this modest contribution – "symbol of a symbol."

SEXUAL SYMBOLISM IN THE ŚVETĀŚVATARA UPANISHAD

R. C. ZAEHNER

The *Śvetāśvatara* Upanishad is not an easy text, for it is full of ambiguities. One of its main themes is, of course, the union of *puruṣa*, the male principle, spirit, with *prakṛti* (or *pradhāna*), the female, matter. The clearest statement of this theme is in 4.5:

> With the one unborn female, red, white, and black
> Who gives birth to many a creature like unto herself,
> Lies the one male, unborn, taking his delight.
> Another male, unborn, forsakes her, for she has had her pleasure.[1]

The same idea occurs in 1.9:

> Two unborn [males] there are: one knows, the other knows not;
> One master, Lord, the other lacking mastery.
> One unborn female there is too, close-linked
> To what is the object of the experience of him who experiences (*bhoktṛ-bhogy'ārtha-yuktā*).

The individual *ātman* ("self" or "spirit"), as it exists empirically, is "powerless (*anīśa*) over whatever causes pleasure or pain" (1.2) because it is bound to matter. Only God is by nature *kevala* ("absolute, alone," 6.11), but the individual self can attain to this condition by contemplating him (1.11).

[1] *bhukta-bhogām*. Hume, followed by Radhakrishnan and Aliette Silburn, unaccountably translates "with whom he has had *his* delight." This is probably due to Deussen's "die genossen." (E. Hume, *The Thirteen Principal Upanishads* [London, 1921]; S. Radhakrishnan, *The Principal Upaniṣads* [New York, 1953]; A. Silburn, *Śvetāśvatara Upaniṣad* [Paris, 1948]; P. Deussen, *Sechzig Upanishads des Veda* [Leipzig, 1897].)

It would seem that this sexual symbolism, used of spirit and matter, must be extended to all those passages in the Upanishad which speak of *yoni*. It is the purpose of this article to show that *yoni* always means "womb" or the female principle in this Upanishad, not "origin," for which *udbhava*, *prabhava*, or *saṁbhava* (3.4; 4.12, cf. 3.1) are used. This is clearly so in 1.7, where "those who are merged in Brahman, intent on it, are released from the womb," that is, from matter and rebirth. It is also so in 1.2, where the possible first causes are discussed. *Yoni* and *puruṣa* occur next to each other, and it is natural to take them as the male and female principles, particularly as they are followed by the words *saṁyoga eṣām* ("or by the union of the two"). For this one may compare 6.5, where Śiva is said to be "the efficient cause of the *saṁyoga*." In 1.2 there is difficulty if we read *cintyā* (feminine singular) as Śankara did, since there seems to be no obvious reason why a feminine form should be used here. A variant *cintyam* agreeing with *kāraṇam* is cited by Radhakrishnan, but this seems to be based on a misunderstanding of Śankara's commentary; Aliette Silburn prints *cintyāh* in her 1948 edition though she does not quote her authority. The grammar of the sentence, however, remains problematical.

Apart from these passages in which the male and female principles are clearly regarded as the dual origin of the whole phenomenal world, there are other passages in which the word *yoni* is less clearly used. Let us start with 4.11 and the closely parallel 5.2. The first reads:

> yo yoniṁ yonim adhitiṣṭhaty eko
> yasminn idaṁ sa ca vi c'aiti sarvam . . . .

He, the One, who approaches womb after womb
In whom the whole universe comes together and drifts apart. . . .

The second is similar, the first hemistych being the same:

> yo yoniṁ yonim adhitiṣṭhaty eko
> viśvāni rūpāṇi yonīś ca sarvāḥ . . . .

> He, the One, who approaches womb after womb,
> All forms, and all wombs . . . .

Here Hume (followed by Radhakrishnan) has "the one who rules over every single source," while Silburn has "celui qui régit à lui seul chaque matrice" (which leaves a pleasing ambivalence between "womb" and "source"). Deussen, however, stuck to "Mutterschoss," and it seems he was right, for there are two parallel passages in the *Gītā* which have to be taken into consideration in this context. In both cases it is with *prakṛti* that he consorts with or over which he rules to produce the world of multiplicity. In *Bhagavad Gītā* 4.6 we read:

> ajo 'pi sann avyay'ātmā, bhūtānām īśvaro 'pi san,
> prakṛtiṁ svām adhiṣṭhāya saṁbhavāmy ātma-māyayā.

Though I am unborn [like the "unborn" male quoted above] and of changeless self, and though I am Lord of [all] creatures, yet by my creative energy do I consort with Nature – which is mine – and come to be [in time].

Here Śankara glosses *adhiṣṭhāya* as *vaśīkṛtya*, "submitting Nature to me," which seems to refer to the sexual act. So Deussen translates "indem ich eingehe." Krishna here refers to his incarnations, but he is probably particularizing the more general idea expressed in *Śvetāśvatara* Upanishad 2.16:

> He is the God who pervades all regions:
> He is the first-born, He is in the womb.
> He is born indeed and will be born again:
> Over against [his] creatures does he stand,
> His face turned every way.

This is typical of the thought of this Upanishad. God transcends both spirit and matter, the perishable and the imperishable of 5.1, and he "emits" himself into matter to form individual selves. This is made absolutely clear in 6.12:

> He it is who makes the one seed manifold,
> The One holding sway among the inactive many:
> Wise men who see him in [their] selves[2] subsistent
> Enjoy everlasting joy, no others.

The "inactive many" refers to individual selves as it does in the Sāṁkhya system, for "the self has no power of itself" (1.2). This again is paralleled in the *Gītā* (9.8):

[2] Or, "in himself."

Subduing (*avaṣṭhabhya*, var. *adhiṣṭhāya*) my own material Nature (*prakṛti*) ever again I emanate this whole host of beings — powerless (*avaśa*) themselves — from Nature comes the power (*vaśāt*).

Even closer to *Śvetāśvatara* 6.12, however, is *Gītā* 14.3–4:

Great Brahman is to me a womb; in it I plant the seed: from this derives the origin (*saṁbhavaḥ*) of all creatures. In whatever womb whatever form arises and grows together, of [all] those [forms] Great Brahman is the womb, I the father, giver of the seed.

Now, in *Śvetāśvatara* 5.4–6, the word *yoni* ("womb") occurs three times. In 5.4 it is said of the "Lord God" that *yoni-svabhāvān adhitiṣṭhaty ekaḥ*. This is already familiar and means that the One God approaches, rules over, or impregnates all things "that have the nature of a womb"; that is, all that has its origin in material nature. Here Deussen, Hume, Radhakrishnan, and Silburn all have "born of a womb." This seems to be inaccurate: *svabhāva* means "individual nature" or "essence," not "born from." What the text says is rather that the one God impregnates all individual manifestations of matter with spirit and so controls them. This is clear from the use of *svabhāva* in the following couplet, and it is rather far-fetched to suppose, as Hume appears to do, that the two words *yoni* and *svabhāva* have a different sense in that couplet. The next line reads:

yac ca *svabhāvaṁ* pacati viśva-*yoniḥ*
pācyāṁs ca sarvān pariṇāmayed yaḥ,
sarvam etad viśvam adhi riṣṭhaty eko
guṇāṁś ca sarvān viniyojayed yaḥ . . . .

Again Hume, Radhakrishnan, and Silburn translate, with minor variations:

The source of all who develops his own nature
And brings to maturity whatever can be ripened . . . .

But why should *yoni* and *svabhāva* completely change their meaning from one line to the next? Certainly the Upanishads are difficult texts, but they do have a certain consistency which translators who so often ignore the obvious grammatical and semantic interpretations fail to recognize. It would seem perfectly obvious that the passage should be literally rendered thus:

He who ripens that which is an individual nature, whose womb is all [material] things, and who develops all things so ripened. . . .

In other words, he plants the seed (as in the *Gītā*), or makes it manifold (*Śvetāśvatara* 6.12), and material nature then takes care of the rest. Similarly, in the next couplet *brahma-yonim*, like *viśva-yoniḥ* in our last passage, must be taken as a *bahuvrīhi* compound if the whole passage is to be seen as consistent. Here again all recent translators including myself[3] seem to have gone astray. I would now translate:

> That which is hidden in the secret Upanishads of the Veda,
> Brahmā knows that that has Brahman as its womb. . . .

The whole passage should then be translated as follows:

> As the sun shines forth, illumining all regions, above, below, athwart, so does this One God, the Blessed Lord adorable approach [and impregnate] all things that have the nature of a womb.
>
> [He it is] who ripens whatever is an individual nature, whose womb is all [material] things, who develops all things so ripened, who alone approaches [and impregnates] this whole universe, and who assigns [their proper] attributes to all.
>
> That which is hidden in the secret Upanishads of the Veda, Brahmā knows that that has Brahman as its womb. The ancient gods and seers who knew it shared in its nature and become immortal.

So translated the whole passage is perfectly consistent in itself and fits in with and is explained by *Bhagavad Gītā* 14:3–4, where *brahman*, or rather *mahad brahman*, is, as all admit, used as a synonym for material nature or *prakṛti*. "What is hidden in the secret Upanishads of the Veda" must then be the "seed" that God injects into material nature in the *Gītā*.

So too in 6.16 I would take *ātma-yoni* to mean "he whose womb is himself or in himself," since as *pradhāna-ksetrajña-pati* Śiva already includes matter as well as spirit within himself: he is both *liṅga* and *yoni*, transcending the sexes as much as he does the perishable (the feminine principle) and the imperishable (the masculine principle, spirit).

Perhaps I may take this opportunity to point out what seems to me to be a hoary mistranslation transmitted by Deussen to his successors. This is 2.14–15. Here the Sanskrit reads:

[3] In my *Hindu Scriptures* (London and New York, 1966), p. 213.

yath'aiva bimbaṁ mṛday'opaliptaṁ
  tejomayaṁ bhrājate tat sudhāntam
tad v' ātma-tattvaṁ prasamīkṣya dehī
  ekaḥ kṛt'ārtho bhavate vīta-śokaḥ.

yadā'tma-tattvena tu brahma-tattvaṁ
  dīp'opamen'eha yuktaḥ prapaśyet
ajaṁ dhruvaṁ sarva-tattvair viśuddhaṁ
  jñātvā devaṁ mucyate sarva-pāśaiḥ.

It would appear that only Max Müller has translated the passage logically and in accordance with the order of the words.[4]

In 5.1 it is made perfectly clear that the personal God, Śiva, transcends both the perishable and the imperishable which together constitute Brahman (whether we read *brahma-pare*, which is difficult, or the more convenient *brahma-pure*, "city of Brahman"). It would, then, not be surprising to find him exalted over Brahman in this passage too, and this is in fact the only natural way to read the passage. It should be obvious that the words *ajaṁ druvam sarva-tattvair viśuddhaṁ* agree with *devam*, not with *brahma-tattvaṁ*, if for no other reason than that the *tattva* ("essence") of Brahman cannot at the same time be "devoid of all *tattvas*." Deussen, with his usual monistical bias, was quite happy to make logical nonsense of the text to preserve the "absoluteness" of Brahman (despite 5.1, where it is explicitly denied), and in this he has been uncritically followed by Hume, Radhakrishnan, and Silburn. In fact, there are *three* stages in liberation described in this passage: (a) the purgation of the individual self, described as a "reflection" or "mirror" (the *imago Dei* of the Christian and Muslim traditions); (b) the illumination of the essence of eternal being – Brahman – by the individual self so cleansed; and (c) "knowledge" of the personal God who is beyond all essences. Hence the correct translation would appear to be:

Even as a mirror begrimed with clay
Shines brightly once it is well cleaned,
So too the embodied [self], once it has seen
  Self as it really is (*tattva*),
Becomes one, its goal achieved and freed from sorrow.

[4] F. Max Müller, *The Upanishads*, part II, *Sacred Books of the East*, 50 vols. (Oxford, 1884), vol. XV, pp. 231–67.

When by means of self as it really is as with a lamp
An integrated (*yukta*) man sees Brahman as it really is,
[Then] knowing the unborn, unchanging God
Devoid of all essences as they really are,
He is from all fetters freed.

In himself, God is beyond all *tattvas*, and it is only in the creative process, when he enters into union first with the "one *tattva* of *tattvas*" (*tattvasya tattvena . . . ekena*), which can only be Brahman, and then with others, that he can be described as having a *tattva* at all (6.3). This doctrine seems to be maintained fairly consistently throughout the *Śvetāśvatara* Upanishad, as it is throughout the *Gītā*. It is due to persistent mistranslation that this has so often escaped notice before.

MANASĀ, GODDESS OF SNAKES

The Ṣaṣṭhi Myth

EDWARD C. DIMOCK, JR.

One of the most curious and interesting aspects of Manasā's complex character is that she is associated in various ways with the bearing and protection of children.[1] Perhaps because of her powers of regeneration, offerings are made to her by childless women.[2]

There is also in Bengal a goddess whose name is Ṣaṣṭhī, who has as her entire domain the giving and protection of children, especially sons. This goddess is worshiped on the sixth day of a child's birth, at which time the god Bidhātā comes to inscribe the child's fate upon its forehead; she is worshiped on the twenty-first day as well.[3]

Many villages in Bengal have a place called *Ṣaṣṭhītolā*, the place where the goddess resides; in other villages there may be no public place for her worship, but it may be carried on inside the house. Sometimes there is no image, sometimes the image is that of Manasā. And sometimes, especially in East Bengal (East Pakistan), the *Ṣaṣṭhītolā* and the *Manasātolā* are the same.[4]

This is the third in a series of studies on Manasā, the goddess of snakes in Bengal. The first two appeared in *History of Religions*, Winter 1962, pp. 307–21, and Winter 1964, pp. 300–322. These will be referred to in the notes as *GS* I and *GS* II. It should be noted that since these two studies were published, a book on the subject has appeared, written by P. K. Maity (*Historical Studies in the Cult of the Goddess Manasa* [Calcutta: Punthi Pustak, 1966]). The interested reader is referred to this useful work.

[1] *GS* I, pp. 319–20.

[2] *GS* I, p. 319.

[3] A sketchy description of the proceedings can be found in the translation of the Vidyā-sundara episode of the *Manasā-maṅgal* of Ketakā-dāsa, in Edward C. Dimock, *The Thief of Love* (Chicago: University of Chicago Press, 1963), pp. 225–26.

[4] Āsutos Bhattācārya, *Bāṅgalā maṅgalkāvyer itihāsa* (Calcutta: A. Mukherji and Co., 1958), p. 709.

Clearly, at some point in time, Manasā and Ṣaṣṭhī either came together or were separated as aspects of the nature of a single goddess. In Kṣirahara village in Rājśāhi district of East Pakistan, there is a four-armed image of Ṣaṣṭhī which strongly recalls the icons of Manasā: she holds a child in her lap and her right foot is placed upon a cat, her *vāhana*, which has its face turned toward her. In her right hand she holds a leafed branch.[5] In Mayurbhañj there is a Ṣaṣṭhī image even more reminiscent of Manasā.[6]

> The image is two-armed, seated on a lotus, with various ornaments; seven snakes spread their hoods over her head. A child is seated on her left thigh, held by her left hand. In her right hand she holds a snake.[7]

Satyanārāyaṇa Bhaṭṭācārya, editor of the *Ṣaṣṭhī-maṅgal* of Kṛṣṇa-rāma-dāsa, says that "in the Tantras," Skandaṣaṣṭhī, one of the goddess' twelve main forms, has among her epithets "two-armed" (*dvibhujaṃ*), "young woman" (*yuvatīm*), "she who grants the boon of safety" (*barābhayayutāṃ*), "golden colored" (*gauravarṇāṃ*), "decorated with many ornaments" (*nānālaṁkārabhūṣitāṃ*), "holding a beautiful boy on her left thigh" (*vamakroḍe suputrikāṃ*), and "dwelling in the Vindhya Mountains" (*vindhavāsinīṃ*).[8] Although some of these epithets are applicable to almost any goddess, some of them, especially that indicating the presence of the child, are reminiscent of those of Manasā. The lack of snakes is interesting, however.

The history of Ṣaṣṭhī, like that of Manasā herself, is obscure. She is known and accepted in Bengal by the early sixteenth century, as is witnessed by the *Caitanya-bhāgavata* of Vṛndāvana-dāsa: Śacī, the mother of the saint Caitanya, accompanied by female companions, goes to bathe in the Ganges after her son's birth, and then to "the place of Ṣaṣṭhī" to perform the rituals of that goddess.[9] And in the same text the names of Ṣaṣṭhī and Viṣahari (one of the epithets of Manasā—"holder of poison" or "destroyer of poison") are curiously linked:

> They all know the deities Ṣaṣṭhī and Viṣahari [or Ṣaṣṭhī-viṣahari], and serve them with great pride.[10]

[5] See *GS* II, p. 305, n. 16.
[6] See *GS* I, pp. 316–17.
[7] Satyanārāyaṇa Bhaṭṭācārya, *Kavi kṛṣṇarām-dāser granthāvali* (Calcutta: Calcutta University, 1958), *Bhumikā*, p. 53.
[8] *Ibid.*
[9] *Caitanya-bhāgavata*, *Ādi* 4:19, 15:115.
[10] *Antya* 4:414.

The goddess is also mentioned in the sixteenth-century text *Tantrasāra*, compiled by Kṛṣṇānanda Āgamavāgīśa, and in at least two of the Purāṇas, though these are of uncertain date. In the *Skanda-purāṇa*, Ṣaṣṭhī is described in the following terms: wife of Kārtikeya, by name Devasenā, a special *mātṛkā*,[11] protectress of children, giver of sons and grandsons, whose *pūjā* is to be performed in each of the twelve months, as well as on the sixth and twenty-first days after the birth of the child, for the child's welfare. And in the probably late *Brahmavaivarta-purāṇa* the following interesting story is told:

> In the Svayambhuva manvantara[12] there lived a king, Priyavrat by name. This king passed his days deeply engrossed in ascetic practices. But one day, for the sake of progeny, he was ordered by Brahma to marry. But even long after his marriage, his wife remained childless. So, with the aid of the ṛṣi Kasyapa, he performed a *putreṣṭi* sacrifice. His wife became pregnant, and a son was born; but the child was born dead. The king then took the dead child and went to the burning ground, and there a goddess in a fiery chariot appeared to him. Listening to the king's story, the goddess said: "I am the daughter of Brahma, wife of Kārtikeya, Devasenā by name, chief among the *mātṛkās*. I am sprung from the six parts [*aṅga*] of material nature, and therefore I am called Ṣaṣṭhī." Then she restored the dead child to life, and was about to embark with him, when the king began to praise and glorify her. Pleased with his prayers, the goddess said: "If you establish my *pūjā*, I shall restore your son to you." The king agreed, and thus Ṣaṣṭhī-*pūjā* was established on the earth.

In an alternative version of the Ṣaṣṭhī-maṅgal story given by Āśutoṣ Bhaṭṭācārya in his *Maṅgalkāvyer itihāsa* (p. 711), though not in the Kṛṣṇarāma-dāsa version, the goddess also wants to be worshiped on the earth, a theme in *maṅgal* literature. But even apart from that, there are many similarities between this story and the skeleton of the Behulā-Lakhindar episode of the Manasā saga: abduction, resuscitation of the dead, restoration to the worshiper on promise of *pūjā*.

Not much more can be said from the historical point of view, though speculations (for example, that the characteristics of the goddess are related to the custom "still current among Munda-

[11] Literally, "mother"; divine mothers, usually eight or sixteen in number.

[12] The first of six ages, each of which are equal to 12,000 years of the gods or 4,320,000 human years.

speaking tribals of Orissa,"[13] to whom the spirit of the paternal grandfather is the guardian deity of the male child [*Maṅgalkāvyer itihāsa*, p. 708]) are of course rife. And an examination of the goddess' name seems equally fruitless. In the story from the *Brahmavaivarta purāṇa* she herself gives one explanation. Satyanārāyaṇa Bhaṭṭācārya provides another. He suggests that the numbers six or sixty (which may be what "Ṣaṣṭhī" means) are often used to symbolize very large, indeterminable numbers, and that therefore her name expresses her expansive grace. It is more likely, however, that she is "the goddess of the sixth day."

It is true, as will be seen in the *maṅgal* itself, that the grace of the goddess is more expansive and ungrudging than that of Manasā. Manasā takes life and restores it with seeming arbitrariness. Ṣaṣṭhī herself is never malevolent. It was suggested that in the case of Manasā, the destructive aspect of her two-fold nature might be objectivized in the person of Neto ("eye"; perhaps the empty eye of the goddess wherein her poison is stored), Manasā's constant companion. But the case is not entirely clear. It is more clear in regard to Ṣaṣṭhī. Ṣaṣṭhī's *vāhana*, her vehicle, is the black cat. And in her *maṅgal*, the functions of Ṣaṣṭhī and the cat are in complementary distribution: the cat steals the children, Ṣaṣṭhī restores them to their mother. Where one of these aspects functions, the other does not.

This fact has led some scholars, among them Satyanārāyaṇa Bhaṭṭācārya, editor of the Ṣaṣṭhī *maṅgal* translated below, to conclude that one of the ancestresses of Ṣaṣṭhī, and therefore possibly of Manasā as well, is the Buddhist goddess Hāritī, who, as her name suggests, was a killer or stealer of children, and thus to be propitiated. Āśutoṣ Bhaṭṭācāryya, in his *Bāṅglā maṅgalkāvyer itihāsa* (pp. 694–96), while discussing still a third goddess, Śitalā, the goddess of smallpox, gives us the following information: In the Buddhist tantras Hāritī is described as a *yakṣinī*, wife of Kuvera. Despite her being a *yakṣinī*, she came to have *pūjā* offered her, and in Nepal her temple is side by side with temples of the Buddha and of Dharmaṭhākur. There is a story in Chinese Buddhist literature which seems to have entered that literature from India, though it has disappeared from the Indian corpus. The story is that there was a *yakṣinī* who lived in a palace in Magadhā and was known as the protectress of that place. Gradually, how-

[13] *Maṅgalkāvyer itihāsa*, p. 54.

ever, she took to stealing the children of the city and eating them. For this reason the people of the city gave her the name Hāritī or Hārankārinī. The people went to the Buddha, and he, having brought her back to the proper path, restored peace to her and to Magadhā.

Thus it is with the malevolent nature of Ṣaṣṭhī, or rather of her *vāhana* the cat. She must be propitiated. The other side, of course, is a goddess of benevolence, the granter of children and their protector, and thus to be worshiped with devotion. Unlike Manasā, Ṣaṣṭhī is basically merciful.

There are twelve forms of Ṣaṣṭhī, one for each month. Their physical characteristics may vary; for example, there is no cat associated with Skanda-ṣaṣṭhī. But the Ṣaṣṭhī discussed in the *maṅgal* below is known as Aranya-ṣaṣṭhī or Jāmāi-ṣaṣṭhī, who is ordinarily associated with the month of Jyaistha. The *maṅgal* is by a writer named Kṛṣṇarāma-dāsa, who lived in the latter half of the seventeenth century. A chronogram in a manuscript of a *Kālikā-maṅgal* which he wrote may be deciphered as 1676–77 A.D. The present text can be dated as 1645 A.D. The poet lived in a village of Kalikātā district in the Saptagrām area, by name Nimita (modern Nimte, just to the north of modern Calcutta), was Kāyastha by caste, and was the son of one Bhāgavati-dāsa. Nothing else is known of him. He has left a large number of short *maṅgal* poems to various gods and goddesses and fragments of others. The *Ṣaṣṭhī-maṅgal* associated with his name is in a broken manuscript. Here is the translation of that which remains to us:

Ṣaṣṭhī-maṅgal of Kavi Kṛṣṇarāma-dāsa

Swiftly passing through heaven and hell, the *sakhī* [companion] reached the earth where, passing one by one through Rāṛha and Gauṛ and Delhi and Kaliṅga, Gayā, Prayoga, Kāśi, and Nepal, she witnessed the *pūjā* of the Devi performed in various ways. Needy women fasted, only in devotion, with as much strength as they possessed. Saptagrām (as it is called on earth)[14] was without equal in this; the people dwelt in houses along the banks of the Bhāgirathi, people pious, givers of limitless sacrifice; there was no untimely death nor any misery or sorrow. The ruler of this place was called "Conqueror of Enemies"; how can I describe his manifold qualities? His glory was like the moon in pure water, his majesty like the sun; his house outshone the splendor

[14] The parentheses are in the printed Bengali text, obviously an interpretation by the editor.

of the Immortal City. In the guise of an old Brahman woman,[15] the *sakhī* Nilavatī entered the city of this king. On her hip was a small basket, and in her hand a *tulsi* leaf, and the many kinds of flowers which grow in Ganges soil, and a staff; so the old woman Māyādhari[16] went slowly to the apartments of the queen, unhindered by the guards, and the queen offered her a seat to sit upon. So the poet Kṛṣṇarām sings the *maṅgal* of Ṣaṣṭhī: its date the earth, the void, the seasons, and the moon.[17]

The queen, seated upon her golden throne, was eating baked fish with great pleasure. She asked the Brahman woman: "Tell me truly, who are you, and where is your home? Do you want wealth, or clothing, or jewels? Why are you, an old woman, alone?" Hearing the words of the queen, Nilavatī said: "I shall tell you of myself, and then you do the same. I live in Burdwan, but I have always wanted to bathe in the Ganges; this is why I have come. I have seven sons and four daughters, and unequaled wealth, for with the grace of Ṣaṣṭhī there is never trouble. Today is the *pūjā* for that Aranyaṣaṣṭhī who is famous in the world;[18] I would offer *pūjā* to the Devī, but I have no offering to give. With this constantly in my mind, I came to the house of the queen; I wanted to worship the highest Devī with her. But having come to you, I perceive difficulty.[19] Let it be. There is danger in performing *pūjā* if there is no offering. I see, troubled, that you are eating flesh. I conclude that you are not without sons. What is there for me to do here; let me then go to another city." The queen replied: "Tell me, let me hear. Who is Ṣaṣṭhī? If one worships her, how is one favored? The *sakhī* said: "The goddess is of the greatest mercy. Through her, the receptacle of *kula*[20] is long-lived. Through her all the women of the three worlds will bear sons. There is no mercy greater than hers. A mother loved by her son is never drowned in the sea of grief for him."[21] The queen replied: "If I am to have a son, I shall certainly perform *pūjā* to Ṣaṣṭhī. But tell me of her who, serving the goddess, obtains the most excellent of sons."

[15] A characteristic feature of all *maṅgal* poetry; see *GS* II and Dimock, *Thief of Love*.

[16] "She who holds or controls *māyā*." *Māyā* is here the divine power of the deity.

[17] The chronogram is: the earth is 1, the void is 0, the seasons are 6, and the moon is 1. Reading the chronogram forwards, 1061 would be 1645 A.D., which fits the dates given in other texts.

[18] In the month of Jaistha; the auspicious days are given at the end of the text.

[19] Or "opposition."

[20] Family honor or pride; a *kulin*, then, is an individual family which possesses such honor.

[21] The Bengali is by no means clear in this couplet.

"Hear, O powerful and true queen, famed among as many gods and men as there are in the three worlds. A woman, having made the preparations, gains all auspicious things as a result of the *pūjā* of Ṣaṣṭhī. There is a house in Sanokā city,[22] where lives a merchant, by name Saya.[23] He has seven sons, and the sons have seven wives, all women true to their wifely vows [*pativratā*]; all is due to the power [*māyā*] of the Devī. Now hear this marvelous thing: on the day of Ṣaṣṭhī all these true wives brought great offerings; what shall I say of their devotion, or of its power to cause the goddess pleasure. They prepared many offerings and went to bathe, leaving the youngest of them as guard. She was so foolish that she immediately took the offerings and stole them to fill her belly. When her mother-in-law came to the place, she did not see the offerings and was very angry. And that woman of evil deeds deceived her [mother-in-law] and put the blame on a black cat: 'It ate and ate, and still was not satisfied.' The cat was greatly angry and wanted to take revenge for this unjust accusation of having eaten greedily.

"The young woman's womb was full, and a son was born to her; and the child cried, in the three worlds. Seeing that, the black cat picked him up in his mouth and brought him to the place of Ṣaṣṭhī. Six sons were delivered in this way, and the black cat brought them all there. The unhappy woman wept: 'Who has stolen my sons? My time has come.'[24] Now hear this wonderful thing I relate: when again it was time for her to give birth, she fled to a distant forest, taking none with her, laying a string along her path.

"In that dense forest she was delivered. And then she went to sleep, her son in her lap and joy in her heart. The black cat was furiously angry; he found them nowhere. But then he found the string, and went along the forest path, and saw the child sleeping peacefully in the woman's lap. He took the boy in his mouth and fled, in great love [*pirīti*] paying no attention to the thorns.

"The boy's crying awakened the merchant's wife. She raised her hands and saw that there was no child in her lap; she was senseless with grief and fled through the forest weeping: her garments were in disarray, her hair was undone, tears streamed from her eyes. When she saw the cat go, taking the boy, she struck herself on her moon-like face decorated with kohl and ringlets; she ran through the forest, stumbling and shrieking. Her only thought was for her son, and the thorns ripped her clothes as she ran.

"Ṣaṣṭhī was sitting there, the treasure-house of all the virtues of

[22] In the *Manasā-maṅgal* of Ketakā-dāsa, Sanakā is the wife of Cando, Manasā's primary antagonist.

[23] In Ketakā-dāsa, Saya is the name of the father of Behulā.

[24] That is, "I am about to die."

woman, and the black cat came to her with the child in its mouth and delight in its heart. He opened his mouth and released the child before Ṣaṣṭhī; he made a bow and remained there in great delight. The goddess said: 'O cat, you have no mercy. How will the wife of the merchant be able to retain her life? When you brought her seventh son you left her breast empty. You have no sympathy; how her heart must be constricted. Why have you given her such sorrow? Such punishment is too much for such a small offense. Now do a little good; return her son.'

"'Now hear me, mother. That evil woman does not worship you, even when her womb is full. She sits there and eats all the good things there are, and then blames me. But however many wrong things she does, and however often, I do not kill her, only in fear of you.' The Devī said: 'She blames you, but do not be so angry. Be tolerant because of her mother-in-law, who is greatly devoted, and offers me *pūjā* often, with all her strength. By the opposition of God, everything is struck by misfortune; by his qualities all are saved . . . .'[25]

"After the cat had left, the wife of the merchant came before the Devī. Trembling, with tears in her eyes, she fell to the earth and praised the Devī in a low, choked voice: 'You are the mother of the world, granter of boons.' She held the feet of Ṣaṣṭhī. 'You tricked the wife of Indra, and then were merciful to her; you gave her the shelter of your feet. You sit upon the lion-throne, with sons around you, some on your lap, some on your hip. I entreat you, that all children may feel your kindness. I had seven sons; what was my offense, that the black cat brought them here. I burn as in a fire; how long shall I bear it?' The goddess said: 'Why do you weep, O merchant's daughter? I do not understand your actions. You constantly give offense; how much more can I bear? On the day of Ṣaṣṭhī, have fish cooked and prepare four portions of rice; I forgive quickly, I shall give you sons, for such is my nature. I shall forgive abuse and opposition, and shall grant a boon. So go quickly to your own house. You stole and ate the food-offerings, and blamed the cat: that was the offense for which you have fallen into difficulty.' The merchant's wife replied: 'I have done wrong, as you say; I know my offense. I have not worshiped you, so all this has occurred. I blamed the black cat, but it was really I who stole and ate the things. As was done, so has been the result, and I must make amends for it. Forgive my transgression, be merciful; give me back my seven sons. If you do not grant me this boon, I shall not return home; I shall take my life right here. I bore my sons, and watched them with my eyes over seven days[?]. I have not held them in my lap, nor ever kissed their faces. Hear me, compassionate one: if you do not show me mercy, I shall stab myself in the throat with a hook.' And she

25 The translation omits one line, which I cannot decipher.

took a glittering knife, and said to the goddess: 'I went into the forest, and lost him there. Shall I take him home?'[26]

"The Devī said: 'Hear me, wife of the merchant. My compassion is aroused by your weeping. See your seven sons, O true wife. Take them and go home. Take your sons; let me not keep them. Call out their names, and they will come to you.' The merchant's wife then went weeping to the place where all the boys were seated and she drenched her seven sons with the tears of her eyes. 'My sons, my sons,' she said, pressing them to her, 'dolls of my heart, come to me. Your mother will take you to your own house.' And weeping, she went on like this. But although they listened, they did not understand the meaning of the words. 'Who are your children, whose mother are you? Why are you so upset for no reason? We are in our mother's house. Where would you take us, woman?' And the seven sons pushed away the hand of their mother. They went to Ṣaṣṭhī and pleaded with her thus: 'We are your sons; let us stay with you. She calls us her sons, and wants to take us away.'

"The Devī was very pleased with these words. She summoned the weeping merchant's wife to her and said: 'I gave you your seven sons. If they do not know their mother, what am I to do?' 'You have caused all this by your power [*māyā*]. By what right do you keep the children of another? I shall worship at your feet, with all the power I possess. Give your consent, and let my sons come with me.' The Devī said: 'I shall instruct you a little every day. On the day of Ṣaṣṭhī there are many gifts for *pūjā*. Black cats are parts [*aṁsa*] of me; if you maltreat one of them, a son will be stolen. Do not falsely accuse one of these cats, or your sons will be affected.[27] I shall be very angry. On the day of Ṣaṣṭhī anoint your son with oil and water . . . .'[28] 'I shall do as you say,' said the merchant's wife.

"'Give us, O Devī, the shadow of your feet, your highest mercy.' And as she was well disposed toward the boys, they made obeisance in devotion, and holding their mother's feet, they said, 'Let us go to our own house.' So on that auspicious morning the unhappy woman regained her seven sons and departed. Saying 'Let us go, children,' she took them on her hips . . . .'[29] Some said: 'Mother, give me bright-colored clothes; if I do not have them I shall not go home. My feet do not move.' And some saw brightly-colored fruit in the top of a tree, and they said: 'Get that for us.' And they saw many kinds of birds flying about, and they said: 'Catch those and give them to us.' And while

[26] The *bhanitā*, or signature line, which is "Kṛṣṇarāma says, 'The merciful goddess began to speak to her,'" has been omitted, as have *bhanitās* throughout the translation.

[27] Or: "If you strike a son, my anger will be very great."

[28] There is a line omitted since it is very unclear.

[29] There is a hiatus in the manuscript at this point.

this was going on, the wife of the merchant was walking, and soon she reached her own land.[30]

"*Hariyā*, balls of *tāl*, and *auser guṛi* – as much as is prescribed, the mother-in-law used to prepare.[31] In Āśvin, in joy, they worshiped Ṣaṣṭhī in the name of Durgā;[32] each boon which was asked was inevitably granted. In Kārtik is the *pūjā* of Ṣaṣṭhī of the burning *ghāṭ* [*smāsana-ṣaṣṭhī*]: she is worshiped with folded hands that sons might return from the burning ground. No illness, grief, or sorrow ever visits the houses of the women who thus worship Ṣaṣṭhī the twelve months around. But on Monday and Friday there is no *pūjā* anywhere on earth."

Hearing the words of the *sakhī*, that jewel of women, the queen asked again very carefully. . . .[33] The *sakhī* said: "Listen while I speak of the cause of this; I know for certain, as I am her servant. Pay careful attention to [this description of] the greatness of Ṣaṣṭhī. She saved the life of Kārtik in battle, and because of this the three worlds resound with shouts of gladness. From the first, Pārvati herself did *pūjā*: who is there living in heaven, earth, or hell who does not worship the greatness of Ṣaṣṭhī one day a month? Śacī and the other wives of the gods, chief among them Saradā Mahāmāyā, perform Ṣaṣṭhī *pūjā* on the day of Aśokaṣaṣṭhī. For on that day sons will go to the heavenly place. One should always worship with devotion on Rohini,[34] for that is the day of the cat-*vāhana*. In anger, Bhavānī was about to make Gokula ashes; she refrained because of the plea of Kṛṣṇa. And the Devī Mahāmāyā said in the court of the gods where and when the *pūjā* of Ṣaṣṭhī should be regulated: in those months when the Ṣaṣṭhī-*tithi*[35] is on Monday, *pūjā* will be performed only in heaven. Whoever in earth or hell undertakes *pūjā* on that day will be without sons. In those months in which the Ṣaṣṭhī-*tithi* falls on Saturday, *pūjā* will be held in hell, nowhere else. On earth, worship on Sunday and Saturday [sic], and on Wednesday and Thursday: she who does so will bear excellent sons. If one does not respect this and does otherwise, not even the wives of the gods [can prevent] their sons from dying. So, O queen, worship thus on these days – and listen to the advantages of fasting. If you do not understand, and worship Gāndhārī on Monday, one hundred sons will die, and great peril will come about."

30 The editor notes that the last several lines do not occur in one of his manuscripts. It is possible that the manuscript is broken at this point, as there seems to be a lack of continuity.

31 *hariyā*: unknown; *tāl*: fruit of the *tāl* palm; *auser guṛi*: a preparation made from *aus* (winter rice).

32 Whether this means "as Durgā" or "taking the name of Durgā" is unclear.

33 There is a hiatus in the manuscript.

34 Rohini is the fourth of the lunar mansions.

35 The lunar day dedicated to Ṣaṣṭhī.

THE "PASSIVITY" OF LANGUAGE AND THE EXPERIENCE OF NATURE

A Study in the Structure of the Primitive Mind

WERNER MÜLLER

Two intellectual disciplines are exceedingly indebted to Mircea Eliade, *Religionswissenschaft* and ethnology. His name will always be mentioned in connection with the profound change occurring today in the study of the history of the human soul. Prior to Eliade, all attempts to study the structures of the human mind – or better, the valences of experience (*Erlebniswerte*) – made no progress. Everyone still remembers the demolition of the idea of *Paideuma* by the second successor to Leo Frobenius.[1]

To understand the significance of this turning to human experience, one need only remember the impact which Eliade's *Le Mythe de l'Eternel Retour* has made on every sensitive reader. The rejection of all -isms and the emphasis on the primordial symbols – mountain, tree, and tower as symbolic of the middle; temple and city as representations of the cosmos; mythical time as continuously recurring rebirth – have produced a new understanding of archaic man, a clearer image of the distinct structure of his mind.

The following essay, an excerpt from a larger work on the Sioux Indians, is intended as a contribution to the expansion of this new approach. By examining a primitive language we hope to illustrate the way in which linguistics might further stimulate the Eliadian view. We base our presentation on Dakota, a Sioux language, which was formerly spoken across the entire northern prairie of the United States but which today is limited to a few

[1] C. A. Schmitz, "Vorwort" to *Mitteilungen zur Kulturkunde*, 1 (1966): 3–4.

reservations in the two states that bear this name. Those who speak this language, because of their colorful appearance, have become known all over the world: they are the horseback-riding Indians decorated with feathered headdresses, the nomads of the Great Plains armed with bow and shield who dwell in tepees and whose livelihood depends almost entirely upon hunting buffalo. After 1870, the total extinction of the buffalo herds forced the transition to reservation life and the adoption of European plow-agriculture. The process of acculturation is bringing about the gradual disappearance of the old culture; even the language more and more approaches English.

Dakota, like almost all Indian idioms, is essentially a language of verbs. But while European linguistic feeling associates the verb with the idea of energetic activity, the majority of Dakota verbs are neutral; there are very few active verb stems. At the very beginning of his Dakota grammar, Boas points to this difference:

> There is a fundamental distinction between verbs expressing states and those expressing actions. The two groups may be designated as neutral and active. The language has a marked tendency to give a strong preponderance to the concept of state. All our adjectives are included in this group, which embraces also almost all verbs that result in a state. Thus a stem like "to sever" is not active but expresses the concept of "to be in a severed condition," the active verb being derived from this stem. The same is true of the concept "to scrape," the stem of which means "to be in a scraped condition." Other verbs which we class as active but which take no object, like "to tremble," are conceived in the same way, the stem meaning "to be a-tremble."[2]

Precisely these uniquely passive forms constitute the core of the Dakota language.[3] The preponderance of these so-called neutrals shapes the structure of this language. With the appearance of these many verb roots as words that express a condition, the attitudes of suffering, of enduring, and of passive acceptance dominate the character of the entire language.

> The concept of a condition [as Boas defines it more precisely] extends over almost all inanimate objects that may be brought into a

[2] Franz Boas and Ella Deloria, "Dakota Grammar," *Memoirs of the National Academy of Sciences*, 23 (1941): 1.

[3] *Ibid.*, p. 23: "By far the majority of verbal stems are neutral."

condition. "To scratch" is not primarily an activity; the active verb is derived from the condition of a scratched surface. These stems can be made active only by adding instrumental prefixes which express the means by which the condition is brought about, or by locative elements which apply the condition to a certain object.[4]

In other words, even the active verbs are basically words that express a condition (*Zustandswörter*). Their "passivity" is suspended only by use of the instrumental prefix. Among the majority of examples which Boas mentions for the usage of instrumental prefixes, the reflexive *ma-* ("me") occurs repeatedly as the unmistakable characteristic of the neutral verb. The personal *wa* ("I") appears relatively seldom. So, for example, na*ma*homni ("I turn around by means of my own power") is formed from the instrumental prefix for "inner power" (*na*), then from *ma-* ("me"), and finally from *homni* ("to turn around"). Actually and literally this means "my inner power turns me around." Na*wa*homni, on the other hand, means "I turn it around with the foot."[5]

The Dakota language seems to employ in every conceivable and possible instance neutral and passive forms. The activeness which is so familiar to us is thus excluded.

Our finding corresponds precisely to the linguistic typological studies of the Swede Holmer.[6] Through an examination of their use of pronouns, he has divided the American primitive languages into types. Two basic contrasting species are shown: the pathocentric type of "passivity" and the egocentric type of action. The criterion is found in the possessive adjective "my." If it corresponds to the reflexive "me," we are dealing with a language of "passivity" (*eine Sprache des Erleidens*) — that is, "my call" corresponds to "calling in regard to *me*." If, however, the possessive word corresponds to the personal "I," we are dealing with a language of action (*eine Sprache des aktiven Handelns*) — that is, "my call" corresponds to "*I* call."

The Dakota language with all its branches belongs to Holmer's pathocentric type. As a model, let us compare the following groups of pronominal sound formations:

4 *Ibid.*, p. 23.
5 *Ibid.*, pp. 46 ff.
6 Nils Holmer, "Amerindian Structure Types," *Sprakliga Bidrag*, 2 (1956): 1–29.

wa-	I	*ma-*	me	*mi-*, *ma-*	my
ya-	you	*ni-*	you (*dich*)	*ni-*	your
ung-	I + you	*ung-*	me + you	*'ung-*, *'ungki*	our[7]

As can easily be seen, the "my" corresponds to the "me," and thereby Dakota becomes a classical example of a pathocentric language. As we have already seen, it avoids whenever possible the active form of "I," and retreats to a view in which all actions and events are understood as happening to oneself (as a *Widerfahrnis*).

Thus, one says in Dakota há*ma*sapa ("I am a black man"), which actually means "to be a black man in regard to me," derived from *hásapa* ("black-skinned") + *ma-* ("me"). Similarly, ho*ma*bŭ ("I have a soft voice") is literally "to have a soft voice in regard to me," derived from *hobu* ("to have a soft voice"). Then there is la*má*kota ("I am a Dakota")—actually, "a Dakota in regard to me." Wi*ma*haha ("I am happy") means "happy in regard to me" and is derived from *waíhaha* + *ma-*. Similarly, *imá*-winkta ("I am really proud of it") actually means "proud of it in regard to me." Wa*má*tŭka ("I am tired") means "to be tired in regard to me." Indeed, even children at play may be heard to say 'i*má*gmŭ ("I am a cat"), which literally means "to be a cat in regard to me."[8]

The tendency of the Dakota language is precisely to replace the possessive with the reflexive pronoun. While it is quite possible to say "my horse has died," the normal expression is "the horse has died in regard to me."[9]

With its pathocentricity, the Dakota language reveals one primordial fact, the fact of our being an object—regardless of whether at a certain moment the telluric realities intrude on us or whether vital processes, feelings, and passions overwhelm us. This tendency is also present in those instances where an instrumental prefix would allow the personal pronoun "I" to be quite as appropriate: an indefinite performer of the action appears in the use of the prefix *ka-*, to which the German *es* corresponds quite closely. For example, *makáischtingma* ("I am falling asleep") is derived from *ma-* ("me"), *ka-* (the instrumental "to cause that"), and *ischtingma* ("to fall asleep"), and thus results in some-

[7] Boas and Deloria, "Dakota Grammar," pp. 76, 127.
[8] *Ibid.*, pp. 22–23, 31, 85.
[9] *Ibid.*, p. 128.

thing like "me cause to fall asleep," or "I am sleepy." Likewise, *makáhomni* ("I have changed [myself]") is derived from *ma-* ("me"), *ka-* (the instrumental), and *homni* ("to turn around"); the combination results in "to cause me to turn around." Similarly, *makát'a* ("I am shocked") means literally "to make me be dead," derived from *t'a* ("to be dead").[10]

Sparing ourselves further examples, we conclude that the Dakota language has a passive nature. The aim of the word formation is to capture impressions, that is, to capture them in the literal sense of the word. This process of capturing impressions has an effect on the speaker. This "passive" (*duldende*), receiving, and feminine structure indicates an attitude which is miles apart from an active will. The "I" imposes itself on the world, the "me" adapts itself to the world; the "I" wants to act, the "me" wants to absorb; the "I" wants to change, the "me" wants to preserve.

Further elaboration upon Holmer's classification of the American primordial languages and their value to the psychology of language is unnecessary. Here linguistic research has made possible a clarification of the structure of the human soul, and indeed this insight first of all permits a clarification of the Indian's concept of nature, his attitude toward the surrounding phenomenal world.

Nevertheless, one might object to our conclusion by pointing out that the closeness of the primitive peoples to telluric reality makes our approach illusory; a feeling of distance, which is absolutely necessary for forming a concept of nature, is unlikely at this stage. Yet this is not the case: the Dakota is quite able to grasp his environment by ordering and structuring it.

It is especially important for us to recognize that the Indian structuring of nature attests to the "passivity" of the language as an expression of the fundamental attitude of the soul. The Dakota accepts all phenomena with a kind of loving reverence. The obsession to conquer, rule, and subdue the world is completely absent in him.

Since about 1850, the coming of the white man to the prairies has placed the tribes of the plains in a position where they can experience and observe the behavior of a more action-oriented people. Perhaps these impressions made them more aware of their

[10] *Ibid.*, p. 47.

own orientation; in any case, however, we may evaluate these Indian utterances as genuine data.

The best observations have been made by Gilmore; his works deal with the tribes settled along the Missouri River and especially with the Arikara. He thinks that Americans are unable

to comprehend the grief and pain experienced by Indians when they see the native forms of life ruthlessly and wantonly destroyed. It was not primarily the realization of economic loss, the loss of a valuable source of food, which caused distress to Indians when, for instance, they witnessed the destruction of wild rice fields and lotus beds, but it was the sense of a fearful void in nature ensuing upon the extinction of a given species where it had formerly flourished. They were pained to contemplate the dislocation of nature's nice balance, the destruction of world symmetry.[11]

In conversations with members of various prairie tribes, Gilmore has learned that this feeling for the balance in nature is already implanted in children:

Do not needlessly destroy the flowers on the prairie or in the woods. If the flowers are plucked there will be no flower babies (seeds); and if there be no flower babies, then in time there will be no people of the flower nations. And if the flower nations die out of the world, then the earth will be sad. All the flower nations and all the different nations of living things have their own proper places in the world, and the world would be incomplete and imperfect without them.[12]

An old Omaha man, with whom Gilmore conversed about the slaughtering of the buffalo, expresses his feelings in the following sentences:

When I was a youth, the country was very beautiful. Along the rivers were belts of timberland, where grew cottonwood, maple, elm, ash, hickory, and walnut trees, and many other kinds. Also there were various kinds of vines and shrubs. And under these grew many good herbs and beautiful flowering plants. In both the woodland and the prairie I could see the trails of many kinds of animals and could hear the cheerful songs of many kinds of birds. When I walked abroad I could see many forms of life, beautiful living creatures which Wakanda had placed here; and these were, after their manner, walking, flying, leaping, running, playing all about. But now the face of all the

[11] M. R. Gilmore, *Prairie Smoke* (New York, 1929), pp. 34–35.
[12] *Ibid.*, p. 35.

land is changed and sad. The living creatures are gone. I see the land desolate, and I suffer an unspeakable sadness. Sometimes I wake in the night and I feel as though I should suffocate from the pressure of this awful feeling of loneliness.[13]

An extraordinary perception of the oneness of the world (*Weltganze*) is expressed here. Just as his language stands open to all impressions, so the Indian sees in the throng of forms between sky and earth a unity, a cosmic order. Both aspects are dependent: the language expresses what observation has perceived. As Gilmore formulates it in his reflections,

In Indian religious thought the universe is conceived as a living, unified community in which all living things, plants as well as animals and men, from the lowest and most humble to the highest and proudest, the spirit beings, and all the elements and powers of the earth and heaven, have their proper and useful places. Man, as one of the forms of living beings in this universal community, is in vital relation with all others.[14]

From an entirely different point of view, C. McCone, by examining the Dakota concepts of time, has arrived at the same conclusion. His thorough investigation was prompted by the meager development of tenses: the Dakota grammar knows no past tense, only present and future tenses.[15] Thus it negates the "historical" time of Western peoples, their linear calendar with its beginning somewhere in time. It pays homage instead to a "mythical" time in which the most distant past is understood as contemporaneously present.

Dakota consciousness knows only an all-embracing duration which is neither measured or measurable. It is essentially "a free good." . . . The perspective of Western civilization may be termed "historical" and that of the Dakota culture called "mythical." . . . The eternal present of the myths regulates and motivates the behavior of every member of the society.[16]

This last sentence of McCone, the interpretative power of which cannot be underrated, is somewhat modified by E. Deloria

13 *Ibid.*, p. 36.
14 *Ibid.*, p. 74.
15 Vernon D. Malan and R. Clyde McCone, "The Time Concept, Perspective, and Premise in the Socio-Cultural Order of the Dakota Indians," *Plains Anthropologist*, 5 (1950): 12–15.
16 *Ibid.*, pp. 12–13.

without basically changing its meaning: "We Indians lived in eternity."[17]

This mythical value system also lies at the heart of the Dakota's feeling for nature (*Naturgefühl*). For this consciousness, nature is a part of that eternal order which is unchanging. To live within a Dakota social group implies, according to McCone,

> to live in close harmony with nature. In contrast the efforts of Western men were directed to the conquest of nature. In the mythical value system nature is regarded as part of the eternal order and thus could not be challenged or altered.[18]

Accordingly, the economy of the Dakota rests upon its adaptability to the natural order, and exactly this orientation toward the universal oneness effects a completely different style of living.

Some of these views must have been familiar to other Indian peoples also. We may consider the following speech of the Kickapoo chief, Kenekuk:

> The white men ruin our land, they make all nature moan. They cut the plants with long knives, they damage the plants and the plants weep. They kill the trees with murderous iron, they wrong the trees and the trees weep. They tear open the viscera of the earth, they hurt the earth and the earth weeps. They poison and muddy the waters of our clear rivers, the fish die, and the fish and the rivers weep. So you see the fish and the rivers weep, the trees weep, the earth weeps, the herbs in the meadows weep – indeed, the entire nature is made to weep by the white men. O these thankless ones! But punishment will overtake them too.[19]

Here again is evident a sense of affinity, a mysterious knowledge of the relationship between man and the living world. This feeling of affinity, of man's unity with the earth and her children in their suffering, determines also the systematization of nature: in addition to the tribes of people there are also "the tribes of quadrupeds," "the tribes of the air," and "the tribes of plants," all having equal rights.[20] This affinity has its model in primeval times.

[17] *Ibid.*, p. 13, from the correspondence between McCone and Ella Deloria, a Teton Indian lady who had already assisted Boas in preparing his "Dakota Grammar."

[18] *Ibid.*, p. 13.

[19] J. G. Kohl, *Reisen im Nordwesten der Vereinigten Staaten* (St. Louis, 1859), p. 497.

[20] Gilmore follows in his *Prairie Smoke* this Indian structure: tribes of men, quadruped tribes, tribes of the air, and tribes of plants.

According to the Arikara genesis, all living things emerged from the belly of the earth and wandered toward the West. When they crossed a large body of water, those who remained behind became fish, those lagging behind on a high cliff turned into birds, and those who stayed in a thick forest took on the shapes of quadrupeds: deer, moose, bear, and porcupine. Those remaining grew up to be human beings.[21]

An outstanding example of how the Indian adapts himself to the world is noted by Gilmore in connection with the ground bean (*Falcata comosa*). This bush, found along the edges of Missouri forests, grows beans about two centimeters in length from its lowest branches into the topsoil, as does the peanut. These beans are a favorite dish of Indian cookery, but they are difficult to obtain because they grow in a heavy thicket. Therefore, the Indians enlist the help of the meadow mouse (*Microtus pennsylvanicus*) in acquiring this food. This animal diligently hoards the beans in its store rooms, and since during the winter it eats nothing else, it pays to dig up the burrows.

Still, no Indian would dare to empty the burrow completely, taking from the helpless mouse its entire food supply. The people not only leave behind a portion of the beans, but, as a means of payment, they also leave a corresponding amount of corn, some lard or bacon, or some other tasty morsel. It is considered mean and unjust to rob the mouse of its entire harvest without a gift in return. The Indians even express a strong feeling of respect: "The meadow mice are very industrious people; they even help human beings!"

For such a bean hunt certain spiritual preparation is needed. Heart and soul must be cleansed, bad thoughts must be banished, and the mind must be awakened to the rights of all living beings, plants and animals. Only with humility and reverence may the mouse be approached and asked to share a portion of its stores.

An old Teton Dakota of the Standing Rock Reservation had gone searching on an autumn day and, believing himself unobserved, addressed the mouse with the following prayer:

Thou who art holy, pity me and help me, I pray. Thou art small, but thou art sufficiently large for thy place in the world. And, though weak, thou art sufficiently strong for thy work, for Holy Wakantanka con-

[21] M. R. Gilmore, "The Arikara Book of Genesis," *Michigan Academy of Science, Arts and Letters*, 12 (1929): 101.

stantly strengthens thee. Thou art also wise, for the wisdom of holiness is with thee constantly. May I be wise in my heart continually, for if an attitude of holy wisdom leads me on, then this shadow-troubled life shall come into constant light.

Only after this prayer did he begin to dig. Gilmore has found this attitude among all Dakotas; he emphasizes here that the Indians allow themselves to be guided by some inner compass, by a feeling for a fixed order in the world which assigns to each its place.[22]

The Indian view of nature, with its sensitivity to integration and relatedness, is epitomized by the name "Mother Earth." The rituals contain numerous expressions of love and reverence for the sacred Mother Earth in general and for one's own homeland in particular. "In their thought of their homeland they did not regard it as a possession which they owned, but they regarded themselves as possessed by their homeland, their country."[23] Gilmore cites in this connection a ritual song of the Pawnee which vividly portrays the old Pawneeland of Nebraska.

> Dark against the sky yonder distant line
> Lies before us. Trees we see, long the line of trees,
> Bending, swaying in the breeze.
>
> Bright with flashing light yonder distant line
> Runs before us, swiftly runs, swift the river runs,
> Winding, flowing o'er the land.
>
> Hark! O hark! A sound, yonder distant sound,
> Comes to greet us, singing comes: soft the river's song,
> Rippling gently 'neath the trees.[24]

The Dakotas express their feeling for the earth just as eloquently: they regard it as a living and conscious being. In Dakota folk music every living being has its own song in which the essence of this particular species is concentrated. This is a remarkable concept of a religious nature. In the hymn of the wild rose (*Rosa*

[22] M. R. Gilmore, "The Ground Bean and Its Uses," *Indian Notes*, 2 (1925): 178 ff.

[23] Gilmore, *Prairie Smoke*, p. 29.

[24] A. C. Fletcher, "The Hako: a Pawnee Ceremony," *Twenty-second Annual Report of the Bureau of American Ethnology*, 1900–1901 (Washington, 1904), pt. 2, p. 303.

pratincola) it is sung about the earth, the mother of all life, that she is not dumb, for flowers are her songs:

And all creatures that live are her songs,
And all creatures that die are her songs,
And the winds blowing by are her songs,
And she wants you to sing all her songs.[25]

Yet it would be a mistake to limit this reverence to the earth, to its animals and plants. Gilmore assures us that the Indians also revered the elements of the universe – sunshine, wind, and the rippling waters in lakes and rivers: "Devout persons would often voice in prayers of gratitude and appreciation their pious contemplations of the wonders of nature."[26]

Let us return once more to our linguistic considerations. The pathocentricity of the language represents an ability of the soul to experience the world in its oneness. The wealth of idiomatic expressions in Boas' Indian grammar, which undoubtedly are part of the everyday language, give us a sense of the extreme receptiveness (*Allempfänglichkeit*) of this language. The lightening and the darkening of the atmosphere, the procession of wandering armies of clouds, the echoing of the countryside with the voices of children, the barking of dogs, the songs of birds, the fading of the wakeful day into sleep and dream, the hue of the morning sky and the change of seasons, the cedar and the flowing river, fiery anger and zealous talk, motherly care and fatherly advice, the wing-beats of the thunderbird and the practical jokes of the trickster – all these countless and passing experiences of the inner and outer world make an impression on the soul and are pregnantly expressed by the Dakota language. This "passive" language and the Indian world view, which is completely given to experience, fit together perfectly. It seems as though the one has created the other.

The importance of the conclusion we have reached, namely, that the cosmos is completely interrelated with its component parts, cannot be underestimated, especially in relation to one area – Dakota religion. The first and oldest information on this subject comes from the nineteenth-century missionaries who in 1834 be-

[25] M. R. Gilmore, "Uses of Plants by Indians of the Missouri River Region," *Thirty-third Annual Report of the Bureau of American Ethnology, 1911–1912* (Washington, 1919), p. 86.

[26] Gilmore, *Prairie Smoke*, p. 32.

gan their work in today's Minnesota, in the vicinity of the former Fort Snelling. Not unpredictably, these men measured the heathen forms of piety by the categories of their theological education. They knew from the Old Testament how "heathen" are supposed to look; worse yet, they compared non-Christian religion with two textbook examples, Greece and Rome. And precisely these models were destined to fail here, for Dakota piety at first sight seemed to lack any system and any order.

Just at this point begin the complaints of the missionaries who were accustomed to classical clarity. The beliefs of the Indians are confused, unsettled, and contradictory; they have no fixed, uniform belief; their mythology lacks a well-defined system; a discordant and chaotic mass of materials engulfs the observer — so groans S. W. Pond.[27]

His brother G. H. Pond had also apparently received the impression that the Dakota sees gods everywhere: "it runs out like the division of matter, to infinity; there is nothing they do not revere as god"; and again, the Dakota actually has "tens of thousands of divinities."[28]

Along the same lines, J. W. Lynd writes:

> Their religious system gives to everything a spirit or a soul. Even the commonest stones, sticks, and clays have a spiritual essence attached to them which must needs be reverenced — for these spirits, too, vent their wrath upon mankind. Indeed, there is no object, however trivial, but has its spirit. The whole material or visible world, as well as the invisible, is but one immense theatre for spirits and fiends to play their torments upon mankind.[29]

It is not surprising that these opinions finally lead to the claim that the Dakotas are pantheists, with an "inextricable maze of gods, demons, spirits, beliefs and counter-beliefs, earnest devotion and reckless skepticism, prayers, sacrifices and sneers, until the Dakota with all his infinity of deities appears a creature of irreligion."[30]

If we remember the extremely receptive nature (*Allempfän-*

[27] G. H. Pond, "The Dakota or Sioux in Minnesota As They Were in 1834," *Minnesota Historical Society Collections*, 12 (1908): 401–2.

[28] G. H. Pond, "Dakota Superstitions," *Minnesota Historical Collections*, 2 (1889): 217.

[29] J. W. Lynd, "The Religion of the Dakotas," *ibid.*, p. 154.

[30] *Ibid.*, p. 150.

glichkeit) of the language, together with the all-encompassing feeling for nature (*Naturgefühl*), then these missionary evaluations automatically fall into their proper place: Dakota piety is nothing less than the reverence for the totality of phenomena, an integration into the total cosmic house (*Welthaus*), the acknowledgment of man's kinship with all the figures and forms of the cosmos. Everything aims at this understanding: the passive structure of the language as well as the appreciation of all natural phenomena.

But the European-American ideological straitjacket of the nineteenth century did not permit such conclusions. This final epoch of invincible faith in European ideas lacked the ability to rid itself of all its own opinions and prejudices and thereby to open the door to foreign worlds of experience and feelings. The intellectual disciplines in those days produced interpretations to suit reason rather than understanding. Thus we are able now to survey the road which we have traveled. And among those who have pointed the way has been Mircea Eliade.

ORDEAL BY FIRE

ERNST BENZ

The mass of material available about ordeals has been most carefully evaluated in the excellent studies by Hermann Nottarp in his *Gottesurteil-Studien*, and by K. Beth in his excellent article in the *Handwörterbuch des deutschen Aberglaubens*. They have convincingly shown that the ordeal by fire was a form of adjudication prevalent among all the Indo-European peoples. At the time of their confrontation with Christianity, ordeal by fire was still commonly practiced, especially by the Germanic tribes, and was so firmly established in the religious consciousness of the people that the Christian church was unable to forbid it.[1] Instead, the Christian church preferred to transform the practice, allowing it to be expressed in the framework of a Christian liturgy and giving it a new theological basis.

Mention of the existence of the ordeal by fire as the form of invoking divine judgment can be found in Greek tragedy. In Sophocles' *Antigone*, a messenger announces to King Kreon the

[1] Hermann Nottarp, *Gottesurteil-Studien* (Munich, 1956): K. Beth, in *Handwörterbuch des deutschen Aberglaubens*, ed. Hans Bächtold-Stäubli, 10 vols. (Berlin and Leipzig, 1934–35), vol. 3, pp. 994 ff.; Ludwig Rockinger, "Quellenbeiträge zur Kenntnis des Verfahrens bei den Gottesurteilen des Eisens, Wassers, usw.," in *Quellen und Erörterungen zur bayerischen und deutschen Geschichte*, ed. L. Rockinger, 9 vols. (Munich, 1958), vol. 7; J. Grimm, *Deutsche Rechtsaltertümer*, 2 vols., 4th ed. (Leipzig, 1899), vol. 2; Ad. Kaegi, "Alter und Herkunft der germanischen Gottesurteile," in *Festschrift zur 39. Versammlung deutscher Philologen* (Zurich, 1887); Ch. Leitmaier, *Die Kirche und die Gottesurteile* (Vienna, 1953); H. Glitsch, "Gottesurteile," *Voigtländers Quellenbüchern*, 44 (1913); Hans Fehr, "Gottesurteil und Folter; Eine Studie zur Dämonologie des Mittelalters und der neueren Zeit," in *Festgabe für Rudolf Stammler zum 70. Geburtstag* (Berlin, 1926); C. de Vesme, *Le Ordalia* (Milan, 1945); P. Browe, *De Ordaliis*, 2 vols. (Rome, 1932–33), text collection.

forbidden burial of Polyneikes, and, at the same time, uses the report of this desecration to clear himself and his friends of any suspicion of complicity in this crime. He says:

We roared bad words about, guard against guard, and came to blows. No one was there to stop us. Each man had done it, nobody had done it so as to prove it on him – we couldn't tell. We were prepared to hold to red-hot iron, to walk through fire, to swear before the gods we hadn't done it, hadn't shared the plan when it was plotted or when it was done.[2]

The judgment of the fire is supplemented here by an oath of purification. Even in pre-Christian times, oath and divine judgment were closely related. According to its original religious meaning, the oath itself represents an ordeal since it not only summons the gods to witness the innocence of the person taking the oath but also provokes divine punishment in case a false statement is made unintentionally by the witness. In the latter case the divine punishment can take effect at a later time, while in the case of the ordeal by fire, the immediate execution of God's judgment is provoked.

The medieval ordeal liturgy is distinguished by the fact that in it old forms of pre-Christian ordeal liturgy are transformed into Christian liturgy.[3] In the pre-Christian liturgy, the fire itself was understood to be a divine power which could differentiate between right and wrong, innocence and guilt; in the Christian liturgy, however, the fire appears as an element and creature which is used in the hand of Almighty God, the Lord of Justice. The pre-Christian charms which were pronounced over the *probandus* and also over the fire and the iron are replaced by the ecclesiastical benedictions and exorcisms which are supposed to hinder the evil powers from intervening in the immediate execution of divine justice. In place of the magic potions and foods with which the *probandus* was made immune to the power of the fire in pre-Christian times, in the Christian ordeal by fire the *probandus* receives the Eucharist during the Mass and drinks holy water immediately before the start of the ordeal. The berserker who, filled with magical strength, is capable of taking the fiery iron

[2] Sophocles, *Antigone*, ll. 260–67 (Elizabeth Wyckoff, trans., in *Sophocles*, ed. David Grene and Richmond Lattimore [Chicago, 1954]).

[3] Texts of ordeal liturgies are presented by Adolph Franz, *Die Kirchlichen Benediktionen im Mittelalter*, 2 vols. (Graz, 1960), vol. 2, pp. 364 ff.

or of walking barefoot on the fiery coals, is transformed into the charismatic who, by the strength of the Holy Spirit, testifies to his power over the elements.

The Church sanctioned the ordeal by fire, together with other forms of ordeals such as the duel and ordeals by both cold and hot water, as a legal means of adjudication; this was obviously a reflection of Germanic law which throughout the Indo-European region employed this method of ascertaining guilt. In its Christianized form the ordeal is found in most Germanic law books of the Christian epoch and was also incorporated into the ecclesiastical canons of many Western synods. Its performance is reflected in its own liturgy, which experienced astonishing growth and development between the ninth and eleventh centuries. In its final form the ordeal liturgy consists of a celebration of the Mass either preceded by or interspersed with a great number of benedictions, exorcisms, and adjurations.

The real intention of the ordeal by fire is shown most clearly in the benedictions with which the ordeal begins, in the blessing of the fire and the iron, and in the blessing of the *probandus* himself. The *probandus* is not simply subjected to the elements, the iron and the fire, in their natural state, but both elements are first blessed. According to the old conception of physics, fire is one of the four basic elements of the world. Thus, in the *benedictio ferri* and in the *coniuratio ferri*, fire is addressed as a creature of God and is consecrated for the purpose of determining the truth. The benedictions begin with the prayer from the blessing of the fire in the Easter Saturday liturgy.[4] The magical differentiating power of fire is raised to a spiritual plane in this prayer. The heating of the iron by the blessed fire is made directly analogous to the spiritual warming and illumination of the heart of the *probandus*. This places the *probandus* in a condition in which he is able to examine himself in view of the imminent ordeal and to confess his own guilt or innocence.

The iron is blessed just as the fire. It is personified and addressed as *creatura ferri*.[5] The early church's cosmological understanding of redemption is assumed: Christ's passion has brought salvation not only to mankind, but also to the whole cosmos and all its elements. Supplementing the *benedictio* is the exorcism of the fire

[4] *Ibid.*, vol. 1, pp. 513–14.
[5] *Ibid.*, vol. 2, pp. 366–67.

and the iron. Just as the creatures of fire and of iron are receptive to the divine blessing, they are also receptive to the effects of demonic powers. Therefore an exorcism of the fire and the iron must precede the rite of the ordeal in order to drive out the demonic powers which use these creatures of God to distort the truth and to hinder its revelation. There are different exorcistic prayers in the liturgy of the ordeal by fire which recur to some extent also in the liturgy of the ordeal by hot water. After the Mass which precedes the ordeal by fire there follows a new benediction of the fire and the iron.[6]

The exorcism concerns two additional objects of the ritual of the ordeal by fire: the place where the ordeal occurs and the *probandus* himself. If the ordeal was held in the church itself, no additional benediction of the place would be necessary, since the church is a holy place by virtue of the liturgy of consecration. If the ordeal was held in the vestibule of the church, in the churchyard, or in another place, as was often required by the complex preparation for making a big fire to heat the pieces of iron or the plowshares, then there first had to be a benediction of the place, in order to keep away all demonic powers from the area of the ordeal.[7] After this preparation, the Mass begins with the introit, which introduces the actual ordeal.

Finally, the *probandus* himself, who after communion walks to the burning pyre to undergo the ordeal, is exorcised by the priest standing beside him.[8] Through these exorcisms the *probandus* is reminded for the last time that his decision to undergo the ordeal by fire can be attributed to demonic influence, to the devil's counsel; on the other hand, however, he is given a final consolation: if after this last warning he is completely certain of his case and trusts in God, the protector of truth, then he can in all safety—*securitas*—seize the hot iron or walk upon it.

The liturgy of the ordeal by fire cites an astonishingly large number of Biblical prototypes in its invocation of God. Seven major prototypes are mentioned:

The rescue of Abraham from the fire of the Chaldeans (Gen. 11:31)
The burning bush (Exodus 3:2)

[6] *Ibid.*, pp. 366–75.
[7] *Ibid.*, p. 369.
[8] *Ibid.*, p. 372.

The rescue of the three youths from the fiery furnace (Daniel 3)
The rescue of Lot from the fire of Sodom and Gomorrah (Gen. 19)
The rescue of Israel from the hands of the Egyptians by the wandering pillar of fire (Exod. 14:19–20)
The outpouring of the Holy Spirit in the form of flaming tongues (Acts 2)
The rescue of Susanna from the charges of her two accusers (Susanna)

"Deus, qui Abraham puerum tuum de incendio Caldeorum salvasti."[9] Here we have a typical, early medieval spiritual etymology, as was often used in deciphering the "mystical" meaning of the letters of Scripture. The Vulgate Genesis 11:31 says about Abraham and his family: "Et eduxit eos de Ur Chaldeorum, ut irent in terram Chanaan." The pious author of the liturgy brought the "Ur" of the Chaldeans together with *urere* ("to burn"), and translated: "de incendio Caldeorum." Already the first rescue of the first bearer of God's promise was a rescue from fire.

The Biblical prototype to which the liturgy of the ordeal by fire and by hot water most often refers is Daniel's story of the three men in the fiery furnace. The most striking feature of this story is that the three men, Shadrach, Meshach, and Abednego, actually provoke King Nebuchadnezzar to submit them to an ordeal by fire. Any thought of entreating God is absent from their minds, as we see from their ready refusal to worship the golden image even if the awaited miracle does not take place.

The three men in the fiery furnace glorify in song the just judgments of God, who proves to be just in the miracle of the ordeal by fire. In the liturgy of the ordeal by fire the whole hymn is sung with the antiphon of the *benedictio ferri.* In one prayer different liturgical traditions (Roman and Greek) seem to have merged,[10] for in it the three men appear in rapid succession under different names: Sidrach, Misach, and Abdenago are the names which are found in the text of the Vulgate, while the names Ananias, Azarias, and Misahel are taken from the Greek text of the Septuagint. The reference to the three men in the furnace constantly recurs in the liturgy of the ordeal by fire and by hot water, as well as in the prayer of exorcism which is spoken over the *probandus.*[11]

[9] *Ibid.*, p. 367.
[10] *Ibid.*, pp. 366–67.
[11] *Ibid.*, p. 372.

The image of the burning bush is directly related to the archetype of the men in the fiery furnace. Moses is not, to be sure, himself rescued from a fire, but the fire which appears to him does not consume the bush. In this respect it resembles the fiery furnace in which the three men walk about singing.[12]

As a third Biblical prototype of the ordeal by fire, there appears in the liturgy a reference to the rescue of Lot from the fire of Sodom and Gomorrah. Here too the fire is an instrument of divine judgment: in contrast to the three men in the fiery furnace, Lot is not rescued from the fire itself, but escapes before the fiery judgment passes over Sodom and Gomorrah.[13]

Further prototypes of Biblical rescue from fire appear somewhat more far-fetched to the modern reader, for instance, the rescue of the Israelites from the hands of the Egyptians by the pillar of fire which moves before them during the flight in the night. Here another meaning of fire appears: the differentiating power of fire which separates gold from slag, the faithful from the faithless. Thus, in the same *benedictio ferri*, God is praised "who separated your faithful from the faithless by the light of fire."[14] About this passage Franz remarks, "which event is meant here remains doubtful." He supposes it is an allusion to the fiery judgment over Sodom, the judgment against the Baal priests (1 Kings 18), or to the exodus of the Israelites from Egypt under the guidance of the fiery pillar. But the assumption that this passage alludes to the exodus seems supported by the reference, in the postcommunion prayer in the Mass designated for the fire ordeal, to God "who art the light which freed the people of Israel from Egyptian bondage."[15] The notion of the differentiating power of fire brings in the prototype of the descent of the Spirit in fiery tongues at Pentecost. This fire too separates the faithful from the faithless.[16] The flaming tongues of Pentecost are also mentioned after reference to the pillar of fire during the exodus.[17]

One last archetype is grouped with the Old Testament prototypes of the ordeal by fire. Although fire plays no part in it, the

12 *Ibid.*, pp. 370, 367.
13 *Ibid.*, pp. 367 ff.
14 *Ibid.*, p. 368.
15 *Ibid.*, p. 370.
16 *Ibid.*, p. 368.
17 *Ibid.*, p. 370. The Biblical examples can also be found in ordeal prayers as early as the so-called Prayers of Cyprian, Migne PL, IV, cols. 987–90.

story of Susanna and her two accusers expresses the same differentiating function of the ordeal by fire – God's judgment proves the innocence which is threatened by false accusations. This story of Susanna, which is added to the book of Daniel as an apocryphal thirteenth chapter, is constantly used in the liturgy of the ordeal by fire. Indeed, the Vulgate version exhibits all the classical characteristics of a divine ordeal. One feature of the Susanna story must have appeared to be particularly important to Germanic legal philosophy: Susanna had no witnesses for her innocence; she was accused by false witnesses and had no compurgator who could swear under oath to her innocence. This was precisely the legal situation in which the medieval feeling for justice demanded a judgment of God in the form of an ordeal by fire or hot water. Sentenced to die on the basis of the accusations of the two false witnesses, "Susanna cried out with a loud voice, and said, 'O eternal God, who dost discern what is secret, who art aware of all things before they come to be, thou knowest that these men have born false witness against me. And now I am to die! Yet I have done none of the things that they have wickedly invented against me!' The Lord heard her cry." (Susanna, verses 42–44.) God's judgment does not occur through an ordeal by fire but through the young boy Daniel, whose spirit is aroused by God and who convicts Susanna's accusers. A particular significance is attached to the Susanna prototype because the ordeal by fire was often used against women who were accused of adultery but who had no compurgators, as in the famous legal case of Queen Kunigunde, the wife of King Heinrich.

The detailed Biblical justification for the practice of the ordeal by fire is the result of a violent theological battle which the supporters of the practice of ordeal waged against opponents from the camp of the canonists and the supporters of an enlightened theology. Thus Hinkmar of Reims turns against the opponents of ordeals.[18] He regards the Flood as a divine judgment, as an ordeal by cold water; similarly, the Sodomites were punished by fire, but Lot and his family were saved. Hinkar likewise interprets the martyrdom of the apostle John as a divine judgment. Even the Last Judgment itself is understood as a universal ordeal by fire. The apostle Paul's expectation that those who are chosen for the

[18] See his pamphlet "De divortio Lotharii regis et Thetbergae reginae," Migne PL, CXXV, 1, cols. 659–66.

Kingdom, and who are still alive at the time of the Lord's descent on the clouds of the heavens, "shall be caught up together with them in the clouds to meet the Lord in the air" (1 Thess. 4:17), is associated with the idea of a judgmental fire: the ungodly will perish in the fire burning on the earth; the redeemed will be raised uninjured and unsinged above the zone of fire on the earth into the sky toward the Lord, who is hurrying down from the clouds.

Following this, the rescue of Lot from the fire of Sodom, as a divine ordeal by fire, is once more brought together with the divine ordeal judgment of Doomsday and with the rescue of the three men from the fiery furnace. In Hinkmar's works the fiery pillar which led the Israelites in their exodus from Egypt is also regarded as an ordeal by fire. Thus, most of the Biblical archetypes occurring in the fire-ordeal liturgy already appear in this theological pamphlet by Hinkmar in which he defends the ecclesiastical legitimacy of the ordeals by fire and water!

Significantly, the prayers of the liturgy of the ordeal by fire are directed not only at the *probandus* but also at the whole attending congregation. This congregation understands itself to be a judicial community responsible to God, in a Christian sense, and responsible for reaching a judgment. Through the ordeal by fire, it is not only the *probandus* but also the congregation as a judicial community which is brought before God's judgment. The prayer of the exorcism of the iron,[19] which is said immediately before the Mass begins, exorcises the "creature of iron," not only in the name of the triune God, but also in the name of all the heavenly witnesses who are assembled around God's throne – the 12 apostles, the 72 disciples, the 12 prophets, the 24 elders who continually praise God (Apoc. 14:4), and the 144,000 innocents who follow the Lamb (Apoc. 14:1) – in order to reveal all of Satan's tricks which hinder the revelation of the truth. The community of the earthly witnesses is incorporated here into the community of the heavenly witnesses of God's glory, truth, and justice.

In this context, the invocation of the Holy Spirit has a special significance. The rite of the ordeal by fire attains its specifically Christian interpretation precisely through this reference to the Holy Spirit. As the Pentecost story shows, the Holy Spirit is di-

[19] Franz, *Kirchlichen Benediktionen*, vol. 2, p. 368, "coniuratio ferri."

rectly related to fire. The appearance of the flaming tongues is understood as the fulfillment of the promise of John the Baptist regarding the man who will come after him: "he will baptize you with the Holy Spirit and with fire" (Matt. 3:11). The blessing of the iron contains a prayer to God in which the ordeal by fire, that is to say, by hot water, appears as the "mystery of fire or water of the Holy Spirit" which brings truth to light and disperses the fog of ignorance that surrounds human judgment. The same is said of the exodus from Egypt of the chosen people in the reference to the differentiating power of fire. It is the Holy Spirit who works through fire and carries out this differentiation, which also enables the witnesses to differentiate the truly faithful from the faithless.[20]

The relation of the ordeal by fire to the original Christian conception of the nature of charisma becomes clear in a prayer addressed to the Holy Spirit before the iron is laid in the fire.[21] The gifts of the Holy Spirit include not only rational gifts, such as the gifts of gnosis, wisdom, and teaching, but also prerational gifts, such as the gift of mastery over the elements, the gift of healing, and the gift of performing miracles. To be sure, the Gospels do not contain any story in which Jesus or one of the apostles commands fire; they only contain reports of the mastery over the storm, the walking across the water, and the power over scorpions and snakes (Luke 10:19). Nevertheless, mastery over fire and invulnerability to fire are among the oldest characteristics of Christian saints and appear in the earliest martyr stories. In the martyrdom of Polycarp of Smyrna, for example, it is reported that the flames from a bonfire refused to burn him and billowed out in front of him "like a sail filled by the wind."[22] Moreover, the Old Testament promises God's chosen people power over the element of fire. In Isaiah 43:2, God speaks to his chosen people: "When you walk through fire you shall not be burned."

From this it becomes understandable how the Christian ordeal by fire was at first staged and even provoked by the Christian saints in order to demonstrate the power of man filled with the divine spirit. In the history of the Germanic mission, the Christian

20 *Ibid.*, pp. 367–68.
21 *Ibid.*, p. 372.
22 Passio Polycarpi, chap. 15.

missionaries deliberately provoked ordeals by fire to carry out the apologetic task of demonstrating the superiority of the Christian God over the demons. Thus Bishop Poppo of Hamburg, who submitted to one ordeal with a red-hot iron before King Harald of Denmark, is said to have undergone another form of ordeal by fire. He walked through a bonfire dressed in a shirt saturated with wax to prove to the heathen Danes the power of the Christian God.[23]

For the same reason, the ordeal by fire is used by the Christian charismatics in their struggle against heresy. As Rufin reports, the Egyptian monk Copres, during an argument with a Manichean, challenged his opponent to undergo an ordeal by fire. Copres was unharmed by the fire while the fearful Manichean, who had to be pushed into the fire, burned.[24] Gregor of Tour reports a similar case.[25] During a quarrel with a heretic, a Catholic proposed to throw a ring into a fire and to reach in after it with his bare hand. Whoever remained unharmed by the fire would have the true religion. The heretic refused to undergo this dangerous test, but the Catholic, after an appeal to God to attest to the true faith, fetched the ring from the fire unharmed. The Christianization of Iceland was carried on under Olaf Tryggvason by Dankbrand, a cleric from Bremen. When an Icelandic woman told him that Christ, after having been challenged by Thor to a duel, had not appeared because he was afraid of defeat, Dankbrand confirmed the Christian faith in a duel against the berserkers who were armed with magic powers.[26]

St. Francis of Assisi also offered to undergo an ordeal by fire before a sultan in Egypt to prove the superiority of Christian faith over that of the Muslims. In 1498 Savonarola wanted to undergo an ordeal by walking through a bonfire to prove the truth of his sermons. Nevertheless, his attempt was thwarted by the Pope and the cardinals.[27]

[23] Adam von Bremen, *Gesta Hammaburgensis* (Hanover, 1876), Monumenta Germaniae historica, Scriptores VII, p. 318.

[24] Rufin, *Historia Monachorum*, chap. 9, Migne PL XXI, col. 426.

[25] *Liber in gloria Confessorum* (Hanover, 1885), chap. 14, Monumenta Germaniae historica, Scriptores rerum Merovingicarum I, p. 756; see Franz, *Kirchlichen Benediktionen*, vol. 2, p. 348.

[26] Nottarp, *Gottesurteil-Studien*, p. 234.

[27] Joseph Schnitzer, "Savonarola und die Feuerprobe," in *Quellen und Forschungen zur Geschichte Savonarolas*, Veröffentlichung des kirchenhis-

According to thoroughly reliable historical traditions, countless persons have survived the ordeal by fire unharmed. One must not dismiss these cases as "legends." We are dealing here with a religious event. Its spiritual prerequisites are fundamentally based upon the *probandus*' religious life, his religious consciousness, his emotions, and his whole environment.

A prerequisite for the ordeal by fire, both for the *probandus* and for those administering it, is the conviction that in this act God himself intervenes in human affairs as judge and witness for the truth. In the religious consciousness of the participants it is really a judgment of God which is called forth because it is God who is called upon to bear witness to the innocence of the accused in a way which must be adjudged a miracle in the religious consciousness of the accused himself, those administering the ordeal, and the witnesses and spectators: it is a miracle of mastery over the element of the fire, the marvelous effect of a charisma, a gift of the Holy Spirit with which God arms his people and thus designates a person as a man of God.

Modern psychology refuses to speak of such an event as a miracle in the sense of a suspension of natural laws. It prefers to speak of "borderline phenomena" (*Grenzphänomene*). Correctly recognizing that we have not thoroughly investigated the interaction between spirit, soul, and body, modern psychology acknowledges that in this interaction "borderline phenomena" can appear which suspend the normal behavioral patterns of the human personality. At any rate, one thing is certain: such "borderline phenomena" do not appear without cause, but are the result of a long preparation of the *probandus*.

To understand the internal and external preparation for the ordeal by fire, the modern investigator must keep in mind a significant religious prerequisite of the ordeal itself: the accused is sentenced to the ordeal only after careful consideration and often only at his own request. The decision to invoke God as judge and helper in a hopeless situation for the accused, who is without the help of witnesses and compurgators, is for the *probandus* an extremely significant decision which profoundly affects his whole spiritual life. It amounts to a decision to deliver himself over to the judg-

torischen Seminar, ed. Alois Knoepfler (Munich, 1904); Karl Hase, *Neue Propheten* (Leipzig, 1851), pp. 61 ff.

ment of the living God and thus to agree to an anticipation of the Last Judgment while being still alive in this world.

But the decision does not end here. It motivates the *probandus* to prepare himself spiritually, emotionally, and physically for the realization of his resolve. He is placed in the position of the penitent who prepares himself for the decisive confrontation with God in the fire.

The first element of the preparation is fasting by the accused and the witnesses. In this respect the law books point to the demonological significance of fasting: by fasting the power of the devil is broken. According to the medieval regulations, fasting means not only abstention from food and drink, but also abstention from marital intercourse. The prescription for cultic purity applies to the priest administering the sacrament as well as to the *probandus* of the ordeal by fire, since the ordeal is also understood to be a sacrament.[28] According to the Anglo-Saxon ordeal laws, sexual abstinence is required also of the witnesses: as soon as the ordeal by fire is prepared, two neutral parties who are sober and have not slept with their wives in the preceding night should come from both sides of the nave of the church and confirm that the iron is red-hot.[29]

Similarly, part of the preparation for the ordeal by fire is an honest confession by the *probandus*; he is to undergo the ordeal in a state of absolution which he receives from the priest at the end of his confession. This confession presupposes careful self-examination and thorough spiritual meditation. The concrete grounds for the accusation as well as his whole life are illuminated in view of the imminent confrontation with the divine judge and are considered in the light of guilt and atonement, of punishment and grace.[30]

All these preparatory stages precede the actual liturgical act of the ordeal. This liturgy is constructed according to the principle of a dramatic intensification leading to a climax. In its definitive form, the liturgy of the ordeal consists of a celebration of the Mass, which is preceded by or interspersed with a great number of benedictions, exorcisms, and adjurations. After the blessing of the place, a Mass is performed in the church, in the vestibule of

28 Nottarp, *Gottesurteil-Studien*, p. 232.

29 F. Liebermann, *Die Gesetze der Angelsachsen*, 3 vols. (Halle, 1903), vol. 1, p. 386; Nottarp, *Gottesurteil-Studien*, p. 249.

30 Franz, *Kirchlichen Benediktionen*, vol. 2, p. 350.

which the ordeal by fire will occur; or, the Mass is performed in a church which is near the place where the ordeal is to occur The forms of the Mass were not everywhere the same; however, the Mass with the *introit* "Iustus es, domine" ("Righteous art thou, O Lord," Psalm 119:137) was generally used.[31] In the Collect and in the lesson from Isaiah 55:6–7 which follow, one is exhorted to repent; in the Gradual one is reminded of divine providence and justice. The Gospel is Mark 11:22–25, which discusses the faith that moves mountains; the *probandus* is exhorted to have that faith, which is capable of accomplishing the most astonishing miracles. This spiritual encouragement is intended to convince him that, having the true faith, he can even dare to undergo the ordeal by fire. The offertory "De profundis" (Psalm 130) follows with its tremendous tension between confidence and the longing for salvation—"I trust confidently in the Lord, my soul trusts in him and I hope for his word"—while the secret prayers ask for protection against the deception of the devil.

Before communion, the priest turns to the *probandus* and adjures him in the name of the triune God, in the name of his baptism, in the name of the Gospels and of the relics located in the church, not to come to the altar if he knows himself to be guilty. If, despite the warning, the *probandus* then comes to the altar, the priest administers communion to him in both kinds with special words of administration which are keyed to his situation: "Corpus et sanguis domini nostri Jesu Christi sit tibi hodie ad comprobationem. Amen." The reception of the sacrament is to have the effect of confirming the innocence of the *probandus*. This act anticipates the divine judgment, for whoever receives the sacrament "unworthily," while knowing his concealed guilt, "eats and drinks judgment upon himself" (1 Cor. 11:29). This formula acts as a powerful strengthening agent for the religious consciousness of the faithful receiver of the sacrament; having partaken of the body and blood of his Savior, he can approach the ordeal with calm certainty. The communion verse repeats the words about faith which moves mountains and ends with Mark 11:24: "Therefore I tell you, whatever you ask in prayer, believe that you receive it, and you will." The postcommunion Collect repeats the request that God grant through the mystery of this sacrament that evil will not triumph over justice.

[31] *Ibid.*, p. 369.

After finishing the Mass, the priest with the *probandus* and the whole congregation proceed from the church to the place where the ordeal by fire is to occur. There a further strengthening of the *probandus* follows: the priest offers him a draught of holy water as further protection against the burning power of the fire. This is followed by a blessing of the fire and of the iron or the plowshares. If the penitential psalms and the litany were not recited immediately after the Mass, they are recited at this time. A prayer concerning divine judgment is inserted into the litany. Then follow the prayers described above, which all focus upon the one request that God may reveal guilt and lead innocence to victory, and that the red-hot iron may be a refreshment for the innocent but a burning fire for the guilty. After further exorcistic prayers, the *probandus* is made to swear upon the cross or upon the Gospels or upon the relics that, in undergoing the ordeal, he will trust in God alone, not "in the devil and his magical arts."[32]

In the practice of Germanic law the practical execution of the ordeal by fire assumed different forms in which older pre-Christian traditions have to some extent been preserved. Thus the Frankish *Lex Ribuaria* of the sixth century contains the rule "to hold the hand in the fire."[33] The carrying of the red-hot iron nine steps became established as a general practice in the Frisian laws of the early Middle Ages and in the Carolingian common law, from which it was incorporated into the canons of the synods of Mainz in 847 and of Tribur in 895. The carrying of the red-hot iron was also accepted early by the Anglo-Saxons and became the preferred ordeal form for free men. In the regulations of Anglo-Saxon laws the weight was determined according to the seriousness of the crime; it varied between one and three pounds. The iron had to be red-hot.

According to Andreas Suneson, Scanian law was acquainted with still another type of ordeal by fire which was used in cases of suspected theft. The *probandus* had to throw the hot iron into a basin or tub twelve steps away from the burning pyre. He had

[32] Rockinger, "Quellenbeitrage zur Kenntnis," p. 378; Nottarp, *Gottesurteil-Studien*, p. 352.

[33] *Lex Ribuaria* (Hanover, 1889), 30, 1, and 31, 5, Monumenta Germaniae historica, Leges V, pp. 221 ff.; Grimm, *Deutsche Rechtsaltertümer*, vol. 2, p. 567.

to do it in such a manner that the iron remained in the basin and did not jump out again because of too great an impact. If this happened, or if the iron missed its target, the ordeal had to be repeated until the iron landed in the basin.[34]

Another kind of ordeal by fire consisted of walking between two burning pyres. This is credibly reported by another source about Petrus Igneus in Florence in 1067 and also about Petrus Bartholomaeus in 1098.[35] In Frisian law there is the walking through a burning pyre. The *probandus* was dressed in a shirt saturated with wax. Wearing this, he had to walk through the fire or between two fires, or the shirt was set aflame while he was wearing it.[36]

Walking across plowshares was provided for especially prominent cases. The *probandus* walked barefoot across a certain number, usually nine red-hot plowshares. The plowshare is an iron implement which has had sacred significance since the most ancient times. According to religious ideas popular among Germans of pre-Christian times, the plowshare possessed a power which protected against magic. Thus, the plowshare was used for healing diseases. The patient had to be blessed while standing on an inverted plowshare and holding another iron with his right hand upon his right shoulder. The magical power of the plowshare is increased by making it red-hot. Just as plowing the first furrow of the year with a red-hot plowshare keeps away wolves, according to pre-Christian ideas, so, according to medieval Christian ideas, encircling a field with a furrow keeps away witches. Thus, for the sacred act of ordeal by fire, an iron is taken which already has a magical significance in popular belief. This magical significance of the plowshare in the ordeal liturgy is made Christian by consecration with a special benediction. For this benediction the general formula for the *ferrum ignitum* is used, but there are also special forms for the benediction of the plowshares.[37]

34 Charles du Fresne Du Cange, *Glossarium mediae et infimae latinitatis*, ed. G. A. L. Henschel (Paris, 1840–50), under *ferrum candens*; Grimm, *Deutsche Rechsaltertümer*, vol. 2, pp. 569 ff., "Im Streit gegen einen simonastischen Bischof."

35 On Petrus Igneus see also Herbert Thurston, S. J., *Die Körperlichen Begleiterscheinungen der Mystik* (Lucerne, 1956), p. 210; Horace K. S. Mann, *Lives of the Popes*, 6 vols. (London, 1902–36), vol. 6, p. 302.

36 Rockinger, "Quellenbeiträge zur Kenntnis," p. 374.

37 *Handwörterbuch des deutschen Aberglaubens*, vol. 6, col. 1724; see also Du Cange, *Glossarium Mediae*, under *vomeres*; Grimm, *Deutsche Rech-*

Just as the red-hot iron must be carried nine feet, so the *probandus* must walk across nine plowshares, stepping on them firmly with the whole sole. This form of ordeal by fire was used especially for women among the highest circles of nobility who had been accused of adultery. Since they had no compurgator, they had to submit to this form of ordeal by fire to prove their innocence. The following details are reported in the *Annales monasterii Wintonensis* about Queen Emma, the mother of Edward the Confessor, who walked across the plowshares in Winchester Cathedral in 1043. The queen sought to clear herself by means of an ordeal of the accusations of marital infidelity raised several times against her. Nine red-hot plowshares were placed on the church floor, which first had been swept. They were spaced according to the length of the step. After they had been briefly blessed – the benediction had to be brief, so that the plowshares would not get cold in the meantime – the queen, barefoot and coatless, her outer garment tied up high, walked praying across the nine plowshares, accompanied by two bishops who guided her steps. She did it in such a manner, as the chronicler especially stresses, that the whole weight of her body rested every time on her feet. The queen withstood the ordeal uninjured, a fact which the chronicler considers a miracle.[38]

The walk across plowshares by the Empress Kunigunde, wife of Heinrich II, in the Cathedral of Bamberg in the year 1007, attained even greater fame. She too was accompanied by two bishops who led her across nine plowshares. Ebernand of Erfurt glorified this event in a heroic poem.[39] A Latin report hints that the empress was in a kind of trance during the ordeal,[40] an explanation which presumably comes closest to the truth if one considers that the *probandi*, conditioned by fasting, could very well be transported through the preceding prayers, benedictions, confession, communion, and the words of the liturgy into a psychophysical borderline condition.

Empress Kunigunde's endurance of the ordeal by fire was also

tsaltertümer, vol. 2, pp. 570 ff. For special plowshare benedictions see K. Zeumer, *Formulae Merovingici et Karolini aevi* (Hanover, 1882), Monumenta Germaniae historica, Leges, section V, p. 665.

38 Annales Monasterii Wintonensis Mabillon. Acta Sanctorum Ordinis Benedicti IV, 2, p. 71.

39 Mabillon VI, 1, p. 456; *Vitae Henrici Additamentum*, col. 3, Monumenta Germaniae historica, Scriptores IV, p. 820.

40 Nottarp, *Gottesurteil-Studien*, p. 258.

considered a divine miracle. The official recognition by canonists of the ordeal on this occasion is one of the very rare cases in which ecclesiastical authorities recognized an ordeal as a miracle, even in the theological-canonical sense. For canonization, proof of at least three miracles was necessary. On the occasion of the canonization of Empress Kunigunde, the fact that she "proceeded unharmed,"[41] was recognized as a miracle by Pope Innocent III in the bull of canonization in 1200 and it was also incorporated into the liturgy of the saint's festival.

It is characteristic of the social position of the sexes within the patriarchical structure of medieval society that the ordeal by fire was required exclusively of women as proof of marital fidelity, as in the Old Testament model where divine judgment is used to prove the marital fidelity of a woman, Susanna, the wife of Joachim. In medieval legal history, there is scarcely a case in which a man declares himself ready to seize a hot iron as proof of his marital fidelity or was ordered by judges to do so.

Nevertheless, Caesarius of Heisterbach attributes a fire miracle to at least one cleric, as a proof of his keeping the vow of celibacy.[42] This cleric was a private chaplain for a noble Franconian family whose male members had already succumbed to the wiles of a meretrix who belonged to the court. When the cleric demanded her expulsion from the household, she told the master of the house that she had also seduced the chaplain and that he now wanted to remove her from the court because of his jealousy. Since the master of the house doubted the truth of her claim, she tried to make it come true, at least later. With the craftiest methods she tried to force the chaplain into an embrace, but without success. Finally she threatened to kill herself if he still refused her. The chaplain apparently agreed to her demands. He had a sumptuous bed made on top of very flammable material which was covered with a sheet. Upon the arrival of the meretrix, he set fire to the bed on which he was lying and asked her to share his flaming bed with him. He remained unharmed in the midst of the burning flames; his clothes and his hair also remained unsinged; he felt the fire "as a soft cool wind." The meretrix, however, was horrified. Repentant, she went to her master and con-

41 *Ibid.*, p. 258; Browe, *De Ordaliis*, vol. 1, no. 30. On Kunigunde see also Hans Fehr, *Das Recht in der Dichtung* (Bern, n.d.), p. 185.

42 Caesarius von Heisterbach, *De miraculis*, II, 10, col. 34: "de clerico qui a meretrice infamatus incendium non sensit."

fessed the innocence of the chaplain whom she had slandered. The chaplain left the sinful house and entered the Dominican order.

Significantly, the husband who submits to the ordeal by fire to prove his marital fidelity to his accusers appears only in the later caricature of the ordeal as portrayed by the humanistic enlightenment of the urban middle classes. Hans Sachs exposes the venerable institution of ordeal by fire to the laughter of his fellow citizens by reversing the classical model of ordeal by fire. In his rhymed farce *Das heis Eyssen*, a husband who is accused of infidelity by his wife is to clear himself of the charge by an ordeal by fire. The husband, however, secretly protects the hand in which he is to carry the red-hot iron with a wood shaving. Thus he remains completely unharmed during the ordeal, to the great delight of the audience, which is well aware of his guilt.

To be sure, the practice of arriving at a judgment did not require from the *probandus* the immediate and total miracle reported of the two empresses. It was not required that the red-hot iron leave no traces whatsoever of a burn on the bare hand or the bare feet; instead, what was required was a rapid healing, so that no festering wounds remained. Therefore, the burned part — arm, hand, or feet — was immediately bandaged and after a few days carefully examined to determine the state of healing. According to Andreas Suneson's Scanian law, a glove was put on the *probandus*' hand after the ordeal. It was then officially sealed. The ordeal was considered to be withstood if healing was ascertained upon the official opening of the sealed bandage or glove.[43]

Finally, there remains the question of what caused the church to abandon the practice of ordeal by fire, as well as of ordeals in general, after it had developed through the centuries an ordeal liturgy so rich in theology and so well-founded biblically, and after the legal practice of the ordeal by fire itself had become so strongly rooted in the religious consciousness and the legal philosophy of the clergy.

Here we must first of all point out the fact that the rational and pragmatic spirit of Roman law was, from the very beginning,

[43] Zeumer, *Formulae Merovingici*, section III, p. 645; Nottarp, *Gottesurteil-Studien*, p. 249.

very skeptical toward the practice of ordeals. This pragmatic legal philosophy of Roman law also found its way into the canonical law of the church. From its inception, canonical law criticized or completely rejected the legal practice of the ordeal by fire which was rooted in Germanic legal consciousness and had been carried into the civil and ecclesiastical life of Germanic tribes and from there into the whole Holy Roman Empire. Since canonical law conceived of itself as containing the divinely sanctioned method of legal process, no other method was permissible.

This conception had a rationalist feature – Roman law was of course considered the "ratio scripta."[44] As early as the Carolingian Renaissance, the canonical legal conception is united with the arguments of a rationalistic theology which tried to rid itself of the prevailing magical or mystical interpretation of Christianity. The ordeal by fire, as well as the invocation of divine judgment in general, is considered a "superstitious invention."[45]

This superstition was not, however, rejected as inadmissible because it was attributed to the lack of education or to the imagination of the people; rather, it was rejected on the basis of an important theological argument. In the polemics against the ordeal by fire, the most important argument which constantly recurs in civil and ecclesiastical promulgations is the notion that the ordeal by fire is a violation of the divine commandment stated in Deuteronomy 6:16: "You shall not put the Lord your God to the test." There is also a rationalistic view which underlies the canonical understanding of this biblical quotation. It assumes that one must not demand or expect that God will act in the world in a way contrary to the rules and laws which he himself has instituted, and that a testing of the Lord is an offense against "reason" and against "nature." Significantly, it was the Archbishop Agobard of Lyon (816–40), the champion of an early phase of European enlightenment based on Roman education and Roman thought, who not only turned against the contemporary belief in witches and magic – "the stupidity of the miserable people has gone so far, that the Christians now believe in nonsense, to which a heathen never succumbed in former times," is one of his sayings – but who also polemicized against ordeals and branded them as a

[44] This formula can still be found in the *Constitutio Apostolica* of Benedict XV (1917), "Providentissima Mater Ecclesia."

[45] Nottarp, *Gottesurteil-Studien*, p. 216.

violation of the Christian faith. Only foolish people, he thought, could call the ordeal by fire or hot water, or the duel, a divine judgment, as if the Almighty God had to serve the passions and inventions of men and thus act contrary to Himself; if the results of ordeals were really divine judgments, then one would not need courts and other authorities.[46]

These protests of Carolingian enlightenment did not at first succeed in destroying the traditional folk piety and the prevailing practice of law, yet in subsequent centuries the protests grew increasingly loud. Proof of this is the development of the ordeal liturgy itself. Basically, the rich development of the ordeal liturgy already presupposes, in all its parts, opposition. Against the objection that ordeals are not Christian, the Old and New Testament substantiations of the ordeal by fire become more elaborate in the ordeal liturgy and the number of biblical archetypes greater.

The voices of an early rationalistic enlightenment are also heard occasionally in Carolingian literature. A poet of Freising, probably Erchambert, gives his opinions about ordeal in 834 in his "Carmen de Timone comite."[47] The Freising poet very correctly recognizes the eschatological character of the divine judgment which the ordeal involves and for this reason he rejects the use of the ordeal. The direct divine judgment takes place only on Doomsday; until then the statute law and the way of arriving at a judgment prescribed in it applies. This corresponds to the statement by Augustine which is often quoted against the ordeal by fire in canonistic literature: "No one should test God when he knows what to do from human reason."[48]

While the practice of the ordeal by fire was thus being undermined by canonical law and its underlying rational and pragmatic legal philosophy, as well as by the beginnings of European enlightenment, another objection brought about the downfall of the belief in the validity of the ordeal by fire. This objection was the idea that the devil himself could misuse the ordeal and make falsehood triumph. The frequency of the use of ordeals by fire and hot water and of the duel led even the most credulous to realize that many of the divine judgments arrived at by these means were actually misjudgments. At first, however, people did

[46] *Ibid.*, p. 333.

[47] *Ibid.*, p. 337; *Poetarum Latinorum II, 1*, ed. E. Dummler (Berlin, 1884), Monumenta Germaniae, p. 120.

[48] Nottarp, *Gottesurteil-Studien*, p. 354.

not explain this fact rationally, but saw in it proof of the presence of a satanic deception. The fear of such deception is already expressed in the fact that exorcism plays such a dominant role in the ritual of the ordeal by fire; the *probandus* is even carried from the church to the place of the ordeal to prevent demonic powers from flowing into him from below when he touches the ground.[49]

The idea of demonic deception on the occasion of the ordeal by fire developed above all in association with the belief in witches. Hexenhammer (1498) expresses strong reservations against the use of the ordeal by fire in the cases of women accused of witchcraft, since he feared that the expected divine miracle could also be brought about in demonic ways by witches who knew magic.[50] Moreover, this view confirms that the ordeal by fire was still regarded more as a magical process which could be thwarted by magical practices than as a marvelous expression of divine omnipotence and justice. In the sixteenth century, this fear had reached the point where the ordeal by fire was denied witches who wanted to use it to prove their innocence.

From this time onward, the religious idea of "testing God" receives special emphasis: by adjuring or forcing a direct decision from Almighty God, people are, in reality, succumbing to a *machinatio diabolica*! The offense against God's omnipotence must have appeared all the greater since the provoked divine miracle was in reality a victory for the devil! This conviction appeared in the *Verbum abbreviatum* (1187) by Petrus Cantor, one of the most decisive opponents of the ordeal by fire.[51]

The relationship between enlightenment and the abolition of the ordeal by fire appears especially clearly in the figure of the Hohenstaufen emperor Friedrich II. He rejected ordeals "with the proud mockery of the scientific mind." In 1231, in his Sicilian code, the constitutions of Melfi, he forbade all judges to use ordeals because only simpleminded people could believe that the true state of affairs would be revealed in this fashion; ordeals

49 Instead of nakedness the Christian Middle Ages demanded that the *probandus* be partially undressed and barefoot, with all hair removed to prevent the hiding of a charm. In some rites the *probandus* was vested in the clothing of a deacon or exorcist, thus entering the ranks of the minor clergy (see Nottarp, *Gottesurteil-Studien*, p. 235).

50 Institoris, Henricus, *Der Hexenhammer*, 3 vols., vol. 3, pp. 105 ff. (3d part, quaestio 17).

51 Browe, *De Ordaliis*, vol. 2, no. 197; Nottarp, *Gottesurteil-Studien*, pp. 364, 383.

were incompatible with the nature of things and with the truth which they did not illuminate, but rather obscured. Thus, the traditional theological argument against ordeals, namely that they were a testing of God, is abandoned. The only valid argument remaining is that they are incompatible with the laws of nature and of reason.[52]

Of course, this attitude was representative of the upper classes, but enlightenment slowly began to prevail among a growing educated class. The mystical and magical folk piety of the Middle Ages experienced increasing rationalization. The belief in the magical power of the fire became just as discredited as the fear of the immediate presence of God and of the direct miraculous intervention of reigning divine justice in the daily lives of the faithful.

The reduction of Christian faith to a "rational religion" which was undertaken by humanism soon took effect in the circles of the educated urban middle classes. In the books of the Alsatian Franciscan Johannes Pauli, published in 1522, divine judgments like the ordeal by fire or the ordeal by hot water are the subjects of very amusing farces.[53] In the rationally illuminated climate of urban enlightenment, the prerequisite for a faithful acceptance of the ordeal by fire, the belief in the omnipresence of the divine judge and his power to demonstrate justice through a miracle, has disappeared.[54]

The attempts which are evident from the very beginning to induce a favorable outcome of the ordeal by "assisting" it with measures which reduced or prevented the burning of the bare skin by the red-hot iron belong half in the sphere of countermagic and half in the realm of magical medicine. In an obvious imitation of pre-Christian practices in which the *probandus* tried to limit the harmful effect of the red-hot iron by magical herbs and by application of certain oils, the priest gave the *probandus* the chrism, which was considered to be a particularly strong apotropaism. Charlemagne had to issue decrees in which the clergy was forbidden on the pain of cutting off one hand to make this

[52] J. L. A. Huillard-Breholles, *Historia diplomatica Friderici secundi*, 7 vols. (Paris, 1854), vol. 4, pt. 1, pp. 102 ff., "Constitutiones regni Siciliae, liber II tit. 31, 33."

[53] Fehr, *Das Recht*, pp. 340, 360, 549.

[54] Only the fire-eater who produces the "miracle" for pay at the fair is left.

chrism available to the *probandus* for drinking or rubbing into his hands.[55] The drinking of holy water immediately before undergoing the ordeal by fire is probably the ecclesiastical substitute for the prohibited and magically "more potent" chrism.

Medicine also offered concoctions which presumably protected against burns.[56] Even in its early stages, the liturgy of the ordeal Mass refers to these attempts to fasify the ordeal by magical practices or by treating the hand with medicinal herbs. Thus the liturgy affirms the early presence of an attitude which presupposes a basically rationalistic way of thinking.[57] The fact that God is asked in the text of the liturgy to prevent the fraud which the *probandus* might intend to commit by using medicinal preparations on his hands presupposes that one had to reckon rather frequently with such attempts to "*corriger la fortune.*" According to the report of Georgio Pachymeres, in Byzantium and in Asia Minor in the middle of the thirteenth century, the *probandus'* hand was wrapped in an officially sealed cloth three days *before* the ordeal by fire while he was preparing himself with fasting and prayer. This was done to prevent the use of salves which might possibly make the hand immune to burns.[58]

In addition to this progress of enlightenment and in addition to the natural tendency to try to influence the outcome of the ordeal by fire by magic or by medicines, there was also an internal element founded in the religious understanding of the ecclesiastical sacrament of penance which contributed to the dissolution of the ordeal by fire. Before undergoing the ordeal by fire and before receiving communion in the ordeal Mass, the *probandus* was required to make a general confession to the priest. As part of the confession he received absolution. Absolution meant that God pronounced the sinner free of the sins which he had confessed to the priest. Could God in the ordeal by fire damn the guilty if He had previously, in the absolution through the mouth of the priest, pronounced him free of all guilt? Thus, after he had confessed his guilt to the priest and after he had received absolution from him, a *probandus* who knew he was guilty could undergo with a clear conscience the ordeal by fire, which normally would

55 See another capitulary of Aachen in 809.
56 Nottarp, *Gottesurteil-Studien,* p. 266.
57 *Ibid.,* p. 267.
58 Browe, *De Ordaliis,* vol. 2, no. 76 (Pachymeres).

have turned out unfavorably for him. Caesarius of Arles tells of a fisherman in the bishopric of Utrecht who had been living for a long time with a woman who was not his wife. Because it was well known, he feared that he would be accused by the synod and then, if he admitted his guilt, would be forced to marry her. If, however, he denied everything and subsequently was proven guilty by the iron ordeal, he feared he would fare even worse. Therefore he went to a priest, confessed, and asked for advice. The priest told him that if he firmly intended to better himself, he could deny (!) his sin, because he had been freed of it through the confession, and then calmly carry the hot iron.[59] And thus it happened, to the great astonishment of all who knew only too well of the fisherman's affair with the woman. Similarly, Johannes Kantakuzenos, the emperor emeritus and later monk and historian, tells of an adulteress who withstood the ordeal by fire although she was guilty only because earlier in the confession she had vowed to be faithful in the future.[60] Therefore, a more subjectivized conception of confession and grace, of human guilt and divine forgiveness, also contributed to the decline of the ordeal by fire, whose religious presuppositions belonged to a more archaic stage of religious consciousness.

[59] *Ibid.*, no. 67 (Caesarius).
[60] Nottarp, *Gottesurteil-Studien*, p. 269.

DOCETISM

A Peculiar Theory about the Ambivalence of the Presence of the Divine

U. BIANCHI

Professor Eliade's discussion of image and symbol gives us an occasion to contribute some reflections on docetism as a peculiar theory of the ambivalence of the presence of the divine in the world, as expressed by particular gnoseological-ontological categories. We are convinced that it is also possible to find "docetistic" attitudes outside the classical field of docetism, which is gnostic Christology. Leaving this particular task to specialists in the religious literatures and faiths of southern and eastern Asia, we shall concentrate our investigation on some gnostic and nongnostic sources, all belonging to the Greek and Hellenistic areas, which perhaps may suffice to give an idea of docetism as a peculiar feature of religious typology.[1] It is a feature whose investigation is the more momentous as far as that particular field is concerned; that is, the modes of the relation between the divine and the mundane, both in the realm of cognition and of ontology, are of first importance in the description of a religious system.

It appears to us that the entire problem of gnosticism amounts to defining a specific mode of presence for heavenly beings in this world. In other words, it is the problem of docetism. The best point of departure in approaching this problem seems to be an

The following exposition was prepared as a communication to the Symposium on Heresies and Schisms held at Berlin in November, 1966, on the occasion of the seventy-fifth anniversary of the Kommission für spätantike Religionsgeschichte.

[1] As for docetism in Buddhism, for example, see E. Conze, "Buddhism and Gnosis," in *Le origini dello gnosticismo* ("The Origins of Gnosticism"), Colloquium of Messina, 1966 (Leiden, 1967), pp. 657–58. Obviously, not every theology of image is docetistic or gnostic; we find it also in orthodox, or in any case nongnostic, Christianity.

important text from the *Hypostase of the Archons* (134, 17–18) from Nag Hammadi: "The psychic can never reach the pneumatic."[2] The context of these words is the fate of the archons who are infatuated with the beauty of the Divine Image manifested in the waters. These same archons later become infatuated with the beauty of the heavenly Eve, who is consubstantial with light, and they try to defile her. Eve, attacked by such horrible and material beings, temporarily shuts the eyes of the archons and substitutes for herself her counterpart, the earthly Eve, who is an "image" of the heavenly Eve. This counterpart is defiled by them and gives birth to Cain.[3]

We believe that we have here the prototype of gnostic docetism. As the latter is closely related to the whole of gnostic metaphysics and theology, it would be a mistake to approach it only in connection with Christology—even gnostic Christology. On the contrary, the problem also involves figures like the heavenly woman, the Anthropos, and in general, as I have indicated, all of the heavenly beings who, according to the gnostic mythology, are present in this world in some way or another, whether actively or passively. Therefore, we must remember that the gnostic ideology has never simply restricted itself to the framework of an anticosmic dualism.[4]

On the contrary, it analyzed on their own presuppositions the various threads that bound together the heavenly and the earthly worlds. Now, docetism is a very specific kind of union, and at the same time a separation, between the two worlds; it is a kind of union well-fitted to correspond to the dualistic-monistic presup-

[2] See J. Leipoldt and H. M. Schenke, *Koptisch-gnostische Schriften aus den Papyrus-Codices von Nag Hamadi* (Hamburg and Bergstedt, 1960).

[3] See also the report of Irenaeus, *Adversus omnes Haereses*, I, 24, 1, on Saturninus' theory: "When a shining image appeared from above, from the Absolute Sovereignty, they [the angels, powers, etc.] were not able to hold it because it immediately returned upward again. They exhorted themselves and said, 'Let us make a man after the image and after the likeness' [note that the 'our' of the Genesis text is deleted here]. When he had been made, and what was formed could not stand erect because of the angels' weakness but wriggled like a worm, the Power above took pity on him because he was made in its likeness, and it sent a spark of life which raised the man and made him upright and made him live. . . ." (translated by R. M. Grant in his *Gnosticism* [New York, 1961], p. 31). The text goes on to say: "The Saviour is unbegotten, incorporeal, and without form. He appeared as a man in semblance." The teaching of Saturninus should be compared with that of the *Apocryphon of John* (translated in *ibid.*).

[4] Marcion is only a partial exception to this, see "Marcion théologien biblique ou docteur gnostique," in *Studia Evangelica* Series.

positions of the gnostic cosmology and metaphysics. According to gnosticism, everything endowed with form, with life, and with order originates in the heavenly world; this presupposes a clear and at the same time complex formulation of the relationship between the two worlds. To give such a formulation was the aim of docetism.

We must, for example, attribute to docetism the common ophitic idea that the upper world is not really physically contained in this world, but only impresses a "seal" in the lower world (and thus leaves something that is in itself empty, that is, with reference to the pneuma; still, however, there is *something* that can give to things below a form and a somewhat "real" semblance of life); one can also speak of an "aroma" or a "dew."[5] All of these are expressions that suggest a very elusive kind of presence-absence of the pneuma within this material world; that is to say, they are formulations of docetism.

Outside of gnosticism as well as within it, the history of docetism is as long as the area it covered was broad. Leaving to one side an interpolated Homeric verse (Odyssey XI 602) contrasting the *eidolon* of Herakles in the Hades to his person, his self (*autos*), as dwelling among the gods, we find the oldest western example of docetism in the post-Homeric legend of Helen as it appears in the *Palinodie* of Stesichoros,[6] a legend and a personality that were to be readopted by Simonianism in a very peculiar way.[7]

Understanding docetism in such a way, namely, as a kind of separation and relation between the lower and upper worlds, al-

[5] Hippolytus, *Refutation of All Heresies*, V, 17, 7–8, and V, 19–22; compare Irenaeus *Adversus*, I, 30, 1–14.

[6] See Plato, *Phaedrus*, 243a, and particularly *Resp.* IX, 586 c: *ὥσπερ τὸ τῆς Ἑλένης εἴδωλον ὑπὸ τῶν ἐν Τροία Στησίχορός φησι γενέσθαι περιμάχητον ἀγνοία τοῦ ἀληθοῦς*. Perhaps already by Hesiod? (cf. schol. Lycophr. 832, as discussed by Bergk, *Poetae lyrici Graeci*, III, p. 215). Or a Pythagorean invention? (see Grant, *Gnosticism*). On the Helen of Stesichoros, see M. Doria, *La Parolo del Passato*, 84 (1962).

[7] Irenaeus, *Adversus*, I, 23, 2: "*qua propter et Stesichorum per carmina maledicentem eam, orbatum oculis; post deinde poenitentem et scribentem eas, quae vocantur, palinodias, in quibus hymnizavit eam, rursus vidisse.*" This is reminiscent of one of the antitheses of Eva in a new gnostic text from the Nag Hammadi, VI, 13, 16: "I am the Honored and the Despised. I am the Prostitute and the Woman of Good Repute . . ." (M. Krause, *ADIK Kopt.* Series II, pp. 23–24). See also *Origini dello gnosticismo*, p. 82, and our remarks in the same place, p. 725. This is a question of an acute expression of the typically gnostic "devolution," degradation, and fracturing of the divine Sophia.

lows us to make further distinctions between different modalities of this relationship. Two types of docetism were already distinguished in Irenaeus' texts on Simonianism. There was the situation of the Megale Dynamis, the Supreme God, who was manifest in Simon: "*ut et in hominibus homo appareret ipse, cum non esset homo; et passum . . . in Iudaea putatum, cum non esset passus.*"[8] And there was the somewhat different situation of the Ennoia, who descended *ad inferiora* and bore the angels and the powers, by whom she was eventually imprisoned *propter invidiam* into the lower world and caught in increasingly unworthy bodies, from the Helen of Sparta down to the whore Helen of Tyrus, whose liberator was Simon. Unlike the Ennoia, the manifestation of the Supreme God was never bound to anything inferior; nonetheless, there was a true consubstantiality between him and the Ennoia, and salvation came to man through hope *in eum* (as manifested in Simon) *et in Helenam.*

We also have a true docetism in Helen. It is therefore up to the gnostic to know enough to "recognize" in her the divine principle, that Ennoia (thought) God which men may never abuse, not even when it is manifested in degraded form. The quotation of the *Palinodie* of Stesichoros in the Simonian document is important. There we have a true instance of heathen docetism: the post-Homeric legend of Helen, who came to Ilion only as *eidolon*, while her person lingered in Egypt, so that the poet, who in following the popular aedic version has blasphemed her, is struck by blindness – that is to say, in the Simonianist eyes – and he must suffer a true *contrappasso* for his *agnosia.*

Nonetheless, the Ennoia has – unlike the Megale Dynamis – really disappeared into matter; *et hanc esse perditam ovem.* If Simon is only a *savior*, Helen is only *saved*, and she is the cause of salvation for men only in respect to the hope that they may join her in her own salvation. In the Simonianism of Iranaeus there is no saved savior, but this in no way contradicts its gnostic character since salvation here too occurs only through recognition of the hidden nature of a being noetic in itself.

In the Song of the Pearl of the *Acts of Thomas* the situation is more complex.[9] In considering the gnostic significance of this

[8] Irenaeus, *Adversus*, I, 23, 3.

[9] Edgar Hennecke, *Neuteslamentliche Apokryhen*, ed. W. Schneemelcher, 2 vols., 3d ed. (Tubingen, 1959), vol. 2, pp. 349 ff.

text, we note that the prince and the pearl seem to be distinguished, yet both are lost in the lower world of Egypt. A prince who forgets his duty and his identity could never have been identified with Christ in any variety or heresy of Christianity. If the pearl is the soul to be saved, the lost sheep, then who, really, is the prince? There is almost surely a kind of consubstantiality between these two, but the situation here is more complicated than that of the saved-savior formula. The prince in the Song of the Pearl is in a position midway between that of the pearl, which has only to be saved, and that of the savior who, in other gnostic texts (for example the *Hymn of the Naassenes*),[10] clothes his impassibility with archontic forms when he descends and thus dupes the archons. In the Song of the Pearl the prince is recognized by the archons and is *himself* duped.

In brief, the situation of the pearl is reminiscent of the degraded Anthropos among the Naassenes, in Poimandres and in the *Untitled Writing* of Codex II, while the prince in the Song of the Pearl recalls the Manichaean Anthropos, whose task first completes the *tertius legatus*: these relationships with a gnostic Anthropos who is fundamentally one and the same figure underscore the *homoousia* of the prince and the pearl. On the other hand, the gnostic savior who appears in his pure docetic garb in the Naassene *Hymn of the Soul* corresponds better to the Basilidianic Jesus, who is replaced at the cross by Simon of Cyrene and laughs at his persecutors; in this connection he also resembles the heavenly woman who in the *Hypostase of the Archons* substitutes her *eidolon* for herself and laughs at her persecutors.

For the moment let us put aside all of these figures – Sophia, the Anthropos, the prince, and the Logos (among the Perates) – who represent, to varying extents, saviors and at the same time saved beings, and consider only two categories within the gnostic text: (a) the savior who is not in need of salvation, and (b) the being who is – through gnosis – saved by him. Do these categories have something in common that can still vindicate the legitimacy of the use of the conception of the "saved savior"? In other words, is there a *homoousia* between these two categories? And what kind of docetism do we have in this specific instance?

We can look for an answer to this question in the *Gospel of Thomas,* as H.-Ch. Puech's penetrating study of the theology of

10 Hippolytus, *Refutation,* V, 10, 2.

image, clothing, angels, and the heavenly Self in this gospel shows us.[11] The savior in the *Gospel of Thomas* is an excellent example of the not-to-be-saved savior. But he is a savior who is fashioned completely in the gnostic style, as is shown by this book's constant doctrine of gnosis as the specific means of salvation. This problem is also important with regard to the question of Christian and heathen elements in gnosticism, for the not-to-be-saved gnostic savior better recalls the New Testament Christ—even with substantial qualifications—whereas the gnostic saved savior, like the prince in the Song of the Pearl, more closely resembles the figures of the Greek-gnostic Sophia, the Anthropos, or the Naassenes' Adonis and Attis. Yet it seems to us that the problem of gnosticism and Christology in the *Gospel of Thomas* is completely contingent upon the problem of metaphysical docetism in the same text, though this metaphysical docetism does not have that abstract and absolute formulation (which on the other hand is characteristic of the gnosticism of India) of a passage in the *Odes of Salomos* (34, 4–5): "the model of that which is below is above, for above there is everything and nothing is below. Only he who does not possess this knowledge believes that something exists below"—that is to say, in this world. The true *ousia* is therefore in the upper world, and it is the prototype of everything that "appears" in this world.

Thus it says in the *Gospel of Thomas* (logion 84): "If you see your likeness, you should rejoice; but if you see your images, that have come into being before you, and do not die, and do not manifest themselves, how great will be that which you will experience" (but compare log. 83). Here is a "manifestation" that does not really occur in this world, for it contains the real presence of a pneumatic that is to be known only by means of gnosis and in an eschatological perspective—as opposed to the *dokein*, which is a kind of presence and effect of the heavenly being in this world.

We shall see how this conception, which leaves an opening for the engagement of the pneumatic being in this world (see below, pp. 271–72), concurs with the gnostic idea of the totality, the "All," and its relation to the world. Before we consider this central aspect of gnostic theology, including that of the *Gospel of*

[11] "Annuaire du Collège de France," 63 (1963–64): 201 ff.; 64 (1964–65): 212 ff. The translation of the logia of Thomas follows that of the Leyden edition; reference is sometimes made to the translation by Grant.

Thomas, we shall quote a few other logia of this gospel that illustrate the ambivalent presence and absence of the heavenly substance.

Thus we have logion 110, "to find the world" (that is, to perceive the world as empty, to unmask the world), and logion 80, "Jesus said: He who has known the world has found a body, and that same one who has found the body, of him the world is not worthy." This logion – which is identical to logion 56, except that the latter has "corpse" instead of "body" – uses the same expression in connection with the body that logion 110 uses with the world. We shall find the same world-body parallel in logion 28, which is very important for the problem of docetism and the figure of the savior in the *Gospel of Thomas*. Let us note that this expression "to find the body" (or "the corpse") is parallel to that knowledge of the world that *a contrario* defines gnosis as the knowledge of the heavenly *ousia*, the *ousia* that must be sought forever and ever (log. 2; compare log. 111: "he who will find himself [his *ousia*, his "image"], of him the world is not worthy").[12]

As we have said, the place of the *ousia* is the heavenly world whereas the lower world is empty, or rather (in the *Gospel of Thomas*) deficient.[13] This becomes clear in those logia which mention the "All." This All is not to be understood in a merely pantheistic sense; it is much more the fullness of the *ousia*, of the heavenly substance which exists *ontōs*,[14] which is rich and whole. Thus we have logion 77: "I am the light that is over all. I am the All, [from me] the All has gone forth, and the All has reached to me. Split wood, and I am there: lift the stone, and you will find me there." Therefore, there is in things something external, which is an appearance (the stone), and something internal, which is the fullness of the *ousia*. The nature of this relationship of the All to the world is not described in either cosmological or *heilsgeschichtlich* terms in the *Gospel of Thomas;* such description does, however, occur in tractates like the *Hypostase of the Archons* and the *Untitled Writing*, which mention the God of the All (an

[12] On these terms see the discussion by R. M. Grant, *The Secret Sayings of Jesus According to the "Gospel of Thomas"* (Garden City, N.Y., 1960), p. 155, with reference also to the "corpse" of the Naassenes, Hippolytus, *Refutation*, V, 8, 22.

[13] Puech, "Annuaire du Collège de France," 65 (1965–66): 250; 64 (1964–65): 212 ff.

[14] See note 12.

expression which in the contemporary orthodox texts has obviously another meaning, i.e., creationistic) and the Pronoia of the All. This All also embraces the lower world, or, better, the vicissitudes that take place in it. The lower world is governed by heavenly providence; its protagonist is the divine *ousia* which imprints form and life on the lower world. Now docetism is a particular interpretation of this providential presence of the Full and the Rich (and of Life) in the emptiness and poverty and death of the material world, a presence developed most extensively in the ophitic tractates quoted by Hippolytus.

As for the pneumatology and the soteriology of the *Gospel of Thomas* and its conception of the presence-absence of *ousia*, we can quote a text of Hippolytus which mentions a Naassene idea about "the blessed nature of past, present, and future things, which is at the same time hidden and manifest."[15] This blessed nature is identified with the heavenly realm that is in man, and the Naassenes say that it is mentioned in the *Gospel of Thomas*. And logion 3 mentions the kingdom that "is within you and outside you" (the second half only in the Coptic version, not in the fragmentary Greek [*Oxyrhynchus Papyri* 654]).[16]

The Christology of the *Gospel of Thomas*, which is characterized by the idea of the not-to-be-saved and not-to-be purified Christ, has nonetheless been influenced by this idea of the ambivalent presence and absence of the pneumatic in the world. Here we can cite the remarkable logion 28: "I stood in the midst of the world and revealed myself to them in the flesh." The *parallelismus membrorum* with its above-mentioned identification of world and flesh (which is foreign to the Johannine "became flesh") also shows the analogy between the expressions "to stand in the midst of the world" and "to reveal . . . oneself." Therefore, like the savior Jesus of the Naassenes' psalm who takes on the form of the archons, or like the saving Logos of the Sethianes[17] who descends into the lower world, the *metra*, and thereby dupes it, this revelation of the savior of the *Gospel of Thomas* who brings about gnosis is accomplished entirely through his "standing in the midst

[15] Hippolytus, *Refutation*, V, 7, 20; compare V, 8, 8.

[16] See J. Doresse, *L'Evangile selon Thomas ou les paroles secretes de Jesus* (Paris, 1959), pp. 124–27). Doresse presupposes, as does our argument, a correspondence between the "within you and outside you" and the "hidden and manifest" of the Naassene text.

[17] In Hippolytus, *Refutation*, V, 19.

of the world." This kind of docetism—like all docetism—is to be sharply distinguished from incarnation and *unio hypostatica.* But it is a kind of docetism that makes a clear distinction between the savior and the men to be saved. The theory of the *homoousia* of the gnostic with the heavenly image does not prevent the *Gospel of Thomas* from saying that men come "empty"[18] into this world and that they belong to this world until the *gnosis* unites them with their heavenly counterparts.

As far as the savior is concerned, it is evident that his (more or less real) transcendence *vis-à-vis* the cosmos and men in the *Gospel of Thomas*—in contrast to the cosmicized Anthropos of the Naassenes and the Logos of the Perates—owes very much to the influence of the common, nongnostic Evangelical catechese and literature. But despite this, it would be misleading to neglect, *inter alia*, the fact that the *Gospel of Thomas* was used as a textbook by the Naassenes themselves, as the report by Hippolytus explicitly states (see above and note 15). The transcendence of the savior in the *Gospel of Thomas* is heavily conditioned by the usual pneumatology of gnosticism, as our analysis of all these docetic texts has shown.

[18] Because the world itself is empty (see note 12). The integration of log. 28 within the gnostic pneumatology is supported by log. 97.

A VANISHING PROBLEM

JACQUES DUCHESNE-GUILLEMIN

Between Christmas and Epiphany, in certain regions of Christendom, three boys carrying a paper star fixed at the end of a decorated stick go singing from farm to farm and beg for a few pennies. They are often in fancy dress but sometimes content themselves with wearing their coats inside out. They smear their faces and hands—one black, with soot; another white, with flour; the third red, with pig's blood. This usage is a remainder of medieval mysteries which originated in France and spread through most of Europe and in which the three wise men at Bethlehem were impersonated as an old man, an adult, and a beardless youth. This differentiation is first attested, in the literary sources, in the Venerable Bede (eighth century), and in art, two centuries earlier.[1]

The division of human life into three phases seems hoary, and certainly reaches back to classical antiquity. It was shared by many authors, including Aristotle. Admittedly, no earlier pictorial representation of it has survived than the eighth-century A.D. fresco in the small bath of Quseir Amra in the Jordanian desert: this decorative and symbolic painting, made by Greek artists using ancient, traditional motifs, shows, in three medallions, a white-bearded old man, an adult with black hair, and a red-cheeked, blond youth.[2]

[1] Compare J. Duchesne-Guillemin, "Die drei Weisen aus dem Morgenlande und die Anbetung der Zeit," *Antaios*, 7 (1965): 234 ff. A gross misprint appears on p. 248; the third line from the bottom should read "primus fuisse dicitur Melchior, senex et canus." Another edition, in Italian, of the same lecture has fewer notes but more illustrations: *I Magi di Betlemme nelle tradizioni occidentali, Vita e Pensiero* (Milan, 1966).

[2] Alois Musil, *Quseir Amra* (Vienna, 1907).

To apply this notion to the three wise men in order to differentiate them was a rather obvious step to take, and it may be that we have to do here with simply one more instance of the absorption into Christianity of a banal pagan feature. Yet there was perhaps in this particular case a special reason for this absorption.

On a silver plaque from the Iranian province of Luristan, dating back at least to the eighth century B.C. and brought to light a few years ago (it is now in the Cincinnati Museum), there appear before a mythical figure three sets of worshipers: children, adults, and old men.[3] This distribution seems particularly suitable to the case of worshipers of a being otherwise characterized as a god of time, for he has wings as well as two faces – symbols of the bisexuality which is normal in a god of origins. An allusion has been recognized here to the god Zurvan, who had in a Syriac text three companions, Ashoqar, Frashoqar, and Zaroqar, terms adapted from Avestan epithets which clearly allude to him as god of youth, manhood, and old age.

Did the pictured ceremony take place at certain seasons? We do not know. Yet it is perhaps not a mere chance that in the Christian world the three corresponding wise men – the youth, the adult, and the old man – do not merely present themselves before God but figure as worshipers of a god who manifests himself at the very time of year in which the year – and hence Time itself – is renewed.

In fact, Zurvan was called in Greek Aion, and it was Aion-Dionysos whose anniversary was celebrated on January 6, that is to say, on the very day which became the feast of the Three Kings. But Aion was conceived of and represented sometimes as a child (by Heraclitus, Euripides, etc.), sometimes as an adult in the fullness of his age (in the picture described by John of Gaza, under Justinian), and sometimes as an old man (by Claudian, in 400 A.D.): in other words, he contained in himself the three ages which were to be distributed among the three wise men.

How can this filiation be demonstrated? Our documents concerning Iran are, as usual, rare and not easily dated, but we do have the medieval tradition on the three ages of the Magi. The problem is therefore posed in historical terms. It would be different if we did not have that tradition: we would then be inclined

[3] R. Ghirshman, "Le dieu Zurvan sur les bronzes du Luristan," *Artibus Asiae*, 21 (1958): 37 ff.

to look for another explanation. But even if the historical approach imposes itself, it should not blind us to the possibility of an underlying structure.

In other words, if the distinction between the Negro, the white-bearded old man, and the red-cheeked youth succeeded in imposing itself and becoming permanent, is it not partly because it fitted into a pattern of colors which was already in existence in European folklore and perhaps even in the Indo-European ideology, or earlier yet?

Quite a few publications seem to have paved the way to an answer. First was Jan de Vries' article "Rood, wit, zwart" in the Belgian-Dutch periodical *Volkskunde* (n.s. 2 [1942]), which was followed by Georges Dumézil's discovery of the color symbolism of the three functions in Indo-European society and religion[4] and Lucien Gerschel's long article on dyeing techniques in ancient and medieval Europe in which he shows that red was the almost exclusive color for dyeing linen, whereas white was the color of the bleached linen and black or brown or any other dark hue the natural color of the unbleached, unwashed fabric.[5]

Gerschel's article appeared too late for C. Scott Littleton to mention it in his excellent book *The New Comparative Mythology* (Berkeley and Los Angeles, 1966), which offers the interesting suggestion that the Dumézilian tripartition may have been reflected in the European preference for triplicity, for instance in the doctrine of the Holy Trinity. We might add several examples, among them the scholastic axiom, rooted in classical antiquity, *omne trinum perfectum*.

But the question is even wider, since we read in Paul Radin's *Primitive Man as Philosopher* (New York, 1927), for instance, that Indians in the western United States use in their decoration, as the three *natural* colors, white, red, and black.

A vanishing problem. . . .

[4] Dumézil, *L'Idéologie tripartie des Indo-Européens* (Brussels, 1958); *La religion romaine archaïque* (Paris, 1966).

[5] Gerschel, "Couleur et teinture chez divers peuples indo-européens," *Annales* (*Economies, Sociétés, Civilisation*), 21 (1966): 608 ff.

CHAINS OF BEING IN EARLY CHRISTIANITY

ROBERT M. GRANT

In his well-known study *The Great Chain of Being* (Cambridge, Mass., 1936), A. O. Lovejoy discussed the philosophical – chiefly Platonic – origins of this idea and traced its history in later times. The purpose of this essay is to show that within Christianity the idea had religious rather than philosophical roots, and to argue that even among Christian philosophical theologians the links in the chain, whatever may be said of the "chain" notion itself, were derived not from the kinds of considerations noted by Lovejoy but from nonphilosophical data expressed primarily in the New Testament and in its Jewish-Christian background. Thus, our theme is eminently suitable for discussion in a group of essays presented to a distinguished scholar who has insisted upon the importance of the study of religious themes as peculiarly religious.

We are not directly concerned with the showing that ideas about such chains circulated in the Graeco-Roman world. A. J. Festugière, in discussing the brief psalm which Hippolytus quoted from the Gnostic teacher Valentinus,[1] has pointed out that these ideas were well known in the empire and has cited the *Platonic Epistle* II, 312 e and following, as well as three texts from the *Hermetica*.[2] Instead, we shall turn directly to the New Testament.

According to Romans 13:1–3, there is a cosmic power structure which implies that subordinates obey their superiors. Every

[1] "Notes sur les Extraits de Théodote de Clement d'Alexandrie et sur les fragments de Valentin," *Vigiliae Christianae*, 3 (1949): 205–7.

[2] *Corpus Hermeticum* 11, 2 ff.; 11, 15; 10, 13.

living thing must obey the powers above it, for there is no authority except from God and authorities exist by God's ordinance. Resistance to authority is resistance to God. At this point Paul is thinking primarily about the state and its officials, as the succeeding verses show. What he has to say about cosmic structures, however, has broader implications. We shall consider (1) his picture of the relations among God, Christ, and Christians; (2) his picture of family life; and finally, (3) some early Christian ideas about angels and archangels.

God, Christ, Christians

At Corinth a small group of "emancipated" Christians seems to have taken Paul's teaching about their new condition to mean that they now lived as wise men, rich and royal; they made use of the Stoic paradoxes about the ideal wise man, rich because needing nothing, royal because ruling himself. Everything belonged to them, for they were free from all. Just so, the Cynic Diogenes was said to have taught that "everything belongs to the wise," for "the property of friends is held in common" and "the wise are friends of the gods"—and "everything belongs to the gods"![3] Paul had little sympathy with the Corinthians' ideas about the wise man, which he viewed as unrealistic (see I Cor. 4:7–13). He agreed with them that everything belonged to Christians, but in opposition to their "democratization" of divine property he set forth a hierarchical scheme. Everything did, indeed, belong to them: "Paul or Apollos or Cephas, or life or death, or things present or things future." All were theirs, but they belonged to Christ and, in turn, Christ belonged to God (I Cor. 3:22–23).

Their ownership of everything, like other aspects of their status, was not due to anything they had achieved but to divine favor (4:7). In the future the same God who gave his Son on behalf of Christians would freely give them everything else (Rom. 8:32). And nothing—death, life, angels, rulers, things present, things future, powers, height, depth, any other created thing—could separate them from the love of God as expressed in Christ Jesus (Rom. 8:38–39).

For our purposes the hierarchical structure is of primary importance. It is a structure grounded in the creation because, ac-

[3] Diogenes Laertius 6, 37.

cording to a semicredal formula expressed in I Corinthians 8:6, for Christians there is one God the Father, the source and goal of all existence, and one Lord Jesus Christ, the mediator of both creation and redemption for Christians. The pattern is the same: God–Christ–Christ's people.

It is a pattern reflected in the final triumph. First God raised Christ from the dead; later he will raise Christians (I Cor. 15:23). Christ will overcome every hostile power but will remain subordinate to "the one who subordinated everything to him" (15:24–28), just as Christians will remain subordinate to him; he remains Lord.

It is also a pattern for imitation. Paul describes his sufferings and asks the Corinthians to imitate him (4:16; compare Phil. 3:17); he asks them to imitate him as he imitates Christ (I Cor. 11:1). "Become as I am," he says (Gal. 4:12). In a less exhortatory mood, he tells the Thessalonians that they did become imitators of him and of the Lord and in turn provided an example to other churches (I Thess. 1:6–7). In suffering they also became imitators of churches in Judaea (2:14). Some of them need to imitate his working day and night and not living in idleness (II Thess. 3:7–9). In any event, the situation is much the same: Christians imitate an apostle who imitates Christ; they are being transformed into the image of God (II Cor. 3:18) – who is Christ (4:4). By forgiving one another as God forgave them in Christ, they can become imitators of God himself (Eph. 4:32–5:1).

The place of the apostle in this chain of being is evidently above that of his converts. He is their father, and in Christ Jesus he begot them through the gospel (II Cor. 4:15; compare Philemon 10); he suffers birth pangs until Christ is formed in them (Gal. 4:19). In turn, he and they owe their existence as a "new creation" to being in Christ (II Cor. 5:17); it is now not he who lives but Christ who lives in him (Gal. 2:20). Though he describes Christ as the Son of God and Christians as his own sons, he does not describe his own relation to Christ as that of son to father. The chain is incomplete at this point and remains so in the New Testament.

The function of the apostle in relation to Christ and the church can, however, be described in the matrimonial language to which we shall presently turn. Paul wanted to betroth the church as a pure virgin to her husband, Christ (II Cor. 11:2). Thus, he took the place which Jewish tradition had assigned to Moses in the betrothal of Israel to God. The difference is partly due to Paul's cosmic structure. The church is, to be sure, the equivalent of Israel (Gal. 6:16; compare I Cor. 10:18, Rom. 9:6). But she is not the bride of God, for God's mediator on earth, and in heaven as well, is Christ. Paul would never speak of the Father as anyone's husband. The sons of God (Rom. 8:14, 8:19, 9:26; II Cor. 3:18; Gal. 3:26, 4:6–7) are sons by adoption (Gal. 4:5, Rom. 8:15). He never discusses the generation of the Son of God.

Christ, the Church, Men, Women

We have now touched upon another significant aspect of Paul's cosmic structure. If the church can be regarded as the bride of Christ, what does this view imply for her relationship to him? Certainly it implies a very close unity. Not only in Ephesians 5:31 but also in I Corinthians 6:16 we find the Old Testament text about "one flesh" (Gen. 2:24) quoted. The Corinthians passage needs to be treated first because of its probable historical priority. Paul is discussing the emancipated Corinthians' argument, borrowed from the Cynics, that just as the food one eats is all "natural," so in matters of sex whatever comes naturally is permissible. He almost agrees with the premise but absolutely rejects the analogical inference. "The body is not for fornication but for the Lord, and the Lord is for the body" (6:13). Since the bodies of Christians are "members of Christ" they cannot make them members, for instance, of a prostitute. Sexual intercourse, on the basis of the "one flesh" text, results in "one body," whereas union with the Lord results in "one spirit" (6:15–17). The Lord is thus viewed as the spiritual husband of the Christian, a member of the church which is his bride. Christians belong not to themselves but to the Lord (6:19–20, 7:23).

The hierarchical aspect of marriage is not stressed in I Corinthians 7, where Paul is more concerned with mutuality in marriage, perhaps under the influence of contemporary Stoic teaching. In chapter 11, however, the hierarchical pattern comes to the fore since Paul is concerned with the behavior of women who do not wear veils in church. There is a chain of being from God through Christ through a husband to a wife (11:3). A man wears nothing on his head to suggest subordination for he is the image and glory of God; his wife is his "glory" and subordinate to him. She was taken from his side and was created for him (11:7–9). Admittedly there is an element of mutuality, since everything is from God (11:12). But Paul is almost obsessed with his point. He argues that the veiling of women is "suitable," that it is taught by "nature," that women's long hair indicates that they need a covering, and that in any case the veiling is a custom of the churches of God (11:13–16). Evidently Christian women at Corinth were difficult for him to deal with.

At Corinth, however, he continued to insist on subordination. "Women are to remain silent in the assemblies, for it is not permitted for them to speak; they are to be subordinate, just as the law says. If they wish to learn anything, they are to ask their own husbands at home, for it is a shameful thing for a woman to speak in church." Once more he appeals to the practice of other churches (14:34–36). The reference to the laws has to do with Genesis 3:16, which insists on the rule of Adam over Eve because she led him astray. Paul agrees with Josephus and rabbinic interpreters: "A woman is inferior to her husband in every respect; therefore she must obey him, not to humiliate her but so that she may be ruled, for God gave the power to the man" (*Contra Apionem* 3, 201).

Had the Corinthian women read Galatians 3:28 they might have found Paul's position somewhat inconsistent. There he says that in Christ Jesus there is neither Jew nor Greek, slave nor free, male nor female. Perhaps they did read it. In II Corinthians he does not return to the subject. Perhaps his encounter with them taught him something. In I Thessalonians, written while he was still at Corinth, he regards wives chiefly as the private property of their husbands (4:4–6) and this view does not appear later.

It is not absolutely certain that Paul wrote either Colossians or Ephesians, to which we now turn, but the ideas we find on this subject in these letters are much like what we have already encountered. Both letters contain sections on household duties which in form resemble what Stoic teachers provided on the subject. These sections are concerned with the mutual responsibilities of inferiors and superiors: wives and husbands, children and fathers, slaves and masters. In each instance the inferior party owes subordination or obedience to the superior, while the superior as husband offers love, as father lack of irritation, as master what is just and equitable (Col. 3:18–4:1).

In the case of the husband, his love for his wife is characteristic of a superior being who voluntarily abandons his rights (as in I Cor. 13:4–7). He is thus like Christ, the Son of God who "loved me and gave himself for me" (Gal. 2:20), who was in the form of God but became obedient (Phil. 2:6–8), who knew no sin but became sin (II Cor. 5:21), who was rich but became poor (II Cor. 8:9).

In Ephesians 5:22–6:9, the section on household duties is more fully developed, although its basic structure remains the same. The longest section has to do with the relation of wives and husbands. Wives are to be subordinate as to the Lord, for the hierarchical relationship is parallel to that of the church to Christ. Similarly, the love of husbands for wives is analogous to Christ's love for the church and his giving of himself for her. In addition, husbands should love their wives as their own bodies. Indeed, "he who loves his wife loves himself, for no one ever hated his own flesh but nourishes and cherishes it." The analogy is drawn with Christ and the church, the "one flesh" passage in Genesis is quoted and applied to Christ and the church, and the section concludes with injunctions for the husband to love his wife as himself—she is thus the neighbor of Leviticus 19:18[4]—and for her to fear her husband.

Can an inferior love a superior? Paul never says that a wife loves her husband or that a child loves a parent or that a slave loves his master. Certainly Christians can love one another, and are urged to do so. God loves; Christ loves. Do Christians love God? Yes, they can, although Paul very rarely says so (Rom. 8:28; I Cor. 2:9, 8:3). Do they love Christ? Not according to the Pauline epistles, where they believe in him or obey him. Indeed, one might even ask if an ordinary Christian can love an apostle. Perhaps the personal relations of Paul with his converts were such that he did not feel he could speak of such love, though he comes very close to mentioning it in the case of the Philippians, who have him in their heart (Phil. 1:7) and—though as usual Paul insists on his independence—have sent him a gift (4:10–20). The fact that questions like this are suggested by the texts shows how far we have come from the "chain of being" ideas found in Platonism.

After Paul's time we encounter what looks like hierarchical

[4] See Gal. 5:14, 6:2; Rom. 13:8–10.

language in the first epistle of Clement, where the sequence of high priest–priest–levite–layman is mentioned (40, 5). Within Christianity, however, an analogous hierarchy — God–Christ–apostles–bishops and deacons — is based on mission and appointment (42, 1–2). It is based on God's will in history, not on the nature of things. Similarly, we read in John 17 that as the Father sent Jesus into the world, so he is sending his disciples.

The Johannine idea that the disciples are to be received as the one who sent them is reiterated in the letters of Ignatius of Antioch (Eph. 6, 1), but Ignatius almost transmutes mission into metaphysics. The bishop is to be regarded as the Lord himself. Agreement with him is agreement with the Father of Jesus Christ, who is the universal bishop. Hypocrisy toward the visible bishop is hypocrisy toward the invisible one (Magnesians 3, 1–2). The bishop presides in God's place (6, 1); he is a copy of the Father (Trallians 3, 1). Below the bishop is the college of presbyters, analogous to the council of the apostles (Magnesians 3, 1; compare Trallians, 2, 2; 3, 1; Philadelphians 5, 1; Smyrnaeans 8, 1).

Christians are to be subject to the bishop and to one another as Jesus Christ was subject to the Father and the apostles are subject to Christ and the Father (Magn. 13, 2).

The hierarchy is not fully metaphysical. As Ignatius points out, even things in heaven such as the glory of the angels and the rulers visible and invisible will be condemned if they do not believe in the blood of Christ — that is, in his death. Office must not puff anyone up, for faith and love are all-important (Smyrn. 6, 1). But in actual practice "one who does anything without the bishop's knowledge worships the devil" (9, 1).

One must assume that Ignatius' ideas are related in part to his own exaltation of episcopal office. Since, however, he knew by heart Paul's letter to the Corinthians, it is likely that he derived his attitude in part from the Pauline notions of hierarchy. Pauline ideas recur in Ignatius' letter to Polycarp (5, 1): "tell my sisters to love the Lord and to be content, in flesh and spirit, with their husbands; similarly instruct my brothers in the name of Jesus Christ to love their wives as the Lord the church." Like Paul, Ignatius speaks often of love, rarely of loving God or Christ (Eph. 9, 2; 15, 3).

The full coordination of mission with metaphysical theology occurs only with the writings of Clement of Alexandria, who explains that the orders of bishops, presbyters, and deacons are analogous to the ranks of three kinds of angels.

Angels and Archangels

In the New Testament, and especially in the Pauline epistles, we encounter a bewildering array of supernatural beings. There are angels and *archai* ("principalities," Rom. 8:38); there are *archai* and *exousiai* ("authorities," I Cor. 15:24; Eph. 1:21, 3:10, 6:12); there are even "thrones, dominations, principalities, and authorities" (Col. 1:16). There are also *archontes* or "rulers," as in I Corinthians 2:6–8. In many instances it is not absolutely clear whether supernatural or natural powers are in view, for most of these terms were also used with reference to earthly authorities. *Archai* and *exousiai* are indubitably political in Luke 12:11 and Titus 3:1, as they are in the Platonic *Alcibiades* I, 135 a–b. *Exousiai* and *archontes* are political in Romans 13:1–3, according to the universal early Christian tradition outside Gnostic circles (see Irenaeus, *Adversus Haereses* 5, 34, 1). The *archontes* of I Corinthians 2:6–8 may be angelic, but they are political in Acts 13:27.

What this ambiguity shows is that, on the one hand, there is a certain confusion between the supernatural and the natural meanings of the words and, on the other, that the supernatural and the natural somehow correspond to each other. If there is a hierarchy on earth we should expect to find a hierarchy in heaven, and vice versa.

Paul mentions an "archangel" only once, in a passage depicting the coming of the Lord from heaven. Here his details are derived from Jewish apocalyptic thought, and at the end there is a "word of command" presumably given by the archangel (I Thess. 4:16). He does not, however, discuss the various ranks of angels, even though differentiations in ranks may be involved in the list in Colossians 1:16: *thronoi, kyriotētes, archai, exousiai.*[5]

The word "thrones" itself suggests some idea of locality, though this is not made explicit in the Pauline epistles.[6] It is made explicit in Ignatius' letter to the Trallians (5, 2). As a prospective martyr he is able to comprehend heavenly matters such as "the angelic locations and the archontic conjunctions"—phrases in

[5] For *thronoi kai exousiai* in the seventh heaven see *Testament of Levi* 3, 8.
[6] For "height" and "depth" related to angelic powers see Rom. 8:38–39.

which astrological terminology is blended. The author of the interpolated version of his letters makes the language more explicit, referring it to archangels and (heavenly) armies, to powers and dominations, to thrones and authorities, and even to "aeons" and the cherubim and seraphim; this terminology, however, is considerably later.

The Valentinian Gnostics, as we should expect, were concerned with the ranks of angels; they spoke of the archangels as images of the aeons and of the angels as images of the archangels.[7] When they quoted Colossians 1:16 they mentioned *thronoi, kyriotētes, basileiai* ("kingdoms"), *theotētes* ("deities"), and *leitourgiai* ("ministrations") – which, with angels and archangels, would make a total of seven classes.[8] One may add that Basil of Caesarea filled out the text in the same way, adding "powers," "angels," and "archangels" – again to a total of seven.[9] The idea of seven classes was quite common. Irenaeus (*Adv. haer.* 2, 30, 3–5) lists groups of five and six but concludes with a list of seven. Various Gnostic groups, however, allowed for various classes.

It was Clement of Alexandria who was most concerned with angels; indeed, he planned to write a treatise on the subject (*Stromateis* 6, 32, 1), of which U. Reidinger has found some traces in a work ascribed to Caesarius.[10] If his assignment of the source of this to Clement is correct, we do not learn much about the doctrine. The functions of Michael, Gabriel, and Raphael are discussed,[11] and we learn that according to Jude (verse 6) there are seven orders of angels! The point is proved by a combination of Ephesians 1:21 with Colossians 1:16.[12]

More valuable information is given in Clement's extant writings, in which we find seven first-born or first-created angels or, rather, archangels, for the angels differ in glory from the archangels (Clement thinks he is quoting I Corinthians 15:40 for this point).[13] They are the seven eyes of the Lord (see Rev. 5:6).[14]

[7] Clement, *Excerpta ex Theodoto* 47, 3.

[8] *Ibid.*, 43, 3; see also Irenaeus, *Adv. haer.* 1, 4, 5 (thrones, deities, dominations).

[9] *In Hexaemeronem* 1, 5.

[10] *Zeitschrift für Kirchengeschichte*, 73 (1962): 253–71.

[11] *Patrologia graeca* 38, 916.

[12] *Ibid.*, 912–13.

[13] *Strom.* 6, 143, 1; see also *Excerpta ex Theodoto* 11, 2.

[14] *Strom.* 5, 35, 2.

These are the archangels whom Paul calls *thronoi* because they are closest to God.[15]

The source of Clement's angelology in primitive Jewish Christianity is made clear not only by the occurrence of "first-created angels" in Hermas (*Vision* 3, 4, 1) and by Clement's quotation of the Jewish-Christian *Apocalypse of Zephaniah* on the angels in the fifth heaven,[16] but also by his transmutation of apocalyptic eschatology at this point. After death men become angels and are instructed for a thousand years; then they become archangels, attaining to the nature of the first-created angels.[17]

Thus, there is continuity between earth and heaven, and a gradual ascent in the ranks of the hierarchy. More important, Clement definitely speaks of the situation of the church here below and its relation to the church above. The progressions (*prokopai*) of bishops, presbyters, and deacons are "imitations" (*mimēmata*) of the angelic glory in the heavenly world,[18] as the earthly church is an "image" (*eikōn*) of the heavenly one.[19]

The reason this passage is important is that while in Ignatius we find both angelic hierarchy and the correspondence of ministers to divine beings, he does not seem to have put the two notions together. For Clement, however, the ecclesiastical hierarchy is a copy of the celestial hierarchy, and we are therefore well on the way to the ideas of Dionysius the Areopagite in the fifth century.

We need not fill in the gaps between Clement and Dionysius.[20] Suffice it to say that for Dionysius there are three triads of angelic beings. Closest to God are thrones and the cherubim and seraphim; below them come authorities, dominations, and powers; after these come angels, archangels, and principalities.[21] He begins his "Ecclesiastical Hierarchies" by discussing baptism, eucharist, and chrismation; he then turns to hieratic orders, of which three are higher (bishops, priests, and deacons) and three are lower (monks, laymen, and catechumens or penitents).

With Dionysius we reach the end of the ancient Christian con-

15 *Eclogae propheticae* 57, 1.

16 *Strom.* 5, 77, 2.

17 *Eclog. proph.* 57, 4–5.

18 *Strom.* 6, 107, 2.

19 *Strom.* 4, 66, 1.

20 See G. Heil, *Denys l'Aréopagite: La Hiérarchie céleste* (Paris, 1958), pp. lix–lx.

21 *Caelestis Hierarchia* 6, 2.

sideration of the theme discussed in *The Chain of Being.* No doubt, for the history of the idea in general, Plato is more important than Paul. But our investigation has clearly shown that for its history within the Christian religion Paul's ideas gave the impetus and Paul's successors were influenced much more by purely religious considerations, often derived from Judaism, than by the Platonism with which Clement, for example, was certainly well acquainted. Even for Dionysius, the content of the hierarchies, as distinct from their neo-Platonic "ennead" form, is Jewish-Christian and ultimately Jewish in origin.[22] This applies to the Pauline ideas with which we began, to the conceptions developed in Ignatius, and to the angelic hierarchies discussed later.

At this point we cannot discuss the political implications which these ideas certainly possessed. We must content ourselves with merely mentioning the comparison of Marcus Aurelius and Commodus to the Father and the Son (made by the apologist Athenagoras [*Leg.* 18]) and the comparison of Constantine's sole rule to the divine monarchy (expressed by Eusebius and combined with mention of the myriads of angels who serve the divine King).[23] These comparisons take us beyond Judaism and, for that matter, beyond early Christianity; they are more closely related to Hellenistic ideas about divine kingship.

[22] See J. Daniélou, *Théologie du judéo-christianisme* (Tournai, 1958), pp. 167–98. E. Peterson (*Das Buch von den Engeln* [Leipzig, 1935], p. 114 = *Theologische Traktate* [Munich, 1950], p. 391 n. 3) insisted that in Jewish angelology the structure was military but not strictly hierarchical; but military structure *is* hierarchical.

[23] *Laus Constantini* 3, 5–6.

HITOTSU-MONO

A Human Symbol of the Shinto Kami

ICHIRŌ HORI

The Person Who Manifests Himself as a Kami

The most significant phenomenon in Japanese folk religion seems to me to be that traditional art by which a man temporarily disguises himself as a Shinto kami.[1] Moreover, a kami sometimes possesses a particular person. Again, a particular person is sometimes enshrined as a kami not only after his death, but also in his lifetime. These phenomena seem to be intimately connected with the Japanese concepts of kami and human nature. As such, they should be considered an important part of the history of religion in Japan.[2]

I should like, first of all, to discuss this problem by introducing one peculiar example. This is a local myth concerning the origin and history of the Shinto priestly family named Kasa (literally, "umbrella") and their tutelary kami named Wakasa-hiko and his consort Wakasa-hime. These two are the officially authorized

I wish to thank Dr. Robert Ellwood, now of the University of Southern California, for reading the first draft of this paper and for making a number of helpful suggestions and corrections.

[1] The Japanese concept of *kami* is very complicated, so that it should not be translated by the English terms "god" or "deity." See D. C. Holtom, "The Meaning of Kami," *Monumenta Nipponica*, 3 (1940): 2–27, 32–53; *ibid.*, 4 (1941): 25–68.

[2] Elaborate work from these perspectives in the ethno-folkloristic field has been done by Kunio Yanagita, Shinobu Orikuchi, Masao Oka, and Enkū Uno, among others. See Yanagita, *Yanagita Kunio Shū* ("Collections of Yanagita Kunio's Works"), (Tokyo, 1962–64); Orikuchi, *Orikuchi Shinobu Zenshū* (Complete Works of Orikuchi Shinobu"), (Tokyo, 1956); Oka, "Ijin Sonata" ("Strangers and Others"), *Minzoku*, 3 (1929): 1069–1109; Uno, *Shūkyō Minzokugaku* ("Religious Ethnology"), rev. ed. (Tokyo, 1948).

guardians of Wakasa province (the present Fukui prefecture).[3] The first retainer of the Wakasa-hiko, Setsumon of the Kasa family, traveled in attendance on his lord (the kami) to search for a permanent residence for the kami, and served as chief priest after the kami had settled down at the present shrine. Afterward, according to the myth, the kami made a contract with Setsumon by which he should be promoted in status from human being to kami as a reward for his ardent and pious services. Setsumon then appeared as a kami named Kuro-dōji-no-kami ("black servant boy") and was enshrined in a small temple in the precincts of the main shrine. The kami permitted Setsumon's direct descendants who succeeded in the position of chief priest to become kami in every other generation. For example, the second priest, Toshibumi, was a human, while the third generation incumbent, Toyobumi, became a kami named Kuro-ko-gami ("black child"). The fourth, Toyonaga, was a human priest, while the fifth, Mochikage, became a kami named Misaki ("front" or "guide"). The tradition that the chief priests who succeeded in odd-numbered generations became kami was transmitted from generation to generation at least until the middle of the Tokugawa period, according to the pictorial lineage (*e-keizu*) which was painted successively. As far as I know, this case seems to be unique even in Japanese Shinto tradition. The tradition does not reveal what differences in daily life or ritual behavior existed between the kami priests and the human priests.

Miko-gami ("Children of the Kami") and Hito-gami ("Man-god")

It is a characteristic of Japanese Shinto traditions that kami and human beings often alternate and interchange with each other. There is no strict distinction between them.

Shinto kami often appear in this world disguised as humans or they may reveal their will through a chosen person's mouth. A man with charismatic power who has acted as an intermediary

[3] This myth is found in a manuscript entitled Wakasa-no-kuni Ichi-ni-nomiya Engi ("Origin and History of the First and Second Shrines in Wakasa Province") and in the picture scroll entitled "Wakasa-no-kuni Ichi-ni-nomiya Jinin E-keizu" ("Pictorial Lineage of the Priestly Family of the First and Second Shrines in Wakasa Province"). This picture scroll is judged by specialists to have been painted in part, at about the beginning of the fourteenth century by an unknown painter.

between kami and humans is often considered to have been a child of the kami (*miko*) and an ancestor or ancestress of a shamanic priestly family.[4] The Japanese word *miko* has two meanings: a child of the kami and a person possessed or chosen by the kami. Thus, according to the *Hitachi-fudoki*, an ancient account of the present Ibaraki prefecture, as early as the eighth century A.D. there existed three shrines dedicated to the *miko-gami* of the Kami of Kashima and Katori.[5] According to the official historical record entitled *Sandai-jitsuroku*, in 866 A.D. more than thirty-eight shrines in the seacoast areas of present Fukushima and Miyagi prefectures were dedicated to the same *miko-gami* as Kashima.[6] The official record explains that the *miko-gami* are offspring of Kashima. But I wonder whether all these shrines dedicated to Kashima-no-miko-gami might not be understood as children of the kami. Persons who carried the kami's spirit on their backs, preaching and revealing the kami's will or mythology as well as disguising themselves as the kami, were also called *miko* or *miko-gami*. It must be remembered that shamanesses are also called *miko* in several rural areas in present-day Japan.

It is thought that in prehistoric ages *miko* were mainly shamanesses or priestesses, but in historical times powerful shamans or priests have also appeared. Moreover, another name for *miko*, *kan-nagi* ("a person who calls the kami") has been used of both sexes. The family lines of shamanesses or priestesses are supposed to represent a special matrilineal inheritance system which was maintained for a long time after the rest of society had changed to a patrilineal system under the strong influence of the Chinese social system. In the course of history, however, patrilinealism promoted the male shaman or priest to a higher status than that of his female counterpart.[7]

[4] Kunio Yanagita, "Raijin-shinkō no Hensen" ("Transformations of the Beliefs in the Kami of Thunder"), *Yanagita Kunio Shū*, 35 vols. (Tokyo, 1962–64), vol. 9, pp. 63–81.

[5] The *Hitachi-fudoki* describes three *miko-no-yashiro* of the Kashima Kami and one *miko-no-yashiro* of the Katori Kami.

[6] According to the *Sandai-jitsuroku* (the official record under the reigns of Emperors Seiwa, Yōzei, and Kōkō, from 858 to 887 A.D.), the distribution of the *miko-no-yashiro* of the Kashima Kami is fifteen shrines in the seacoast areas of present Fukushima prefecture and twenty-three shrines in the seacoast areas of present Miyagi prefecture.

[7] A faint survival of the past is observed in the belief in *onari-gami* of the Ryukyu islanders. See Yanagita, *Yanagita Kunio Shū*, vol. 9, pp. 23–40, 41–62. It might be added that the *miko* of the Kami of Usa-Hachiman was,

In this connection, we must discuss further the development of the concept of *hito-gami* ("man-god"), one of the most characteristic manifestations of Japanese folk religion.[8] Within the *hito-gami* system of belief we have to mention as typical, if not a stereotype, the *ara-hito-gami* ("ferocious or violent man-god"). In general, a *hito-gami* is the person possessed or elected by the kami. But at the same time the word may also indicate a deification of a person who has superhuman charismatic power, or who died an unusual death with the possibility that in the future he may show hostility and hatred toward the world. Therefore, the word *ara-hito-gami*, indicating the most violent and powerful of these man-gods, also has two meanings. Moreover, this word has also been used of a sovereign's charisma or powerful magico-religious character, and sometimes of the august virtue of the emperor, the *mi-itsu* of the Mikado. In the case of the emperor, however, the characters which read *ara-hito-gami* were changed from those meaning "violent man-god" to others meaning "manifest personal-god." Nevertheless, historically speaking, the most typical and well-known *ara-hito-gami* were the Kami of Hitokoto-nushi, the Kami of Sumiyoshi or Suminoye, the Kami of the Hachiman Shrines, the Kami of the Kitano Shrine, and so on. All of these *ara-hito-gami* were first great deities associated with oracles and magical curses or spells who next descended and appeared in disguise as human figures. Finally they appeared in this world accompanied by several dependent small kami or semi-kami who served and assisted their lord, the *ara-hito-gami*.

The kami called Hitokoto-nushi of Mount Katsuragi in Nara prefecture first appeared before the Emperor Yūryaku with a figure and imperial *cortège* like the emperor's. The *Kojiki* says that the kami introduced himself to the emperor by saying, "I am the kami who dispels with a word the evil, and with a word the good," and thus he was called Hitokoto-nushi ("the lord of the one word").[9]

The Kami of Sumiyoshi or Suminoye are the violent or active spirits of three kinds of Kami of the Sea (the upper, middle, and

as I shall explain later, converted to Buddhism and called *negi-ni* ("Shinto-priestly Buddhist-nun").

[8] Ichirō Hori, *Folk Religion in Japan: Continuity and Change* (Chicago, 1968).

[9] See W. G. Aston, trans., *Nihongi: Chronicles of Japan from the Earliest Times to A. D. 697*, 2 vols. (London, 1890), vol. I, pp. 341–42.

bottom), who first appeared as washings in the purification rite practiced by Izanagi-no-kami after his return from an adventurous journey to the netherworld where he sought his departed consort Izanami-no-kami.[10] Then, in the reign of the Emperor Chūai, these three Kami of the Sea revealed themselves again through the mouth of the Empress Jingū, who had fallen into a trance. According to the *Nihongi*, the three Kami of the Sea gave instructions, saying, "A gentle spirit (*nigi-mitama*) will attach itself to the Empress' person and keep watch over her life; a rough spirit (*ara-mitama*) will form the vanguard and be a guide to the squadron."[11] In folk religion, however, the Kami of Sumiyoshi are often said to appear in disguise as old men with white hair and white beards. His oracles were mostly in the form of poems (*waka*) delivered by the Tsumori family, the main priestly family of the Sumiyoshi Shrine. Accordingly, the kami was later worshiped as the kami of the *waka* as well as of literature. Moreover, the myth relates that when the kami was about to descend from heaven, several miraculous pine trees suddenly appeared near the shrine. These pine trees are called *aioi-no-matsu* ("pine trees that sprang up simultaneously with the kami's appearance") and are a symbol of the Sumiyoshi Shrine.[12]

According to the local myth, the Kami of the Usa-Hachiman Shrine in Kyushu first revealed himself as a three-year-old boy to an old blacksmith who later became the ancestor of the chief priestly family. According to another myth, the kami himself appeared in disguise as a blacksmith on the top of the sacred mountain called Omoto-yama.[13] In the Nara period, the Hachiman Kami was very active in political and religious activities. In 749 A.D. a shamaness named Morime of the Miwa family, the chief priestly family, was possessed by the kami. Following the kami's oracle, she went all the way from Kyushu to the capital city, Nara, to worship before the newly completed Great Vairocana Buddha of the Tōdai-ji temple. This was a turning point in the history of the mixture of Buddhism and Shinto. Morime was converted to

[10] *Ibid.*, pp. 27 ff.

[11] *Ibid.*, pp. 226–29.

[12] See Manyō-shū, vol. 6, no. 1020–21, in *Iwanami Bunko* Series No. 1–4, p. 246.

[13] *Hachiman Uso-ni-miya Go-takusen-shū* ("Collections of the Divine Oracles given by Usa-Hachiman Kami"). The manuscript of this collection has survived; it is owned by the Kokugakuin University Library.

Buddhism and became a Buddhist nun. After this she was called a *negi-ni* ("Shinto-priestly Buddhist-nun").[14] Again in 769 the Hachiman Kami revealed a divine message through the mouth of one of the priests, saying that the ambitious Buddhist archbishop Dōkyō, the Empress Shōtoku's favorite retainer, should succeed to the imperial throne to pacify the whole empire.[15] Once again, in 859, the Hachiman Kami moved to Kyoto from Kyushu because of an oracle revealed to a Buddhist monk, Gyōkyō. The kami settled on top of Mount Otokoyama at a shrine named Iwashimizu-Hachiman Gokoku-ji near the capital to became the guardian of the capital and of the imperial household.[16] Moreover, in each of his many shrines this kami controlled several *waka-miya* or *ima-miya*. Literally these names mean "young deity" or "newly appeared deity." Actually they were vivid and newly appeared small, malevolent kami dependent on Hachiman.[17]

To give another example, the sudden appearance of the Kitano Tenjin in the middle of the Heian period (tenth century) was a world-shaking event at the time. Kitano Tenjin ("Heavenly Kami of Kitano") was believed to be the deification of the prime minister Michizane Sugawara (845–903 A.D.), who died in exile because of a false accusation. Afterward, the spirit of Michizane revealed himself through the mouths of several persons including a humble shamanic woman named Ayako, a Buddhist monk named Dōken, a little boy of seven years named Tarōmaru of Miwa, and a son of the priestly family of Mount Hira Shrine. The spirit of Michizane announced that he had become an angry and violent kami, in fact the greatest kami of plague and misfortune of this world, and that he controlled 105,000 dependent devils and demons who distributed epidemics and evils. This idea of accompaniment by many dependents shows the same pattern as that of Hachiman. Again, the myth tells us that when the spirit of Michizane appeared as Kitano Tenjin, the oracle announced that several thou-

14 *Shoku Nihongi*, vol. 17, in *Kokushi Taikei* series, 59 vols. (Tokyo, 1929–59), vol. 2, p. 206.

15 *Ibid.*, vol. 30, pp. 368–69.

16 Gyōkyō, "Iwashimizu Hachiman-gū Gokoku-ji Ryakki" ("Origin and History of the Temple Dedicated to Hachiman Kami, Guardian of the Nation"), cited in the *Chōya Gunsai*, vol. 16, Sec. Buddhist Matters I, in *Kokushi Taikei series*, vol. 29, no. 1 (Tokyo, 1964), pp. 392–93.

17 Naoichi Miyaji, *Hachiman-shin no Kenkyū* ("Study on the Hachiman Kami"), in *Miyaji Naoichi Ikō-shū* ("Posthumous Works of Naoichi Miyaji"), (Tokyo, 1956), vol. 2.

sand pine trees would spring up in only one night as a sign of the kami's appearance at the site of the present Kitano Shrine. This reminds us of the myth of Sumiyoshi concerning the *aioi-no-matsu*. It is also interesting that both the Kami of Sumiyoshi and the Kami of Kitano later became guardians of poetry, literature, and caligraphy, and that, according to medieval legends, both kami often appeared in this world disguised as old men.[18]

Naïve but easily possessed little boys were often called *shidō*, *yori-warawa*, or *gohō-dōji* in Japanese classical literature; they also had a strong influence on the history of Japanese folk religion.[19] The early *ara-hito-gami*, as mentioned above, seem to have been most significant as *goryō-shin* (malevolent kami who were deified angry spirits of the dead) or *takusen-shin* (kami of oracles). These were quite different from the peaceful and static *uji-gami* (tutelary kami of a village, clan, or family). *Ara-hito-gami* generally appeared suddenly through the mouths of particular ecstatic persons. Therefore, they were at first enshrined and worshiped by the *yori-mashi* or *yori-warawa*, the possessed or chosen person through whom they were first revealed. The original meaning of *waka-miya*, which frequently appears in medieval literature, is "newly appeared kami," or "vivid and young kami." Later it came to mean the child-kami of a great kami or controller, which might be equivalent to the *miko-gami* of the Kashima Kami mentioned above. The term *waka-miya-be* refers to the priestly family of the *waka-miya*, that is, a priestly family having powerful shamanic ability. In the course of history, the *ara-hito-gami* gradually changed their character to become humanistic guardians or kami of literature or caligraphy. Then the original functions of *ara-hito-gami* had to be transferred to a dependent *waka-miya* with its *waka-miya-be*. In medieval times, for example, the *uchifuse-no-miko* ("shamaness of lying down," a nickname given because of her posture during séance) at the Waka-miya Shrine of the Kamo-jinja in Kyoto[20] or the shamaness at the

[18] "Kitano Engi" ("Origin and History of the Kitano Kami"), preface to vol. 2, *Gunsho Ruijū* series, vol. 19 (Tokyo, 1959), pp. 129–30, 145–50.

[19] Yanagita, "Kaijin Shōdō" ("Kami of the Sea Appearing as a Little Boy"), in *Yanagita Kunio Shū*, vol. 8, pp. 37–74; "Matsuō Kondei no Monogatari" ("Legends of the Young Warrior Named Matsuō"), *ibid.*, pp. 99–114; "Raijin Shinkō no Hensen," *ibid.*, pp. 63–81; "Hito wo Kami ni matsuru Fūshū," *ibid.*, pp. 472–98.

[20] *Ōkagami*, vol. 1, *Kokushi Taikei Series*, vol. 21, no. 1, p. 36.

Waka-miya Shrine of the Iwashimizu-Hachiman Shrine may have been models of *waka-miya-be* priestesses or shamanesses. These models should be traced back to the ancient myths of the *Kojiki* and *Nihongi* concerning the relationship between the great shamaness Tamayori-hime ("princess possessed by the kami") and the kami of Mount Miwa named O-mono-nushi ("great controller of the spirits"). Tamayori-hime was said to be the ancestress of the politically and religiously powerful Miwa and Kamo families which later scattered and settled in various provinces, keeping their traditional magical, religious, and shamanic abilities.[21]

The *ara-hito-gami* cult originally arose outside normal agricultural communities integrated by the *uji-gami* (tutelary kami) system. At first it attracted believers. For this reason, *waka-miya-be* priests or shamans were necessarily very sensitive to the signs of the times; they had to grasp tendencies among the common people and exercise keen insight into human nature. They also had to acquire sufficient skill in magic and the techniques of ecstasy to cause followers to yield to their opinions and teachings.

As Frazer has pointed out, persons possessed either temporarily or permanently by gods or spirits have been commonly worshiped as man-gods.[22] In Polynesia and some other Pacific islands, such persons are believed to be incarnations of gods or spirits. This is also true of Japanese folk religion; newly revealed *goryō-shin*, *waka-miya*, or *ima-miya* (newly appeared kami) are seen as being gradually brought under the control of great *ara-hito-gami* and made dependent on them. On the other hand, in the course of history the *waka-miya-be* priests or shamans are gradually deified and enshrined as subordinate kami. The very curious subordinate shrines in the precincts of big shrines of the *ara-hito-gami* type should be understood as survivals of this history of deification of *waka-miya-be* priests and shamans.[23]

21 *Kojiki*, vol. 2 under the reign of the Emperor Sujin; Aston, *Nihongi*, vol. 2, p. 153.

22 James G. Fraser, *The Golden Bough: A Study in Magic and Religion*, abridged ed. (New York, 1955), pp. 83–101.

23 For example, in the precincts of the Iwashimizu-Hachiman and Kitano Shrines in Kyoto and the Kasuga Shrine in Nara there exist subordinate shrines called *Matsu-warawa-no-yashiro* and *Shō-dō-sha* respectively, which indicate a shrine dedicated to the "pine-tree boy." We may compare them with the mythical legends concerning the *Oi-matsu* ("old pine tree"), an attendant of the Kami of Kitano, or with *Matsuō Kondei* ("young warrior of the pine-tree king"), an attendant of the Iwashimizu-Hachiman. We may also cite the many subordinate shrines dedicated to so-and-so *Tayū* (or *-dayū*)

It would therefore be imaginable that the relationship between the Kami of Wakasa-hiko and the priestly Kasa family mentioned at the beginning of this paper should be classified as belonging to the *ara-hito-gami* or *waka-miya* and *waka-miya-be* pattern because the first revealer of the kami and the ancestor of the priestly Kasa family, Setsumon, appeared at first in disguise as the *dōji*, a young attendant of the kami, but later was promoted to the status of a kami named Kuro-dōji. However, he was painted in the *e-keizu* ("pictorial lineage scroll") as an old man with long mustache and penetrating eyes. There is also a legend concerning the selection of the kami's permanent shrine in which it is said that several thousand pine trees sprang up in only one night as a sign of the kami's selection. This legend reminds us of appearances of the kami of Kitano and Sumiyoshi.

It may be concluded that the Kami of Wakasa-hiko was a typical *ara-hito-gami* and Setsumon of the Kasa was a typical *waka-miya-be* belonging to the same pattern as the *matsu-warawa* at Kasuga, Kitano, and Iwashimizu shrines. I will discuss later the magical meaning of the family name Kasa ("umbrella").

Persons Who Disguise Themselves as Kami

Cases among Tōya-kannushi

Although the special forms mentioned above do not necessarily obtain at all Shinto shrines, something of the ancient man-god pattern can be found in the functions of certain village Shinto

in the precincts of the great oracular or *hito-gami* shrines, such as *Hyaku-dayū-sha* ("shrine dedicated to the priest named Hyaku-dayū") at the Ebisu-jinja in Nishinomiya near Osaka, or the *Gen-dayū-sha* at the Atsuta-jingū in Nagoya. Yanagita Kunio concludes from this that Matsu-warawa, together with *Hyaku-dayū*, *Gen-dayū*, and others, should be understood as having originated as the main kami's attendants as well as the kami's chosen or possessed mediator, afterward deified and enshrined as subordinate kami by descendants who maintained their position as the chief priestly family (Yanagita, "Matsuō Kondei no Monogatari," *Yanagita Kunio Shū*, vol. 9, pp. 99–114). I would like to note in this connection that the term *matsu* uses the character meaning "pine tree," but phonetically the word also means "waiting," which has some etymological relation to the term *matsuri* ("ritual" or "festival"). Also, in the Heian period the term *tayū* originally meant the fifth rank of imperial court officers, but this word was later used as a common noun for the Shinto priest as well as for the magico-religious artist in medieval drama and ballads. Moreover, the terms *warawa* and *dō* (or *dōji*) uses a character meaning "boy" or "youth," but in ancient Japanese literature they should be understood to mean a great charismatic or magico-religious person or a kami's attendant.

priests. *Tōya-kannushi* is the title of an unauthorized but customary Shinto priest elected yearly from among the heads of duty-houses (*tōya*) of parishioners. In several villages where no professional Shinto priest serves at the village shrine, the *tōya-kannushi* takes his place according to a yearly shift system. He is chosen either by divine lot or by turns from the duty-houses. Therefore, he is often called *ichinen-kannushi* ("one-year priest") or *tō-nin* ("duty-man"). The duty-house system (*tōya-seido* or *miya-za*) is strictly limited to a group of houses which transmits from generation to generation the mythical tradition of the relationship between the village kami and their common ancestors. They have the responsibility and privilege of taking the role of temporary priests of the village shrine to guard the whole life of the community. For example, Tenma-tenjin-sha Shrine in Komatsu-mura in Shiga prefecture has been served by a group of duty-houses called *kongen-sanjūnin-gumi* ("group of original thirty houses"), all of which families are believed to be the descendants of Tarōmaru of the Miwa family, first revealer of the Kami of Tenma-tenjin. (This is the Kitano Kami.) It consists of five subgroups from which ten persons are elected, one being the *tōya-kannushi* and the other nine his assistants.[24]

After the Meiji Restoration, the government appointed official Shinto priests at every governmentally registered shrine. As a result, the *tōya-kannushi*'s status and functions have necessarily degenerated to that of assistants of the professional priests. Nevertheless, when strong and ardent believers still existed among the villagers, struggles frequently occurred between the two kinds of priests, professional and *tōya*, concerning the division of functions. We can find many strong *tōya* systems and *ichinen-kannushi* still surviving, especially in western Honshu.

Outstanding research has been done by Higo Kazuo[25] and Inouye Yorihisa[26] in the Kinki area and by Wakamori Tarō[27] in Shimane prefecture, where the most elaborate *tōya-kannushi* sys-

[24] Yorihisa Inouye, *Kyoto Ko-shū-shi* ("Traditional Customs and Festivals in Kyoto"), (Osaka, 1940), pp. 236 ff.; Kazuo Higo, "Ōmi ni okeru Miyaza no Kenkyū" ("A Study on the Duty-House System in Shiga Prefecture"), in *Tokyo Bunri-ka Daigaku Kiyo*, no. 16 (Tokyo, 1938).

[25] Kazuo Higo, *Miyaza no Kenkyū* ("A Study on the Duty-House System"), (Tokyo, 1942).

[26] Inouye, *Kyoto Ko-shū-shi.*

[27] Tarō Wakamori, *Miho-jinja no Kenkyū* ("A Study on the Festival-system at Miho-jinja"), (Tokyo, 1955).

tems have survived. In the Kinki area, the *tōya-kannushi* is often called *kō-dono*, which means "Mr. Kami" or "Mr. Head." This term suggests a hidden meaning and reveals the original sacred functions of the *tōya-kannushi*. He must obey traditional religious abstinences and taboos in daily life during his duty-year. He is isolated not only from the common people but even from his own family. He must purify himself by bathing in water every morning and evening; he must wear special clothes, attend and render service to the kami's shrine every day, and perform prayers, divinations, rituals, and magical performances at the parishioners' request.

For example, in the case of the *tōya-kannushi* system at Mihogaseki in Shimane prefecture, where the Miho-jinja is located, there are three steps in *tōya* duties, each step existing to promote the *tōya-kannushi*'s religious as well as social status. First there is the *tōya* of the great festival in April called *Aofushigaki-no-shinji*; second is the *tōya* of the Marōdo ("guest")-jinja, a subordinate of the main shrine; and last is the *ichinen-kannushi* ("yearly priest") or *tō-nin* ("head man"). All these *tōya* are chosen by divine lot from among the duty-houses in Mihogaseki. There are several traditional abstinences and taboos observed by each of the three *tōya* and for the two interval periods between them. The strictest, however, are required of the highest rank, the *ichinen-kannushi* or *tō-nin*. During the whole duty-year the *tō-nin* must go to the sea early every morning to purify himself by bathing; he must then worship and serve the kami at the shrine, whatever the weather. He must keep away from all impurities and defilements, visible and invisible; he must abstain from certain foods and avoid certain words; he must keep his own pure fire, which may not be mixed with other fires or used by another person even accidentally; he must cook his own meals by himself using his own fire; he must sleep and remain alone in an isolated room where all the sacred symbols and instruments are installed. No one may touch him or talk carelessly with him. In front of the gate of the *tō-nin*'s house are built symbolic pillars called *ohake*, decorated by the sacred tree-leaves and cut-papers which show all the parishioners in the town as well as the kami itself that the whole house is now taboo and sacred. Sometimes the Buddhist altar with its memorial tablets for dead ancestors and relatives is sealed and carried out of the house to avoid the influence of Buddhism as well as that of the spirits of the dead. According to writings of the Tokugawa period, the *tō-nin* had to fall into trance artificially and deliver divine messages at parishioners' request or on festival days. It was believed that the fortune, weather, harvest, and fishing success of the whole community might depend simply upon the abstinence and religious service to the kami rendered by the *tō-nin*.[28]

The examples mentioned above seem to be rather extraordinary cases, but it is noticeable that the secluded and tabooed way of life during the duty-year is far more strict and severe than that required of professional Shinto priests. It is also much more rigid than the practice of the unauthorized popular priest at the small village shrine. Moreover, the *tōya-kannushi* wears quite different clothes from those of common people, such as special headgear, court dress or white dress, and white socks, not only on festival days but also in daily life.[29]

From this evidence we may conclude that the *kō-dono* should be considered a survival of men who disguised themselves as kami and acted out the kami's behavior, although the techniques of ecstasy and real communion are lost.

Hitotsu-mono

In the holy of holies in Japanese Shinto shrines, a mirror, a piece of jade, or a sword is installed as a symbol of the kami's body. The sacred *sakaki* tree with cotton cloth tied to it or a sacred stick with silk or cut paper on it may also be regarded as symbols possessed by the kami. These symbols are the objects

28 *Ibid.*; Shingi-in ("Governmental Headquarters of the Shrine Shinto"), ed., *Kan-Kokuhei-sha Tokushu-shinji Shirabe* ("Researches on the Particular Annual Festivals Performed at the Governmentally Authorized Higher Ranked Shinto Shrines"), (Tokyo, 1941), vol. 4, pp. 39–80.

29 For example, the *kō-dono* at the Tenman-gū Shrine in Yase-mura in Kyoto goes to the shrine twice a day to worship and offer lighted lanterns to the shrine. At these times the *kō-dono* must wear special clothes with a plum-blossom crest which is thought to be a symbol of Tenma Tenjin, another name of the Kami of Kitano. He also has a special hat and wears a white robe in the morning, while in the evening he wears a *hakama* (a divided skirt for men's formal wear) with a crest of cherry blossoms. A black robe is worn on festival days. When he rides a horse in festival processions, all attendants herald him in a manner usually reserved for expressing reverence for superhuman beings or for the emperor. When he walks on the street on festival days, one attendant holds an umbrella over him from behind (Inouye, *Kyoto Ko-shū-shi*, pp. 316–17).

of worship. After the introduction of Buddhism into Japan, the Japanese confronted the brilliant statues and paintings of Buddhas and Bodhisattvas for the first time, and they gradually became accustomed to worshiping them. Despite the strong influence of Buddhist art, however, there was no early tendency to make figures of Shinto kami for worship.[30]

On the other hand, strong tendencies have existed to see the kami as incarnate in actual human beings. Many local myths and legends from the medieval period depict kami revealing themselves in such disguises as an old man with a long beard and white hair, a brilliant and august youth, a graceful and elegant woman, a fairy, a beautiful child, or even a Buddhist monk. Given these tendencies toward conceptualization and the general pressure of syncretism, one would have expected statues of kami to appear in profusion. Curiously, however, the first examples of Shinto kami statues do not occur before the tenth century (mid-Heian period), the approximate date of the wooden sculpture displaying the Kami of Hachiman in the figure of a Buddhist monk, the Sōgyō-Hachiman owned by Yakushiji Temple in Nara. Thereafter, the numbers of kami images gradually increased, but their artistic sensibility and technique do not seem to have developed markedly. There are many among the existing statues classified as kami figures which probably were not really installed in the holy of holies of a shrine as the object of worship. Why did the use of images of kami as objects of worship not develop in Shinto? This question is a problem not only in the field of Japanese art but also in the history of Japanese religion. There are various factors involved, including the underdevelopment of Shinto theology and the unsystematic character of Shinto iconography. I would say, however, that a key to the solution of the problem lies in the relationship between the kami and human beings. The existence of living kami, living objects of worship, should be especially noted. These embodiments have shown themselves to be the most concrete images of the kami and have transmitted the kami's will

[30] In the course of history, Shinto has become mixed with Buddhism in various other ways: *jingū-ji* temples dedicated to Shinto kami under Buddhist titles were built in the precincts of almost all Shinto shrines; Buddhist statues called *honji-butsu* (a statue of Buddha manifesting the prime noumenon) were installed inside or in front of the holy of holies at the Shinto shrines. These were results of the development of the theory that kami and Buddha alike manifest the prime noumenon (*honji-suijaku*).

to the parishioners. The tradition of the Kasa family is an extraordinary case of the practices and ideas of the deification of the special living kami or human image of the divine in the medieval period.[31]

It is difficult to decide whether men disguised themselves as kami because the idea of kami appearing in this world in human form already existed, or whether the reverse was true. However, the original meaning of the Japanese word *matsuri* ("Shinto festival") should be understood to be "inviting and waiting for the kami's visit," or "submitting to or obeying the kami." For these festivals, the people selected a holy place which they enclosed by hanging sacred straw festoons as a taboo sign. Within it they erected the sacred *sakaki* tree as the object of worship. There they confined themselves and burned large fires.[32] Immersed in this atmosphere, they could see the kami in human form descend from heaven riding on a horse or a white cloud. In Okinawa it is often reported that the actual figure of the mountain-kami was seen descending to this world. According to the *Ryūkyū Shintō-ki* ("Report of the Ryukuan Shinto") written by Taichū (1552–1639), immediately before the new kami Kimitezuri appears some five-colored umbrella-like symbols appear on the sacred mountaintops. Thereupon the king's court prepares for the celebration of the descent of the new kami by erecting more than thirty large umbrellas in the royal courtyard; they then invite the new kami with sacred music and dancing.[33]

I have already mentioned in previous pages the symbolic umbrellas used by the *kō-dono*. Originally the umbrella seems to have been an important symbol of the appearance of the kami, and was next applied to a man who was disguised as a kami or had a charismatic nature.[34] That the family of the Kasa ("um-

31 Also, the family name of the chief priests at the Suwa-jinja in Nagano prefecture was *Jin-shi* ("kami family"), which signifies a consciousness of the holiness of the family. At the *tatae-no-shinji* ("festival called *tatae*"), formerly held on the Day of the Cock in the third month of the lunar calendar, a virgin child was selected from among the family members to be a divine messenger. He made a tour to all the parishioners' villages of the Suwa-jinja in Suwa and Chiisagata counties.

32 *Wakun no Shiori*, comp. Kotosuga Tanigawa (Tokyo, 1898), vol. 1, p. 29.

33 Taichū, *Ryūkyū Shintō-ki*, ed. Genchi Katō (Tokyo, 1943), pp. 80–81.

34 Shinobu Orikuchi, *Kodai Kenkyū*, vol. 1 in *Orikuchi Shinobu Zenshū* ("Collected Works of Shinobu Orikuchi"), 32 vols. (Tokyo, 1954–59), vol. 2, pp. 182 ff., 248 ff.

brella") should also have such a symbol means that it is the *waka-miya-be* of the *hito-gami.*[35]

One survival of the ideas that recall the kami's visit by human proxy may be seen in the *hitotsu-mono*, who appears in the processions of various Shinto festival days bearing symbolic pheasant feathers.[36] But there exists another kind of *hitotsu-mono* with other symbols. The *hitotsu-mono* who appears in the *Ofuna-matsuri* ("divine ship festival") at Hayatama-jinja of Kumano in Wakayama prefecture has been transformed into dolls which are dressed in a braided hat and a gold-laced hunting suit (*kari-ginu*, a formal dress of the medieval *samurai*, "warrior class") with twelve ears of miscanthus and twelve paper symbols called *gō-ō* attached. It is said, however, that in former times youths of the parish were selected to play the role of the *hitotsu-mono.*[37] For this reason it is possible that the symbolic figures of old men and women, or of youths or children, which are often installed on the portable shrines or festival cars in the festival processions at various other Shinto shrines, should be understood as trans-

[35] The mountain-kami at the Otake ("sacred mountain") in the Amami Islands is served and celebrated by five *noro* (shamanic priestesses), two *waki-gami* (female assistants of the *noro*), and a *kuji* (a male assistant and transmitter as well as interpreter of the divine myth called *Omoro*). The male members of the village were strictly prohibited from attending the festival, or even catching a glimpse of it, but it is said that they were able to watch from the entrance of the sacred mountain the figure of the kami descending from the mountain on horseback in times when belief in kami was very ardent and pristine among the villagers.

[36] For example, at the *Oide-matsuri* ("festival of the kami's coming") of the Rikyu-Hachiman in Uji, Kyoto prefecture, the *hitotsu-mono* wears a white dress and white *hakama* as well as a hat with Japanese pheasant feathers and many hanging white cut papers as taboo signs. He heads the festival procession just behind the large, sacred *sakaki* tree which is regarded as a symbol possessed by the kami (see Inouye, *Kyoto Ko-shū-shi*, pp. 98–100). The *hitotsu-mono* at the Nifu-jinja in Kaisō county, Wakayama prefecture, is played by a celestial child in the festival procession. He wears the fourth rank's formal costume and a hat with Japanese pheasant feathers as well as many long cut papers as tokens of consecration. He rides horseback and marches in a procession just before the portable shrine (*mikoshi*). In the annual festival of Waka-miya of the Kasuga-jinja in Nara, the *hitotsu-mono* also wears a hat with pheasant feathers. Therefore, we may take the symbolic hat with such feathers to be a common symbol of all *hitotsu-mono.* See Ichirō Hori, *Wagakuni Minkan-shinkō-shi no Kenkyū* ("A Study on the History of Japanese Folk Religion"), 2 vols. (Tokyo, 1953), vol. 1, pp. 471–72, n. 11.

[37] Hori, *Wagakuni*, vol. 1; Heibon-sha, ed. *Shintō Daijiten* ("Encyclopedia of Shinto"), 6 vols. (Tokyo, 1940), vol. 3, p. 196.

formations of the original *hitotsu-mono*. These symbolic roles would have been originally played by selected living persons. The change from living persons possessed or chosen by the kami or spirit as their proxy to the figures or dolls is comparable to their also taking the form of magico-religious players who visited from door to door to celebrate at the beginning of the year.[38]

Concluding Examples

In the case of *hitotsu-mono*, the hat with pheasant feathers is a symbol of a possessed and consecrated person who is a kami's proxy. In the myths of the *Kojiki* and *Nihongi*, however, a straw hat and straw raincoat, or a mask, are also regarded as a sign of a superhuman or mythical figure.[39]

Such symbolic garb was a means to annihilate the profane human personality and to engraft the mythical figures or kami-like personality.[40] That simple forms of *hitotsu-mono* became decorative dolls or the celestial children at the festival processions of several Shinto shrines may be gathered from folk religion more than authentic Shrine Shinto. The functions and behavior of the *kōdono* and some *tōya-kannushi* mentioned above are only a few examples among many.[41]

38 See Hori, *Wagakuni*, vol. 2, pp. 566–96; see also his paper, "Mysterious Visitors from the Harvest to the New Year," in *Studies in Japanese Folklore*, pp. 76–103.

39 See Aston, *Nihongi*, vol. 1, pp. 50 ff. and 105–17.

40 Until the medieval period, it was common for Shinto priestesses, shamanesses, magicians, and certain other magico-religious players or reciters, as well as court ladies, to wear especially thick facial paint.

41 Two kami named *Aka-mata* and *Kuro-mata* ("red one" and "black one") annually appear from the sacred cave in Miyara-mura on Yaeyama Island at the Pouri festival (harvest festival) in June. They are personified by two village youths of good conduct and good health, each of whom wears a different, terrible mask and covers his body with miscanthus and other grasses. The two visit from door to door to give each house encouragement and celebration. The old men and women in the village believe that they are real kami and their voices real kami voices, and in no small numbers are moved to tears, begging them to come again the next year at the time the kami proxies are leaving the village for the Eternal Land (*Toko-yo*) overseas through the sacred cave. The kami named Maya and Tomo-maya ("male and female cat kami"), who appear at the autumn festival in Ishigaki Island, wear masks of male and female cats, raincoats made of *adan* grass, and hats made of *kuba* leaves. They visit from house to house in the village to celebrate in advance the good harvest of the next year (see *Yanagita*, "Kainan-Shōki," *Yamagita Kunio Shū*, vol. 1, pp. 287–89).

On the main islands of Japan, many mysterious visitors appear at the end and the beginning of the year to purify houses, especially the sunken hearth, and to drive off evil, impurities, and faults, as well as to celebrate the New Year and promise a good harvest in the coming year. This custom has presumably existed since ancient times.[42]

In this connection, we must recognize that the existence of such mysterious seasonal visitors might be a folk custom derived from kami proxies or consecrated persons chosen or possessed by the kami.[43] I would like to add a word to call to the readers' attention the fact that all these visitors, without exception, appear in symbolic disguise, wearing a special hat, mask, or straw raincoat, or carrying some kind of symbolic object.

I will conclude this paper by introducing five very suggestive poems which were presumably recited at the *Chin-kon* festival of the imperial court preceding the Harvest Festival (*Nüname*). The *Chin-kon* is the initiatory ceremony of shaking of the emperor's soul for the purpose of renewing the emperor's life power, which was believed to have a direct connection with the fortunes of the harvest of the coming year and of the whole nation. The *Chin-kon* poems read as follows:

We want to bring down the Great Soul,
  Of the Kami Toyohirume ["Brilliant Sun Goddess"],
Who resides in Heaven;
  The Root [substance] is a gold halberd,
And the Branch [shadow] is a wooden halberd!

Oh! the August Umbrellas
  That stand on the mountaintop of Mount Miwa!
If they do not flourish now,
  When shall they be able to flourish?

Oh! My Sister!
  At the mountain-foot of Mount Anashi,
You must wear mountain-creepers as a crown
  Because many people look at you now!

42 See Yanagita, *Saiji Shūzoku Goi* ("Folk Vocabulary of the Annual Functions"), (Tokyo, 1939), pp. 296 ff.; "Yukiguni no Haru" ("Spring in the Snowy Provinces"), *Yanagita Kunio Shū*, vol. 2, pp. 3–136.

43 Richard M. Dorsen, ed., *Studies in Japanese Folklore* (Bloomington, 1963), pp. 76–103.

Let us take a *tamachi*,[44]
  Let the Kami whose August Spirit has ascended,
Whose Spirit has ascended,
  Come just now!

Let the Kami who holds the Soul-box,
  Let She [the same kami] whose spirit has ascended and left
Now come!
  Let the Soul [of the emperor] which is now leaving
Let this Soul return![45]

[44] The meaning of *tamachi* is now obscure. Many scholars suppose that it was miscopied in ancient times from a term like *tamashi*, which may have signified a soul or soul power (see Hori, "Mysterious Visitors from the Harvest to the New Year," in *ibid.*, p. 102, n. 36).

[45] *Nenjūgyōji Hishō* ("The Secret of the Annual Rites") was a manuscript written by an unknown author in the latter years of the Heian period (twelfth century). It was first published in the *Gunsho Ruijū series*, vol. 86 (Tokyo, 1931), pp. 518–19.

AINU MYTH

JOSEPH M. KITAGAWA

Those who are acquainted with the writings of Mircea Eliade are invariably impressed by the breadth of vision in his attempts to delineate the unity and continuity of the religious experience of man throughout history as well as the multiplicity of the myths, symbols, and other religious forms that have emerged in various parts of the world. More immediately, Eliade is also aware of the existential necessity of confrontation between the two types of mentality, namely, the "traditional," characteristic of man in archaic and Oriental societies, and the "modern," characteristic of man in modern societies of the Western type. He feels that, while Asia and Africa have entered the main stage of world history, "the Western world has not yet, or not generally, met with authentic representatives of the 'real' non-Western traditions."[1]

Seen from another perspective, the problem is not that the confrontation between Western and non-Western mentalities has not taken place, because it has been going on for the last three centuries at least. The real issue is that such a confrontation was one-sided, undertaken by the West's initiative, and occurred primarily on economic, political, and technological planes. But one of the inevitable consequences of the East-West encounter in the modern period is that Western ways of managing practical affairs as well as Western modes of thinking have undercut the traditional foundations of Eastern societies and cultures. For example, the Western notion of history, which came to have a decisive influence on the East, altered the traditional Eastern view of "history," ac-

[1] Mircea Eliade, *Myths, Dreams and Mysteries*, trans. Philip Mairet (New York, 1960), pp. 8–9.

cording to which cosmic and human, archaic and historic, and sacred and profane were held to be mutually inclusive and interpenetrating. Nevertheless, a great change has taken place in this respect since the end of World War II. The so-called resurgence of Eastern religions and cultures indicates the increasing self-conscious awareness of the East that the task of shaping history, for which the East is destined to share the burden with the West, demands not the reshaping of the East according to the image of the West but the actualization of religious and cultural resources of the East for the benefit of all humanity. This is easier said than done, of course. Thus far much effort has been directed toward affirming the intrinsic values of the major religions and cultures of Asia, but relatively little attention has been given to archaic and folk elements which are also integral parts of the Eastern heritage. In this situation the task of a historian of religions, especially if he comes from the Eastern milieu, is to be uniquely sensitive to the total religious and cultural experiences of the East, including both the archaic and historic traditions, which, to be sure, cannot be understood in isolation from the experience of the rest of humanity. With this in mind, a modest attempt is made in this essay to elucidate the significance of the Ainu myths.

Much has been written, but little is actually known, about the origin and ethnic identity of the Ainu.[2] Most scholars agree, however, that the Ainu were probably one of the Paleo-Siberian groups which slowly migrated eastward during the prehistoric period and eventually settled in Sakhalin, Hokkaidō, and the Kurile Islands shortly before the Christian era. During the course of slow migration the Ainu undoubtedly came in contact with a number of ethnic groups, such as the Samoyed, the Ostyak, the Vogul, the Tungusic, and the Turkic, which accounts for similarities that exist between some of the words, symbols, and rituals of the Ainu and those of other Paleo-Siberian and Neo-Siberian groups. Even after they settled in the present localities, the Ainu lived in close proximity to the Gilyak and other tribes and maintained some trade contact with various tribes in eastern Siberia and northern Manchuria. Ironically, the question regarding the extent to which

[2] For various theories and speculations concerning the identity of the Ainu, see J. M. Kitagawa, "Ainu Bear Festival (Iyomante)," *History of Religions*, 1 (1961): 99–106.

cultural influences were exerted between the Ainu and the dominant Japanese group is far from clear. However, concerning the once controversial question of whether the term *kamuy* ("spirit, divine, sacred") is of Ainu origin as Batchelor believed,[3] or is a slightly changed form of the Japanese word *kami* ("spirit, deity, sacred, high, above") which the Ainu must have borrowed, as Chamberlain held,[4] most scholars today are inclined to agree with Chamberlain's theory, although they acknowledge that the meaning of *kamuy* was derived from the Ainu's own tradition.

It is important to note that while some of the Ainu words, symbols, and rituals have been influenced by and/or borrowed from neighboring groups, the Ainu to a great extent have preserved to the present century their own unique cultural and religious structure in continuity with the ancient past. For example, Kindaichi, a leading scholar of the Ainu language, holds that the "incorporating" and "polysynthetic" characteristics of the Ainu language find no affinities with neighboring languages such as Japanese, Korean, Tunguse, Chinese, and Malayo-Polynesian. While some scholars attempt to find a possible connection between Ainu and Gilyak because both have "object conjugation," Kindaichi dismisses such a possibility on the grounds that they share no common roots in their vocabulary. In fact, he goes so far as to assert that "the language of the Ainu forms by itself a linguistic island."[5] More significant, from our standpoint, is the Ainu attitude toward language, for, in sharp contrast to the prevailing notion of language as a means to convey an idea of a reality from which it is once removed, the Ainu consider language as a reinforcement of the immediacy of their relations to *kamuy*. That is, physical objects, beings, and events are experienced as inextricable components of sacred reality. This notion of language provides an important

[3] John Batchelor, "On the Ainu Term 'Kamui,'" *Transactions of Asiatic Society of Japan*, 16 (1888): 17–32.

[4] Basil Hall Chamberlain, "Reply to Mr. Batchelor on the Words 'Kamui' and 'Aino,'" *Transactions of Asiatic Society of Japan*, 16 (1888): 33–38. Incidentally, the present writer agrees with Chamberlain concerning the word *kamuy* or *kamui*, but agrees with Batchelor concerning the usage of *Ainu*.

[5] Kyōsuke Kindaichi, "The Ainu," *Proceedings of the Third Pan-Pacific Science Congress* (Tokyo, 1926), p. 2322. Kindaichi acknowledges the fact that the Hyperboleans and the American Indians speak incorporating languages, or even polysynthetic languages, but he still finds it signficant that the Ainu managed to preserve the integrity of their language so fully despite their long period of exposure to so many tribes.

key to our understanding of the nature and meaning of the Ainu myths.

It might be helpful for us to classify the Ainu language, following the analysis of Chiri, a noted scholar of linguistics and himself an Ainu, into two forms—"ordinary language" (*yayan-itak*) and "ornamental language" (*atomte-itak*), or "spoken words" (*rupa-itak*) and "rhythmic words" (*sa-kor-itak*).[6] Most Ainu men and women, being musical and fond of humming, singing, and dancing, tend to speak any sentence with a certain natural rhythm. In fact, the Ainu verb "to speak" (*ru-cha-no-ye* or *ru-pa-no-ye*) literally means "to utter words with semi-rhythm." But on formal or ceremonial occasions, when, for example, they offer prayers and incantations or when they engage in debate or negotiation, they are expected to "chant" or "sing" (*sa-ko-ye*; "speak with rhythm") because they believe that without proper rhythm the real potency of words cannot be fully actualized. Thus, a semiformal greeting is to be "chanted," for it means not only the meeting of two persons, but, as implied in the Ainu term for "greetings" (*ukoyaykurekarpa-itak*), it signifies "words of encounter between one's *kamuy* and another person's *kamuy*."

The extent to which the Ainu use "rhythmic words" can be seen in the wide variety of their magical formulas and incantations, which are designed to meet every conceivable occasion. Any young girl can recite the simple formula "*nupki san/ pē san*" ("muddy water, go down/ water, go down") as she goes to a brook to draw a bucketful of drinking water. And any old woman, while peeling the stem of a wild plant, can recite "*siwa-kina tōpen/ kina tōpen*" ("O bitter grass, be sweet/ O grass, be sweet"). Although there are serious occasions which require the expert service of shamanesses (*tusukur*), in many cases ordinary Ainu men and women are expected to know the proper words of incantation as well as accompanying magical acts which invoke the benevolent *kamuy* and ward off the malevolent spirits. Significantly, the Ainu term corresponding to a spell or incantation is *sitak*, an abbreviated form of *si-itak* ("true word"), which implies that the true word properly recited brings about the desired state of affairs, and the

[6] Mashio Chiri, *Ainu ni denshō-saretaru kabu-shikyoku ni kansuru chōsa-kenkyū* ("A Study on Songs, Dances, and Music Preserved by the Ainu"), (Tokyo, 1960), pp. 23 ff.

expert in the art of incantation is called *sitak-kon-kur* ("one who has mastered the true word"). On this subject, thanks to Chiri's lifelong research, we now have at our disposal carefully classified data of spells and incantations which have been preserved by the Ainu in various districts of Hokkaidō and Sakhalin.[7] For example, believing that solar eclipses are caused by the giant fox in the sky swallowing the sun, the Sakhalin Ainu put on hats made of fox skin and hit hard on any round object, such as drums or trays, while chanting "*chux eatu/ chux eatu*" ("vomit the sun/ vomit the sun"); the Hokkaidō Ainu, who believe that the sun is swallowed by a monstrous fish of the ocean, hit a boat and shoot arrows toward the sky while chanting "*chup-kamuy hōy/ e-ray nā hōy/ yaynu-pa hōy*" ("O sun/ you are dying/ recover your breathing"). There are also elaborate formulas of incantation to pacify earthquakes, typhoons, rainstorms, and tidal waves, and to avoid fire, sickness, and the falling of trees. There are even formulas to be chanted when the baby sneezes or when he keeps on crying at night. More important are a series of formulas to be used in connection with hunting and fishing, the two activities essential to their livelihood.[8]

On some critical occasions which threaten the welfare of the total community, as, for example, when there is an accidental death or a great fire, the entire village engages as a group in a magical act of marching, dancing, and shouting. In different Ainu territories this phenomenon is variously called *kewehumse* ("groaning to ward off the evil spirit"), *niwen-horippa* ("ritualistic shouting and dancing"), or *rimimse* ("group singing and dancing"). Even today, should someone be killed by a wild animal on the mountain, for instance, it is common practice for the men and women of the village to march, singing, dancing, and stamping all the way, to the spot where the death took place and to bury the deceased there. Such a misfortune occurs, according to their view, because of negligence on the part of the *kamuy*. Parenthetically it might be noted that the *kamuy* are believed to be working in their own world, which faces in the opposite direction from that of man; the male *kamuy* is said to be engaged in engraving and the female *kamuy* in embroidering, so that they do not hear ordinary human

[7] *Ibid.*, pp. 4–23.

[8] I have cited the formula to be used when one encounters a bear in the mountain in Kitagawa, "Ainu Bear Festival," p. 135.

voices. Hence the groaning, dancing, and noisy stamping! (It is said that women's singing and shouting are more effective than men's in calling the *kamuy's* attention.) While this noisy magical ritual is going on, the village elders step out of the group and chant prayers, saying, in effect, that it was because the *kamuy* were not duly attentive that the evil spirits took advantage of the situation and caused such misfortunes, and they mildly admonish the *kamuy* to be more vigilant henceforth.

As might be expected, the Ainu's predisposition toward "rhythmic words" has engendered a rich variety of verses, songs, and ballads, including nursery rhymes, children's play songs, boat songs, hunting songs, drinking songs, and love songs. It is taken for granted by the Ainu that just as each animal, bird, and insect has its unique mode of singing, each person in every situation can and should express himself in the appropriate form of singing or chanting. When several families or the entire village get together for feasts and ceremonies on special occasions such as weddings, funerals, and the bear festival, the Ainu engage in various kinds of formalized dances accompanied by singing and clapping of hands as well as by the beating of drums and/or other objects. Some of these dances are called *tapkar*, *rimse*, and *horippa* and developed from the tradition of the communal magical act, *kewehumse*, which, as mentioned earlier, is aimed at warding off evil spirits and invoking benevolent *kamuy*. The songs for these dances are variously known as *tapkar-sinotcha*, *rimse*, *upopo*, and *hechiri*. Incidentally, the term *sinotcha* originally meant *si-not-sa* ("melodies for the dances by the shamaness"), although today it refers to any lyrical song. Of special interest for the understanding of the Ainu mentality is the name of a certain kind of song called *yaysama*, which literally means "imitating oneself." These songs, which are marked by the frequent repetition of the phrase *yaysamanena* ("thus I sing my mind"), usually unfold the inner sentiment of a person. It is also interesting to note that there are many songs and dances which "imitate" the voices and movements of animals, birds, and insects, all of which are believed to share with human beings the common *kamuy* nature.

The motif of "imitation" which runs through the songs and dances of the Ainu also underlies their manner of telling *iso-itak* ("personal adventures, stories"), *upashkuma* ("old stories"), and *uwe-*

pekere ("anecdotes, fables, legends, sagas"). Whenever an Ainu tells a story, according to Kindaichi, "the story-teller assumes the character of the hero of the story, who is sometimes a great man or a wicked one, and sometimes a [*kamuy*] or a devil, or even the spirit of a bear or a wolf. This is . . . one of the most peculiar characteristics of the Ainu stories."[9] This notion of "imitation" is especially pertinent to our understanding of the Ainu myths, sacred legends, and epics, which are collectively called *yukar*. Significantly, the term *yukar* means literally "to imitate" (*i-ukar*) in the sense that the reciter imitates either the manner of the animals or birds which are to be hunted or the personal adventures and stories (*iso-itak*) told by "the *kamuy* whom we imitate and follow" (*A-e-yukar kamuy*).[10]

We must bear in mind, however, that the Ainu notion of "imitation" does not mean simply to impersonate or copy the voice and movements of another being, be it *kamuy*, hero, animal, or bird. To be sure, it has that dimension too. But, more basically, what is implied is the notion that when one imitates some other being one can, by the magical potency of the rhythmic language, fully participate in the person or being whose words he is reciting or chanting. An analogy to the Ainu notion of "imitation" is probably found in the idea of the ancient Egyptian who, according to Wilson, "did not distinguish between symbolism and participation; if he said that the king was Horus, he did not mean that the king was playing the part of Horus, he meant that the king *was* Horus, that the god was effectively present in the king's body during the particular activity in question."[11] The significant difference in the case of the Ainu, however, is that such a prerogative is shared by every Ainu man and woman, so that by chanting or by listening to the rhythmic words of the *kamuy*, hero, animal, and bird, all of whom are endowed with the *kamuy* nature, the indivisibility of man (which is the meaning of the term "Ainu") from the *kamuy* becomes renewed and reinforced as their experienced reality. In this sense, the recitation of the rhythmic words of *yukar* is in itself a sacramental act, although the *yukar* are often chanted as an important ingredient of ritual.

[9] Kindaichi, "The Ainu," p. 2310.

[10] *Ibid.*

[11] John A. Wilson, "Egypt," in *The Intellectual Adventure of Ancient Man*, by H. Frankfort, H. A. Frankfort, J. A. Wilson, T. Jacobsen, and W. A. Irwin (Chicago, 1946), pp. 64–65.

Students of Ainu religion and culture cannot help being amazed by the fact that the Ainu have transmitted orally the rich variety of *yukar*, many of which contain 2,000 to 3,000 lines, while the longest ones extend to 10,000 lines, without any aid of written notes. It is conceivable that if they had wanted written words, they could have adopted a written language from any one of their neighbors. On this score, we are inclined to believe that the numinous quality of the rhythmic words is such that the *yukar* could only be handed down orally from generation to generation. The pioneer of the modern study of the *yukar* was an English missionary, John Batchelor, who collected and translated many of them under the designation of folklore.[12] More recently, scholarly research on the *yukar* has been greatly advanced by the careful linguistic research of Kindaichi with the cooperation of Chiri Mashio and Chiri's sister and aunts.[13]

Considering the bewildering variety of existing *yukar*, it is not difficult to understand why there is no definitive method of classifying them.[14] Most scholars, however, would be reasonably satisfied with the simple scheme of classification which has been suggested by Chiri.[15] According to him, the *yukar* may be divided into 1) the shamanistic chants or witch songs (*tusu-sinotcha*) believed to be the utterances of the *kamuy* given through the mouth

[12] See his "Specimens of Ainu Folklore," *Transactions of the Asiatic Society of Japan*, 16 (1888); *ibid.*, 18 (1889); *ibid.*, 20 (1892); *The Ainu of Japan* (New York, 1895); *The Ainu and Their Folklore* (London, 1901); *Uwepekere or Ainu Fireside Stories, As Told By One of Themselves* (London, 1925); and *Ainu Life and Lore* (London, 1927).

[13] Kyōsuke Kindaichi, who had earlier published *Ainu seiten* ("Sacred Tradition of the Ainu"), (1923); *Jojishi, yukara no kenkyū* ("A Study of Yukar"), 2 vols. (1933); *Ainu bungaku* ("Literature of the Ainu"), (1933); *Ainu no shinten* ("Scriptures of the Ainu"), (1943); and *Ainu jojishi, itadorimaru no kyoku* ("Ainu Yukar, 'Kutune Shirka'"), (1944) has recently undertaken a monumental enterprise of editing and translating a series of *yukara-shū* ("collections of yukar"). Already published are vol. 1, *Pon Oina* (1959); vol. 2, *Poro Oina*; vol. 3, *Ponsamorunkur* and *Kamuikarsapa Kamuitartumam* (1963); vol. 4, *Kemka Karip* (1964); vol. 5, *Nishimakunmat* (1965); vol. 6, *Iyochiunmat* (1966); and vol. 7, *Uchiu Ninkari* and *Akeusutu* (1966). Several more volumes are forthcoming. It is an almost unbelievable fact that all these *yukar* have been recorded from the memory of one lady, Kannari Matsu, who happens to be the maternal aunt of Mashio Chiri.

[14] On this subject, see Richard W. Howell, "The Classification and Description of Ainu Folklore," *Journal of American Folklore*, 64 (1951): 361–69, and Bronislaw Pilsudski, *Materials for the Study of the Ainu Language and Folklore* (Krakow, 1933).

[15] See Chiri, *Ainu ni denshō*, pp. 84–90.

of the shamaness (*tusu-kur*) during the state of ecstatic possession; 2) the songs of the *kamuy* (*kamuy-yukar*) which are tales about the *kamuy* narrated by themselves; 3) the sacred inheritance or legends (*oina*, also called *oina-yukar* or *kamuy-oina*) which contain the teachings and traditions of the most popular character in the Ainu pantheon, who as such is the prototype of the Ainu and whose name is variously known as Oina-kamuy or Aeoina-kamuy ("the *kamuy* whose inheritance we preserve"), Pon Okikurumi ("smaller Okikurumi," meaning the son of Okikurumi, whose name he assumes later), or Ainu-rak-kur ("the one who smells like the Ainu"); 4) the epics of the hero (*Ainu yukar* or simply *yukar*), which are autobiographical accounts of the intricate adventures of the Ainu hero par excellence, Poiyaumbe, who is also known as Poy-Sinutapkaun-kur ("son of Sinutapuka"), Pon-Otasam-un-kur ("son of Otasam"), and Pon-Otasut-un-kur ("son of Otasut"); and 5) the romantic poems, or more literally the epics of women (*menoko yukar*), which describe the love affairs of Sinutapka-un-mat ("daughter of Sinutapka") or Otasam-un-mat ("daughter of Otasam").

Attempts have also been made to divide the *yukar* into mythico-religious and nonreligious categories. Indeed, many scholars hold that the *tusu-sinotcha* ("shamanistic chants"), *kamuy yukar* ("songs of the *kamuy*"), and *oina* ("sacred inheritance") belong to the first category while the *Ainu yukar* ("epics of the hero") and *menoko yukar* ("epics of women") belong to the second. There is some truth in this view because of the *Ainu yukar* and *menoko yukar* are usually chanted on festive occasions or when people get together to enjoy themselves on long winter nights, whereas it is taken for granted that the *oina*, for example, "is not merely to be heard with pleasure, but to be believed in."[16] Nevertheless, if applied rigidly, such a division is bound to be arbitrary and to falsify the nature of the *yukar* because even the war tales of the *Ainu ukar* and the romantic scenes of the *menoko yukar* are shot through with mythico-religious motifs and symbols. In fact, the *oina* and the *Ainu yukar*, for instance, are so similar that many sections of these two are hardly distinguishable except for the names of the main characters and place names.[17] On the other

[16] K. Kindaichi, *Ainu Life and Legend* (Tokyo, 1941), p. 71.

[17] K. Kindaichi, *Ainu bunka-shi* ("A Study of the Ainu Culture"), (Tokyo, 1961), pp. 292–93.

hand, there are some noticeable stylistic differences among the various kinds of *yukar*. For example, the *oina*, which is considered by some scholars as a part of the *kamuy yukar*, does not have the rhythmic refrain (*sakehe*) which is the characteristic mark of the *kamuy yukar*. Also, the *oina* and the *Ainu yukar* are far more developed in poetic sophistication and more grandiose in scope than the *tusu-sinotcha* and the *kamuy yukar*. Obviously, the *Ainu yukar*, which took its present form about five or six hundred years ago, was modeled after the *oina*, which had existed earlier as a "sacred charter of the Ainu," to use a recent writer's phrase.[18] Parenthetically we might mention that it required expert, and more often than not hereditary, reciters—the *oina-kur* and the *yukar-kur*—to memorize faithfully these long and complicated verses as as well as the manner of chanting them in order to transmit them orally from one generation to the next. It is most plausible that originally the *oina* developed out of the tradition of the *kamuy yukar*, which in turn was derived from the *tusu-sinotcha* uttered by the shamanesses. This accounts for the fact that we find in the simple rhythmic words of the *kamuy yukar* and the *tusu-sinotcha* some of the key motifs of Ainu myth which were elaborated subsequently in the *oina*, the *Ainu yukar*, and the *menoko yukar*.

The significance of the *tusu-sinotcha* and the *kamuy yukar* can be readily seen in the light of the decisive role played by the shamaness in the life of the Ainu. In this connection, Kindaichi cites a famous *yukar* concerning a certain princess who grew up without any care of adults. "As I cried for hunger," the *yukar* states, "I entered, through my crying, into the state of ecstasy, and I grew up chanting the *tusu-sinotcha* unaided until I became a maiden."[19] All Ainu women, according to Kindaichi, are potentially capable of becoming the shamaness (*tusu-kur*) by the power of the serpent, which is believed to be the *turen-kamuy* ("the *kamuy* who possesses").[20] Even today, when the chieftain is confronted with a serious problem he offers liquor to the *kamuy*, and,

[18] Richard W. Howell, "The Kamui Oina: A Sacred Charter of the Ainu," *Journal of American Folklore*, 65 (1952): 379–417. In this article, the author provides a translation of the *oina* (pp. 381–86) and an analysis of Ainu society, culture, and religion through the study of the *oina*.

[19] Kindaichi, *Ainu bunka-shi*, pp. 216–27.

[20] The Ainu woman's full dress is nothing but the attire of the shamaness. See Kindaichi, *Ainu Life and Legend*, p. 27.

after drinking half of it himself, gives the rest to the shamaness. She drinks it and begins to sing a *tusu-sinotcha.* "While singing, the woman becomes possessed with a spirit. The tone of her voice changes into an extraordinary one. At last it becomes the voice of the [*kamuy*] and sings something suggestive. The chieftain guesses the meaning of the song, and thereby judges or decides. . . ."[21]

Some of the rhythmic words repeated in the *tusu-sinotcha*, such as *sa-a-e-e-e/ hayussa-a/ taa-taa/ hayussa-a/ rankee/ saa-eee*, for example, must have been the voices of certain *kamuy* whom the shamaness "imitated," because they are unintelligible to human ears. When the shamaness is called upon to help in a difficult childbirth, she repeats the song of the *kamuy* of the water imp, who is believed to come from a distant lake in order to protect the pregnant woman. The shamaness chants "*hai hussa tata. . . .*" Sometimes more than one *kamuy*, one at a time to be sure, communicates through the same shamaness. Chiri mentions the example of a shamaness who, in dealing with a case of a dying woman, chanted the utterances of the male and female *kamuy* of the spider, followed by those of the *kamuy* of the dragon snake, with marked changes in her voice, gestures, and the content of her message. In this case, the voice of the *kamuy* of the spider stated, "*aynu mataynu/ sermak ka ta/ naa pase kamuy/ astoma kamuy/ horarpa wa okay*" ("this woman's soul is possessed by a *kamuy* who is heavier" [which means greater] "and more powerful than I am"). Then, the voice of the dragon serpent, which is loud and resounding, announced that the woman's sickness was caused by the spirit of the rabbit chewing the string of her heart.[22] There are various kinds of the *tusu-sinotcha*, some of which are very short while others are of considerable length; they have been preserved either independently or as parts of the *yukar*.

The *kamuy yukar* resembles, at least stylistically, the *tusu-sinotcha* in the sense that it too repeats some seemingly meaningless phrases as refrains (*sakehe*), such as: *oway oway tururke/ oway oway tururke/ oway oway tururke*, although it is more poetically sophisticated than the other. On the other hand, unlike the *tusu-sinotcha*, which deal with such specific matters as difficult child-

[21] *Ibid.*, pp. 68–69.

[22] The text of this *tusu-sinotcha* and Chiri's translation are found in his *Ainu ni denshō*, pp. 85–88.

birth, serious sickness, or a critical issue of the village, the *kamuy yukar* shares with the *oina* the quality of being the songs about the *kamuy* narrated by themselves. The basic difference is that while the *oina* is the autobiographical account of a *kamuy* with identifiable human characteristics, the *kamuy yukar* is attributed to the *kamuy* who are visiting man's world in animal, bird, and other nonhuman disguise. Popular in the *kamuy yukar* are the *kamuy* of the bear (the *kamuy* of the mountain), wolf, fox, water weasel, owl, dolphin (the *kamuy* of the sea), snake, frog, and swamp shellfish, as well as the *kamuy* of such plants as aconite, bulbous plant, and yew tree. Natural phenomena are represented by the *kamuy* of fire, wind, and thunder; even the boat, anchor, and other material objects are not excluded from the list.

Among all the characters of the *kamuy yukar*, one who is favored by many is the owl, affectionately called *kamuy-chikap* ("divine bird") or *kamuy-ekasi* ("divine elder"). He assumes the all-important task of maintaining the order and welfare of the village (*kotan*), which is the basic unit of Ainu society and the model of the various worlds of *kamuy*; thus he is given the titles of *kotan-kor-kamuy* ("guardian *kamuy* of the village") and *mosir-kor-kamuy* ("guardian *kamuy* of the world"). He is also known as *kunne-rek-kamuy* ("the *kamuy* who caws as night") and is believed to lead men to the bear cave by singing "*pewrep! pewrep cikoyki! kot! kot! kot!*" He announces the coming of rain by the sound "*ca! ca!*" and warns men about an impending calamity with the sound "*co! co!*" Indeed, the owl is *iso-sanke-kamuy* ("the *kamuy* who provides the fortunes of sea and mountain") to the Ainu.

In a well-known *kamuy yukar*, the owl recalls the time when he wanted to protest, on behalf of man, to the *kamuy* in charge of the game and fish because they refused to release deer and fish to man. To transmit his plea to these *kamuy* he needed a messenger endowed with the qualities of eloquence and expertise in negotiation, because, in his words, "Once I was an eloquent speaker but am now getting too old." At that time, a crow volunteered for the job, but fell asleep while the owl was instructing him. Then a jay volunteered, but he too fell asleep during the instruction. Finally, a water weasel was found worthy for the task and flew to heaven with the owl's message. A few days later he returned from heaven with a reply. Evidently, it was reported, when men caught deer and fish, they hit them with rotten wood and, after taking meat, threw away the carcasses on the ground. Thus the deer and fish returned to the world of the *kamuy* empty-handed, that is, without proper presents from the world of man, weeping over their misfortunes. And that is why the *kamuy* in charge of the game and fish threatened man with famine unless he learned to respect animals and fish. Hearing this, the owl goes on to say, "I taught men in their dreams how to treat the deer and fish with better care and respect, including the use of beautifully decorated sticks for killing them, whereby the deer and fish returned to their world with lovely gifts. The *kamuy*, delighted by this, provided abundant amounts of deer and fish to man. . . ." The song, which is narrated in the first person singular throughout, ends with the characteristic closing phrase "Thus uttered the *kamuy ekasi* ("*divine elder*"), *kotan-kor kamuy* ("guardian *kamuy* of the village"). . . ."[23]

In another *kamuy yukar* the owl portrays himself as the benefactor of the poor and the preserver of peaceful interhuman relations.[24] It begins with the description of the owl flying over the village, singing "dews of silver are dripping down all around/ dews of gold are dripping down all around" ("*shirokanipe ranran pishkan/ konkanipe ranran pishkan*"). This verse, which itself sounds like the dew dripping down, is effectively repeated and enhances the musical quality of the song. At any rate, the owl notices that some families which were once rich and respected are now poor and ill-treated by the new rich. As the owl flies by the beach, children of the new rich try to shoot him with golden arrows. Soon he notices a small, poorly dressed boy apart from other children, and allows himself to be shot by an ordinary wooden arrow by this boy and to be taken to his humble cottage. The boy sends the owl into the house through the ceremonial window, which is reserved to bring in the bear, fish, and other *kamuy*. The boy's parents, poorly dressed but obviously persons of good background, worship the owl, saying "*kamuichikap kamui*

23 This account is an abbreviated translation of "Kamuichikap kamui yaieyukar 'Konkuwa,'" recorded in Yukiye Chiri, *Ainu shinyō-shū* ("A Collection of the *kamuy yukar* of the Ainu"), (Tokyo, 1923), pp. 74–85. The author is the sister of Mashio Chiri. She published this small, elegant volume before she died at the age of twenty-one.

24 The full text of this account is found in *ibid.*, pp. 2–23.

pase kamui" ("O divine bird, O great *kamuy*"). They apologize for their humble cottage, which is not good enough to house the guardian *kamuy* of the village, but promise to make many *inau* (whittled sticks used as offerings to the *kamuy*) and put him in the place of honor.

When everybody goes to sleep, the song continues: "I started flying around inside the house singing *shirokanipe ranran*. . . , and as my wings flapped, lovely divine treasures descended around me, filling the house. Also, by singing *shirokanipe ranran*. . . I transformed the humble cottage into a big golden mansion, full of nice furniture and fine clothes. . . ." Then, in the morning, the boy of the house is dispatched, clothed in rags, to invite the villagers to a feast. Upon looking at the transformed house, the arrogant new rich who came to laugh at the audacity of the boy's family were overcome by the wisdom of the *kamuy* and repented, and all of them became good friends and neighbors again. In the end, they held a big feast and worshiped him. Although the owl returned afterward to his own world with many gifts, he says, "I always sit behind the world of man and protect it."

As one can see in these two examples, the *kamuy yukar* are based on very simple themes and, unlike the case of the *oina*, the cosmogonic and theogonic motifs of the *kamuy yukar* are not very well articulated. Nevertheless, the *kamuy yukar* as well as the *tusu-sinotcha* portray the cosmos as a community, not of things but of beings, all sharing the *kamuy* nature; thus, for the Ainu, sacral reality can be experienced in and through the world of nature. This central theme, it should be remembered, runs through all aspects of the life of the Ainu as exemplified by the rituals and the *yukar*. It must be admitted that the Ainu never developed great religions and cultures as did other peoples in Asia. But they have preserved the legacy of a very creative way of committing their sacred tradition of myths, history, law, art, science, and religion to the rhythmic *yukar*, which have been "imitated," respected, enjoyed, and followed as the foundation of the community of shared experience of being both the *kamuy* and the Ainu (which means "man"). To casual observers the life of the Ainu may have little to recommend it. But to the Ainu, what appears to be a drab life in the barren northern islands is enriched by the numinous potency of the rhythmic words, and to them this world is the "cradle of the *kamuy*," the most beautiful among all the worlds of the *kamuy*, which the *kamuy* wish to visit in various disguises. Thus, through reciting and hearing the *yukar*, the Ainu are reminded and reassured of the fact that this world of nature is constantly permeated by the harmony of poignant rhythmic voices of the *kamuy*.

Shirokanipe ranran pishkan,
konkanipe ranran pishkan . . . .

III

LITERARY . . .

DRUGS AND ECSTASY

ERNST JÜNGER

> Qu'elle soit ramassée pour "le bien" ou pour "le mal," la mandragore est crainte et respectée comme une plante miraculeuse — En elle sont renfermées des forces extraordinaires, qui peuvent multiplier la vie ou donner la mort. En une certaine mesure donc, la mandragore est "l'herbe de la vie et de la mort."
>
> Mircea Eliade, "Le culte de la mandragore en Roumanie," *Xalmoxis*, 1938

The influence of drugs is ambivalent; they affect both action and contemplation, will and intuition. These two forces, which seemingly exclude each other, are often produced by the same means, as everyone knows who has ever observed a drinking party.

It is, however, questionable whether wine can be considered a drug in the strict sense of the word. Perhaps its original power has become domesticated in the course of millennia of use. We hear of its greater power, but also of its greater mystery, from myths in which Dionysus appears as the lord and host of feasts with his entourage of Satyrs, Sileni, Maenads, and beasts of prey.

The triumphant conquest of Dionysus took place in a reverse order from Alexander's — from India across the Near East to Europe — and his conquests were of a more lasting nature. Dionysus is considered, like Adonis, to be the founder of orgiastic festivals, whose periodic recurrences are deeply interwoven with historical event. An exuberant phallic worship was connected with these festivals. Phallacism was not the content of the Dionysia but one of the revelations which confirmed the mystery and its binding power. In contrast to the Dionysia, according to an ancient author, "the festivals of Aphrodite in Cythera might be called the pious games of children."

This original power of wine has vanished; we see it return, in a milder form, in the autumn and spring festivals of the wine countries. In rare instances only the intensification of the lust for life, colors, melodies, and grotesque pictures reveals a trace of the ancient mystic world with its uncanny, contagious power. Archaic features then appear in the faces, leaps, and dances. More than anything else, the mask is essential in this as a symbol of the "reversed world."

If we compare the triumphs of Alexander and Dionysus, we touch upon the difference between historical and elemental power. Success in history, as the conquest of Babylon, for example, shows, is fleeting and tied to names. The moment does not return in the same form; it becomes a link in the chain of historical time. But if we consider changes in the elemental world, neither names nor dates are important and yet changes take place time and again, not only below historical time but also within it. They burst forth like magma from its crust.

But let us stay with wine. Alexander was forced to retreat from India, while Dionysus even today reigns as a nameless host. Wine has changed Europe more forcefully than has the sword: even today it is considered to be a medium of cultic transformation. The exchange of new poisons and ecstasies, and also of new vices, fevers, and diseases, lacks the kind of definite dating by which coronations or decisive battles are remembered. Such exchanges remain in the dark, in the entanglement of the roots. We can surmise the events, but we can neither know their extent nor penetrate their depth.

For Europeans, Cortez' landing in Mexico in 1519 belonged to the historical order; for the Aztecs, this event belonged to the magical order of the world. In the latter world order dream is more powerful than consciousness; the presentiment has greater binding force than the word. In those contacts there is an oscillating element which is understood sometimes as booty and sometimes as a gift, then again as guilt or expiation—for example, in the sacrifice: on the one hand Montezuma, on the other Maximilian, both emperors of Mexico. Below the surface seeds, images, and dreams are given and received in an alternation which destroys some tribes and strengthens others. Yet its effect cannot be exactly described or dated.

Statistics, even if they are precise, can only extract figures from a problem. The problem in its depth is not touched by them; it remains in the strict sense of the word "a matter in disguise." This applies especially to domains that border on the psyche, as well as to any "behavior," including animal behavior, and no less to our subject of drugs and induced ecstasy.

To mention in this connection one of America's great gifts to Europe, tobacco, we have rather precise figures concerning the relation between nicotine and a number of diseases. These findings belong to the field of statistics. If we are to acknowledge them, however, we must first accept the idea of "utility" under which they were established.

Usefulness, in this case, is of a hygienic nature. Yet, from a different point of view, smoking could also imply something beneficial—the word "enjoyment" itself indicates this possibility. One might think of the easing of conversation, of the shortening of a tedious hour or the rapid passage of a gloomy one, of some association that may be prompted in this way, or simply of any moment of happiness. Any concentration, but any relaxation, too, must be paid for. Is the enjoyment worth the price? Here lies the problem for which statistics can only supply data. It arises for the smoker every time he thinks of lighting a cigarette.

Statistics merely confirm a fact which has always been known: drugs are dangerous. He who becomes involved with them takes a risk which becomes greater the less he calculates. In this respect, however, in comparing loss and gain, statistics are of value.

We include wine and tobacco in our consideration because it is advisable to start from rather well-known factors. Both are only marginals of our subject proper. They will be touched less the more exactly we define the word "drug." For Baudelaire wine opens, along with hashish and opium, the gate to artificial paradises. Justifiably, the friend of wine is disinclined to consider wine as a drug. He prefers wine growers and coopers rather than chemists and manufacturers to be occupied with wine. Still, from the growing of the wine to the resurrection of the grapes from the cellar, the care and skill of wine growers and craftsmen are devoted to wine; it is still regarded as a divine gift of miraculous, transforming power. It is blood of the earth and blood of gods.

To consider wine as a drug would mean no more than one comment among others — for instance, that wine contains alcohol. Tobacco seems to fit better in this category. Nicotine gives us an idea of what is possible in the sphere of alkaloids. In the smoke offerings which are made daily on our planet, there is an indication of the lightness, the spiritual liberation of the great dreams of flight. But compared with the magic power of opium, nicotine gives only a slight uplift, a mild euphoria.

Like many other etymological explanations, the one for the word "drug" is unsatisfactory. Its origin is obscure. As in the case of the word "alcohol" there are derivations from the Spanish-Arabic and also from medieval Latin. The origin from the Dutch *drog*, dry, is more likely. Drugs were materials obtained from many countries; they were traded through herb lofts and pharmacies and used by physicians, cooks, and perfumery and grocery dealers. From the beginning the word had a tinge of mystery, of magical manipulation, especially if the materials were of oriental origin.

In our definition a drug is a substance which produces a state of ecstacy. It is true, however, that something specific must be added to distinguish these substances from others used as medicine or simply for enjoyment. This specific factor should not be sought in the substance itself, but rather in the purpose of its use, because medicine too, as well as other stuffs taken for the sake of pleasure, may be used, in this restricted sense, as intoxicating drugs.

In a passage of his *Midsummer Night's Dream* Shakespeare speaks of the "common" sleep, which he distinguishes from stronger, magical states. The former brings dreams, the latter visions and prophecies. In a similar way the ecstasy produced by a drug shows particular effects which are difficult to describe. He who seeks this type of intoxication does so with specific intentions. And he who uses the word "drug" in this sense presupposes an understanding on the part of his listener or reader which cannot be defined more exactly. He sets fact on a border line.

Infusions and concentrations, decoctions and elixirs, powders and pills, ointments, pastes and resinous substances, all these can be used as drugs in this specific sense. The substance may be solid, liquid, gaseous, or smoke-like; it may be eaten, drunk, inhaled, smoked, sniffed, or injected. To attain a state of ecstasy not only a certain kind of substance is required, but also a certain quantity and concentration thereof. The dosage may be too low or too high; in the former case it will not lead beyond soberness, and in the latter it will cause unconsciousness. It is well known that in the case of drug addiction it becomes more and more difficult to adhere to the golden mean—on the one hand lies depression, and on the other the dosage becomes ever more threatening. The price that must be paid for pleasure rises ever higher. Then, the only choice is to reform or to perish.

As the effect of the drug diminishes, either quantity or concentration can be increased. That is the case with the smoker or drinker who first increases his usual consumption and then reaches for stronger kinds. This indicates at the same time that mere pleasure no longer suffices. A third possibility lies in a change in periodicity—in the transition from daily habit to rare, festive excess. In the third case, not the dosage but the receptivity is increased. The smoker who can muster up the discipline to be content with one cigarette in the morning will none the less be satisfied, because he achieves an intensity of pleasure hitherto unknown to him despite his greater former consumption. However, this again adds to temptation.

The sensitivity may become very great and, correspondingly, the dosage very slight, even minimal. We have known ever since Hahnemann that even the slightest traces of substances may become effective, and modern chemistry confirms this fact. In every case, however, the prescription must be supported by a special receptivity. For this reason homeopathic medicines do not help everyone. They presuppose homeopathic behavior. For the sensitive person a hint is enough. That is a universal law, not only in the field of hygiene but also in the general conduct of life. In the opposite case, there is an applicable proverb: "a rough log needs a rough wedge."

Thus the dosage may become minimal. Under certain circumstances, some substances which are commonly believed to be neutral may even become intoxicating, such as the air we breathe. Jules Verne's "Idea of Doctor Ox" is based on this principle. Under the false pretense of planning to build a gasworks, Doctor Ox induces an intoxicated state in the inhabitants of a small town by adding pure oxygen to the air. Thus, through concentration, a substance which we inhale with every breath of air we take becomes "poisonous." Paracelsus: "Sola dosis facit venenum."

Doctor Ox distilled the air. From this it can be assumed that for sensitive people it may become intoxicating in itself. And so it is indeed. There are probably few people for whom Goethe's words "youth is intoxication without wine" have not become reality, at least for some moments. Certainly this requires untouched receptivity, one of the signs of youth. In any case, however, external factors will also contribute to that effect, either through "higher potencies" of known or unknown substances or atmospheric influences. In novels we find flowerly phrases such as "the air was like wine"; the inexplicable gaiety arises from almost immaterial sources.

Yet the "happy hour" may bring melancholy as well. It may have an exhorting, warning power, and this quality makes it no less beneficial, because threatening dangers often announce themselves in this manner. Apart from perceptions, which are equally difficult to explain or deny, there are many experiences for which refined receptivity suffices as an explanation. Alexander von Humbold, in his "Reise in die Äquinoktialgegenden" ("Journey to the Equinoctial Areas"), deals extensively with the phenomena which preceded volcanic eruptions and earthquakes. In this connection he discusses the agitation of men and animals that may justly be called premonition as well as perception.

Up to the present day man has tried time and again to extract substances or psychogenic forces out of the atmosphere, so to speak. Mesmer, for example, taking magnetism as his starting point, believed he recognized a "fluid" which emanated from the human body and could be conserved in certain objects, such as storage batteries. In medicine, Mesmerism became hardly more than a fashion; its influence, however, survived in literature. E. Th. A. Hoffmann was especially fascinated by it. Mesmer's dissertation had already caused a sensation: "De planetarum influxu" could as easily have been the title of a piece of writing by Novalis or a contribution to the *Athenäum.*

More significant, although less well-known than Mesmer, is Carl Ludwig von Reichenbach; he excelled not only as a natural philosopher but also as a geologist, chemist, and industrialist. Reichenbach claimed he had found in "Od" a substance whose force or emanation may be compared to Mesmer's fluid. This Od, though present everywhere in nature, is more easily perceived by delicately organized beings, whom Reichenbach called "sensitive," or, in case of special sensitivity, "highly sensitive" creatures. Reichenbach, in whom a gift for natural philosophy was united with the exactness of the natural scientist, attempted to prove the existence of Od experimentally. For this purpose he employed sensitive persons in the same way as a nearsighted person uses spectacles. He developed methods which we would call "tests" today. Although he used no instruments, he nevertheless made very fine differentiations. A person who could not detect a difference in temperature between the small and large ends of a chicken egg held in two fingers did not qualify as a sensitive person. Reichenbach ventures to penetrate into regions which, though neither remote nor closed, are inaccessible to dull senses.

Physicists, however, were just as unwilling to take notice of Od as psychiatrists and neurologists were to give consideration to sensitive persons. As a natural scientist Reichenbach grieved about this; as a philosopher he could disregard it. He came up with his idea at a most unfavorable time. This is even more true of Fechner, who considered the mathematical-physical view of the world as the "night side" of the universe, and drew from Reichenbach's writings the greatest benefit for his "psychophysics."

Fechner's thoughts about the animation of celestial bodies and of plants faded away without an echo in an era in which mechanistic theories forced their way with unprecedented force. In medicine, a massive positivism was in preparation, and out of its hybris a surgeon boasted that he had never seen a soul in his work.

Such opposing views give rise to the impression that the mind of the age was busy in two wings of a building without any doors between the two. One might also think of a double mirror whose two sides are separated by an opaque layer. Nonetheless, there have been and will be periods which approximate a oneness of view. It can never be fully attained because both the mathematical-physical view of the world and the natural-philosophical view of Reichenbach and Fechner are only aspects of the "inner self of nature" (*Inneren der Natur*).

Thus, the dosage which leads to intoxication can be minimal if the receptivity is great enough. In this respect, too, some sensitive persons are especially susceptible. The norms which the legislator feels must be established – in traffic laws, for instance – can only give an approximate standard. It will become ever stricter because the empirical world daily proves anew that intoxication and technology are clashing powers which exclude each other. Truly, this does not apply to drugs as such. On the contrary, their number and the extent of their use increase steadily. There are a growing number of achievements in which the proper use of drugs is not only indicated but indispensable. This becomes a science in itself.

The receptivity which leads to ecstasy can become so strong that mere ways of behavior suffice and drugs become superfluous. This is a prerogative of ascetics; their close relationship to ecstasy has always been known. Added to temperance, staying awake, and fasting is solitude, which the artist and the scholar also need, temporarily at least. The flow of images in the Thebais were "tele-visions" which were not dependent on drugs, let alone on equipment.

The thinker, the artist who is in good form, knows phases in which new light flows toward him. The world begins to speak and responds to the mind with swelling force. Objects seem to charge themselves; their beauty, their meaningful order come out in a new way. This being-in-good-form is independent of physical well-being; it is often in contrast to the latter, almost as if images had easier access in a condition of weakness than at other times. It is true, however, that Reichenbach has already warned against confusing sensitivity and illness – after all, it is not easy to avoid error here. The difficulty becomes especially obvious in disputes in which conclusions are drawn about the psyche of the artist on the basis of his work. It is no coincidence that our own time is so rich in controversies of this kind. Probably states of heightened sensitivity precede not only the productive phases in the life of the individual but also changes of style within a culture. These developments are connected with an almost Babylonian confusion, not only of forms of artistic expression but of language in general.

Jung-Stilling calls this receptivity a "faculty of clairvoyance" and means by this a heightened susceptibility which can be gained by a certain way of life: "finally, however, a pure, devout man may also achieve ecstacies and a state of magnetic sleep through prolonged exercises and a godly way of living." According to him "the soul works in the natural state through the brain and the nerves, in the magnetic state without either." Only after death does man gain the full power of clairvoyant sleep, because he has been completely separated from the body; this capacity is far more perfect after death than it can be in life.

Jung-Stilling's clairvoyants correspond roughly to Reichenbach's highly sensitive men; in the language of the present day they might be understood as extremely rare but recurring mutants. Clairvoyance can be developed, yet it must be inborn. Thereby Jung-Stilling explains, among other things, those cases in which warning dreams or apparitions are perceived not by the person in danger but by a third person who plays the role of the receiver. This faculty need not be coupled with ethical or intellectual endowment; it may appear in a dull existence as well as in a person full of genius. In the figure of Prince Myshkin Dostoevsky describes someone with a highly developed faculty of clairvoyance who seems to be an idiot in the eyes of the people around him. In old and new biographies one comes again and again upon the figure of the highly sensitive person who, before a fire, a stroke of lightning, or some other accident, is seized by indomitable unrest or oppression in breathing and leaves the room where he had been with others who remained unconcerned.

States of excitation or meditation, similar to those of intoxication, may also occur without the use of toxic drugs. This points to the possibility that drugs awaken faculties which are more comprehensive than those produced by a specific intoxication. They are a key—though not the only one—to realms that are closed to normal perception. For that with which one strives to achieve the idea of intoxication is hardly adequate unless it is broadened to comprise manifold and even contradictory phenomena. We started from the observation that drugs influence the will as well as contemplation. Within this ambivalence there is a large scale of variability which leads on either side to unconsciousness and finally to death. Drugs may be wanted as excitants and stimulants, as somnifacients, narcotics, and hallucinogens; they serve both narcotization and stimulation. Hassen Sabah, the old man from the mountain, was familiar with this scale to its full extent. He led the Fedavis, the votaries who were later also called the Assassins, from the peace of artificial paradises to the frenzy of running amok against princes and satraps. Not the same thing but something closely related can be found within the entanglement of our technological world. Its tendencies include both the flight into insensitivity and the intensification of the mechanism of motion through the use of stimulants.

The legislator must simplify this abundance. He considers intoxication "to be the state brought about by the use of drugs, especially the state of acute alcoholic poisoning." It is up to him to decide in every individual case whether or not intoxication had to do with a particular act, which might also be an act of omission. To judge in what state of consciousness the punishable deviation begins is especially difficult because there are drugs which, at least temporarily, further technical achievement. Champion fighters have always known such drugs, but the borderline which separates doping from permitted stimulation is fluid.

Every year there appear in the market new drugs whose dangerous effects are often not recognized until the damage has been done. With others the damage is minimal but accumulates in decades of use to an often disastrous degree. This applies both to stimulating drugs such as tobacco and to narcotics such as mild sleeping pills. Added to this is the fact that stimulants and narcotics are often used in addition to one another, or rather against one another. The saw moves to and fro. One might also think of weights on a scale: for every weight a counterweight is put on the scale. Thus an artificial equilibrium is maintained until one day the scale beam breaks.

The outsider, the sober person, notices above all in the spectrum of inebriation the side on which motion takes place. There the state of being different cannot be ignored; it announces itself far and wide to eyes and ears. The words for this condition refer, at least in the beer and wine consuming countries, to excessive drinking or heightened activity. They are mostly derived from the Latin *bibo* and *ebrius*, or the old high German *trinkan* and the Gothic *drigkan*. On the other hand, *Rauschen* denotes a lively movement, like that of wings, which becomes, also acoustically, noticeable as *Geräusch*. The movement may become violent—the Anglo-Saxon *rush* implying *stürzen* (onrush) should be mentioned here. One should further think of heightened, vibrant vitality. *Rauschzeit* is mating time. It is said of the wild boar that he becomes *rauschig*. Some animals gather in swarms; immediately following the mating flight termites drop their wings.

Rauschzeit is swarming time; men and animals congregate. For this very reason the active, will-determined side of inebriation is best known. The inebriated person does not shy away from society. He feels happy in the festive excitement and does not seek solitude; he often behaves conspicuously, but he enjoys greater license in his behavior than the sober person. One prefers seeing a laughing person to seeing a sad one; the slightly tipsy person is regarded with benevolence, frequently as the one who drives away boredom and cheers up everyone. A messenger of Dionysus enters and opens the gate to a mad world. This is contagious even for the sober individual.

This heightened activity that cannot be overlooked has given the word *Rausch* an important connotation. Generally speaking, in language also the visible side of things claims a greater share than the hidden side. An example of this is the word "day." When we pronounce it we also include the night in it. So the bright side also comprises the shadow. Generally we hardly think about that. Similarly, the word *Rausch*, though it stresses the apparent heightening of the vital, includes also its lessening: the lethargic and motionless states which closely resemble sleep and dream.

Inebriation manifests itself in various, often contrary phenomena; drugs produce the same varying effects. Nevertheless, they both complement each other to create a complex of wide range. It is said of Hassan Sabah that he led his Assassins into a world of blissful dreams or into that of murder through the use of the same drug, hashish.

He who seeks a state of insensibility behaves differently from the person who, in the manner of enthusiasts, intends to attain ecstasy. The former does not seek society but solitude. He is closer to addiction; for this reason he generally seeks to conceal his actions, which are also devoid of any festive element. The "secret drinker" is considered to be a questionable type.

He who takes drugs heavily and habitually must do this secretly for the simple reason that drugs, in most cases, come from dubious sources. Their use leads into a zone of illegality. Therefore it is one of the signs of anarchy if such heavily intoxicated individuals no longer shy away from the public. After World War I, for example, one could watch drugged persons in coffee houses "staring holes into the air."

However, the drugged person avoids society not only because he has to fear it for various reasons. By his very nature he is dependent on solitude; his disposition is not communicative, but receptive, passive. He sits as if he were facing a magic mirror, motionless, absorbed in himself, and it is always his own self that he enjoys, be it as pure euphoria or as a world of visions created by his innermost being and flowing back to him. There are lamps whose fluorescent light can change a gray stone into a piece of gold ore. Baudelaire, who calls hashish "a weapon for suicide," mentions, among other effects, the extraordinary chill following the use of the drug, which he includes in the "category of the lonely joys." This feeling of chill, also produced by other narcotics, is not only of a physical nature. It is also a sign of loneliness.

Narcissus was the son of a river god and the nymph Liriope. His mother was just as much enchanted with his beauty as she was frightened by his coldness. Worried about his fate, she asked the seer Tiresias for advice and heard from him the oracle: her son would be endowed with longevity unless he should recognize himself. The enigmatic prophecy was fulfilled when Narcissus, returning one day from the hunt, thirstily bent over a spring and saw his reflected image. The youth fell in love with the phantom and consumed himself in unrequited longing for his own image until he perished. The gods changed him into a flower of intoxicating scent, the narcissus, which has carried his name to the present day and whose blooms like to bend over quiet waters.

Probably the Narcissus myth, like many others, has only been preserved in its rudiments; its great theme seems to have been his longing. The nymph Echo also became a victim of this feeling;

she longed in vain for the embrace of Narcissus and consumed herself in her sorrow until nothing remained of her but her voice.

Narcissus "became acquainted with himself," but he did not know himself. "Know yourself!" was written above the temple of Apollo in Delphi; Narcissus failed in this most difficult task like so many before and after him. The word "to know" has a double meaning; Narcissus entered into an erotic venture, while Faust chose an intellectual one. Faust wanted, according to Mephistopheles, "Helen in all women"; Narcissus, turned inward, vainly sought his self in his reflected image.

Exactly this consuming longing is also a mark of drugs and their use; the desire again and again remains behind the fulfillment. The images are enticing, like a Fata Morgana; the thirst becomes more burning. We might also think of entering a grotto which branches out into a labyrinth of increasingly narrow and impracticable passages. There threatens the fate of Elias Froböm, the hero of Hoffmann's "The Mines of Falun" ("Die Bergwerke zu Falun"). He does not return, he is lost to the world; a similar thing happened to the monk of Heisterbach who lost his way in the forest and did not come back to his monastery until three hundred years later. This forest is time.

We believe that the substances which produce narcotic intoxication are finer, more ethereal than those which exert the will. Faust, after the great conjuration in his nocturnal study, is first led to the coarse drinkers in Auerbach's cellar and only then into the witch's kitchen.

We speak of "narcotic scent." The word is derived from the Greek *ναρκόω*, "to dull the senses." In southern Europe there are some kinds of narcissi whose scent is considered to be dangerous. Euphoria and painlessness follow the inhalation of volatile substances such as laughing gas or ether. At the turn of the century, the latter was in fashion as a drug, and Maupassant devoted a special study to it. In classical magic, smoke is frequently mentioned, not only as a narcotic but also as an excellent medium for the visions that follow narcotization. We find such scenes in "A Thousand and One Nights" and also in the works of authors like Cazotte, Hoffmann, Poe, Kubin, and others.

The conjecture suggests itself that the aspect of intoxication that is turned toward visions is also more significant with regard to quality. If we want to form an opinion on this, we must go back to the common root from which forms of imagination of such variety arise. The risk that we take in using drugs consists in our shaking a fundamental pillar of existence, namely time. This of course is done in different ways: depending on whether we narcotize or stimulate ourselves, we stretch or compress time. In turn, the traversing of space is connected with this factor: on the one hand, the endeavor to increase the motion, on the other the rigidity, of the magic world.

If we compare time to a stream, as has always been done, to the stimulated person the stream seems to narrow, to flow more rapidly downward in whirlpools and cascades. Thoughts, miming, and gestures adjust to this pace; the stimulated person thinks and acts faster and more impulsively than the sober one, and his actions become less calculable. Under the influence of narcotic drugs, however, time slows down. The stream flows more quietly; the banks recede. As narcotization begins, consciousness floats as in a boat on a lake whose shores it no longer sees. Time appears boundless; it becomes an ocean.

This leads to the endless opium dreams as described by de Quincey. He fancies "to be buried for millennia in the bowels of eternal pyramids." In *Suspiria de Profundis*, a collection of essays that appeared a quarter of a century after the *Confessions of an English Opium-Eater*, he looks back on this tremendous expansion of time and says that to describe it astronomical standards would not be sufficient. "Indeed, it would be ridiculous to measure the span of time one lives through in a dream by generations—or even by thousands of years."

The feeling of being distant altogether from the human consciousness of time is confirmed by others, for instance, Cocteau: "Tout ce qu'on fait dans la vie, même l'amour, on le fait dans le train express qui roule vers la mort. Fumer l'opium, c'est quitter le train en marche; c'est s'occuper d'autre chose que de la vie, de la mort."

Time runs faster at the animal pole, more slowly at the vegetative pole. This fact sheds also some light on the relation between narcotics and pain. Most people become acquainted with narcotics because of their anesthetic properties. The feeling of bliss, of euphoria, connected with their use leads to addiction. The fact that it is especially the depressed who so easily fall victim to morphine is explained by their existence as such being already painful to them. Many narcotics are at the same time hallucinogens. In isolating morphine in 1803, Sertürner separated the pain-stilling potency of opium from the eidetic power. Thereby he helped countless suffering people, but at the same time he robbed of its colors the poppy juice praised by Novalis.

He who strives for visions wishes neither to escape pain nor to enjoy euphoria by means of a narcoticum; he seeks a phantasticum. He is not motivated by the fear of suffering but by curiosity, perhaps also by presumption. In the magic and witchery of the Middle Ages, the world of the alkaloids came in again and again: conjuration with the aid of potions, ointments, and fumes of mandrake, thorn apple, and henbane.

Conjuration was counted among the capital crimes in those days. The phenomena were more credible at the time than today. For Faust the realm of ghosts, though it has largely become a spiritual world, is still "not closed," yet he is only concerned with the success of his conjuration. Religious or moral scruples no longer worry him. Likewise, in our time, the intellectual devoted to the Muses is confronted with the question of what the drug can impart. His final aim cannot be the kinetic intensification of powers, happiness, or even freedom from pain. He is not even interested in the sharpening or refinement of insight but, as in Faust's cabinet, in "that which enters."

This "entering" does not mean that new facts become known. The enrichment of the empirical world is *not* meant. Faust strives to get out of his study, while a man like Wagner will remain there and feel happy the rest of his life. "It is true, I know much, but I want to know all"—there is no end to that, and in this sense the discovery of America also belongs to facts; no spaceship can lead out of that world. No acceleration, even if it carried us to the stars, can annul the primary dictum, "From yourself you cannot flee." This also applies to the intensification of the vital force. Multiplication, even involution, does not change the cardinal number. More is expected from that which enters than intensification of a dynamic or vital kind. At all times it was hoped that it would bring an increase, a complement, an apposition. That does not imply involution but addition.

In conjuration, be it with the aid of asceticism or by other means, formerly no one doubted that something strange would join in. Since then the intellect has gained such superior power that this conviction is only defended by a rearguard. Ultimately, however, it is of mere topographical significance whether an addition comes from outside or from within, whether its origin is the universe or the depth of one's self. Not the point at which the probe is started, but the one that it reaches is decisive. Here the vision is so strongly convincing that there is neither room nor need to question its reality, much less its origin. Where reasons, authorities, or even means of force are necessary to ensure its reality, the vision has already lost its power; it lives on, but henceforth its effect is merely that of a shadow or an echo. Yet, "the readiness is all."

THE LITERARY WORK OF MIRCEA ELIADE

VIRGIL IERUNCA

Two pursuits of the same quest: literary work and scientific research. The career of Mircea Eliade possesses this fertile duality which, however, affords its hazards. One of these hazards, and not the least, is that it may be thought that one can know the scholar while ignoring the novelist. Or that the novelist is simply an illustrator of philosophical theses, which amounts to the same thing. In the West this danger confronts the historian of religions whose renown is already established. In Romania, however, the novelist eclipsed the scholar, for his entry into literature was made in a striking, unprecedented, and confusing manner.

Beginning with *Isabel şi Apele Diavolului* (1930), the "mixture of the *ascesis* of metaphysical exaltation, and of sexuality"[1] appeared explosive to a literary criticism which was hardly reassured by *Maitreyi* (a poem rather than a novel of love, in an India which is a geographical point of the consciousness and not an exotic setting), and fell back into the dread of the unknown with the appearance of some novels in which Mircea Eliade depicts the torments and exacerbated behavior of his generation, *Intoarcerea din Rai* (1934) and *Huliganii* (1935). As for the fantastic, whether its appearance is "folkloric" and autochthonous as in *Domnişoara Christina* (1936) and *Şarpele* (1937), or issues directly from tantric experiences and yoga as in *Secretul Doctorului Honigberger* (1940), it only serves to situate Mircea

[1] Mircea Eliade, *Amintiri: I. Mansarda* (Madrid, 1966), p. 152.

Eliade in a still more singular manner in the context of Romanian literature.

It is not so much the modernism of form which offends (the interior monologue, rupture of linear time, destruction of classical techniques, insertion of the intimate journal, the essay in the novel), for Romanian literature was, at the time, familiar with the boldest experiments, although it did not advance them. (Had it not known surrealism with Urmuz, before the First World War?) It is in relation to Western letters that one tries to situate this enigmatic adolescent who comes, however, to sojourn in India and whose scientific preoccupations should throw light on the matter. One refers to Joyce, speaks of Gide. How should the *Huliganii* ("Hooligans"), furious *négateurs* in quest of a paradise reconquered by the paradoxical weapons of violence and eroticism, not seem to the eyes of a literary criticism oriented toward the West poorly acclimatized brothers of the *Faux-Monnayeurs* of Gide?[2] These are only inimical brothers. To the Gidian dramas of conscience they oppose the conflicts of metaphysical inquietude. To reason menaced by its own excesses they respond with a dangerously lived mystique. In fact, the dangers are not the same, since the interrogative effort is different. The Gidian response, "why not?" in a world deserted by the gods, does not correspond with Mircea Eliade, who seeks with an active nostalgia for the lost paradise. The India present in *Isabel și Apele Diavolului*, in *Șantier*, and in *Maitreyi*, camouflaged in the secret roots of other novels, detaches the works of Eliade from the Western problematic. In the "indirect novel" *Șantier* (a journal of ideas rather than of feelings), Mircea Eliade writes:

> Solitude, meditation, study — I would have been able to find them, under the same conditions, anywhere in Europe. But there is here [in India] a certain atmosphere of renunciation, . . . of control of the consciousness, of love, which is favorable for me. Neither theosophy, nor brahmanic practices, nor rituals — nothing barbarous, nothing created by history. But an extraordinary belief in the reality of the verities, in the power of man to know them and to live them by an interior realization, by purity, and above all by meditation.[3]

[2] Eliade is astonished at the blindness of the literary criticism of his works: "I have read the most amusing interpretations of my novels in *Istoria Literaturii române* by G. Călinescu: one speaks of my 'Gidism' although I did not discover Gide until about thirty." ("Fragment autobiografic," *Caete de Dor*, no. 7 [July, 1953], p. 5.)

[3] *Șantier* (Bucharest, 1935), p. 52.

Hindu thought was not unknown in Romania. But it had little tempted the writers.[4] Mircea Eliade is the first to have a direct experience of it while knowing enough not to be dissolved in it.[5] India did not overwhelm his work and his thought; it only nourished them, opening them to myths, to symbols, to a language to which the West no longer holds the key. This is undoubtedly why Mircea Eliade is not reducible to Western influences even when they are real; [6] it is also why his reaction against the Western "provincialism" of Romanian literature is violent. If the twentieth century reinstates the symbol as an instrument of knowledge, if the West tends at last to renew the dialogue with other forms of spirituality – archaic and exotic – if, as Mircea Eliade affirms, "the origin of a symbol is worth the discovery of a dynasty of pharaohs," [7] Romania knows one of its greatest opportunities to assert its spirituality without any longer suffering from having known neither the Middle Ages nor the Renaissance. Rich in protohistory, having kept an active familiarity with myth and symbol, Eastern Europe, like the Orient, can offer some instruction to the West and no longer content itself merely with demanding it.[8] In the archaic tradition which animates Romanian spirituality, Mircea Eliade finds still living forms which he proposes to integrate into the vast "*musée imaginaire*" of religions.

This exploration is, as we have said, a quest which is pursued by the writer as well as by the scholar. This fact is well worth our attention. The case is rare enough to become exemplary. This coexistence of the scholar and the writer has been explained at length by Mircea Eliade in an important text written in Romanian, "Fragment autobiografic." [9] The distance which appears to separate the two activities is considerably reduced when we learn that Mircea Eliade considers his studies and researches as more philosophical than scientific:

Even when I was occupied with the history of the sciences and tried to understand the meaning of alchemy and Oriental metallurgies, what

[4] The poet Mihai Eminescu had had access to India only through Schopenhauer; the scholar Hasdeu had drowned it in his flamboyant erudition; for Cosbuc it had been material for poetic translations.

[5] This danger existed for him, as he noted much later in his journal.

[6] That of Papini.

[7] *Fragmentarium* (Bucharest, 1939), p. 38.

[8] See on this subject Eliade's study "Probleme de cultură românească," *Indreptar*, 1 (1951).

[9] *Caete de Dor*, no. 7 (July, 1953).

interested me most were the *metaphysical values* present in these traditional techniques and not the eventual scientific discoveries.[10]

The same pursuit in folklore and ethnology:

I was interested only in the spiritual documents which lay buried in the mass of books published by the ethnologists, folklorists, sociologists. In these hundreds of thousands of pages, it seemed to me that there survived a world of myths and symbols which ought to be known and understood in order to be able to comprehend the situation of man in the Cosmos. For, as one knows, this situation constitutes already a metaphysic.[11]

This collaboration of the philosopher and the writer involves its hazards, its difficulties. First, its difficulties: the coexistence cannot be concomitant. At times, the writer will have to sacrifice his time to the scholar and the latter will have equally to give way before the novelist. "I am incapable," confesses Mircea Eliade in his journal dated November 3, 1949,

of living at the same time in two spiritual universes: that of literature and that of science. Here is my fundamental weakness; I cannot remain in the waking state and at the same time find myself in a dream, in a play. As soon as "I make literature," I find again another universe; I call it oneiric, for it has another temporal structure, and above all because my relations with the characters are of an imaginary and not a critical nature.[12]

However confining it may be, this collaboration, even with its periods of sacrifice, is not for that less fruitful. It asserts itself already in the thirteen-year-old child who publishes articles on the life of insects and recounts at the same time, in an unfinished novel of which the manuscript is lost, the history of the cosmos from the appearance of the first galaxies, through the memoirs of a lead soldier. It continues in the adolescent and the grown man and sometimes seems to involve a conscious development. Does not *Secretul Doctorului Honigberger* derive from the treatise on yoga, *Domnişoara Christina*,[13] from his work on the mythologies of

[10] *Ibid.*, p. 1.

[11] *Ibid.*, pp. 1–2. Eliade had insisted much earlier on the role of folklore as an instrument of knowledge (*Insula lui Euthanasius* [Bucharest, 1943], p. 47).

[12] *Caete de Dor*, no. 9 (December, 1955), p. 11.

[13] *Domnişoara Christina* (Bucharest, 1936) is the story of a young dead girl, a vampire who falls in love with a human. It illustrates rather well the

death, etc.? Mircea Eliade would have been able to convince himself of it if a decisive experience had not revealed to him the completely unconscious character of this collaboration. Eliade occupied himself with the symbolism of the serpent in a vast body of folklore when he began to write, as in a second state, the fantastic story *Şarpele*.[14] He felt then that the writer refused the concurrence of the scholar and discovered, when the book was finished, that "the free act of creation was able, on the contrary, to reveal certain theoretical meanings" while "the theoretical activity could not influence the literary activity consciously and voluntarily."[15]

Şarpele represents a decisive experience for Mircea Eliade, for this story reveals to him the theme which he considers the keystone of all his works of maturity: the *unrecognizability of miracle*. The intervention of the sacred in the world is always camouflaged; there is no apparent difference between the sacred and the profane, and the fantastic lies at the heart of the banal. It is not only as a novelist that Mircea Eliade will remember this theme in *Forêt Interdite*[16] or in stories such as "La Ţigănci,"[17] "Ghicitor în pietre,"[18] or "Podul";[19] as a historian of religions he will develop it in all his works.

"The World is what it seems to be and at the same time a cipher."[20] It is to this transparency that the work of Mircea Eliade will open itself henceforth. A new way is thus opened to the fan-

manner in which Eliade intends to avail himself of folklore and to make it serve. In a study on folkloric themes and literary production (in *Insula lui Euthanasius*, p. 371), he warned against the transposition of folkloric motifs. The only valid effort seemed to him to be an approach to the source of folkloric production which is "the fantastic presence, an irrational experience."

[14] In some memoirs entitled "Bucharest, 1937," published in *Fiinta Romaneasca*, no. 5 (1966), Eliade returns to this subject which is close to his heart: "*Şarpele* is my only book written without a plan, without knowing what would be the course of action, and without knowing the end. It is undoubtedly a pure product of the imagination. I utilized nothing of what I knew and of all that I would have been able to know about the symbolism or the mythology of the serpent" (p. 63).

[15] "Fragment autobiografic," p. 10.

[16] "The same dialectic underlies *Forêt Interdite* . . . but this time it is no longer a question of the profound significations of the Cosmos, but of the 'cipher' of historical events" (Eliade, "Bucharest, 1937," p. 64).

[17] Published in his volume *Nuvele* (Madrid, 1963).

[18] *Ibid.*

[19] *Fiinta Romaneasca*, no. 4 (1966).

[20] Eliade, "Bucharest, 1937," p. 64.

tastic,[21] and all the themes which nourish the novels of Mircea Eliade are connected with it in one way or another.

Time, first of all. One could say that Time is the central character in all the literary work of Mircea Eliade; it is his life obsession, his permanent double. The mystery of the rupture provoked by the appearance of Time and by the fall into History, which necessarily follows it, supports the work and the life of the writer. As a child, Eliade awakened to existence through the anguish of the precipitous passage of time. He reckoned time, he felt it, and his *Amintiri* ("Autobiography"), published in Romanian, tells us of the forced vigils, the incessant struggle against sleep, the combat against Khronos which will remain the existential leitmotiv of the adolescent.[22] Action or work – indeed, action through work – will become the only possible therapeutic for escaping the folly of time, the neurasthenia of this continual passage.[23] This therapeutic, or duty, he will quickly extend to his entire generation. He is the only one in Romania to be no longer, apparently, waylaid by History.

The First World War brought an end to a national ideal which had monopolized Romanian culture to the point of making it exclusively militant. The generation of Mircea Eliade is really

21 The originality of which surprises even Western literary criticism which, moreover, does not have at its disposal all of Eliade's novels in translation. Thus Jean Mistler will write with the appearance of *Minuit à Serampore* (Paris, 1956) – the French title of the collection of narratives entitled in Romanian *Secretul Doctorului Honigberger*: "Mircea Eliade, aided by his excellent translator M. A. M. Schmidt, seems to me to trace out a new way to the fantastic. After Hoffmann and Poe, who have ingeniously added alterations of characters, he opens the vast field of the Eastern mystics" (*L'Aurore*, July 24, 1956).

22 Since *Isabel și Apele Diavolului* ([Bucharest, 1930], p. 112), the intolerable flow of time haunts the principal character: "I lived long agonies in experiencing grievously how *time passes*; the slow death of things, the distinct flow of moments poisoned me, wounded me, undermined the base of existence, shook the axis, . . . I could no longer walk in the streets, for I felt men dying moment by moment."

23 In *Șantier*, seemingly an indirect novel but in fact a camouflaged journal, these revealing lines occur on page 30: "This night I have debated with myself for an hour in my bed. I felt, with an extraordinary sensibility, lucidity, attention, clarity, *time flow* about me. Each moment buried the preceding, all that charmed or troubled was only an ephemeral flash. The crisis continues now while I write. Time, Time obsesses me to the point of neurasthenia . . . . When I become conscious of the time which flows without any power being able to stop it, I tremble. Either I am becoming mad, or I ought urgently to accomplish a great action."

available for a nonengaged culture. Mircea Eliade felt the precariousness of this respite, this pause. This is the reason for his haste, for articles addressed to his generation, for the fervent and anguished counsel in a moving article, "Anno Domine," published at the beginning of 1928, to conceive this year as the last and to make of these twelve months a whole life's work. An apocalyptic vision, before the events, but one that events confirmed ten years later when a great "historical" night fell on an entire culture, a night from which it has not yet emerged.[24]

All Mircea Eliade's characters will call to mind this wrestling with the Angel, above all those of *Forêt Interdite*, which remains *par excellence* the novel of Time. Mircea Eliade notes in his journal on August 5, 1951:

> This novel, which unfolds during twelve years, is, in a certain sense, a fresco, but its center of gravity is found elsewhere; in the different conceptions of time which the principal characters assume. . . . I believe one will notice the passage from the "fantastic time" of the beginning (the encounter in the forest) to the "psychological time" of the first chapters, and, in a still more despotic manner, to the "historical time" of the end.[25]

Referring to the Death-Time, the Time leading to Death, of Heidegger, one of the characters in the novel (Birish) says: "We are mystified. We are told that a half hour has passed or that it is six o'clock—as if that had importance. The important fact is that our time, that is, the Time of our life, is a Time of Death."[26]

Stephane, the key character of *Forêt Interdite*, tries by every means to annul time. Birish does not any longer refer to Heidegger to try to understand the effort of Stephane: "Your desire to go outside of Time and to ignore History probably betrays a

24 "Whence arose this apocalyptic vision?" Eliade asked himself later: "In any case not from the political situation of Romania or of Europe. At the beginning of 1928, there were not many people who were living in terror of an imminent war. Besides, I was almost entirely ignorant of the internal and international situation. My fear was of another order; I feared that Time would be hostile to us. . . . On another plane, this was that same "struggle against sleep" that I had waged since the *lycée*, when I had learned that, for all I had to do—thousands of books to read, so many disciplines to study—sixteen hours did not suffice. This time, it was no longer a question of myself alone. I felt responsible for the entire 'young generation,' that I imagined called to grand destinies" (*Amintiri*, p. 153).

25 *Caete de Dor*, no. 9 (December, 1955), p. 15.

26 *Forêt Interdite*, p. 65.

desperate effort to rediscover the blessedness of infancy, to reinstate a lost Paradise."[27] For it is not, as with Proust, a matter of searching for the lost time, but of blotting out Time as psychological, personal, and social memory. A conversation between Birish and Stephane affirms it explicitly:

> "I believe I understand," says Birish. "In a certain sense, you wanted, like Proust, to recover the lost time."
>
> "No, that's not it. It was *another kind of Time.* I had not yet lived it. It was not connected with my past. It was *something other*, as if it came from somewhere else."[28]

The "memory" for which Stephane struggles is a memory of the *illud tempus* and not a personal,[29] historical recollection, for History is in fact destructive of memory.[30] It is a metaphysical effort and in this sense nearer to Dostoevsky and Faulkner than Proust.[31] In his journal, written in the margin of *Forêt Interdite*, Mircea Eliade is the first to make this comparison with Dostoevsky:

> March 4, 1953: I had forgotten this detail of *The Idiot*: Muichkine had understood the decisive importance of time for historical man, "fallen man." Here is what he says: "At this moment . . . I have glimpsed the meaning of the singular expression: time will be no more" (Apocalypse 10:6). This "moment" is the last conscious flash before the attack of epilepsy. It is interesting that Dostoevsky has understood the *metaphysical* value (and not only the *ecstatic* value) of this atemporal "moment," of this *nunc stans* which signifies eternity.[32]

27 *Ibid.*, p. 460.

28 *Ibid.*, p. 507.

29 The "psychological" memory ought itself to be suppressed in order to escape Time. Eliade affirmed this as early as 1934 in a book of essays, *Oceanografie* (Bucharest, 1934), p. 191: "Learn then to ignore Time, not to fear its implications. Suppress every trace of sentimental memory, suppress evanescent contemplations, memories of infancy, autumns, pressed flowers, nostalgias."

30 Stephane says again in *Forêt Interdite*, p. 544: "I think that one is wrong in believing History is bound up with memory. History perpetually modifies memories, ceaselessly accords them new values, negative or positive, until in the end, it annuls them. That is what has happened, for example with Christianity."

31 This difference is underlined by Robert Kanters, after reading *Forêt Interdite*: "Proust tries to liberate himself from the present, or, if one wishes, to render time present. Stephane wants to be liberated from Time itself, to go out of the belly of the whale, and to find there – eternity" (*La Tour Saint-Jacques*, no. 3 [March–April, 1956], p. 86).

32 *Caete de Dor*, no. 9 (December, 1955), p. 27.

Mircea Eliade shares with Faulkner this desire to return to the beginnings in order to suppress time,[33] but while for Faulkner time is lived as a destiny that the characters do not decipher, for Mircea Eliade the anguish arises precisely from the lucidity with which the heroes assume their condition of being tortured by Time, which is to say, by History. If Time is only the malediction of Man after the fall, of Man in History, and, as Berdiaev has said, the ways of escape are simple for an archaic mentality which has only to return to the *illud tempus* in order to be regenerated, they are nevertheless arduous for the Christian obliged to accept History, which is a consequence of original sin, to accept it in the image of Christ and not be able at the same time to keep from dreaming of its abolition by Redemption, from valorizing the eschatological function of the present. This paradoxical attitude of the Christian who accepts history and denies it at the same time, "hoping for salvation outside of it and even against it,"[34] is duplicated in Mircea Eliade's nostalgia for the archaic solution and his obsession with the past of his own country, at this point weighed down with history, having escaped none of its vicissitudes (so that the Romanian philosopher Lucien Blaga could say that the Romanian people have endured only by "sabotaging history"). To sabotage history by action – the paradox is only apparent. It is to observe in any case an antihistorical attitude, an apocalyptic attitude, to assure its remoteness by contempt, to go out of History to find salvation: "My essential preoccupation," writes Mircea Eliade in his journal, "is precisely the means of escaping History, of saving myself through symbol, myth, rites, archetypes."[35] It is absolutely necessary to abolish the distance, the dialectic: "There was not for me any hiatus between the world and myth; there was no dialectic. Objects were objects and, *at the same time*, symbols, meanings."[36]

Is it pure coincidence if precisely the myth of the summer

[33] Dominique Aury insists, in an article entitled "La Forêt profonde" (in *La Nouvelle Nouvelle Revue Française*, 4 [1956]), on this *rapprochement* between *Forêt Interdite* and the *Go Down, Moses* of Faulkner.

[34] See on this subject Eliade's study *Căderea în istorie, Indreptar*, 2 (1952), and 3 (1952).

[35] *Caete de Dor*, no. 8 (June, 1954), p. 27.

[36] *Isabel şi Apele Diavolului*, p. 97. The same effort is recorded in *Soliloquii* (Bucharest, 1932), p. 55: "To go out of self and its destiny. Whence the desire to participate in a super-individual life, whence the thirst for fantastic experience, for symbol."

solstice, which corresponds to a suspension of time, obsesses Mircea Eliade to the extent that it is found connecting by an unconscious process two of his key novels, *Isabel și Apele Diavolului* and *Forêt Interdite*? The writer inquires of himself about it:

I recall that it was exactly 20 years ago, in the torrid heat of Calcutta, that I wrote "The Dream of a Summer Night" in *Isabel.* The same dream of solstice, with another structure and extending to other levels, is also found in the center of *Forêt Interdite.* Would this be a simple coincidence? The myth and symbol of the solstice has obsessed me for many years. But I had forgotten that they followed me since *Isabel.*[37]

Besides Time, love, conceived as an instrument of knowledge, as a metaphysical adventure, informs all the work of Mircea Eliade, and not only what are conventionally called his novels of love, such as *Maitreyi* or *Nuntă în Cer.*[38] Love is a stranger to the world; love cannot find its fulfillment on earth. The adolescents of the early novels of Mircea Eliade regard it first of all as a charm that should be broken by any means. Undoubtedly they call to mind, with Mircea Eliade, the primitive's "negative valorization" of love, his refusal to lose himself in others.[39] But what was natural for the primitive is no longer natural for the man informed by the immense revolution brought about by Christianity, which has encouraged at all levels the loss of self.[40]

For Mircea Eliade, love is antinatural and cannot be lived on earth.[41] It is a souvenir of Paradise, and is impossible of reconquest. It is the instrument *par excellence* of metaphysical knowledge. The exacerbated Don Juanism of the early heroes of Mircea

[37] Journal dated July 5, 1949, in *Caete de Dor*, no. 9 (December, 1955), p. 9.

[38] *Nuntă în Cer* (Bucharest, 1939).

[39] *Caete de Dor*, no. 8 (June, 1954), p. 27: "In primitive poetry, love is never 'natural'; it is the consequence of a charm or of divine caprice . . . . Primitive man does not want to *lose himself*. All that he thinks and desires is centered on ontology. He wants to be real; he wants to be whole. If the rite requires him sometimes to abandon his humanity, it is in order to join himself to absolute reality. In any case, he does not abandon himself for one similar to himself, for another living and derisory fragment."

[40] *Ibid.*

[41] It is significant that two of Eliade's novels indicate even by their titles this incapacity for the human being to realize love on earth: *Intoarcerea din Rai* ("Return from Paradise"), in which the hero, Pavel Anicet, seeks in death the ultimate solution to the laceration of love; and *Nuntă în Cer* ("Marriage in Heaven"), in which the couple break up and the woman disappears, probably in death, for having wished to live this paradisiacal experience on earth.

Eliade cannot be explained otherwise.[42] We are alerted to it begining with *Isabel şi Apele Diavolului*:

In fact, I am not a sensualist. My erotic conquests were conquests of principle, provoked by some ideas, relations, intimate experiences. . . . That is why I have written that Don Juan ought to be a theologian, in the substantial and not the erudite sense. . . . I have loved metaphysics too much not to be an intimate of women.[43]

As this adventure is of a metaphysical order, it occurs at extreme levels, ignoring every law except that of knowledge. In *Intoarcerea din Rai* and in *Huliganii*, Eros breaks free of the social and moral and most often opposes them.[44] But the violence, paroxysm, and the indifference to every ethic are not enough to make love sufficiently antinatural. In order to surpass its fallen condition love should involve a temptation of holiness. The coexistence of two loves, which was already prefigured in an unpublished novel of adolescence ("Gaudeamus"), became a leitmotiv in Mircea Eliade's literary works. Pavel Anicet in *Intoarcerea din Rai* knows until defeat and death the curse of loving two women at the same time and with the same love.[45] Stephane, in *Forêt*

[42] Don Juanism or asceticism are two apparently opposite behaviors having in fact the same end, the dissolution of love, either by its explosion or by its refusal. The character who best assumes the "ascetic" condition in Eliade's work, David Dragu in *Huliganii*, also wishes to preserve his integrity. Among the heroes of Eliade, the Don Juan–ascetic dichotomy is not necessarily antinomian. In these early novels one could speak of an ascetic experience of Don Juan.

[43] *Isabel şi Apele Diavolului*, pp. 82–83.

[44] In his journal of 1942, Eliade returns to these early novels (*Caete de Dor*, no. 8 [June, 1954], p. 25): "I realize, this time, the total absence of the moral problem in these books. The characters do what they want, without any resistance; the women give in easily, no one marries, no one has children . . . . The truth is that with me the obsession with the metaphysical and the biological does not leave any place for another problematic. With me (that which I was 8 or 10 years ago), Eros had a metaphysical function. Love involves and sanctions without the indispensible presence of society . . . . Yet another thing: I have remained marked by the vocabulary and the symbolism of the Hindu mysticism (Vaishnava) which expresses the mystical love in terms of *adultery* and not of *marriage*, precisely in order to signify the transcendence of every mystical experience, its essence being a 'stranger' to the world . . . . My characters fall in love and make love no matter how and no matter whom, because I, their author, am interested exclusively in that experience of love which reveals a destiny and not in its social consequences.

[45] "Human nature," thinks Pavel Anicet, "is so fundamentally tragic that it forces you to direct yourself ceaselessly in at least two parallel, if not op-

Interdite, lives this same tortured destiny that only death resolves. He, too, loves two women at the same time. Another character in the novel says to him:

Both were destined for you, since you love each of them, but you have believed that you could love them at the same time, in the same way that souls can love in heaven, and that is impossible. That has been your illusion. Above in heaven, after death, all things will be given you at once. . . . But you have believed that you could live the heavenly life here on earth.[46]

This "heavenly life" assumed on earth, this angelic temptation, this "paradise of unity" of which Pavel Anicet speaks, is equally the impossible adventure of *Nuntă în Cer*. Two men have loved the same woman.[47] They tell each other of this love during an interminable sleepless night, receiving from one another the revelation of all that this love bears of the "paradisiacal" and thus unrealizable. Hasnas does not recognize this until too late and thus lives fully the covert miracle hidden by apparent banality.[48] For Mavrodin it is cosmic union, the angelic state,[49] the "Marriage in Heaven," the Adamic state which he is bent on preserving in refusing the child which would root him in the world. "Love is

posed, directions . . . . One is macerated, lives in a continual nostalgia for a paradise of Unity, of absolute love" (p. 375).

[46] *Forêt Interdite*, p. 475.

[47] Few of Eliade's novels lack this implacable duality. It is absent, however, in the love novel *par excellence*, *Maitreyi*, in which Gaston Bachelard saw a "mythology of voluptuousness" (see Eliade's "Fragment Autobiografic," p. 11). This uniqueness of *Maitreyi* among the romantic works of Eliade is perhaps due to the fact that in this novel duality arises from the conception of love that the two characters have. For the Hindu heroine, love represents an integration in the Cosmos, while the hero is incapable of escaping the tortured condition of a European. One does not need to find in this, as did an exegete of Eliade in Romania, traces of tantrism. Tantrism tempted the novelist in another work, in the frantastic tale *Minuit à Serampore*. For the cosmic conception of love, see p. 155 of *Maitreyi*, the declaration of love which binds the heroine to her lover and unbinds her from the world, a declaration that makes to the Cosmos in its entirety. This novel was translated into French by Alain Guillermou and appeared under the title *La Nuit Bengali* (Paris, 1950).

[48] "One finds such a love only once in a lifetime," says Hasnas. "It is in a certain sense miraculous, and that is perhaps why it appears as an accident among events which are completely frivolous and lacking in meaning" (*Nuntă în Cer*, p. 265).

[49] Mavrodin, in the same novel: "The presence of the woman loved—which is for every man demonic, which is scattering and shattering—I experienced this time as an angelic fulfillment of my being" (p. 65).

our Paradise," he says to the woman he loves, "a paradise without fruit."[50]

This refused "fruit," this obstinacy in not accepting the human condition after the fall, will lead Mavrodin to the destruction of his earthly love. The same woman vanishes from the life of the two men: from the first because she refuses to give him a child, from the second because she wants one. The contradiction is only apparent. Is not this woman the instrument by which both are punished – Hasnas for not having recognized the miracle and Mavrodin for having wanted, on the contrary, to live it without any compromise with the ephemeral? Do not this nonrecognition and this refusal belong to the same forbidden tree of knowledge?

Only death will be able to resolve the duality, put an end to the rending, and offer the status of Eden. In most of Mircea Eliade's novels, and even in his play *Iphigenia*,[51] we are confronted with an active revalorization of death. "What is it that leads man to confront the real?" asks a character in *Huliganii*, "What is it that causes him to think with his whole being, to go beyond biology and even psychology? One thing only: the contemplation of death, the expectation of death, the thought of death."[52] This "thought of death" ought not to leave us for a moment, for by it we define ourselves and are able to communicate authentically with others. In *Intoarcerea din Rai* Pavel Anicet says to his best friend: "Men ought continually to make confession, to remain *au courant* with their conception of death."[53]

One can apprehend this death even without the impossible Lazarean experience:

> Only from those who have known death, cultivated it, who have conversed with it, in the course of long centuries of waiting, in apocalyptic nights, can we learn death. Only from those who have known death without dying can we learn it. Although this appears paradoxical, this fact is nonetheless true – simple and true. In a real intuition, drawn from folklore, you encounter the reality of death, know its "passages," understand its somber destiny. A man who dies in a legend is worth

[50] *Ibid.*, p. 91.
[51] *Iphigenia* (Valle Hermoso, 1951). Eliade's Iphigenia is an original Iphigenia, bewitched by death, in love with death, and awaiting only death's fulfillment.
[52] *Huliganii*, p. 212.
[53] *Intoarcerea din Rai*, p. 377.

more (from the point of view of knowledge) than all the heroes who die in all the modern novels.[54]

And undoubtedly it is because Mircea Eliade is nurtured by this "knowledge" that his heroes die *differently*. Pavel Anicet in *Intoarcerea din Rai* prepares his suicide like a *fête*, as a glorious return to Oneness, as a reintegration. "Death-rapture. Death, instrument of knowledge. Death in order to embrace Unity, the All."[55]

The symbolism of death takes on a somber character only when it is falsely interpreted, when the law of death is not accepted in its integrity.[56] In most other cases – even when the process is unconscious – death appears as a sign of light. The journal that Mircea Eliade kept while writing *Forêt Interdite* reveals something on this subject. Stephane, the hero, loves, as we have said, two women – Ioana and Ileana. The first dies in a bombardment; he will be reunited with the second only in death, caused by an automobile accident. While he was writing the novel, Mircea Eliade noted on June 26, 1954:

I began to write *Forêt Interdite* five years ago; I knew almost nothing of the book except the end. I knew that after twelve years Stephane would again meet Ileana in a forest and that he would recognize the car which (as it had seemed to him) had disappeared or should have disappeared in the forest of Baneasa,[57] during the night of Saint John in 1936. . . . Their unexpected reunion in 1948 compensated for all their trials and suffering. Until the last moment, even after having begun to write the last chapter and to approach their meeting in the forest of Royaumont, I had believed that the new meeting was going to mean for each of them a "new life" [*renovatio*]. I had homologized Stephane's quest to an initiatory *Quest*. . . . Now, today, I have understood it was an entirely different matter: Stephane was obsessed with "the car which had to disappear at midnight," the car in which Ileana would have had to come to Baneasa in 1936. What appears strange to him in the meeting at Baneasa – stranger than the incomprehensible love for

[54] *Oceanografie*, p. 271.

[55] *Intoarcerea din Rai*, p. 417.

[56] In *Domnişoara Christina* it is not the vampire theme which tempts Eliade, but the drama "without issue of the dead youth who cannot separate herself from the earth, who insists on believing in the possibility of communicating with the living, even hoping to be able to love as human beings love in their incarnate modality," the drama of a "spirit which refuses to assume its own modality of being" (Eliade, "Bucharest, 1937," pp. 57–58).

[57] A forest near Bucharest.

Ileana (for he is still in love with Ioana) – is his obsession with her car. Now, everything is explained if Ileana's car – *real* at Royaumont twelve years later – is the cradle of their death. It seems to me now that Ileana does not love Stephane any longer. The Quest of the latter was thus the quest for Death. Ileana reveals that she is what she was from the beginning: an angel of Death (only, in the beginning, without the *real car*, her true destiny could not be perceived). The cars have an archetypal function in the novel and the attentive reader will quickly observe that each time a "car" enters it provokes a "*rupture de niveau*" and the destinies are realized or become perceptible. The symbolism of Death *imposes itself on me* in writing the last chapter. I do not yet know that both are going to die in an accident that night, although this end is the only plausible one. Stephane has penetrated all the secrets; this comprehension corresponds to the "final understanding" of the sage, which is at the same time his tombstone.[58]

We have quoted this page of the journal almost in its entirety, for it not only clarifies the symbolism of death in the novels of Mircea Eliade[59] but also shows the collaboration between the scholar and the writer taking place at the level of the unconscious, the initiative being largely that of the writer. "It is probable," writes Mircea Eliade, "that a whole series of questions, mysteries, and problems which my theoretical activity refused demanded gratification in the freedom of literary writing."[60]

This freedom insists, indeed insisted, on not having limits. The young Mircea Eliade transforms adolescence into a criterion of value[61] and shakes the foundations of traditional language. With him the novel becomes what it was not before: intimate diary, essay, philosophical discussion, film of ideas, source of knowledge; this unprecedented novel is a "work in progress." Its complete freedom does not spare even its author. The initiative is abandoned to the characters and the writer is the first to be astonished by their extreme behavior, the denouements they impose on

[58] *Caete de Dor*, no. 9 (December, 1955), p. 31.

[59] We also find this conception of death conquered by stages of understanding in another of Eliade's heroes, Pavel Anicet: "With each act of understanding we advance in death; with each act of understanding we advance in peace" (*Intoarcerea din Rai*, p. 373).

[60] "Fragment Autobiografic," p. 11.

[61] Seriousness belongs to adolescence. Petru Anicet says it clearly in *Huliganii*: "It seems to me that people become less and less serious as they age. It is youth which knows the truly serious." To be serious means for Eliade's adolescents "to go to the limit whatever may come" (*ibid.*, pp. 245–46).

him, the interior monologues which take the place of narration and sometimes annul it.[62] A barrier against literature: authenticity; a style against literature: experience.[63] "In the face of originality I raise authenticity."[64] Authenticity which expresses, according to Mircea Eliade, "a powerful ontological thirst for knowledge of the real"[65] is tyrannical enough to prevent the novel from constructing elaborate architecture.[66] Up to a certain point and a certain date the writing is "hooliganical" like the characters; it does not allow hindrances.

"The Hooligans," the title of Mircea Eliade's novel, requires interpretation. The "hooligans" want to be the servants of revolt; they will never be its professionals. No revolutionary party can claim their anger, for it is not directed only against a social order, or even against the parents' generation, but against the status of man in the world. This "revolt of the darkness" does not tend toward the creation of another human condition, but toward the destruction of the foundations of that which exists. This destruction is to be accomplished much less by social violence than by an anarchical exaltation of the biological self.

A "sage" character in this novel, David Dragu, having passed the "hooligan" age and experience, tries to describe this limit situation:

To respect nothing, to believe only in oneself, in one's youth, in one's biology. He who does not begin thus before himself and before the world will not create anything. To be able to forget the verities, to have so much of life in oneself that one becomes impervious to the verities so that one can no longer be intimidated—that is the hooligan's vocation. . . . Some break the windows; others affirm that life begins with them. . . . What proud vitality! What violent affirmation to divide the world into the living and the dead thus, with a simple value judgment or a simple broken window. . . . All of you are ignorant of the established verities, established order, established men. You all be-

[62] See *Lumina ce se stinge* (Bucharest, 1934).

[63] Eliade's "experientialism" has been spoken of in Romania. Eliade himself has written: "I understand freedom through experience, for I am able to escape certain things only by looking them in the face and I can know the true love only by going beyond it" (*Oceanografie*, p. 70).

[64] *Ibid.*, p. 176.

[65] *Ibid.*, p. 152.

[66] In *Soliloquii*, p. 83, Eliade warns us: "This book has neither beginning or end. One could have very well begun on the last page. It proves nothing, destroys nothing."

lieve that the world begins with you, or more modestly, that you can save the world.[67]

And yet it is a "hooligan" who, thinking of the novel he is writing, comes back to the obsession with authenticity:

The novel will be mirror of his life, the reality of any youth. The rest is literature, all that does not arise from fresh, tactile, immediate sensation. Experiences, mud or sun, but only experiences. *Authenticity*: intimate diary, total confession, written quickly, a film of flesh and anger, revelations of the night.[68]

But the "hooliganical" writing, even during this period of youth, did not exhaust all the writing of Mircea Eliade, just as the "hooligans" did not exhaust the gamut of his characters. Beginning with *Isabel și Apele Diavolului*, another key hero asserts himself, a hero absent from his own life—"I listened to the story of my life without paying attention to it"[69]—who will incarnate himself in a still more exemplary manner in Stephane in *Forêt Interdite* and who, caught in a tight web of signs, forgets to live and to pursue his own biography.

If the pure novel ought to be destroyed and the "psychological" heroes abolished, it is not in order to advance a purely anarchical experience of the writing (a "zero degree" of terror), but in order to be replaced, the former by a novel of knowledge and the latter by a "character myth." When Mircea Eliade declares in 1939 that the novel in Romania finds itself in a revolutionary phase, he deplores, at the same time, that with a few exceptions[70] it had not succeeded in creating "character myths" who "live the drama of knowledge" and who have "a theoretical consciousness of the world."[71] By this he defines the ambition of his own exalted, cynical, or mystical heroes, whose experience will be in essence metaphysical.

The novel ought, then, to break its narrow limits, its epic limits, to become a magnifying mirror of the sum of knowledge of an epoch: "The pure novel is a nonsense," writes Mircea Eliade,

67 *Huliganii*, pp. 235–36.

68 *Ibid.*, p. 170.

69 *Isabel și Apele Diavolului*, p. 96.

70 *Patul lui Procust* by Camil Petrescu is one such exception.

71 And Eliade adds: "A people—through its folklore and its history—creates myths. A literature—especially epic literature—creates character myths" (*Fragmentarium*, p. 85).

as is also "pure poetry." A great epic creation reflects in large part, and with the means of knowledge which are proper to it, the meaning of life and the value of man, the scientific and philosophical conquests of the century. . . . It is absurd to prohibit "theory" in an epic work; it is absurd to ask the novelist to limit himself to description, events. . . . "Theory," that is, intelligence, human dignity, courage before destiny, scorn of truisms. Why do the novelists flee before this mission of the novel: to reflect an epoch, not only in its social aspect but also in its theoretical and moral aspect; that is, to reflect the contemporary efforts at understanding, the efforts to valorize life, in order to resolve the problem of death? [72]

The bursting of the traditional epic forms represents for Mircea Eliade something more and other than modernism of form. Discussing in 1966 his *Șantier*, an intimate diary transformed into an indirect novel, and regretting, moreover, its "hybrid form," Mircea Eliade nonetheless sees, in a mélange of genres, one of the possible solutions of the crisis of the contemporary novel:

I believe indeed that the several "crises" through which the novel, theater, and systematic philosophy have passed will encourage a new "literary genre" which one cannot define at the moment, but which will be as far from the traditional expression of the philosophical writings, the essay, the criticism, as from the intimate diary of the type of Goncourt or Amiel. Writings in this new literary genre are apparently hybrid, belonging as much to the notebook or the intimate diary as to the style of the erudite monograph, letters, philosophical reflection, political and social problematic, or historiography. [73]

The breakup of the genres does not correspond to the breakup of narration, and Mircea Eliade has not been at any time the prophet or precursor of an antinovel, a "new novel" stripped of its constitutive elements — intrigue and character — and rejecting meaning at all levels. Since the intervention of the sacred in the world is always camouflaged, the object itself can become the depository of sacred meaning. It is opaque only for those who do not know how to see.

Contrary to the new novel, narration will be reinstated by Mircea Eliade in all its rights, in its complete dignity. Moreover, he proposes to write a study that he would like to entitle "On

72 *Ibid.*, pp. 112–13.

73 "Scriitor la Bucuresti," *Cuvântul in Exil*, nos. 48–50 (May–July, 1966).

the Necessity for the Novel-Novel," and notes in his journal, dated January 5, 1952:

To show the autonomous, glorious, irreducible dimension of *narration* as a form of myth and mythologies readapted to the modern conscience. To show that modern man, as man in archaic societies, cannot exist without myths, without exemplary narratives. The metaphysical dignity of narration, ignored by the realist generations smitten by psychology who have placed in the foreground psychological analysis, then spectral analysis.[74]

Setting himself against the techniques of destruction, which he had used himself ("the fallacy of the interior monologue and the mental film") and even against "the kabbalistic universe of the later Joyce,"[75] Mircea Eliade sees there a sign of the return to chaos to which the adventure of modern art gives witness:

The meaning of it seems clear to me: we refuse the world and the meaning of our existence, as our predecessors have known and accepted it; we manifest this refusal by abolishing the past, breaking the forms, flattening the volumes, disarticulating all the languages, and our ideal would be to obliterate even these ruins and fragments, to return to the pure black, the amorphous without limits, the unity of Chaos.[76]

Is not the adventure of modern art, in this sense, "hooliganical"? Does it not participate in this "revolt of the darkness" described by the young Mircea Eliade? But does it not contain, along with its refusal, an opening toward another world, a renewed world? "The return to chaos is only a moment in a more complex process," continues Mircea Eliade,

Today we are witnessing not only the destruction of languages, as in the times of cubism and futurism, but above all the desire to reach the plenitude of origins. Rare are those who take account of this precosmogonic moment. . . . It is strange that the literary critics, although they have a passion for the archaic and exotic myths, do not take account of the meanings of their own passion and do not understand that myth is above all a narration. . . . Modern man's attraction for myths betrays his hidden desire to listen to stories. . . . In the jargon of literary criticism, this means novel-novel.[77]

[74] *Caete de Dor*, no. 9 (December, 1955), p. 19.
[75] *Ibid.*, p. 19.
[76] "Carnet de vară 1957," *Caete de Dor*, no. 13 (June, 1960), p. 27.
[77] *Ibid.*, p. 27. In his preface to the Portuguese edition of *Forêt Interdite*,

Nevertheless, Mircea Eliade abandoned this novel-novel, of which the most evident illustration remains *Forêt Interdite*, about ten years ago in order to write some short stories. Compared to his symphonic work, which corresponds to very severe chamber music, these stories are the quartets of purity. This sacrifice is not a disavowal. In the concentrated, purified time of the short story, Mircea Eliade finds again the source of the fantastic discovered in *Şarpele*: the camouflage of miracle under the banality of the everyday. Certainly, the unrecognizability of miracle was fundamental to his entire epic universe, a universe full of signs. A hero dominates these stories: the banal man. *Petit bourgeois* from the suburbs of Bucharest or peasant, he is not entirely novel in the prose of Mircea Eliade. But whereas before he represented only a picturesque counterpoint in a universe dominated by "intellectuals," he now reigns as a master. And for the first time miracles are based on him.[78] The fantastic becomes more so, for the banality is now double; it resides in the object or the setting, bearers of the sacred, and in him to whom it is revealed. Banality surrounds us on all sides; it is too perfect not to become suspect. The landscape itself is transformed by it. If this Romania in which the action of most of the stories takes place is more real than reality, transparent to the point of being evanescent, it is because it has become a space inhabited by signs; it belongs to an imaginary geography.[79]

This banality which is found at the source of miracle is augmented by the apparently neutral writing of Mircea Eliade, which willingly ignores what is usually called beautiful style. His indif-

Eliade returns to this "defense and illustration" of the novel-novel. See *Bosque proibido* (Lisbon, 1963).

[78] As an intellectual tormented by meanings, Stephane in *Forêt Interdite* keeps straining to hear signs. Gavrilescu, the little professor of piano in "La Ţigănci," goes through the rites of passage of death in a dazed condition which banishes every temptation of deciphering. The cattle dealer in "Douăsprezece mii capete de vită" is the victim of a leap, of a going back in Time, as is the hero in *Minuit à Serampore*. Unlike the latter, however, he is incapable of questioning himself about his adventure. (Both short stories were published in *Nuvele*.)

[79] Eliade writes on July 24 in his journal *Revista Scriitorilor Romani* (no. 1 [1962], p. 16): "Movila, Tuzla, and Constanţa in 'Ghicitor în pietre' belong to a mythical geography hardly 'resembling' these localities as they were around 1939. I feel more and more the need to free my literature from the geographically and historically concrete. The Bucharest of 'Pe Strada Mântuleasa,' although legendary, is more 'true' than the city that I traversed for the last time in August, 1942."

ference to perfection of form—for which he was reproached by Romanian literary critics at the appearance of his early novels—is not explained only by his feeling that time is limited, by his hurry to construct an *oeuvre* and not to make "beautiful books" [80]—it is essential. Making beautiful is for him the opposite of *making*, and even the idea of a metaphor seems to him to partake of folly.

Mircea Eliade, then, will not have anything to do with "style," but this lack of style is a conquest. It is still more evident in the later stories in the prosaic language of the simple characters. One can speak of a banality in Mircea Eliade's writing only if he sees the snare which this banality lays. It too hides a sign. If it were not so, why would this prose "without style" be so difficult to translate? Why would its limpidity, its transparence, its successive transformations remain prisoners of the magic circle of a single language, Romanian?

This is not the least of the secrets which mark this royal road toward the Center which is the literary work of Mircea Eliade.

[80] In the margin of these criticisms Eliade notes: "I knew besides that for the moment I could write only in a state of fever, hastily, nearly frantically; that in itself this manner of writing was not unfit for literary creation. (Dostoevsky wrote or dictated several of his novels in the same manner.) And then, I knew besides that I did not have much time ahead of me . . . . So I hurried . . . . To the extent that an author is capable of understanding the intention of his own act of creation, I was inclined to believe that it was not formal perfection that would be able to save my works from caducity" (*Cuvântul in Exil*, nos. 48–50 [May–July, 1966].

AUTHENTICITY AND EXPERIENCE OF TIME

Remarks on Mircea Eliade's Literary Works

GÜNTHER SPALTMANN

> It is surprising that so few historians of religion have ever tried to interpret a literary work from their own perspective. . . . On the contrary, as is well known, many literary critics, especially in the United States, have not hesitated to use the findings of the history of religions in their hermeneutical work.[1]

With these words, Mircea Eliade provides us with a stimulus for the following discussion. We recognize that our objective here cannot be a theoretical treatment of our subject or an exhaustive study in this perspective of Eliade's own literary work. We shall have to be content to pursue a few thoughts which have been suggested by Eliade's words.

Anyone who wants to consider literature from the perspective of history of religions will clearly understand that he must first of all check to see whether such an undertaking is legitimate and whether it might not meet with too great a resistance on the part of professional literary criticism. An inappropriate obliteration of the boundaries between the two fields could arouse distrust and probably do harm. It is likely that in every case the first objection which would be raised would be the same, namely, that

[1] Mircea Eliade, "Cultural Fashions and History of Religions," in *The History of Religions: Essays on the Problem of Understanding*, ed. Joseph M. Kitagawa (Chicago, 1967), pp. 22–23.

one would misuse the literary works by employing them simply to illustrate the findings and theses of history of religions. Irving Howe comments in one place on this: "critics, though they can hardly avoid discussing a good many nonliterary topics, should not be expected to do the work of the philosophers, theologians, and politicians."[2] Accordingly, the historian of religions could feel justified in pursuing his own objectives. Yet there is still the question of the legitimacy of his doing it in a field which literary criticism examines with its own characteristic methods.

If one looks around for allies in this undertaking, one's gaze naturally falls, first of all, upon the scholars who are inclined to look upon literature as a vessel for ideas (even nonliterary ideas). In the works of men like Ananda Coomaraswamy one finds every possible support, yet one feels at the same time that one could not simply take over his theories.

> Traditionally, the highest function of art was conceived as the illumination of a thesis. . . . The symbols of traditional art have been "secularized," "emptied of content," and turned into mere "art forms." . . . One of the most characteristic features of works of spiritual art is their pervasive symbolism. Since the form or thesis of a work of art is always a metaphysical content and since this content is something which cannot be observed by the senses, the artist, like the authors of the scripture, is forced to use physical objects or qualities as symbols for that content.[3]

From the perspective of literary criticism, many objections can certainly be raised against such a theory as it is summarized above by Fabian Gudas. Nevertheless, today, after people have learned to abstain from incompetent infringement upon each other's fields, the different fields of research are approaching each other again. New feelers are being extended by religion, theology, and philosophy, as well as by literature. The findings may be of use to all.

John Cruikshank, for example, refers to "this growing similarity of interests in philosophy and literature, and particularly among phenomenologists and novelists."[4] In saying this he is primarily

[2] Irving Howe, "Modern Criticism, Privileges and Perils," in *Modern Literary Criticism*, ed. Irving Howe (Boston, 1958), p. 32.

[3] Fabian Gudas, "Ananda K. Coomaraswamy: The Perennial Philosophy of Art," in *Studies in Contemporary Literature*, ed. Waldo F. McNeir (Baton Rouge, 1962), p. 8.

[4] John Cruikshank, ed., *The Novelist as Philosopher, Studies in French Fiction 1935–1960* (Oxford, 1962), p. 9.

thinking of Sartre and other French modernists, but if we change his words a little, they could also refer to Eliade. Eliade, however, is better known among his current readers as a scholar than as a novelist, since few of his literary works are widely accessible. Thus it is all the more important to study his literary works to see whether there are parallels and oblique associations with his scholarly works.

A certain tension between religion or theology and literature may remain, making such a study even more fruitful. Luckily, literary critics are no longer so intent upon isolating themselves from philosophy, religion, and theology. Just ten years ago, Nathan A. Scott, Jr., attacked leading modern literary critics ("the contemporary movement in criticism") for this self-isolation. Even if at that time he exaggerated somewhat, some of the views he attacked are still relevant today. As Scott sees it, these critics postulate the following:

> The language of poetry does not convey rhetorical propositions about the issues of religion or politics or psychology or science: that is to say, does not conduct the mind beyond itself to anything at all but rather leads us deeper and deeper into itself, a process of exploration.

In contrast to the preceding, Scott makes clear his own views: "the work is oriented by the vision, by the belief, by the ultimate concern of which it is an incarnation; its orientation, that is to say, is essentially religious. And this is why criticism itself must, in the end, be theological."[5]

Perhaps criticism *must* not always be theological, but it *can* always be theological. Unquestionably there is no single legitimate approach to criticism. A genuine collaboration is entirely possible. A. Tate, too, admits that literature has the possibility of transcending itself; according to his view, the plot of a novel, for example, can be extremely concrete, yet with the help of analogy it can transcend time and space.[6]

This dialogue between the different areas of criticism will go on. For us, it is enough to point out briefly here that very little would stand in the way of a student of religions who is genuinely interested in interpreting literary works from his own perspective. We must remember, however, that if the fields are care-

[5] Nathan A. Scott, *The Christian Scholar*, 40 (1957): 279, 292.
[6] Allen Tate, *The Forlorn Demon* (New York, 1953), p. 36.

lessly mixed, dangers will naturally arise along this road. Unquestionably, it would be a mistake to examine literature only to see if religious phenomena, symbols, and ideas are present. The important and decisive thing is the authenticity of the artist's creation.

A further danger, which is no longer as real as it was a few decades ago, is the temptation to replace religion with literature. There have been (and indeed there still are) authors and also critics who dream of literature as a surrogate for religion (*Ersatzreligion*). The new insights regarding the relationship between literature and myth lure them into this. Stephen Spender points out that Michael Hamburger, in one of his essays, cites several authorities who assert that Rilke, for example, really tried to elevate his writings to the status of religion. Spender then continues:

> To F. R. Leavis there is no question but that D. H. Lawrence's message is "religious." Yeats makes a mosaic of fragments of Oriental and Western belief and varieties of mysticism, a religion as eclectic as the picture of art selected from all times and places, which André Malraux in his *Musée Imaginaire* supposes modern men and women to carry round in their heads.[7]

The actual seams between imagination, inspiration, belief, and mythical thought cannot be completely removed by interpretation. A certain tension, owing to the fact that the different areas do not quite correspond, proves to be very fruitful for criticism. Making religions out of literature and literature out of religion must not become a threatening danger.

The difficulty, if we perceive it correctly, will always lie in determining whether the symbols and mythological allusions in a literary work are only external, dogmatic, or just mundane trappings, or whether they are an integral part of the work, so that the literary quality of the work would suffer if the symbols were taken away.

If we thus feel justified in considering Eliade's literary work from this point of view, the question that naturally arises is what we should consider first. His books are full of mythological refer-

[7] Stephen Spender, *The Struggle of the Modern* (Berkeley and Los Angeles, 1963), p. 38.

ences, symbols, and meanings. Eliade himself, however, can give us guidance. In the above-mentioned lecture he says:

> I am not referring to those cases in which the religious context or implications of a work are more or less evident, as, for example, Chagall's paintings with their enormous "eye of God," the angels, the severed heads and bodies flying upside down—and his omnipresent ass, that messianic animal par excellence.[8]

Tempting as it might be to set up an inventory of religious phenomena, ideas, and implications, it would be more advisable, first of all, to find a common denominator by which the many separate phenomena can then be compared. For only in terms of such a common idea will they gain their significance. The occasional use of mythical symbols can be found in the work of many a novelist who himself is anything but mythically inclined. In a more comprehensive study, classifications and deeper connections and transformations could be discussed and oblique associations made. Thus, Eliade's work could be interpreted as a whole. Since we are here only presenting a prologue to such a larger work, our subject has to be limited to just a few topics.

The primary factor uniting all the mythical and religious phenomena, all the ideas, figures, and creations in Eliade's work, is the atmosphere of the *mysterious* (*des Geheimnisses*). It is the mysterious which characterizes all his people, events, feelings, notions—everything seems to transcend itself and to point beyond itself to something that is still to happen, a solution that is expected, an event which will transcend and transform the temporal world. And the aura of the mysterious is not fabricated artificially, even though Eliade of course knows the ingredients as they were classically employed by Poe. One never has the suspicion that Eliade makes use of the mysterious only because he is trying to avoid setting forth his ideas in broad daylight, for he is only too interested in setting forth his ideas and also in promoting their discussion. Kenneth Burke's friendly irony would not be applicable to Eliade: "an ounce of 'mystery' is worth a ton of 'argument.' Indeed, where mystery is, we can be assured that the arguments will profusely flow, as *intellectus* flows from *fides*."[9]

[8] Eliade, "Cultural Fashions," p. 21.

[9] Kenneth Burke, "Mysticism as a Solution to the Poet's Dilemma," in *Spiritual Problems in Contemporary Literature*, ed. S. Hopper (New York, 1953), p. 105.

The "mystery of the world," in the correct sense, is also the most authentic phenomenon of all human ways of experiencing the self. It encompasses and is also the source of true literary creation. Burke himself gives an example of this in his previously quoted essay:

grass on a college campus . . . is not just a "sensory" thing. At the very least, it bodies forth certain principles of order, with related claims, obligations, and promises. It is not merely "empirical." It is "mythic," "ritualistic"; it not just *is*, it *stands* for.[10]

The deeper quality of the mysterious transcends implied meanings and has to do with the world as such. In addition to myth, literature and art in general are well suited to portray this quality of the mysterious. According to E. Underhill there are indeed great similarities between the way the mystic and the artist experience the world.[11]

What we mean when we stress the "quality of the mysterious" is explained by Anton Szerb in an interesting, almost forgotten book. In discussing John Cowper Powys, Szerb says:

Already the atmosphere contains wonder (*Wunder*). The whole novel is mysterious in an uncertain, vague way. It is reminiscent of Dostoyevsky. One is at all times prepared for something dreadful to happen or for some horrible mystery to come to light. In Dostoyevsky's works the dreadful thing does indeed appear. Powys' method, however, is even more terrifying, for the dreadful thing does not appear. The mysterious we sense is nothing other than the mystery of reality. Anyone who is not shielded by the cloak of ideological and moral conventions has his naked self touched by the world. This has a mysterious and terrifying significance. Powys' marvelous art consists in his ability to master this perception of life which assimilates everything under the star of the mysterious![12]

We think that Eliade would probably agree with these observations. In one of his early essays, "Folkloristic Themes and Artistic Creation," he himself says that in the development of the legend

[10] *Ibid.*

[11] Evelyn Underhill, *The Essentials of Mysticism* (New York, 1960), p. 77: "These pictures are seen by the mystic . . . they are not produced by any voluntary process of composition, but loom up, as do the best creations of other artists, from his deeper mind, bringing with them an intense conviction of reality."

[12] Anton Szerb, *Die Suche nach dem Wunder* (Amsterdam and Leipzig, 1938), p. 178.

the anecdote is not important, but rather the presence of the fantastic, "for experience, not formal knowledge, constitutes the phantastic element of the game."[13]

If the atmosphere, the experiential background, is of such decisive importance, then the objection that the consideration of literary works from the perspective of history of religions would be satisfied with listing dry analogies and phenomena disappears. If the latter are authentically experienced, they can point to the decisively important experiential background. Thomas Mann's views on the significance of myth for an author are representative of those of many modern novelists. Mann, who states these views in his great essays about Wagner and Freud, is an intellectual author who did not simply submit to a surrogate for religion but found deepest, ordering life in the nature of myth even for modern times.

Another point is singled out by Novak when he speaks of the relationships between philosophy (*Wissenschaft*) and art:

> The novel does not so much describe man's state, in suggestive metaphor and symbol, so that we can look into it and see ourselves; rather, it invites us to enter into a new horizon. It recreates the standpoint and furnishes the pointers by which we live through a way of conceiving our lives. . . . The novelist is not so much interested in articulating his experience as in living through it by means of his artifact. He is interested in the skillful recreation of an experience within a certain horizon, so that his readers may likewise experience it. . . . The novelist recreates the horizon of the self; the philosopher tries to speak about it in a system of propositions. . . .[14]

Since our task is to set up a parallel between Eliade's scholarly and literary works and to find out whether the same creative spirit that sees myths is present in both, we are faced with the following question: Is there not perhaps a basic danger inherent in his two-fold activity? Is not the author perhaps trying to illustrate in his novels and stories his scholarly theories, insights, and findings? First of all, we would like to reply that even didactic literature has its place. We can also say that Eliade's literary work is not derived from his scholarly activity but that the two types

13 Mircea Eliade, "Teme folclorice şi creaţie artistică," in *Insula lui Euthanasius* (Bucharest, 1943), p. 373.

14 Michael Novak, "Philosophy of Fiction," *Christian Scholar*, 47 (1964): 101.

of work are carried on alongside each other. We must also recognize that from his early youth on Eliade has been inclined toward diversified activity. His work is so many-sided that it is precisely this that causes difficulty in approaching it and surveying it. Any single way of considering his work may prove, after a short time, to be too one-sided in comparison with the many-sidedness of his works and endeavors.

The early ambitions of the author tend toward the life of the polymath, the universal man, the Renaissance man. The name of the great Romanian polymath Nicolae Iorga appears several times as a model; Goethe and Papini are also mentioned. His scholarly work deals with and makes accessible to us a great many different subjects; as a journalist he has at his disposal a great variety of experience; as a student he had already published scholarly essays on remote subjects for the general public.[15] Even in his belletristic work his vision arches far between two poles. Here we may perhaps say that his turning to myth may also be a manifestation of the striving for universality. Thomas Mann, too, believed that the universality which he was striving for could best be realized in mythical figures.

To be sure, it seems questionable and dangerous to limit oneself to a discussion of only one of Eliade's works when his total work is not known to the public. And yet, the more one occupies oneself with his work, the more one realizes that all the seemingly divergent lines converge upon one central point or emanate from this central point, and that even the diversity in style can be explained by means of a *primum movens*.

In Eliade's works one can very quickly discern that he has a horror of imitated life, of conventional writing, and of copied clichés. This is all the more important since the love for genuine myth and for genuine tradition gains in authenticity through it. The desire for authenticity of experience, of writing, of thinking, brings him to seek and postulate the direct confrontation with life, with things, with phenomena. This desire for the authentic can be shown in his scholarly as well as in his literary work. By this we do not mean merely precise documentation, but — if feasible — a test by example, so to speak, "the risking of one's own neck." In his school days Eliade experimented in his laboratory; later he devoted everything to an immediate testing of the im-

[15] Mircea Eliade, *Amintiri: I Mansarda* (Madrid, 1966).

pressions he had received from reading, from conversations with famous authors, or in the libraries of foreign cities. The same desire also led him to India.[16]

This need for authenticity can even be traced in the style of his works: the atmosphere of the mysterious above all in *Șarpele* and *Secretul Doctorului Honigberger*, psychological reality in the interior monologue and *style indirect libre* in *Huliganii*, and, above all, in *Forêt Interdite*. We shall have to return to this in a later part of this study.

In *Fragmentarium*, a collection of short essays, we find several references to the need for authenticity. There Eliade speaks, for example, about the "future destiny of the Romanian novel" and attempts to set up some criteria for it. In future books it is above all important to invent new characters who take part in the drama of existence as fully as possible, who have a destiny, and who experience the struggle for knowledge; for literature creates myth-characters.[17] There we even find an essay entitled "Authenticity" in which he indicates what this concept means for him: authenticity is a moment in the great movement toward the "concrete" which characterizes the last quarter century (for example, the success of phenomenology, the value which one attaches to "irrational experience" in studies of religions, and the interest in ethnography and folklore). Authenticity cannot be a characteristic of the nineteenth century, for it does not confuse the "real" with the tangible; it is also not antimetaphysical, but it is rather the expression of a strong ontological yearning for knowledge of the real. All this seems very important to us, even if it shows that the turning to myth in Eliade's case is not perhaps a flight from reality but is, on the contrary, a thirst for deeper reality. This is why he wants literature to transform itself, why he wants to find the new work, "the book with new people, people who are permeated with deeper conflicts . . . these characters possess a grandiose theoretical knowledge of the world."[18]

This desire for authenticity (*Wille zur Authentizität*) sometimes — at least in the early works — goes to the limits of the gruesome and the crude, and is no doubt one of the reasons why, when reading Eliade's major novels, one very often gets the im-

[16] *Ibid.*

[17] Mircea Eliade, "Despre Destinul Romanului Românesc," in his *Fragmentarium* (Bucharest, 1939), p. 85.

[18] *Ibid.*, p. 84.

pression that everything dogmatic in traditional belief, all the conventions of society and of behavior, are doubted, directly attacked, or not even recognized as existing. Eliade's people seem to be animated by an explosive urge for independence, by a feverish intensity for self-realization and for showing themselves as they really are, cost what it may. Many conventional norms are exceeded – norms of bourgeois morality as well as norms of linguistic style. This is a characteristic of his major novels. It could furnish, in a separate study, the material for a comparison between the wish for authenticity of life and its creation. He works with techniques similar to those of other innovators of the novel: Faulkner, Proust, Joyce, Huxley. In our eyes he sometimes seems to be closest to Virginia Woolf, despite the differences in the direct dealing with life. Moreover, one can readily see from *Intoarcerea din Rai* and *Huliganii* why traditionalists did not at all approve of the author at the beginning of his career as a novelist.

In order to master the onslaught of experience, Eliade had to keep an extensive diary. At any rate, the diary quality of some stories and parts of novels is obvious. Conversely, one can also say that much is contained in his diaries which could be incorporated into a novel with little change. This too is related to the authentic.[19] Moreover, Thomas Mann also confesses how often he has almost directly incorporated into his works material from reality. *Tonio Kröger* and *Death in Venice* are not "made-up."

For the observer it is a constant source of astonishment to see the consistency with which an intensively living human being pursues his life. Perhaps some of the early works are slowly pressing to be reworked in order to get their final form. In any case, some portions of his early works seem to be anticipations of what is to be a later completion. Only outsiders, people who judge superficially, could want to see in these works the danger of their being fragmentary and disjointed. The diary unites the divergent tendencies and becomes an expression of the authentic life. More than once one gets the impression that events and reflections touch the reader most directly in those portions of the book where one believes that he feels the underlying diary quality. If whole passages of a diary, like those of the (published) *Șantier* read

19 The persons here are like characters out of a novel, even though Eliade is dealing with public figures. See Mircea Eliade, *Șantier* (Bucharest, 1935); see also Rabindranath Tagore and others in this book.

exactly like a novel, we can conclude from this that even when writing his diary Eliade approaches the archetypal via the personal element of experience. Here again we can use Thomas Mann for a comparison. Mann remarked that he needed only to speak about himself to open the mouth of the general public.

As soon as the reader accepts the conception of a book as authentic, he also feels inclined to admit the legitimacy of the artistic creation (*Gestaltung*). Michael Novak discusses in his essay the possibilities of recognizing truth or falsity in a work of fiction. He introduces the interesting concept of the "horizon," which one would also like to apply to Eliade's literary work:

> Falsity in fiction is the presentation of a point of view that is no more than rationalization, or shows such little penetration that it does not justify so many pages. Only persons can judge personal authenticity; the truth or falsity of fiction is not judged as directly as the truth or falsity of a scientific theory, for they are established at a level prior to science. The truth or falsity of fiction is verified in living one's life: live in the horizon of Gide, or Mailer, or Camus, and see how it meets the tests of life.[20]

This "horizon" of which Novak speaks is seen in Eliade's case most clearly in the image of time. The problem of time, to which the author is so intensely devoted in his scholarly work, is also one of the chief concerns in his literary works. This links him with most of the important authors of our time.

Since we cannot even hope to trace all the different phenomena and ideas in his books which manifest a concern with the mythical, we turn briefly to a discussion of time. For one thing, we are convinced that we can thus gain insight into the author's nature. Also, from his treatment and experience of time, it might become clear whether the parallel which we have postulated as existing between Eliade's scholarly and literary works can become evident.

> The theme of all novels is Time; a certain time span which is filled out by all the events recounted in the novel. The events give this time span its rhythm; they make it into a time, which is thought of and experienced in the human sense, since time is the sequence of transformations. The novel and time are inseparable, the raw material of both is the event. Therefore the philosophical problem in constructing the

20 Novak, "Philosophy of Fiction," p. 109.

novel is always the problem of how the novelist deals with time. In the story of the novel *every great turning point must lead to a change in the concept of time and vice versa.*[21]

In view of Eliade's unusually strong feeling for the mythical, it follows that he is not concerned with "time" merely as something passing and elapsing, but that he has insights into the deeper connections. He is especially fascinated by the problem of interchanging time and of going from one level of time into another. The mythical phenomena of time are directly approached in several books. The problem is only intimated in *Maitreyi*, the beautiful love story from India, but in *Secretul Doctorului Honigberger* and "Nopți la Serampore" time already assumes a major role. In *Honigberger* a man liberates himself from time and space after extensive study of occult books and vanishes from his surroundings. The story sometimes reads like a handbook for personal penetration of these spheres. Eliade has the first person narrator come upon the diary which the vanished initiate has left behind, examine it, and intersperse it with comments from his own studies and from everyday life, whereby the authentic quality of the novel is again reinforced. For example, after the narrator has again quoted an excerpt from the diary of the vanished Dr. Zerlendi, he immediately adds his own observation in the following manner:

(Note: I must confess that I don't quite understand what Dr. Zerlendi wants to say here; I have nevertheless permitted this excerpt from the text to remain because it seems possible to me that experienced occultists might discern some meaning behind it. A *Sadhu* with whom I became associated in 1930 in Konarak told me – but I don't know whether he spoke the truth – that it was disconcerting, while undertaking certain Yoga meditations, to meet the spirits of sleeping persons who wander about like shadows in the dimension of sleep. One could say that they look at one uneasily, because they cannot comprehend how it is possible that they encounter there an awake and fully conscious human being.)[22]

[21] Szerb, *Die Suche*, p. 105. For further studies in the problem of time see also Emil Staiger, *Die Zeit als Einbildungskraft des Dichters* (Zurich and Leipzig, 1939), Eberhard Lämmert, *Bauformen des Erzahlens* (Stuttgart, 1955), especially pp. 73–91; Franz Stanzel, *Die typischen Erzählsituationen im Roman* (Vienna, 1955), pp. 49 ff.

[22] M. Eliade, *Secretul Doctorului Honigberger* (Bucharest, 1940). Quoted from the German translation, *Nächte in Serampore* (Munich, 1953), p. 141.

In the other story, "Nopți la Serampore," the main characters confront a former time with the assistance of an expert. In mythical fear they experience this former time as their own present time. One of the important mythical problems here is the extent to which they are observers and the extent to which they are participants in an event which they perhaps actually change by their "being thrown into it."[23]

Șarpele too is one of these mysterious stories. Here, even more clearly than in "Nopți," the transformation of people and their levels of experience starts from their mundane lives and finds its fulfillment in myth: some excursionists meet an attractive young man on their way to a lake where they want to pass some time. The young man asks to be taken along. He apparently has a special relationship to nature and to animals; he also has at his command a snake charm with which he brings the excursionists out of their conventional lives and into a dreamlike existence. The atmosphere is full of mysterious presentiments and feelings; the style envelops everything in a simple and transparent dreaminess. Thus, at the end, when the young man, significantly named Andronic, and the young girl whom he has chosen are found naked and embraced asleep in the early morning light on the snake island, a shocking scene by conventional standards is transformed into the mythically symbolic. The arrival of the snake is experienced by everyone as symbolic and enchanting; everyone is brought more closely in touch with his own life. Dorina, the young girl, whom the group would like to marry off to a bourgeois husband, feels herself especially attracted to the mysterious young Andronic. She looks anxiously toward the snake which, summoned by the charm, appears among them.

> She had the impression that the snake was coming directly at her. A sudden horror banished the earlier enchantment, as though she were being confronted with something terrible and dangerous which no girl was allowed to see. It was a strange mixture of death and erotic breathing in this repulsive rolling movement, in the cold line of the reptile.[24]

Related to this are a series of shorter and mostly later stories in which new attempts are constantly made to treat the theme

[23] *Ibid., passim.*

[24] Mircea Eliade, *Șarpele*, 2d ed. (Bucharest, 1944), pp. 109–10.

of time and interchange of time. The author attaches particular importance to the disconcerting effect which an *involuntary* transition from one level of time to another can have, especially if the person subjected to it is mentally unprepared or has no personal relationship to the event that befalls him. In the story "12,000 capete de vite,"[25] there is a coarse man who experiences the change of time without being able to understand what is happening to him. He becomes enraged and believes that someone has played a dreadful trick on him. Moreover, here again is the eerie phenomenon: one can really be transported into another time, one can speak to figures which one sees there, but they do not want to answer. In "La Tigănci," a respectable piano teacher does not fare any better. Here the atmosphere of mystery is heightened by his visit to a strange brothel where he seems to lose (or to find) his identity and where the old woman at the gate has Norn-like features.[26]

We should note the diversity in the effects of the interchange of time upon those who experience it. In *Secretul Doctorului Honigberger* the initiate is basically sympathetic to the occurrence of the mystery; the narrator, to be sure, is confused about what happens to him, but the experience opens a new door to him. On the other hand, the nonintellectual, the coarse man, reacts to what unexpectedly happens to him with anger, indignation, and disgust. But everyone experiences his own time, which of course is not a chronological unfolding but an already experienced time (*erlebte Zeit*).

In both theory and practice, Eliade has found that he cannot treat the problem of the departure from time and the interchange of the levels of time by directly telling the story. He has found other ways which seem less direct (and therefore perhaps also less sensational) to make his purpose clear. By this is meant first of all the *style* of narration. After one has developed a feeling for Eliade's themes from reading the directly told "tall stories," it is very fascinating to see how he – now mainly by stylistic means – strives for the same objective: his major novels, *Intoarcerea din Rai*, *Huliganii*, and *Forêt Interdite*, are very concretely set in modern times in the period between the two world wars

25 Mircea Eliade, *Nuvele* (Madrid, 1963), pp. 137–48.
26 *Ibid.*, pp. 5–42.

and in wartime. He, like Proust, Faulkner, and Woolf, treats the theme of time through his style. He is not content with describing it as an object. Some of his earlier works point in this direction, but the technique attains its zenith in *Huliganii* and *Forêt Interdite*. We can follow the problem of time even in the grammar. Although we cannot go into the total construction of the novels, we want to try to show by means of concrete examples how Eliade's preoccupation with time is also reflected in sentence structure. An excerpt from *Huliganii*:

> Petru resolved, from now on, to decline every invitation to come to tea in the house of his new pupil. (And yet, how often during the winter he had to break his word. How often he found Anisioara sitting at the table and waiting for him, always in front of the same tea pot which had been covered with a pillow to keep it warm. Then she threatened to run away from the piano lesson if he at least didn't drink a cup of tea and eat a piece of cake. At the Lecca house they never ran out of cake which was always served in good sized pieces.)[27]

In these few lines, taken from a seemingly unimportant paragraph, a series of various levels of time is already disclosed: within the plane of narrative time Petru decides no longer to go to afternoon tea in the (his) future. There immediately follows in parentheses a remark by the narrator (or by Petru?), saying that he would break (has broken) his resolution often in the future, which has become the past for the author of the note. At the same time, this future into which the narrator projects himself is not successive but rather reiterative (*iterativ*). There is no progressive action, but rather an almost static contemplation in which again there is a change of time. The last sentence of the quoted paragraph also belongs to the narrator's account of the really appearing future and uses instead of the reiterative "how often" and the durative "never," immediately followed by "always." We should also add that the narrative point of view (*Erzählpunkt*) seemingly alternates between the active Petru and the narrator, and we assume that the latter probably cannot really be the author of the book. The use of the *style indirect libre* and also of the emotionally tinged "how often," justifies our assumption that it is again Petru (perhaps identical with the narrator?) who here – even if on a later plane of narrative time – is reflecting about events which, at the scene of the action, are still

[27] Mircea Eliade, *Huliganii* (Bucharest, 1935), p. 14.

future, but which, in his projection, are already taking place in the present or have become part of the past.

The future is part of the present, or the present is only a facet of the future, and they both belong to the deeper concept of time. Every single action in Eliade's works seems to be associated with, or at least related to, that which has come before and also to that which is yet to follow, which is only intuited by the reader. Through this there also originates a quality of mystery, since new light is shed on past episodes and the reader can eavesdrop on the future in its genesis. This is a source of light which accompanies the reader through the jungle of time. "Components of the narrative, which have an episodic effect in their places, can manifest by retrospective illumination their real integration with the whole."[28]

In continuous synchronization, Eliade has the past, the present, and the future permeate each other. This is perhaps not so much to clarify but rather to show the diversity of the relationships within a single episode. This is why there are in his stories not only projections into the future and flashbacks into the past, but also reiterative and durative summaries in which the viewpoint again changes.

The flashbacks are not meant to be a history of the preceding time, as in classical style, but rather an experiencing by association. Perhaps, in a deeper, vague respect, this is a causal relationship after all. The flashbacks, more than the projections into the future, do not necessarily seem to the reader to be tied to the main action. Sometimes they contribute side plots, but by their color they also help to make the action of the present time into a multifaceted musical composition.

Everything is woven into a tapestry of experience in which every thread is tied to those in front, those in back, and those at the sides. All earthly time is like a tapestry before the eyes of the poet, where the past and the future, together with the present, seem to form one continuous plane. If we can speak of an act of providence here, then it is to be understood as something imagistic rather than rational-causal.

Having tried to show the projections into the future by using *Huliganii* as a model, we would like to quote a passage from *Forêt Interdite* in which the flashback technique is particularly clear.

[28] Lämmert, *Bauformen des Erzählens.*

Ce dimanche-là de novembre, Stéphane s'était surpris à répéter plusieurs fois un nom: Mihai Duma. Il était certain d'avoir entendu ce nom mais n'arrivait pas à se rappeler dans quelles circonstances. . . . Il alluma une cigarette. La grille de fer qui entourait le jardin devant la maison, avait été arrachée et livrée à l'industrie de guerre — comme, d'ailleurs, tous les autres grillages d'Oxford. Mihai Duma, se souvint-il tout d'un coup, était un garçon dont lui avait parlé Birish. Mais il ne réussit à se rappeler rien de plus et il rentra chez lui, irrité, le front baissé, à travers la pluie qui tombait. . . . Puis, il prit un livre et l'ouvrit au hasard. Au bout d'un moment il regarda le titre pour savoir qu'il lisait; c'était un volume de critique littéraire. L'auteur était Virginia Woolf. Birish lui avait parlé de Mihai Duma une nuit . . . "Je viens de chez quelqu'un, de chez Mihai Duma, à Cotroceni. . . . Je suis éreinté. . . . J'ai marché toute la journée. Je suis allé à Cotroceni, jusqu'à Cotroceni. . . ."

Il sentit le froid le saisir.

"Je suis tout de même chargé d'une mission officielle! dit-il soudain. Je ne vois guère de différence entre la Gestapo et vous, la grande démocratie. . . ."

Un policier qui examinait sa chemise, devant la fenêtre, tourna doucement la tête et sourit.

Tout nu, son mégot entre les doigts, Stéphane eut le sentiment d'être plus ridicule encore dans la posture qu'il avait prise, à demi dressé d'indignation. . . .

"Nous, on ne vous arrachera pas les dents," fit l'homme, d'un ton placide.

"J'ai rencontré quelqu'un d'intéressant! lui avait dit Birish cette nuit-là. Un nommé Mihai Duma." Le matin suivant, à la Légation, il s'était décidé tout d'un coup à lui télégraphier. Il se rendait compte de son imprudence, mais il sentait qu'il ne se tranquilliserait qu'après avoir reçu le réponse de Birish. "Prière me communiquer télégraphiquement détails précis sur Mihai Duma. Stop. Suis intéressé plus haut degré par cet homme. Stop. Amitiés Stéphane." Il avait commencé à chiffrer le télégramme dans le code du Ministère de l'Economie, mais il se rappela tout d'un coup que ce code était périmé depuis quelques mois. Il aurait dû demander à Fotescou ou au conseiller de la Légation le nouveau chiffre mais il hésita longtemps et finit par descendre lui-même au bureau de poste. Il envoya le télégramme en clair. Trois jours plus tard, il reçut la réponse: "Homme dépourvu d'intérêt. Stop. Ai cessé depuis longtemps toute relation avec lui. Stop. Heureux cependant du signe de vie que vous m'avez donné. Stop. Amitiés Petre."[29]

The passage begins in the pluperfect, with a past that occurred before the narrated plot (*Erzählhandlung*). But the verb then

[29] Mircea Eliade, *Forêt Interdite* (Paris, 1955), pp. 291–92.

immediately changes into the appropriate narrative time. Thus, we must be dealing here with a recollection of the main character, Stéphane. The recollection gains concreteness through the accurately described details. Stéphane remembers a day in which the ominous name Duma looms up in his memory (second recollection), but he cannot recall the details. While he is then toying with a book (not without reason is it Virginia Woolf, we think), suddenly—*tout d'un coup*, an expression used frequently in this passage—he is living again in a vaguely remembered past. He remembers that a friend, Birish, spoke to him of Duma. With this another step backward is taken, backward in time. This already resembles a cabinet of mirrors with endless reflections.

The conversation with Birish also looms up out of the past. Then the recollection (all the recollections which are encased one within the other) breaks off. He suddenly feels himself physically seized by cold. Now, "suddenly," a new level of experience is present, and we see for a moment the actual time of the narration and of the action which till now had not yet been shown to us: while he is pursuing these memories Stéphane is being interrogated by the police. He compares this to Gestapo interrogations. We see that he immediately slips back again into his recollections while he is standing naked before the officials and smoking a cigarette. Duma, the name he remembers, seems to have a mysterious association with this act of violence. A further image in the mirror of the past opens itself to him; the labyrinth is complete, his confusion has become a spiritual and temporal mystery. He remembers that at that time he had wired his friend Birish for clarification of the Duma mystery. As an ironic end to this mirrored episode, the Duma affair, built up like a detective story and on which so much seemed to hang, disappears into nothingness, whereby the tension is shifted to the interior self.

Out of these multileveled recollections—one door opens after the other, yet without leading anywhere—there unfolds, as the actual event, the plunging into the bottomless well of time and thus into the bottomless well of the "self."

This, unfortunately, is not the place to compare Eliade's conception of time with that of Joyce, Faulkner, and, above all, Virginia Woolf, in whose works remarkable similarities can be found. Completely apart from the theological, or at any rate mythical, intervention of the Great Time into the time of everyday life,

Eliade's characters also possess in everyday life a particularly intense feeling for time. They can have past experiences unroll before their eyes at will like a film; their fantasy and power of imagination exceed the usual measure (see, for example, Mitica in *Huliganii* or the swindler in *Forêt Interdite*, who alone could fill a novel). They share this strong power of imagination with their creator. It seems to go along with the ability to grasp religious phenomena. "The mind of the poet at moments . . . gains an insight into reality, reads Nature as a symbol of something behind or within Nature not ordinarily perceived."[30] One can clearly see the difference between Eliade's novels and traditional forms of narration: "[the difference] is indicated chiefly in the difference in subject matter—which is, for the earlier novelists, motive and action (external man) and for the later ones, psychic existence and functioning (internal man)," as we read in Robert Humphrey's works.[31] But Eliade's novels are also full of intricate action which, together with the narrative style, reinforces the quality of the mysterious. "Knowledge . . . as a category of consciousness must include intuition, vision, and sometimes even the occult, so far as twentieth-century writers are concerned."[32]

Eliade always involves the whole man in the experience, and man is challenged by the experience. Direct narration becomes indirect, the *style indirect libre*, and the interior monologue. The stream of consciousness appears quite naturally; there is a smooth transition back to the indirect style of narration, then direct narration is suddenly used again.[33] The interspersed dialogues remind us of Huxley and of Thomas Mann's *Magic Mountain*, and sometimes also of Malraux.

From this flashing back and forth of the levels of time there arises as the deeper meaning not so much an interchangeability of the time, but to a certain extent, a deeper pattern; the "actual" time becomes discernible in this tapestry on the loom of time. We wish to quote Eliade himself:

Since the relentlessness and emptiness of time has become a dogma for the entire modern world (or more precisely, for all those who do

30 I. A. Richards, quoted by Allen Tate in his *On the Limits of Poetry* (New York, 1948), p. 45.

31 Robert Humphrey, *Stream of Consciousness in the Modern Novel* (Berkeley and Los Angeles, 1959), p. 8.

32 *Ibid.*, p. 7.

33 Lämmert, *Bauformen des Erzählens.*

not identify themselves with the Judeo-Christian ideology), the temporality (*Zeitlichkeit*) which has been possessed and experienced by man manifests itself in the field of philosophy as the tragic consciousness of the vanity of all human existence. . . . A reconciliation with temporality is, however, possible if we adopt a proper concept of time.[34]

In the stories, the personal experience of "departure from time" fills the findings of his scholarly works with a terror which lends new authenticity even to them.

It is a deep, fulfilled time which opens up before us. Emil Staiger (in an essay on Keller) says of a very different, but also (to some degree) timeless time:

A time, which does not pass, above all does not proceed towards anything . . . its significance does not lie in the hereafter (*Jenseits*) which would first have to be attained and not in immortality. It is a stationary present, an eternally inert "present" ("*Da*").[35]

This would be the other pole of Eliade's vision.

We started this study with the concept of mystery and we would now like to return to it. The genuineness of Eliade's concern can also be shown in his stories; he does not try to demonstrate scholarly findings with them. The mysterious, mythical atmosphere includes in itself all individual symbols and ideas which could be investigated from the point of view of their religious quality. How the mystery presents itself and how its atmosphere communicates itself to the reader is the decisive thing in Eliade's literary work. "The conditions for the sense of mystery are present when there is communication between different kinds of being. Not just communication, nor difference—but communication across the gulf of difference," say Burke, who goes on to speak about the oxymoron as a mystical and stylistic phenomenon as if here he were thinking of Eliade's comprehensive view (*Zusammenschau*) of alchemy and the problem of time: ". . . we get to problems of catharsis: purification by the kill. . . . Hence even, we may watch for alchemy. . . ." Although this passage is not directly relevant to Eliade's intentions, we can still partially lean on it.[36]

[34] Mircea Eliade, "Alchemie und Zeitlichkeit," *Antaios* 2 (1961): 187, 188.

[35] Emil Staiger, *Die Zeit als Einbildungskraft des Dichters* (Zurich and Leipzig, 1963), p. 163.

[36] Burke, "Mysticism as a Solution," p. 105.

New interest in myth is shown today in the most diverse quarters. Eliade can feel corroborated in those things which he is deeply concerned with:

if according to modern psychology the myth proves to be still alive even in modern man, then this is less astonishing for the historian of religions than for the theologian, since the former knows from his own discipline about the close attachment and fusion of Christian and non-Christian elements in religious life. To be sure, man thus obviously appears very complex. Is he a Christian or is he a pagan? This formulation of the problem is probably too simplistic and too crude. Myth is alive even today, partly among individuals, no longer among cultic communities.[37]

We wish to end with these words of Thomas Mann, who was so deeply concerned with myth:

in the life of the human race the mythical is an early and primitive stage, in the life of the individual it is a late and mature one. What is gained is an insight into the higher truth depicted in the actual; a smiling knowledge of the schema in which and according to which the supposed individual lives. . . ."[38]

[37] Hans Schar, "Religionsgeschichte, Psychologie und Psychotherapie," in the Festschrift for Gustav Mensching, *Religion und Religionen* (Bonn, 1967), p. 261.

[38] Thomas Mann, "Freud und die Zukunft," in *Adel des Geistes* (Stockholm, 1948), pp. 578–79 (the English translation is from Thomas Mann, *Essays of Three Decades*, trans. H. T. Lowe-Porter [New York, 1965], p. 422).

THE FOREST AS MANDALA

Notes concerning a Novel by Mircea Eliade

VINTILA HORIA

Tempo di uccidere is the title of an Italian novel by Ennio Flaiano which appeared some years ago. The title is eloquent and coincides in part with the theme of the last novel of Mircea Eliade, *Forêt Interdite* (Paris, 1955). In effect, we endure a "time for killing" not because today men die or kill each other more than in other ages—death has always been equal to itself—but because never before has man integrated himself in a more conscious manner into the destructive significance of time. In his research works, dedicated above all else to problems in the philosophy of religions,[1] Mircea Eliade has shown how civilizations prior to our own, the so-called traditional or primitive civilizations, have concentrated upon the theme of the annihilation of time, the destructive current, and, by means of evasion through myth, have succeeded in eluding the consequences of contact with historical time. The people of Romania, for example (Mircea Eliade himself is an exiled Romanian author), throughout the periods of provocations and sufferings through which they have passed, have done nothing other than "sabotage history," as Lucian Blaga would say. They have withdrawn themselves into the myth.

There exist, as a consequence, two kinds of time. One is a time that kills, a historical time without beginning and without end, a time which offers no hope to the man who accepts it, not even the hope of an immortality beyond terrestrial life; this is the nature of time as occidental civilization has conceived it at least since

[1] Vintila Horia uses the term "philosophy of religion" to describe Mircea Eliade's field of research although it is, more properly speaking, the history of religions in which Eliade is interested [*translator's note*].

Descartes. The other kind of time, mythical time, is a time which saves; within it men belonging to the traditional civilizations succeeded in avoiding the disintegrating action of historical time.

It is evident that the Christian religion accepts, beyond any mythical or magical "illusionism," life in historical time, and that Christian doctrine, which postulates the annihilation of the ancient and traditional soteriological techniques and the realization of the human person and of nations in time (Jesus Christ himself is born, suffers, and dies in a historical time), is at the base of Western civilization's conception of time. Nevertheless, as Mircea Eliade demonstrates in *Le Mythe de l'Eternel Retour*, Christianity also foresaw an end to time at the Last Judgment, when each man would achieve a definitive and eternal position. Therefore, Christian time does not contain the illusion of a return but is rather a time that begins on a determined date and finishes on a determined date. According to the Christian conception, in spite of being submitted to the time which kills, man retains the hope of an end, of a perfect realization of himself within an eternity situated beyond history.

On the other hand, postcartesian man, representative of the idealist conception, of Hegelian or Marxist ritual, or the positivist conception, runs the danger of realizing, at a certain moment, his tragic position in time and of coming to be, as he is today, terrorized by history and placed in the position of being able himself to destroy the possibility of returning to a mythic conception of history as well as the hope of an eternal life situated beyond the time that perishes.

For the one who realizes this situation without possible salvation, the terror of time becomes insupportable. Since Kierkegaard, the term "anxiety" has been used to designate the feeling that man appears from nothing and is directed toward a future that contains, it is true, all the personal decisions that shape his existential content, but within whose bounds nothing will be resolved in his favor. The problem of time and the impossibility of the man of today resolving it in one manner or another is the theme of the contemporary novel. In Joyce, Kafka, and Proust, this time for killing, or time for dying, whose permanent crime no one can sanction, becomes the key to the present novel, the literary genre which best expresses and synthesizes our age, much as destiny and the blind fate which it implies had been the key to ancient tragedy.

Without doubt the psychological nuances are multiple within this eschatological postulation of the problem of time in the contemporary novel. There is a type of novel in which the terror of time appears under a Freudian aspect, as, for example, in Marcel Proust, Stefan Zweig, and Alberto Moravia. This novel is profoundly marked by the libido and by the dictatorship of certain complexes, the heritage of infancy, which never surpass the tragic sphere and which do not escape from the individual entity. Nevertheless, the terror of time appears under another psychological aspect through the influence of Jung and the vast perspectives which his theory opens in regard to the collective unconscious, according to which each individual is the scene of a permanent battle between mythical time and historical time. As a consequence, one can speak of an *existential* psychology (I refer, one should understand, to the application of psychology to the novel) based on psychoanalysis, and an *essential* psychology, based on the theory of Jung.

This reference deserves clarification. According to Freud, the unconscious is formed by "the crumbs fallen from the table of the conscious." For Jung, the unconscious is something much more important, and its roots are not, so to speak, existential but essential. This means that our interior world has a much more ample base than that of the strictly personal experiences realized by the individual in the period of infancy and that, in general, our behavior is influenced by innate experiences belonging to a psychic inheritance that precedes the individual and that is related directly to his lineage and race. This whole ancestral complex is called, according to the theory of Jung about our interior world, "the collective unconscious." How did Jung arrive at this important conclusion? Examining the dreams and deliriums of his patients, the great psychologist of Zurich observed that individuals having no relationship with each other can have similar dreams and deliriums. Even more: the images produced by the dreams of his patients have a visible tie to the myths of primitive peoples who still exist or even have disappeared. Upon comparing this impressive coincidence between that which we dream and that which men of other ages have considered the foundation of their societies and cultures, Jung characterizes all these common manifestations as archetypes. Consequently, if for Freud the unconscious was the survival of infancy in the life of the adult, for Jung the collective unconscious is the survival of the traditionally religious in the life of the civilized man. This distinction is very important because the archetypes constitute true "psychic organs" which have formed through the centuries owing to the contact of the psychic being with the universe, in the same way that our corporeal organs have formed during the lengthy contact of our body with the physical forces of the universe. As one can see, this is matter for an anti-idealist theory, since if these psychic or physical organs have adapted themselves in the course of time to certain exterior factors, this is proof that the exterior reality exists and is not only a projection of the subject, as the idealist philosophers affirmed.

Concepts like soul, intuition, and interiority acquire in this fashion a metaphysical significance to which the psychoanalysis of Freud, whose contempt for philosophy is the most important reason for the limitation of his theory to pathology and psychotherapy, could not aspire.

The echo which the theories of Jung have managed to evoke in the philosophy of religions and in literature has been extremely important, and it can well be said that a very clear line of division separates those writers, psychologists, and sociologists who during the last forty years have followed Freud or Jung. The impact of psychoanalysis upon literature has been decisive and, including the North American novelists of recent generations, a whole current of literature has lived under the influence of Freud. Logically enough, psychoanalytical resonances can also be noticed in Sartre and the other existentialists. The influence of Jung is as yet less visible, since the scandal mounted by existentialism has falsified the literary perspective of our time.

Mircea Eliade's novel *Forêt Interdite*, whose mythic signification is evident, also belongs to the current inspired by the depth psychology of Jung. Eliade's book can be defined as the meditation of a man upon the thousand-year history of his people, with all the risks and calamities that this implies. Like Stefan Viziru, the protagonist of *Forêt Interdite*, the Romanian people live a double drama: on the traditional plane they are forced to remain outside history in order to evade the consequences of historical time, a technique that they have followed since they formed themselves as a people and, surely, also before; another force, however, has incited them to participate in history since the time they were integrated into the Western conception of life in 1848.

That fragment of the Romanian people which has remained loyal to the traditional conception, and, situated on the mythical plane, refuses civilization (we refer to the peasants), has the opportunity of saving itself from any disaster, since disasters occur only in historical time. The other fragment (the bourgeoisie and the workers), who became entangled in history, are being destroyed by it. In effect the bourgeoisie has been smashed during recent years. The workers will be destroyed also: if they remain a part of Romanian society they will lose their identity, but it is impossible for them to return to the traditional ways of life.

What takes place in Mircea Eliade's novel? Here also the action is developed on two distinct planes. On the historical plane the the writer Ciru Partenie (the temporal alter ego of Stefan Viziru) and Ioana, the wife of Viziru, both personifications of Romanian humanity situated in full historical time, are carried along and destroyed by events. On the plane of tradition, Viziru, who symbolizes Romanian man tempted to flee from history and to realize himself beyond it in the traditional conception toward which Anisie (the symbol of age-old peasant wisdom) pushes him, and Ileana (the woman whom Viziru loves because, as in the ancient stories, it had been predestined for him) meet again at the end of the novel to disappear together in a death which is not destruction but self-realization in the myth. The coach which Viziru sees when he meets Ileana for the first time, a coach which does not exist in reality, will be the instrument or the means which will facilitate the evasion of time for the two. At the moment when the image of the coach is confused with the image of Ileana, never to be separated from her, Stefan Viziru achieves his first victory over historical time. It is clear that the vision is atemporal, prophetic, and possible only on the basis of the cyclical conception of history. The other people cannot see the coach, since integration into a progressive conception of time excludes the possibility of visionary sight. Prophecy is impossible within unrepeatable time.

This is the ideal schematic structure of Eliade's novel. In its more than six hundred pages a total Romanian universe is set in motion in the period which began around 1935 and ended in 1945 with the victory of the communists. We participate in those anguished years before the war, in the life of Bucharest, in the epoch of Carol II, in the tragedy of the Iron Guard, in the entrance of Europe into war, in the bombing of London, in the revolution of the Iron Guard, in the earthquake of 1940, in the war in Russia, in the bombing of Bucharest in 1944, in the entrance of the Russians into the country, and in the first years of exile. Two decades of Romanian history vibrate in these dense pages, which seem at times a living and powerful literary fresco worthy of the most vigorous naturalism. Beyond what can be described, however, is the obsession with the time for killing and the time that saves, each one resolved on different planes.

In the same way in which he knows how to assimilate the most interesting aspects of the contemporary novel, Eliade revivifies the art of the Romanian novel and allows one to glimpse what contemporary Romanian writers might have been able to accomplish if present-day literature in Romania were not subjected to the unreal exigencies of socialist realism.

The conclusion of the book – self-realization in death, but in a death which is not an end but a myth, or perhaps a completion in, or a return to, an immortal essence – might seem pessimistic. But it is not such – at least not for the reader initiated into Eliade's philosophy or for one who accepts that point of view. We do not believe that the escape from time might bestow salvation upon us, as the end of the novel suggests to us. We do not believe that refuge in the myth can be a solution. "You have made me terribly sad. You have made me sad unto death," says Father Bursuc to Viziru after having listened to his lengthy confession, whose drama resides in the interior struggle of the protagonist, in the conflict between his situation in historical time, in the end inescapable, and his eagerness for an extratemporal perfection. They are words which any reader would be inclined to direct to Eliade upon closing the last page of the book. The character of Father Bursuc is also perfectly realized. He is a fellow apparently malleable, bland, at the same time for God and for the devil, for the Church and for the communists; his mission, however, is important in that area in which the Church can be a form of resistance – the only permitted. This Bursuc, who pretends not to believe in anything but whose intervention is efficacious and permanent in a world conquered by evil, is the only personage who resists the provocation of time in a Christian manner, or, if you will, actively, at times with a sibylline quality – the symbol perhaps of a fifth column profoundly injected into the flesh of communism. His dialogues with Viziru are truly works of art and at times recall Dostoevsky, especially in some pages of *The Brothers Karamazov*.

Invitations to the world of mystery follow each other without interruption in Eliade's novel. Here are some examples: "Il faut chercher à échapper au Temps, à sortir du Temps. Regardez bien autour de vous: de tous côtés vous sont faits des signes. Avez confiance dans les signes, suivez-les. . . ." Further on are found these fragments in which Stefan Viziru describes his encounter with the philosopher Anisie and explains his system:

It is necessary to escape from time, to leave time. Look around you well: There are signs ready for you on all sides. Have confidence in the signs, follow them. . . . This man has discovered a great mystery. He has learned how time passes. He has divined at the same time what he can do to prevent time from going further. . . . Ever since then . . . he no longer lives, like us, according to a more or less complicated schedule. He only takes cosmic time into account: the day, the night, the phases of the moon, the seasons. And even that cosmic time, according to what he said to me, will one day be abolished for him. In listening he must find the metaphysical significance of the word: to take cognizance of its being in its plenitude and its integrity. Nothing more can now distract him or anymore impede his living each essential moment of that cosmic time. For him, the new moon or the full moon, the equinoxes and the solstices, the twilight of the dawn and of the evening are no longer, as they are for us, a simple function of the dates on a calendar. Each of these moments reveals to him a new aspect of the All, of the Cosmos. He accepts no time outside cosmic time and above all he refuses historical time, that time in which, for example, parliamentary elections, the rearmament measures taken by Hitler, or the engagements of the Spanish Civil War are enacted. He has decided to take into account only that time in which cosmic events are inserted: the revolution of the moon, the succession of the seasons, the rotation of the earth. He is content to experience the significance of each one of those grand events. . . . For him Nature starts to become not only transparent, but also the bearer of values. It is not a question of returning to the primitive, let us say bestial, state of humanity. He discovers in Nature not that emptiness of spirit which certain ones among us look for there, but the key to the first metaphysical revelations: the mystery of death and resurrection, the mystery of the passage from being to non-being. And this man who is nearly at the beginning of his experience has already succeeded in escaping from time. Not only from historical time . . . but from physiological time. Although he is some years older than us, he seems ten years younger.

As can be seen, we are invited to go back to Babylonian practices, to the age in which, while the astronomers were discovering the cosmic rhythm, the play of the turning and returning of the stars, they imagined that the life of man follows the same rhythm and that everything that passes by appears again at the same point in the universe: the stars and men. It was when such ideas, together with Iranian literature, became the basis for the cyclical theory of history that it traveled onward to fecundate the folklore of all people and to transform itself into the philosophy of distant peasant civilizations.

To choose cosmic time is all right, but how shall the man of today in the midst of his cities, where the moon is often invisible, manage to situate himself in this "prohibited forest"; how shall he cease to belong to his own civilization in order to integrate himself, body and soul, with another? Neither Mircea Eliade, Mario Meunier, nor the rest of the authors who investigate other styles of life, whether exotic or simply non-Western, tell us this.

All right: our civilization kills time, it is a daily assassin of our peronal time. It carries us at fantastic velocity outside life. But how shall it be avoided? A simple invitation is not sufficient. The philosopher Anisie lived in the country, among flowers and bees, and this allowed him to elude historical time as does any peasant. But for the man of the city, the man who lives in Los Angeles, Paris, Bucharest, Moscow, or Buenos Aires: how will it be possible for him to separate himself from history, to live the cosmic time, to imitate Nature when he has ceased to see her, when his greatest desire is to transform her and not to imitate her? It is as though one were to say to the Argentinians, the Colombians, and the Venezuelans: "Return to Indoamerica!" This is now no longer possible. And besides, to make such a tremendous effort only in order to appear ten years younger: no, the merchandise is not worth the price.

The time for killing, the time that slays. . . . The solution is not in eluding a situation which, in conformity with the traditional cyclical conception, can return again upon us, but in leaving this time for killing, exhausting it, carrying it onward to its conclusion, like the heroes of Malraux. Only thus shall we one day find ourselves beyond it.

Returning to Jung, without whose schema it is difficult to understand Eliade's novel, I find it logical to relate this "prohibited forest," the symbol of a definitive realization in the beyond, in what Eliade himself called in another novel "the celestial marriage," to the Jungian "Mandala." If in effect we conceive the human drama, in general, as the search for equilibrium, according to a process of individualization, it is evident that "to dream in the forest"[2] means that one has arrived at interior equilibrium, at a final phase in a process of psychological healing. And *healing* here means *salvation*, in the most spiritual sense possible. "Santé" and "salut," in French, imply the same finality. And it seems important to me to indicate, at the end of these notes concerning Eliade's novel, that the "prohibited forest," the collective myth of Romanian history, the image of a general salvation (the forest was the place where the Romanians saved themselves during the invasions of the barbarians), represents here a perfect psychic ideal, the visible form of a goal reached in the inner self of the two personages in the novel.

These aspects of Eliade's novel place it in a privileged position with respect to the writing of contemporary novels because it has been worked out according to a plan of the *visible-invisible*, historical, psychological, and metaphysical which few novelists have yet been able to achieve. There is in it a germ of the human totality which rejects and annihilates any partiality or partisanship, signs of the contemporary mediocrity of those who cannot maintain the complex and honest mentality of a philosopher of religions. From this point of view, and because he is who he is, Mircea Eliade is a novelist of the future.

[2] "Soñar con el bosque."

TIME AND DESTINY IN THE NOVELS OF MIRCEA ELIADE

GEORGE USCATESCU

The bipolar, creative personality of Mircea Eliade has uniquely demonstrated a successive attraction for and alienation from the history of religions and ethnological problems, as well as from epic creativity, properly speaking. Nevertheless, a final resolution of an almost ontological nature of this complex personality is possible: of someone who, with surprising facility, produces treatises on the philosophy of religion, essays, literary criticism, memoirs, a diary, research concerning an original theme in reference to myths and symbols, and novels on an ample scale. Eliade as a creative person is easily inclined toward confessional tones and testimonies. His "diary," or autobiographical comments, offers us the necessary keys, destined finally to unlock his personality. There are numerous pages which offer us a vision conjoined with his work and his personality and a sense of himself in complete totality. Speaking one time of his spiritual experiences in India, he writes in his diary of April 21, 1963:

> [I am] astonished at the discoveries that I make in regard to my novels, *Isabel* and *The Quenched Light*. The latter, unreadable, monotonous, unfulfilled – suddenly reveals itself to me as an unconscious reaction against India, a desperate attempt to defend myself against myself – since I had decided in the summer of 1930 to hinduize myself, to lose myself in the Hindu masses. The mystery of the light – that incomprehensible fire which rages one night in the library and which provokes, among other things, the blindness and disorganization of the librarian – was, ultimately, the "mystery" of my existence in regard to Dasgupta. There are very many things about which I know that I do not have the

right to speak. I could, nevertheless, add a typed page, specifying that these notations will never be published.

The resolution which Eliade himself offers us carries the final significance of his work to the field of literature. His concern becomes a type of leitmotiv in his autobiographical pages and in his diaries.

Gide's fear and that of so many other writers at the beginning of the century of becoming *littérateurs*. On account of that Gide searched for life and later on discovered a social conscience. J. P. Sartre continues the same tradition: "literature" must reflect the historically concrete, have cognizance of the social and political. My liberation from "literature" by means of the history of religions and ethnology corresponds to the same tendency: for me this is *real*, not "literature." Because of that the critic who might see in my scientific work an inclination toward the erudite would be mistaken. It is a question of something completely different: of a world that seems to me more real, more alive, than the characters in a novel or novels.

Likewise, on another occasion, Eliade, armed with the weapons of literature and science in a determined search for the *real*, confesses to us:

I realize now that for almost ten years I have sacrificed literature also; I have renounced writing novels (the only literary genre that was suitable to my talent). I have done it in order to inculcate a new comprehension of *homo religiosus*. In a certain sense I have given testimony in a religious war that I knew was lost beforehand."

Thus, the literary work of Mircea Eliade presents itself to us open to a global understanding, through the well-armed and lucid critical spirit of its author. We misjudge the creative personality of this Romanian author if we place the accent exclusively on his vast and solid scientific work. The fundamental elements of his complex subject in the field of scholarship, the search for and comprehension of *homo religiosus*, are present in his literary creation: Mythos, Eros, Thanatos, and Logos are the fundamental resolutions of his literary themes. They are themes which are parallel to Eliade's scientific investigations as a historian of religions; the predominant accent, however, is never philosophical or erudite, but rather literary and artistic. His literary creativity goes *pari passu* with his scientific erudition, and both, in a certain way, reflect the preoccupation of those moments which correspond to the grasping of reality. It is not necessary to seek in one of the forms the means for completing the other; rather, the search should be for a modality which expresses in another way the spiritual disquiet of the author in search of an expressive, creative plenitude.

For that reason we believe that Eliade's literary work (comprehending those moments when he is not on the heights of the solitude of his other productivity – the scientific) offers some profiles of the whole, independently including the themes that are common to the themes of his work as philosopher and essayist and leaving us free from any dogmatic and theoretical freight in an aesthetic experience with its own dignity and economy.

It is important that it should be thus since the extent of Eliade's literary productivity is noteworthy. The first long novels, *Isabel și Apele Diavolului* (1930) and *Maitreyi* (1933), draw their inspiration from Indian themes of a strong erotic character and reveal in the hands of a new author both a solid technique and understanding which assures significant success to the works. His novelistic creativity continues with *Intoarcerea din Rai* (1934), *Huliganii* (1935), *Domnișoara Christina* (1936), *Șarpele* (1937), *Nuntă în Cer* (1939), and *Secretul Doctorului Honigberger* (1940). Contemporaneously with these appears his first scientific work, concerning mythic and religious elements, which, together with his literary work, constitutes an ample fresco of a reality that ideally combines the imaginative with the social and truly historical. In his lucid, penetrating, and intelligent spirit, myth and destiny occupy an important place. Both can be followed and interpreted from the basis of a methodology centered in a "*coincidentia oppositorum*" which will culminate in the field of literature, years later, in the great novel *Forêt Interdite* (1955) and the volume of short stories, *Nuvele* (1963), which are enormously suggestive for the study of the aesthetic economy of Eliade's literary creativity.

His studious tenacity regarding the reality, so actual and passionate, of myths in contemporary sensibility is dominated by another problem which is not precisely that of myth. It is the problem of time, which, in the most significant part of his literary work, he takes delight in presenting as a novelesque theme. In this he follows a particular tradition of Romanian spirituality whose supreme personification is the poet Mihail Eminescu. In Eminescu the problem of time occupies a basic place. Eliade is conscious of that and proclaims in his memoirs, "I discover with surprise how profoundly Eminescu has meditated upon the problem of time."

In Eliade this problem acquires forms of "pathos," and his work thus offers us motifs for reflections of great significance. Time is drama, a dominating drama which extends like an ample veil of melancholy upon the destiny of the characters. In this sense Eliade is a spirit perfectly identified with the sensibility of his age. Although tension has always existed between spirit and the objective reality of the surrounding world, very seldom before our time has man felt with greater dramatic intensity the weight of time upon his destiny. Our age is characterized by the disjunction of beliefs, the hopeless crisis of desires, and the absence of possibilities for completeness – in a word, by the typical state of spiritual crisis. In few previous circumstances has the terrible weight of time been felt as such an inexorable limit and implacable finitude upon human dimensions.

The contemporary novel, which is the instrument in its turn of the expression of a vast feeling of crisis, has undoubtedly been and continues to be one of the most suggestive means for extending this pervasive sense of crisis as a tragic sense of time. In relation to the same area of experience, if the novel is lacking in the passionate quality which surrounds the most original and strained philosophical current of today, existentialism, it abounds, on the other hand, in the plastic and suggestive means by which the drama of time flowing in a hopeless rhythm on an irreversible course may make itself more obvious, more living, and more tragic than ever for us. There is no lack of symbolism in the fact that the first great contemporary fresco of epic dimensions bears the title "A la recherche du temps perdu."

Certainly, it is owing to this typical tension that there exists the formal schematization of the most characteristic and discussed contemporary novelistic technique, the drama of time. Expressed as finitude, of the time without hope, incapable of illuminating itself in the flame of an eternal light, and, as a consequence, incapable of avoiding its own imperfection, this is a drama of modest formal perspectives which does not permit great flights and grand human convulsions. The drama of time displays the paradox of obsessive introspection translated into symbols in the enormous novels contained in the twenty-four hours of the life of a character, typically reflected in the *Ulysses* of Joyce. One day in the life of Mr. Bloom is told to us in 1,200 pages. "The super capacity for hypertrophic expression," writes Hermann Broch, "to which the writer is condemned expresses the incapacity for expression in a world condemned to muteness."

We encounter precisely this central problem in Eliade's great novel *Forêt Interdite*, whose original title in Romanian, *Noapte de Sânziene* ("Night of Saint John"), we consider much more suggestive. Eliade's great novel appears after fifteen years of epic silence. Some of the themes from his novels of the thirties return, but the technique, thematic extent, inspiration, poetic elements, and above all the atmosphere, offer appreciable novelties. It is probable that one day criticism will truly judge to what extent this great novel offers a moment of creative fulfillment without which it would be impossible to explain the essential character of the literary and philosophical creativity of the Romanian author. This novel reveals to us an Eliade at the fullest unfolding of his epic faculties and establishes for the reader a problematical situation of great literary authenticity and verisimilitude, independent of his scientific productivity concerning similar themes. From another point of view, it would be difficult and to a certain extent absurd to analyze this novel and to evaluate the position which it occupies in relation to the contemporary novel (which searches for its boundary situation in the "*nouveau roman*" or in the novel of "silence" of Samuel Beckett or Robbe-Grillet), apart from its author's background as historian and philosopher of religions, distiller of myths, and taster of symbols. Unsatisfied with the historicistic solutions and little disposed to admit any determinism in cultural solutions, Eliade is a writer capable of constructing in the more than seven hundred difficult pages of a very moving novel a world which lives with unaccustomed intensity the contingent reality, projected in the dimensions of symbol, myth, and a sublime necessity for escape. The drama of time lived as finitude, as boundary and Nemesis, and at the same time the tension of life desiring a symbolic dimension, the search for a magic transtemporal feeling in our existence: all these things he presents to us suddenly, using technical literary devices of a modern character in a contemporary mode in a narrative whose calm but firm rhythm does not weaken for a single moment. This is a magnificent novel, the best and most complete in the work of Mircea Eliade.

In a real sense Eliade manages with great skill and mastery, employing living personages who fulfill their destiny on the developed technical plane of the twentieth century and who live their daily existence in Bucharest, London, Lisbon, and Paris in the foreground and whirlwind of great cities. He gives a living, true form to the myths, inserting them perfectly into the destiny of his characters, vivifying them with situations and places, to create a fantastic world as permanent watchman over reality. This time it is very possible that Eliade has reached the ideal of his activity on the most varied levels: the stylistic interpenetration of the sacred and the profane, the dissolution of the fantastic in the real. In his scholarly studies the theme may be said to appear as the leitmotiv for his literary work. Speaking one time of his novel *Șarpele*, he himself anticipates an explanation for us:

> Without knowing it, without desiring it, I have succeeded in showing in *Şarpele* what was going to develop later on in my work in philosophy and history of religions. Apparently, "the sacred" is not distinguished from "the profane," the "fantastic" camouflages itself in the "real," and the world is that which it appears to be and is at the same time a key. The same dialectic – evidently in the context of an epic fresco of large proportions – also sustains *Forêt Interdite*, begun twelve years later in 1949, with the difference that this time it is not a question of the profound meanings in the Cosmos but of the "key" to historical events. The theme of the camouflage of the fantastic in the daily event is found again in some novellas written much later, for example in "La Ţigaňci" (written in 1959 and published in the volume *Nuvele* [Madrid, 1963]) and "The Bridge" (1964). In a certain sense one could say that this theme constitutes the central element in all my mature writings.

In the work *Forêt Interdite*, Eliade offers us proof that to create an original novel at a moment in which the novel as genre appears to have exhausted its possibilities, the author is not necessarily obliged to revert either to the procedure of reporting or to the utopian and futuristic procedure – or to any of that kind of schematization born in reality from the surrealistic tradition.

The original and truly perfected aspects of Mircea Eliade's novel are multiple. Some of these are reflected in the creation of some extraordinary figures who constitute a curious and revelatory antithesis essential to the novel, like that of Vadastra, the solemn gnome, ridiculous but radically sympathetic, who spouts his dicta without plausible reasons on the first level of the action of the drama. Another such character is the no less extraordinary Mrs. Zissu, who is present, we could say, in the destiny of the protagonists of the novel without anyone's knowing truly whether or not she has existed in any form other than that of Circe, the temptress. Yet another example is that solitary prince of the mountains, the wise man Anisie, whose presence is a fountain of unquenchable fable making. All these personages accentuate the atmosphere of the fantastic in the work of Eliade and integrate its typical "*Labyrinth-Erlebniss*" in the destiny of the characters. Without doubt, the labyrinthine construction constitutes one of the essential characteristics of Eliade's epic creation. It reaches its plenitude in the admirable short novel "La Tigañci" a perfect example of the labyrinthine way of life which characterizes the existence of the protagonists. It is a determining factor in Eliade's own destiny and an important element in the technique of the writer.

As we said before, however, that which gives force and authenticity to *Forêt Interdite* is the drama which its central character, Stefan Viziru, lives. It is through him that the drama and conjunction of means which move the novel itself, in its living architecture, in its atmosphere, in its style, and in the drama of time, come to exist. This drama is worked out with magnificent possibilities and resources by the author. But what is most impressive is the fact that by means of the author's permanent, intelligent, and lucid self-control, an atmosphere of lyricism, an ineffable poetry, pervades the drama. This makes of Eliade a worthy and noble tributary to the highest expression of Romanian spirituality. The technique of the novel is managed with undebatable mastery; the author uses the most competent means and is always alert before the almost inevitable interferences of the philosopher in the novelesque structure and those no less inevitable exhalations of a lyricism consubstantial with the world to which it belongs. The novel never becomes for a single moment one of ideology or simply of philosophical "thesis"; it is never dominated by those poetic accents easily produced by the siren song of myth, symbol, and the desire to break the mystery of time. Two revelatory moments that we are pleased to point out here constitute the implicit foundation of the novel, but they are not for that reason less charged with dignity. The first is the page that one of the characters discovers in a book of Hindu mythology, which we judge as a type of motif in the novel: the problem of avoiding time and the means of reconciling this evasion with history itself. This is a theme deeply loved and repeatedly handled by the creative consciousness of this Romanian writer, who has presented it many times in order to transfigure it in very original epic terms. The second is the episode of the torture of one of the characters, the professor of philosophy Biris, by the communist police, who try to make him reveal a supposed message from the national conspiracy against communism. Already in agony, the professor limits himself to the recitation of a sublime message capable of breaking the limits of time and death. This "message" is the popular Romanian poem "Mioritza," to which Eliade refers so many times with sensibility and effect in his studies of ethnology.

"Since you speak of time," Professor Biris says in the first episode we are referred to,

I am going to tell you a legend of India which I read this morning. It is the story of a famous ascetic who was called Narada. Impressed by his holiness, Viṣṇu promised to satisfy any of his desires. "Teach me the secret of your power, the incomprehensible Maya," the hermit asked him. Viṣṇu made a sign to him that he should follow. After a little while, as they were walking along a deserted path in the full heat of the sun and were thirsty, Viṣṇu asked him to go to a neighboring village and bring water. The deity remained waiting for him at the edge of the road. Narada hastened and called at the gate of the first house he found. A young girl opened it. She was so beautiful that, upon seeing her, Narada forgot the reason for his visit. He entered the house and the whole family received him with the honors due a holy man. He remained as a guest of those people for a long time. Finally he married the beautiful young girl and knew the happiness of married life and the good and bad fortune that is woven into the existence of a laborer. And so the years passed. Narada had three sons and at the death of his father-in-law became master of his lands. But in the twelfth year torrential rains flooded the region. In a single night his sheep drowned and his house fell down. Holding up his wife with one arm and with the other his two older sons and carrying the small one on his back, he then went forward with difficulty in the waves. But the burden was too heavy. The boy he carried on his shoulder slipped and fell into the water. Narada abandoned everything and threw himself into the flood to try to reach him. But it was too late. The wave had drowned the boy in a few seconds. Meanwhile his two others sons and wife drowned. Narada himself fell exhausted and his body floated unconscious like a piece of wood on the water. When he awoke, abandoned by the wave upon a rock, he remembered all his adventures and began to cry. But suddenly he heard a familiar voice: "My son, where is the water that you were to bring me? I have been waiting for at least half an hour!" Narada turned his head. In place of the flood that had destroyed everything, he saw only the desert landscape, brilliant under the midday sun. "Have you understood now the mystery of my power?" Viṣṇu asked him. "Have you understood in what Maya consists?"

The second revelatory episode equally implies the imperious necessity of escaping from the time and historical existence which constitute the principal problem of the novel. But there is in it besides, as we have said, a lyrical accent, a sweet atmosphere of poetry which penetrates the most beautiful pages of this novel like a distant, uncontainable song. Professor Biris, who is dying, tortured to the farthest extremity of human suffering, calls out to his jailers that he will reveal the message of the supposed conspiracy in which they think him to be implicated. To the consternation of his implacable guards, he recites the immortal verses of the popular Romanian ballad "Mioritza": "At the foot of the mountain, at the gate of Paradise, it is here that they come along the path. They descend toward the valley. There are three flocks of sheep with three young shepherds." And the verses follow: the integral poetic text of a sublime transfiguration of life in death, of time in eternity, a true solution of the problem of time. Insofar as he is a scholar, Eliade is very familiar with the theme. It appears almost as a permanent tendency in his studies each time that he approaches the subject matter of the philosophy of Romanian culture through mythic elements. Ultimately Eliade places in relief the importance the "Mioritza" has had in the evolution of those modern Romanian intellectuals who have seen in the depth of the poem—this affirmation is important from the pen of a specialist in the history of religions and in the significance of myths—something more than "magico-religious beliefs and practices." In the protagonist of the poem, the shepherd who awaits death with a serene resignation and prepares himself for it as for a supreme act of "cosmic liturgy," Eliade sees someone who by his attitude transcends fatalism, the act of pure contemplation, and the concept of nemesis-pessimism. The primordial basis of the poem has the nature of an oracle; the protagonist of the drama accepts his destiny—already outlined and known to him—clearly and serenely, without any ambiguity. But there is something more important in the significance of the poem. It is the fact that "the Romanian cultural elites have recognized themselves in the destiny" of the protagonist. Eliade proclaims at the same time the nobility and dignity of a Romanian intellectual consciousness of what is absurd: an unspeakable creative grandeur. This creative intellectual consciousness knows the terms of its tragic historical nemesis. It knows that history is against it; nevertheless, it never stops proposing a change in the tragically contrary feeling of this nemesis, "continuing to create and believe in culture as though that history, disposed to destroy and annihilate its creative efforts, did not exist. The Romanian creative act, Eliade concludes, "is compatible with the cry of the shepherd of 'Mioritza' who exalts his own death in nuptial terms." It is natural that with this consciousness Eliade should introduce the terms of this very beautiful myth into his idea of destiny and time which inspires the poetic foundation of his novel *Forêt Interdite*. Because of this, we might say that the elements of the popular poem help him in a certain fashion in his search for a solution to the problem of time, a question of principal importance in the economy of his novel.

This solution is found implicitly in Eliade's novel. The destiny of his principal protagonists, the logical culmination of the tension of their terrestrial existences, allows each one of them to glimpse the open horizons of a necessary plenitude. There is in their glance a last moment of infinite duration. In that instant they find all the hours of desire and suffering of a tormented existence illuminated by supreme beatitude. They are tormented precisely by the problem of time which is a problem lived as a unique drama, a vast metaphysical drama, a tormented existential drama in other circumstances. It contains tragic possibilities of prescinding such other dramas of existence as humiliations, physical and moral sufferings, the loss of beloved beings, and love itself in all its complicated web of manifestations.

Certainly these are not the only relevant aspects of Mircea Eliade's magnificent and unique novel *Forêt Interdite*, an accomplished narrative synthesis of the fantastic and the real in history and myth through the tortured drama of the human existence of its characters. But the aspect that we have wanted to point out, the desire for plenitude achieved by means of escape from time, the background music for epic action majestically woven, allows this important work of Eliade, which opens a new stage and wide perspectives in his literary activity, to be a positive presence in the writing of novels at this time. In addition, it also offers a proof that the so-called crisis of the novel is not definitive, much less without solution.

BEGINNINGS OF A FRIENDSHIP

E. M. CIORAN

It was around 1932 when I first met Eliade in Bucharest, where I had just completed a hazy course of studies in philosophy. In those days the "new generation"—a magical term we proudly invoked—idolized him. We scorned the "old duffers" and "dot-ers"—anyone over thirty, that is. Our mentor was waging war against them; he would take aim and fell them one by one. Rarely did he fire wild, as in the case of his attack on Tudor Arghezi, a great poet whose only failing was that he had been recognized, consecrated. The struggle between generations seemed to us the key to all conflicts, the explanatory formula of every event. Being young was, in our eyes, a certificate of genius. I am aware that such conceit is an historical invariable, but I believe our generation outstripped all previous ones. This self-infatuation denoted our chafing will to create History, our craving to squeeze into it and, above all, renovate it from within. Frenzy was the fashion, and in whom had it been embodied? In someone who had recently returned from India, the very land which had always turned its back on history, on chronology, on process as such. I should not make an issue of this paradox if it did not bear witness to a deep-seated duality characteristic of Eliade, who is drawn, with equal attraction, to essence and to accident, to the intemporal and to the daily, to the mystical and to literature. This duality does not entail any self-mutilation: it is his nature and luck to be able to live simultaneously or by turns on different spiritual levels, to be able, without dramatic soul-searching, to study ecstasy and pursue the anecdotal.

Even in those early days I was already astonished that he could fathom the Sankhya (on which he had published a long essay) and take an interest in the latest novel. I have never stopped being intrigued by the spectacle of a mind so hugely and breathlessly inquisitive that in anyone but him it would be pathological. There is nothing in his composition of the monomaniac's glum obstinacy, nothing of the obsessed man who squats in some one field, dismissing everything outside as secondary and frivolous. The sole obsession I have discerned in him, his polygraphy (and even it has abated with age), is really the reverse of one, as it reflects a mind led by its insatiable hunger for exploration to seize on all subjects. There was one man whom Eliade used to admire passionately—Nicolas Iorga, the Romanian historian, an extraordinary figure, fascinating and disconcerting, who had written more than a thousand works, lively in patches but generally turgid, ill-constructed, unreadable, full of intuitions clogged in the mire. And Eliade admired him the way one admires the elements, a forest, the sea, the fields, fertility for its own sake, everything that sprouts, proliferates, invades, and asserts itself. He is still prey to the superstition of vitality, of productivity. I may be going out on a limb, but I have every reason to believe that subconsciously he places books above the gods. He has made a cult of them. At any rate, I know no one who loves them as much as he. Never will I forget his haste to touch them, to caress them, to riffle through them when he landed in Paris soon after the Liberation. In bookstores he exulted, he *officiated*; it was voodooism, idolatry. That much enthusiasm implies a great fund of generosity, for without it one could not appreciate profusion, exuberance, prodigality—qualities by which the mind imitates nature and surpasses it. I have never been able to read Balzac, never, that is, since my early adolescence. His is a world closed to me, inaccessible; I have never been able to enter it, and I am loathe to. How many times has Eliade sought to convert me! He had read *The Human Comedy* in Bucharest; he reread it in Paris in 1947 and, for all I know, he is rereading it now in Chicago. He has always loved the ample novel, swarming, unfolding on several levels in unison with the "infinite" melody, conveying the massive presence of time, accumulating details and complex, divergent themes. On the other hand, he shuns whatever smacks of *exercise* in Letters, the anemic and refined sport so dear to esthetes, the gamy, exquisitely rotten side of certain productions devoid of sap and of instinct. But there is another way of explaining his passion for Balzac. We can divide minds into two categories: those that love process and those that love result. The former fasten onto the unfolding of things, onto stages and the successive expression of thought or of action, while the latter are riveted by final expressions to the exclusion of all else. Tempermentally I have always leaned toward the latter—toward a Chamfort, a Joubert, a Lichtenberg, who hand you some formula without disclosing the path that led them to it. They cannot, for reasons of modesty or of sterility, tear themselves free from the superstition of brevity. They would like to encapsulate everything in a page, a sentence, a word; sometimes they succeed, but it must be said, rarely. Laconism must resign itself to silence if it hopes to avoid the pitfall of spuriously enigmatic depth. All the same, the person who loves this quintessentialized, or, if you prefer, sclerotic, form of expression has difficulty weaning himself away from it and loving some other. He who has long associated with the moralists is at pains to understand Balzac, yet he can guess what reasons motivate those who do have a weakness for him, who see in him a universe and derive from his work a sensation of life, of expansiveness, of freedom unknown to the fancier of maxims (a minor genre in which perfection and asphyxia cannot be told apart).

However clear Eliade's liking for vast syntheses, nonetheless he could have excelled in the fragment, in the short, fulgurating essay; the fact is, he did excel in it, as his early works—those myriad brief texts he published before and after his voyage to India—demonstrate. In 1927 and 1928 he contributed regularly to a daily newspaper in Bucharest. At the time I lived in a provincial town where I was completing high school. The paper arrived at 11 A.M. During recess I would rush to the newsstand to buy a copy, and it was thus I familiarized myself with more or less weird names like Asvaghosha, Ksoma de Körös, Buonaiuti, Eugenio d'Ors, and many others. I much preferred the articles on foreigners because their works, nowhere to be found in my small town, impressed me as mysterious and definitive; happiness for me amounted to the hope of reading them one day. I thereby placed disappointment out of reach whereas, with native writers, I had it near at hand. What erudition, what verve and strength were poured into those articles of a single day's duration! I am convinced that they were palpitating with interest and that I am not seeing their value enhanced through the distorting glass of memory. I read them as an enthusiast to be sure, but as a lucid enthusiast. What I especially prized in them was the young Eliade's gift of making ideas contagious and vibrant, of investing them with a halo of hysteria, but positive, stimulating, sane hysteria. Obviously this gift belongs only to youth, yet even if one preserved it in afteryears, one would not care to exercise it when broaching the subject of history of religions. Nowhere did it burst forth more brilliantly than in the "Letters to a Provincial" which Eliade wrote upon his return from India and which appeared serially in the same daily. I doubt that I missed a single one of those letters. I read them all; in fact we all read them, for they concerned us, they were addressed to us. Usually we were each of us singled out, and we awaited our turn. One day mine came. I was issued nothing more or less than a global invitation to liquidate my obsessions, to cease raiding the periodical magazines with my sepulchral ideas, to give some thought to problems other than death, my fixation then as now. Was I supposed to meekly accept a verdict like that? I wasn't about to. I discarded every other problem as unworthy of consideration; indeed, I had just published a text on "the vision of death in Nordic art" and I fully intended to persevere in that same direction. Inwardly I reproached my friend for not identifying himself with something, for wanting to be *all* because he couldn't be some one thing, for being incapable, in short, of fanaticism, of delirium, of "depth," which I understood as the ability to deliver oneself to a mania and cling to it. I believed that one could be *something* only by adopting, whole-cloth, an attitude—thereby eschewing availability, pirouettes, constant self-renewal. In my eyes the primordial duty of a mind was to forge a world of its own, a narrowly defined absolute, and to burrow in with all its might. This amounted to the idea of *engagement* if you like, but *engagement* with the inner life as its sole object—a commitment to oneself and not to others. I reproached Eliade for being elusive on account of his openness, his mobility, his enthusiasm. I also reproached him for having interests other than India; it seemed to me that India could effectively supplant everything else, that it was beneath him to fiddle about with other matters. All of these grievances crystallized in an article "The Fateless Man," whose title was purposely surly, in which I inveighed against the versatility of this mind I admired, against his inability to root himself in one idea. I showed the deficiency of his every virtue (the classic method of being unjust and disloyal to someone); I blamed him for being the master of his moods and passions, for being able to handle them tactically, for conjuring away the tragic, and for being unaware of "fatality." This frontal assault blunted its purpose by being too general: it could have been aimed at anyone. Why should a theoretical mind, a man summoned by his problems, figure as a hero or a knave? There is no concrete affinity between ideas and tragedy. But I felt at the time that every idea had to embody itself or else wax into a scream. Persuaded as I was that discouragement signified awakening and knowledge, I begrudged my friend his optimism, his interest in the manifold, his self-squandery in activity which I found incompatible with the demands of true knowledge. Because I was abulic, I considered myself more sophisticated than he, as if my abulia had been the result of some spiritual conquest or of a willful act of wisdom. I recall telling him one day that, to have preserved so much freshness and confidence (and so much innocence as well) he must have fed on nothing but grass in some former life. I could not forgive him for making me feel older than he; I held him responsible for my spleen and my defeats, and it seemed to me that he had gained his hopes by robbing me of mine. How could he bound about in so many disparate realms? His inquisitiveness, in which I saw the work of a demon or, like Saint Augustine, a "malady," was the axe I invariably ground against him. But with him it was, far from being a "malady," a sign of health. And I reproached him for his health and yet envied it. This calls for a somewhat indiscreet digression.

I doubt that I would have written "The Fateless Man" if not for one particular circumstance. We had a woman friend in common, a highly talented actress who, unhappily for her, was haunted by metaphysical problems. Her obsessions were to cripple her career and her talent. On stage, in the middle of a soliloquy or a dialogue, her underlying concerns would catch her by surprise, invade her, lay hold of her mind, and whatever she was in the midst of reciting would suddenly strike her as unbearably inane. Her acting suffered as a consequence. She had too much integrity to be able to, or want to, fake her way through. She wasn't dismissed; she was merely given minor, insignificant roles which could not upset her in the least. She availed herself of this opportunity to give full vent to her questioning and speculative tastes, freighting them with all the passion she had hitherto brought to bear on acting. Seeking answers, she turned, in her distress, to Eliade, and then, less inspired, to me. One day he could stand no more of it, rebuffed her, and would not see her again. She came to pour her resentment into my ear. After that I saw her often; I let her talk, I listened. She was dazzling, to be sure, but so monopolizing, so cloying, so insistent that, feeling fed up and fascinated after each of our meetings, I would invariably make for the nearest bar and get drunk. Imagine a peasant (for she was entirely self-taught, having been raised in a remote village) speaking to you of Nothingness with such unheard-of brio and fervor! She had learned several languages, dabbled in theosophy, acquainted herself with the major poets, and experienced quite a few reversals. None of them, however, had affected her so profoundly as this last. Her virtues, like her torments, were such that, at the beginning of our friendship, it seemed to me inexplicable and inadmissible that Eliade could have treated her so cavalierly. Finding his behavior toward her dastardly, I avenged her with "The Fateless Man." When the article appeared on the front page of a weekly, she was delighted with it, read it aloud in my presence as if it was some deathless monologue, and then analyzed the text paragraph by paragraph. "You have never written anything better" she said to me — a displaced compliment she was really paying herself, for wasn't it she who had, in a sense, provoked the article and furnished me its ingredients? In time I came to appreciate Eliade's weariness and exasperation, and the outlandishness of my biased assault. He never held it against me, however, and even found it all rather amusing. This trait deserves special mention, for experience has taught me that writers — people endowed with prodigious memories — are capable of making any sacrifice for you except when it comes to forgiving, to forgetting some rather too penetrating thrust.

It was during this same period that he began to lecture at the Faculty of Letters in Bucharest. I attended whenever I could. The fervor he lavished on his articles was evident in his lessons as well — the most lively and vibrant I have ever heard. Without notes, empty-handed, carried away in a vortex of lyric erudition, he would convulsively, yet coherently, fling his words, underlining them with jerky hand gestures. One hour of tension after which, miraculously, he did not appear exhausted, and perhaps wasn't. It was as if he possessed the art of withstanding fatigue indefinitely. Everything *negative*, everything that promotes self-destruction on the physical as well as the spiritual plane, was then, and still is, foreign to him—whence his inaptitude for resignation, for remorse, for despair, for all feelings that imply the bogged-down, the rut, the nonfuture. Again, I may be going out on a limb, but I believe that if he has perfect understanding of sin, he lacks a sense of it: he is too feverish for that, too dynamic, too hurried, too full of projects, too intoxicated with the possible. People possessed of this sense are the kind who chew over their past endlessly, who take root in it and cannot tear themselves free, who flail themselves with invented faults through some need to torture their consciences, and who enjoy musing over the memory of any shameful or irreparable act they have committed or, even better, wanted to commit. We are back to the obsessed. They alone have time to descend into the pit of remorse, to vacation there, to wallow in it. They alone are formed of the stuff that makes a genuine Christian, that is, someone gnawed, ravaged, beset with the unhealthy desire to be a reprobate, yet managing all the same to overcome that desire—his victory (never total) being the measure of what he calls "having faith." Ever since Pascal and Kierkegaard, we can no longer conceive of "salvation" without a retinue of infirmities, without the secret delights of the inner drama. Now more than ever, with "accursedness" in fashion (where literature is concerned), everyone is expected to live in anguish and reprobation. But can a learned man be *accursed*? Why should he be? Doesn't he know too much to be able to condescend to hell, to the narrow circles of hell? It is unhappily the case with us that only the dark sides of Christianity still strike a chord. Perhaps, to rediscover the essence of Christianity, we would have to see it clothed in *black*. If such an image, such a version is the true one, then Eliade stands, from all evidence, on the periphery of this religion. But perhaps he stands on the periphery of *every* religion, by profession as well as by conviction. Is he not one of the most brilliant representatives of a new alexandrianism which, like the old, places all beliefs on the same level, without being able to choose some one? Having refused to marshal them into a hierarchy, how can one be partial? Which belief can one sponsor;

which divinity can one invoke? It is impossible to imagine a specialist in the history of religions *praying*. Or, if indeed he does pray, he thus betrays his teaching, he contradicts himself, he damages his *Treatises* in which no *true* god figures, all the gods being viewed as equivalent. It is futile to describe them and comment upon them with insight; he cannot blow life into them, having tapped them of their sap, compared them with one another, and, to complete their misery, frayed them with rubbing until they are reduced to bloodless symbols useless to the believer, assuming that at this stage of erudition, disillusion, and irony there is somebody around who still truly believes. We are all of us, and Eliade in the fore, *would-have-been* believers; we are all religious minds without religion.

CURRICULUM VITAE

Mircea Eliade was born in Bucharest, Romania, on March 9, 1907. After completing the *lycée*, he entered the University of Bucharest in 1925 and took his M.A. in 1928 with a dissertation on Italian philosophy from Ficino to Giordano Bruno. Obtaining a scholarship from the Maharajah Sir Manindra Chandra Nundy of Kasimbazar, Eliade was able to live in India from 1928 to 1932. He studied Sanskrit and Indian philosophy with Professor Surendranath Dasgupta at the University of Calcutta. After another six months in the *ashram* of Rishikesh (Himalaya), Eliade returned to Romania. In 1933 he took his Ph.D. with a dissertation on Yoga, and was appointed Assistant Professor in the Faculty of Letters at the University of Bucharest. In 1940, Eliade was sent to the Romanian Legation in London as cultural attaché, and in 1941 was transferred to the Legation in Lisbon, where he remained until 1945. In 1945 he went to Paris as a visiting professor at the Ecole des Hautes Etudes of the Sorbonne. He also lectured in many European universities. In the autumn of 1956, Mircea Eliade was invited to deliver the Haskell Lectures at the University of Chicago; in 1957 he became a regular professor of History of Religions and in 1962 he was appointed the Sewell L. Avery Distinguished Service Professor at the same university.

BIBLIOGRAPHY OF MIRCEA ELIADE

I. BOOKS

Romanian

Isabel şi Apele Diavolului ("Isabel and the Devil's Waters"). Bucharest: Editura Naţionala Ciornei, 1930. 236 pp.

Soliloquii ("Soliloquies"). Bucharest: Editura Cartea cu Semne, 1932. 83 pp.

Intr'o mânăstire din Himalaya ("In a Himalayan Monastery"). Bucharest: Editura Cartea Românească, 1932. 32 pp.

Maitreyi ("Maitreyi"). Bucharest: Editura Cultura Naţională, 1933. 266 pp.

Intoarcerea din Rai ("The Return from Paradise"). Bucharest: Editura Naţionala-Ciornei, 1934. 419 pp.

Lumina ce se stinge ("The Light Which Fails"). Bucharest: Editura Cartea Românească, 1934. 414 pp.

Oceanografie ("Oceanography"). Bucharest: Editura Cultura Poporului, 1934. 304 pp.

India. Bucharest: Editura Cugetarea, 1934. 279 pp.

Alchimia Asiatică ("Asiatic Alchemy"). Bucharest: Editura Cultura Poporului, 1934. 76 pp.

Şantier ("Work in Progress"). Bucharest: Editura Cugetarea, 1935. 276 pp.

Huliganii ("The Hooligans"). 2 vols. Bucharest: Editura Naţionala-Ciornei, 1935. 270 and 280 pp.

Domnişoara Christina ("Mademoiselle Christina"). Bucharest: Editura Cultura Naţională, 1936. 260 pp.

Şarpele ("The Snake"). Bucharest: Editura Naţionala-Ciornei, 1937. 240 pp.

Scrieri literare, morale şi politice de B. P. Hasdeu ("Literary, Moral, and Political Writings by B. P. Hasdeu"). 2 vols. Bucharest: Editura Fundaţia Regală pentru Artă şi Literatură, 1937. 473 and 420 pp.

Cosmologie şi Alchimie babiloniană ("Babylonian Cosmology and Alchemy"). Bucharest: Editura Vremea, 1937. 136 pp.

Nuntă în Cer ("Marriage in Heaven"). Bucharest: Editura Cugetarea, 1938. 280 pp.

Fragmentarium ("Essays"). Bucharest: Editura Vremea, 1939. 160 pp.

Secretul Doctorului Honigberger ("The Secret of Dr. Honigberger"), (includes "Nopți la Serampore" ["Night in Serampore"]). Bucharest: Editura Socec, 1940. 190 pp.

Mitul Reintegrării ("The Myth of Reintegration"). Bucharest: Editura Vremea, 1942. 110 pp.

Salazar și revoluția în Portugalia ("Salazar and the Revolution in Portugal"). Bucharest: Editura Gorjan, 1942. 247 pp.

Comentarii la legenda Meșterului Manole ("Commentaries on the Legend of Master Manole"). Bucharest: Editura Publicom, 1943. 144 pp.

Insula lui Euthanasius ("The Island of Euthanasius"). Bucharest: Editura Fundația Regală pentru Artă și Literatură, 1943. 382 pp.

Iphigenia (a play). Valle Hermoso: Editura Cartea Pribegiei, 1951. 172 pp.

Nuvele ("Short Stories"). Madrid: Editura Destin, 1963. 152 pp.

Amintiri: I. Mansarda ("An Autobiography: I. The Attic"). Madrid: Editura Destin, 1966. 176 pp.

Pe strada Mântuleasa ("Mântuleasa Street"). Paris: Caietele Inorugului, II, 1968. 129 pp.

Translations into Romanian

T. E. Lawrence, *Revolta în deșert* ("Revolt in the Desert"). 2 vols. Bucharest: Editura Fundația Regală pentru Literatură și Artă, 1934. 250 and 230 pp.

Pearl Buck, *Inger Luptător* ("Fighting Angel"). Bucharest: Editura Fundația Regală pentru Literatură și Artă, 1939. 280 pp.

French

Yoga. Essai sur les Origines de la Mystique Indienne. Paris: Librairie Orientaliste Paul Geuthner, 1936. 346 pp.

Techniques du Yoga. Collection "La Montagne Sainte-Geneviève." Paris: Gallimard, 1948. 266 pp.

Traité d'Histoire des Religions. Preface by Georges Dumézil. Paris: Payot, 1949. 405 pp.

Le Mythe de l'Eternel Retour. Collection "Les Essais," XXXIV. Paris: Gallimard, 1949. 254 pp.

La Nuit Bengali. Translation of *Maitreyi* from the Romanian by A. Guillermou. Collection "La Méridienne." Paris: Gallimard, 1950. 260 pp.

Le Chamanisme et les Techniques Archaïques de l'Extase. Paris: Payot, 1951. 450 pp.

Images et Symboles. Essais sur le Symbolisme Magico-Religieux. Collection "Les Essais," LX. Paris: Gallimard, 1952. 240 pp.

Le Yoga. Immortalité et Liberté. Paris: Payot, 1954. 428 pp.

Forêt Interdite. Translation from the Romanian manuscript by A. Guillermou. Collection "Du Monde Entier," CLX. Paris: Gallimard, 1955. 640 pp.

Forgerons et Alchimistes. Collection "Homo Sapiens." Paris: Flammarion, 1956. 212 pp.

Minuit à Serampore (with "Le Secret du Docteur Honigberger"). Translation of *Nächte in Serampore* from the German by Albert-Marie Schmidt. Paris: Librairie Stock, 1956. 244 pp.

Mythes, Rêves et Mystères. Collection "Les Essais," LXXXIV. Paris: Gallimard, 1957. 312 pp.

Naissances Mystiques. Essais sur Quelques Types d'Initiation. Collection "Les Essais," XCII. Paris: Gallimard, 1959. 276 pp.

Méphistophélès et l'Androgyne. Collection "Les Essais," CIII. Paris: Gallimard, 1962. 280 pp.

Patañjali et le Yoga. Collection "Maîtres Spirituels." Paris: Editions du Seuil, 1962. 190 pp.

Aspects du Mythe. Collection "Idées," no. 32. Paris: Gallimard, 1963. 250 pp.

Le Sacré et le Profane. Collection "Idées," no. 76. Paris: Gallimard, 1965. 188 pp.

English

Metallurgy, Magic and Alchemy. Cahiers de Zalmoxis, I. Paris: Librairie Orientaliste Paul Geuthner, 1938. 48 pp.

The Myth of the Eternal Return. Translation of *Le Mythe de l'Eternel Retour* from the French by Willard R. Trask. Bollingen Series XLVI. New York: Routledge and Kegan Paul, 1955. 208 pp. Reprinted with new Preface as *Cosmos and History.* New York: Harper Torchbooks, 1959.

Patterns in Comparative Religion. Translation of *Traité d'Histoire des Religions* from the French by Rosemary Sheed. London and New York: Sheed and Ward, 1958. 484 pp.

Birth and Rebirth. The Religious Meaning of Initiation in Human Culture. Translation of *Naissances Mystiques* from the French by Willard R. Trask. New York: Harper and Brothers; London: Harvill Press, 1958. 190 pp. Reprinted as *Rites and Symbols of Initiation.* New York: Harper Torchbooks, 1965.

Yoga. Immortality and Freedom. Translation of *Le Yoga. Immortalité et Liberté* from the French by Willard R. Trask. Bollingen Series LVI. New York and London: Routledge and Kegan Paul, 1958. 552 pp.

The Sacred and the Profane. The Nature of Religion. Translation of *Le Sacré et le Profane* from the French by Willard R. Trask. New York: Harcourt, Brace and Company, 1959. 254 pp.

Myths, Dreams and Mysteries. Translation of *Mythes, Rêves et Mystères* from the French by Philip Mairet. With Foreword to English translation. New York: Harper and Brothers; London: Harvill Press, 1960. 256 pp.

Images and Symbols. Studies in Religious Symbolism. Translation of *Images et Symboles* from the French by Philip Mairet. New York: Sheed and Ward; London: Harvill Press, 1961. 190 pp.

The Forge and the Crucible. Translation of *Forgerons et Alchimistes* from the French by Stephen Corrin. London: Ridder and Company; New York: Harper and Brothers, 1962. 208 pp.

Myth and Reality. Translation of *Aspects du Mythe* from the French by Willard R. Trask. World Perspective, XXXI. New York: Harper and Row, 1963; London: George Allen and Unwin, 1964. 204 pp.

Shamanism: Archaic Techniques of Ecstasy. Translation of *Le Chamanisme et les Techniques Archaïques de l'Extase* from the French by Willard R.

Trask. Bollingen Series LXXVI. New York and London: Routledge and Kegan Paul, 1964. 634 pp.

Mephistopheles and the Androgyne: Studies in Religious Myth and Symbol. Translation of *Méphistophélès et l'Androgyne* from the French by J. M. Cohen. New York: Sheed and Ward, 1965. 224 pp. Also published as *The Two and the One.* London: Harvill Press, 1965.

From Primitives to Zen. A Thematic Sourcebook on the History of Religions. London: Collins; New York: Harper and Row, 1967. 670 pp.

German

Das Mädchen Maitreyi. Translation of *Maitreyi* from the Romanian by Günther Spaltmann. Munich: Nymphenbürger, 1948. 227 pp.

Andronic und die Schlange. Translation of *Şarpele* from the Romanian by Günther Spaltmann. Munich: Nymphenbürger Verlagshandlung, 1949. 152 pp.

Nächte in Serampore. Translation of *Secretul Doctorului Honigberger* from the Romanian by Günther Spaltmann. Munich-Planegg: Otto-Wilhelm-Barth-Verlag, 1953. 178 pp.

Der Mythos der ewigen Wiederkehr. Translation of *Le Mythe de l'Eternel Retour* from the French by Günther Spaltmann. Düsseldorf: Eugen Diederichs Verlag, 1953. 252 pp. Reprinted as *Kosmos und Geschichte.* Munich: Rowohlt Deutsche Enzyklopädie, no. 260, 1966. 148 pp.

Die Religionen und das Heilige. Elemente der Religionsgeschichte. Translation of *Traité d'Histoire des Religions* from the French by M. Rassem and I. Köck. Munich: Otto Müller Verlag, 1954. 601 pp.

Das Heilige und das Profane. Vom Wesen des Religiösen. Translation of *Le Sacré et le Profane* from the French. Munich: Rowohlt Deutsche Enzyklopädie, 1957. 154 pp.

Schamanismus und archaische Ekstasentechnik. Translation of *Le Chamanisme et les Techniques Archaïques de l'Extase* from the French by Inge Köck. Zurich and Stuttgart: Rascher Verlag, 1957. 472 pp.

Ewige Bilder und Sinnbilder. Translation of *Images et Symboles* from the French by Theodor Sapper. Olten and Freiburg im Breisgau: Walter Verlag, 1958. 264 pp.

Yoga. Unsterblichkeit und Freiheit. Translation of *Le Yoga. Immortalité et Liberté* from the French by Inge Köck. Zurich and Stuttgart: Rascher Verlag, 1960. 515 pp.

Schmiede und Alchemisten. Translation of *Forgerons et Alchimistes* from the French by Emma von Pelet. Stuttgart: Ernst Klett Verlag, 1960. 249 pp.

Mythen, Träume und Mysterium. Translation of *Mythes, Rêves et Mystères* from the French by Michael Benedikt and Matthias Vereno. Salzburg: Otto Müller Verlag, 1961. 344 pp.

Das Mysterium der Wiedergeburt. Initiationsriten, ihre kulturelle und religiöse Bedeutung. Translation of *Naissances Mystiques. Essais sur Quelques Types d'Initiation* from the French by Emile Hoffmann. Zurich and Stuttgart: Rascher Verlag, 1961. 264 pp.

Spanish

Los Rumanos. Breviario historico. Madrid: Editorial Stylos (Publicaciones del Instituto Rumano de Cultura), 1943. 95 pp.

La Noche Bengali. Translation of *La Nuit Bengali* from the French by Manuel Peyrou. Collección "Grandes Novelistas." Buenos Aires: Emecé Editores, 1951. 194 pp.

El Mito del Eterno Retorno. Translation of *Le Mythe de l'Eternel Retour* from the French by Ricardo Anaya. Collección "Grandes Ensayistas." Buenos Aires: Emecé Editores, 1952. 188 pp.

Tratado de Historia de las Religiones. Translation of *Traité d'Histoire des Religions* from the French by A. Madinaveitia. Madrid: Biblioteca de Cuestiones Actuales, Instituto de Estudio Politicos, 1954. 453 pp.

Imágenes y Simbolos. Translation of *Images et Symboles* from the French by Carmen Castro. Madrid: Ediciones Taurus, 1955. 196 pp.

Yoga, Immortalidad y libertad. Translation of *Le Yoga. Immortalié et Liberté* from the French by Susana de Aldecoa. Buenos Aires: Ediciones Leviatan, 1957. 439 pp.

Herreros y Alquimistas. Translation of *Forgerons et Alchimistes* from the French by the publisher. Madrid: Taurus, 1959. 211 pp.

El Chamanismo y las técnicas arcaicas del éxtasis. Translation of *Le Chamanisme et les Techniques Archaïques de l'Extase* from the French by Ernestina de Campourcin, revised by Lauro José Zavala. Mexico City and Buenos Aires: Fondo de Cultura Economica, 1960. 454 pp.

Tecnicas del Yoga. Translation of *Techniques du Yoga* from the French by Oscar Andrieu. Buenos Aires: Compañía General Fabril Editora, 1961. 232 pp.

Mitos, Sueños y Misterios. Translation of *Mythes, Rêves et Mystères* from the French by Lysandro Z. D. Galtier. Buenos Aires: Compañía General Fabril Editora, 1961. 277 pp.

Lo Sagrado y lo Profano. Translation of *Le Sacré et le Profane* from the French by Luis Gil. Madrid: Ediciones Guadarama, 1967. 231 pp.

Mito y Realidad. Translation of *Aspects du Mythe* from the French by Luis Gil. Madrid: Ediciones Guadarama, 1968. 239 pp.

Italian

Passione a Calcutta. Translation of *Maitreyi* from the Romanian by Giovanna Calvieri Caroncini. Rome: Casa Editrice "La Caravella," 1945. 221 pp.

Tecniche dello Yoga. Translation of *Techniques du Yoga* from the French by Anna Macchioro de Martino. Turin: Edizioni Einaudi, 1952. 232 pp.

Lo Sciamanismo e le tecniche dell'estasi. Translation of *Le Chamanisme et les Techniques Archaïques de l'Extase* from the French by C. d'Altavilla. Rome and Milan: Fratelli Bocca Editori, 1953. 378 pp.

Trattato di Storia delle Religioni. Translation of *Traité d'Histoire des Religions* from the French by Virginia Vacca. Turin: Edizioni Einaudi, 1954. 538 pp.

Il Sacro e il Profano. Translation of *Le Sacré et le Profane* from the French by Edoardo Fadini. Turin: Paolo Boringhieri, 1967. 171 pp.

Mito e Realtà. Translation of *Aspects du Mythe* from the French by Giovanni Cantoni. Turin. Borla Editore, 1966. 252 pp.

Il mito dell'eterno ritorno. Translation of *Le Mythe de l'Eternel Retour* from the French by Giovanni Cantoni. Turin: Borla Editore, 1968. 205 pp.

Portuguese

Os Romenos, Latinos do Oriente. Translation from the French manuscript by Eugénio Navarro. Collecçao "Gládio." Lisbon: Livraria Classica Editora, 1943. 95 pp.

Noite Bengali. Translation of *Maitreyi* from the Romanian by Maria Leonor Buesco. Lisbon: Editora Ulisseia, 1961. 230 pp.

O Sagrado e o Profano. A Essencia das Religiões. Translation of *Le Sacré et le Profane* from the French by Rogério Fernandes. Lisbon: Livros do Brasil, 1962. 174 pp.

Bosque proibido. Translation of *Forêt Interdite* from the French by Maria Leonor Buescu. Lisbon: Editura Ulisseia, 1963. 621 pp.

Dutch

Het gewijde en het profane. Een studie over de religieuze essentie. Translation of *Le Sacré et le Profane* from the French by Hans Andreus. Hilversum: C. de Boer Jr. / Paul Brand, 1962. 133 pp.

Beelden en symbolen. Opstellen over symboliek in magie en godsdienst. Translation of *Images et Symboles. Essais sur le Symbolisme Magico-Religieux* from the French by Anton Monshouwer. Hilversum: C. de Boer Jr. / Paul Brand, 1963. 173 pp.

De Mythe van de eeuwige terugkeer. Translation of *Le Mythe de l'Eternel Retour* from the French by Anton Monshouwer. Hilversum: C. de Boer Jr. / Paul Brand, 1964. 165 pp.

Danish

Helligt og Profant. Translation of *Le Sacré et le Profane* from the French by Gerda Lipowsky and Carl Nielsen. Copenhagen: Biilmann and Eriksen, 1965. 152 pp.

Myten om den evige tilbagekomst. Translation of *Le Mythe de l'Eternel Retour* from the French by Vagn Duekilde. Munksgaardserien, no. 19. Copenhagen: Munksgaard, 1966. 177 pp.

Swedish

Heligt och profant. Translation of *Le Sacré et le Profane* from the French by Alf Ahlberg. Stockholm: A. B. Verbum, 1968. 205 pp.

Greek

Kosmos kai Istoria. O mythos tes aenaoy epanalepsieos. Translation of *Le Mythe de l'Eternel Retour* from the French by Themistokles Th. Lazakis. Athens, 1966. 160 pp.

Polish

Traktat o historii religii. Translation of *Traité d'Histoire des Religions* from the French by Jan Wierusz-Kowalski, with an Introduction by Leszek Kolakowski. Warsaw: Ksiażka i Wiedza, 1966. 556 pp.

Japanese

Ei-en kaiki no shinwa. Translation of *Le Mythe de l'Eternel Retour* from the French by Ichirō Hori. Tokyo: Miraisha, 1963. 236 pp.

Daichi, Nōkō, Josei. Abridged translation of *Patterns in Comparative Religion* by Ichirō Hori. Tokyo: Miraisha, 1968. 314 pp.

Works in Collaboration

Petru Comarnescu, Mircea Eliade, and Ionel Jianu. *Témoignages sur Brancusi*. Editions d'Art. Paris: Arted, 1967. 63 pp.

Edited Works

Nae Ionescu. *Roza Vânturilor*. (With Afterword by Mircea Eliade.) Bucharest: Cultura Națională, 1936. 458 pp.

Edited Works in Collaboration

Mircea Eliade and Joseph M. Kitagawa. *History of Religions: Essays in Methodology*. Chicago: University of Chicago Press, 1959. 164 pp. (German translation, 1963; Japanese translation, 1962.)

II. JOURNALS FOUNDED AND EDITED

Zalmoxis. Revue des Etudes Religieuses. Vols. 1–3. Paris: Librarie Orientaliste Paul Geuthner, 1938–42.

Antaios (with Ernst Jünger). Stuttgart: Klett Verlag, 1960–.

History of Religions (with J. M. Kitagawa and Charles Long). Chicago: University of Chicago Press, 1961–.

III. STUDIES, ESSAYS, AND ARTICLES

"Les religions des mystères dans les publications récentes." *Logos* 1 (Bucharest, 1928): 117–31.

"La vision chrétienne d'Ernesto Buonaiuti. A propos de ses derniers livres." *Ibid.*, pp. 283–92.

"Problematica filozofiei indiene: linii de orientare." *Revista de Filozofie* 15 (1930): 50–72.

"Introducere în filozofia Sâmkhya." *Ibid.*, pp. 152–75.

"Il male e la liberazione nella filosofia Sâmkhya-Yoga." *Ricerche Religiose* 6 (1930): 200–221.

"Contribuții la psihologia Yoga." *Revista de Filozofie* 16 (1931): 52–76.

"Cunoștințele botanice în vechea Indie." *Buletinul Societății de Științe din Cluj* 6 (1931): 221–37.

"Il Rituale Hindu e la vita interiore." *Richerche Religiose* 8 (1932): 486–504.
"America văzută de un tânăr de azi." *Revista Fundaţiilor Regale* 1 (1934): 196–201.
"Activitatea institutului de cultură comparată (Oslo)." *Ibid.*, 2 (1935): 116–39.
"Elemente pre-ariene în hinduism." *Ibid.*, 3 (1936): 149–73.
"Inainte de miracolul grec." *Ibid.*, pp. 397–402.
"Istoria medicinii în România." *Ibid.*, pp. 664–69.
"Muzeul satului romănesc." *Ibid.*, pp. 193–99.
"O carte despre moarte." *Ibid.*, pp. 439–45.
"Un nou fel de literatură revoluţionară." *Ibid.*, pp. 439–45.
"Despre o 'filozofie' a lunii." *Ibid.*, pp. 655–60.
"Despre o etică a 'Puterii.'" *Ibid.*, 4 (1937): 187–92.
"Câteva cărţi de istoria religiilor." *Ibid.*, pp. 422–31.
"Inainte şi după miracolul biblic." *Ibid.*, pp. 657–61.
"Folklorul ca instrument de cunoaştere." *Ibid.*, pp. 136–52.
"Ananda Coomaraswamy." *Ibid.*, pp. 183–89.
"Efemeride orientale." *Ibid.*, pp. 417–23.
"Barabudur, templul simbolic." *Ibid.*, pp. 605–17.
"Lo Yoga e la spiritualità indiana." *Asiatica* 3 (1937): 229–40.
"La moartea lui Rudolf Otto." *Revista Fundaţiilor Regale* 4 (1937): 676–79.
"Intre Elephantine şi Ierusalim." *Ibid.*, pp. 421–26.
"Demonologie indiană şi o legendă românească." *Ibid.*, pp. 644–49.
"Cosmical homology and Yoga." *Journal of the Indian Society of Oriental Art* 5 (1937): 188–203.
"Limbajele Secrete." *Revista Fundaţiilor Regale* 5 (1938): 124–41.
"Lucian Blaga şi sensul culturii." *Ibid.*, pp. 162–66.
"Un amănunt din Parsifal." *Ibid.*, pp. 422–26.
"Alegorie sau 'limbaj secret?'" *Ibid.*, pp. 616–32.
"Religia evreilor nomazi." *Ibid.*, pp. 171–75.
"Locum refrigerii." *Ibid.*, pp. 418–22.
"Viaţa unui 'maestru' Tibetan." *Ibid.*, pp. 668–71.
"Un savant rus despre literatura chineză (Basile Alexiev)." *Ibid.*, pp. 437–42.
"La concezione della libertà nel pensiero indiano." *Asiatica* 4 (1938): 345–54.
" 'Treptele' lui Julien Green." *Revista Fundaţiilor Regale* 6 (1939): 662–68.
"Cărţile populare în literatura românească." *Ibid.*, pp. 132–47.
"Moartea doctorului Gaster." *Ibid.*, pp. 395–99.
"Insula lui Euthanasius." *Ibid.*, pp. 100–109.
"Vechi controverse . . . (despre Paul-Louis Couchoud)." *Ibid.*, pp. 446–51.
"Simbolismul arborelui sacru." *Ibid.*, pp. 675–80.
"Mediterana şi Oceanul Indian." *Ibid.*, pp. 203–8.
"Piatra şerpilor." *Meşterul Manole* (1939): 1–12.
"Ierburile de sub cruce. . . ." *Revista Fundaţiilor Regale* 6 (1939): 353–69.
"Metallurgy, Magic and Alchemy." *Zalmoxis* 1 (1938): 85–129.
"Mélanges: I. Notes de démonologie; II. Locum refrigerii. . . ." *Ibid.*, pp. 197–208.
"Le culte de la mandragore en Roumanie." *Ibid.*, pp. 209–25.
"Comentarii italiene." *Revista Fundaţiilor Regale* 7 (1940): 189–94.
"Les livres populaires dans la littérature roumaine." *Zalmoxis* 2 (1939): 63–78.

"Notes sur le symbolisme aquatique." *Ibid.*, pp. 131–52.

"La Mandragore et les mythes de la 'naissance miraculeuse.'" *Zalmoxis* 3 (1940–42): 3–48.

"Dor, a saudade romena." *Acção*, no. 89, December 31, 1942.

"Cançoes romenos do Natal." *A Voz*, December 23, 1942.

"A lenda de Mestre Manole." *Acção*, no. 106, April 14, 1943.

"Un mito romeno da morte." *Ibid.*, no. 178, September 29, 1944.

"Le problème du chamanisme." *Revue de l'Histoire des Religions* 131 (1946): 5–52.

"Les sacrifices grecs et les rites des peuples primitifs." *Ibid.*, 133 (1947–48): 225–30.

"Le 'dieu lieur' et le symbolisme des noeuds." *Ibid.*, 134 (1947–48): 5–36.

"Science, idéalisme et phénomènes paranormaux." *Critique*, no. 23, April, 1948: 315–23.

"*Dūrohaṇa* and the 'waking dream.'" In *Art and Thought*, edited by K. Bharatha Iyer. London: Luzac, 1948. Pp. 209–13.

"La mythologie primitive." *Critique*, no. 27 (August, 1948): 708–17.

"Origines et diffusion de la civilisation." *Ibid.*, no. 29, October, 1948: 897–908.

"Pour une histoire générale des Religions indo-européennes." *Annales. Economies. Sociétés. Civilisations* 4 (1949): 183–91.

"La souveraineté et la religion indo-européennes." *Critique*, no. 35, April, 1949: 342–49.

"La Vigne mystique." *L'Amour de l'Art*, December, 1949: 39–45.

"Shamanism." In *Forgotten Religions*, edited by Vergilius Ferm. New York: Philosophical Library, 1949. Pp. 297–308.

"Sapta padani kramati." In *The Munshi Diamond Jubilee Commemoration Volume*, Part I: Bhāratīya Vidyā, vol. IX. Poona, 1949. Pp. 180–88.

"Phénoménologie de la Religion et Sociologie religieuse." *Critique*, no. 39, August, 1949: 713–20.

"Introduction au tantrisme." In *Approches de l'Inde.* Marseille: Cahiers du Sud, 1950. Pp. 132–44.

"Les Sept Pas du Bouddha." In *Pro Regno, Pro Sanctuario* (Hommage Van der Leeuw) edited by W. J. Kooiman and J. M. van Veen. Nijkerk, 1950. Pp. 169–75.

"Actualité de la Mythologie." *Critique*, no. 43, December, 1950: 236–43.

"Redécouverte du symbolisme." *Combat*, December 27, 1951.

"Le Dieu lointain dans les religions primitives." *Témoignages. Cahiers de la Pierre-qui-vire* 28 (1951): 22–27.

"Psychologie et Histoire des Religions: à propos du symbolisme du 'Centre.'" *Eranos-Jahrbuch* 19 (1951): 247–82.

"Einführende Betrachtungen über den Schamanismus." *Paideuma* 5 (1951): 87–97.

"Eléments chamaniques dans le Lamaïsme." *France-Asie*, no. 61/62, 1951: 96–106.

"Le Temps et l'Eternité dans la pansée indienne." *Eranos-Jahrbuch* 20 (1952): 219–52.

"Chasteté, sexualité et vie mystique chez les primitifs." *Mystique et Continence (Etudes Carmélitaines)*, (1952): 29–50.

"Symbolisme indien de l'abolition du temps." *Journal de Psychologie* 45 (1952): 430–38.

"Mythes indiens du Temps." *Combat*, March 13, 1952.

"Le Bouddhisme et l'Occident." *Ibid.*, August 7, 1952.

"Rencontre avec Jung." *Ibid.*, October 9, 1952.

"Le Symbolisme du 'Centre.'" *Revue de Culture Européenne* 2 (1952): 227–39.

"Mythe et Histoire dans la littérature orale." *Bulletin du Centre Roumain de Recherches* 1 (1952): 26–31.

"Mythes cosmogoniques et guérisons magiques." *Proceedings, Seventh Congress for the History of Religions*. Amsterdam, 1950. Pp. 180–81.

"Le symbolisme religieux et la valorisation de l'angoisse." In *L'Angoisse du temps présent et les devoirs de l'esprit*. Neufchatel: Editions de la Baconnière, 1953. Pp. 55–71.

"Le problème des origines du Yoga." In *Yoga. Science de l'homme intégral*. Marseille: Cahiers du Sud, 1953. Pp. 11–20.

"Chamanisme et techniques yogiques indiennes." *Ibid.*, pp. 98–115.

"Techniques de l'extase et langages secrets." In *Conferenze, Istituto Italiano per il medio ed estremo Oriente*, 2 vols. Rome, 1953. Vol. 2, pp. 57–79.

"Les mythes du monde moderne," *La Nouvelle Nouvelle Revue Française* 1 (1953): 440–58.

"Puissance et Sacralité dans l'histoire des religions." *Eranos-Jahrbuch* 22 (1953): 11–44.

"La Nostalgie du Paradis dans les Traditions primitives." *Diogène* 3 (1953): 31–45.

"Apport de la synthèse: René Grousset." *France-Asie*, no. 88/89, 1953: 827–29.

"Dos tradiciones culturales y la situacion actual de la cultura rumana." *Oriente* 3 (1953): 213–18.

"La Nostalgia del Paradiso nelle tradizioni primitive." *Diogène* 3 (1953): 279–91.

"La nostalgia del paraiso en las tradiciones primitives." *Diogène* 3 (1953): 33–46.

"The Yearning for Paradise in Primitive Tradition." *Diogenes* 3 (1953): 18–30.

"Das Heimweh nach dem Paradies in den Überlieferungen der primitiven Völker." *Diogenes* 3 (1954): 301–15.

"Expérience sensorielle et expérience mystique chez les primitifs." *Nos Sens et Dieu (Etudes Carmélitaines)*, (1954): 70–99.

"La Terre-Mère et les hiérogamies cosmiques." *Eranos-Jahrbuch* 22 (1954): 57–95.

"Symbolisme et histoire des religions." *Critique*, no. 83, April, 1954: 323–37.

"Psychology and Comparative Religion: A Study of the Symbolism of the Centre." In *Selection*, vol. 2, edited by Cecily Hastings and Donald Nicholl. London and New York: Sheed and Ward, 1954. Pp. 17–43.

"The Problem of the Origins of Yoga." In *Forms and Techniques of Altruistic and Spiritual Growth*, edited by Pitirim A. Sorokin. Boston: Beacon Press, 1954. Pp. 63–70.

"Shamanism and Indian Yoga Techniques." *Ibid.*, pp. 70–84.

"Les représentations de la Mort chez les primitifs." *La Mort et l'Au-delà* (*Témoignages. Cahiers de la Pierre-qui-vire*), no. 41, January, 1954: 166–74.

"Eranos." *Nimbus* 2 (1954): 57–58.

"Der Mythos der ewigen Wiederkehr." In *Handbuch der Weltgeschichte*, edited by Alexander Randa. 2 vols. Olten: Verlag Otto Walter, 1954. Vol. 1, 189–92.

"Die Mythen in der modernen Welt." *Merkur*, no. 78, August, 1954: 724–35.

"Los mitos en el mundo moderno." *La Torre* 2 (1954): 69–85.

"Les danseurs passent, la danse reste." *Du* 15 (1955): 60.

"Smiths, Shamans and Mystagogues." *East and West* 6 (1955): 206–15.

"Nouvel An, peau neuve." *Le Courrier* 8 (1955): 7–32. (As "Rituals and Symbols of Time Reborn," *The Courier*; as "Dias que prefiguran el Ano," *El Correo.*)

"Mythologie et histoire des religions." *Diogène* 9 (1955): 99–116.

"Terra Mater and Cosmic Hierogamies." *Spring* (1955): 15–40.

"Symbolisme et rituels métallurgiques babyloniens." In *Studien zur analytischen Psychologie C. G. Jung*, edited by C. G. Jung Institute, 2 vols. Zurich: Rascher Verlag, 1955. Vol. 2, pp. 42–46.

"Note sur Jung et l'Alchimie." *Le Disque Vert* (1955); 97–109.

"Note sur l'alchimie indienne." *Rencontre Orient-Occident* 1 (1955): 3–10.

"Mystère et régénération spirituelle dans les religions extra-européennes." *Eranos-Jahrbuch* 23 (1955): 57–98.

"Aspects initiatiques de l'Alchimie occidentale." *Archivio di Filosofia: Studi di Filosofia della Religione*, no. 2 (1955): 215–25.

"Le Mythe du Bon Sauvage." *La Nouvelle Nouvelle Revue Française* 3 (1955): 229–49.

"El Mito del buen salvage o los prestigios del origen." *La Torre* 3 (1955): 49–66.

"Note sur l'érotique mystique indienne." *La Table Ronde*, no. 97, January, 1956: 28–33.

"Littérature orale." In *Encyclopédie de la Pléiade*, edited by Raymond Queneau. *Histoire des Littératures. 1: Littératures anciennes orientales et orales* (Paris: Gallimard, 1956), pp. 3–26.

"Symbolisme du 'vol magique.'" *Numen* 3 (1956): 1–13.

"Les savants et les contes de fées." *La Nouvelle Nouvelle Revue Française* 4 (1956): 884–91.

"Terra Mater—Petra Genitrix." *La Tour Saint-Jacques* 5 (1956): 2–9.

"Masse und Mythos." In *Handbuch der Weltgeschichte*, edited by Alexander Randa. 2 vols. Olten: Verlag Otto Walter, 1956. Vol. 2, col. 2302–4.

"Kosmogonische Mythen und magische Heilungen." *Paideuma* 6 (1956): 194–204.

"Time and Eternity in Indian Thought." In *Man and Time*, edited by Joseph Campbell. Bollingen Series XXX. New York, 1957. Pp. 173–200.

"La funcion creadora del mito." *La Gaceta*, July, 1957.

"La vertu créatrice du mythe." *Eranos-Jahrbuch* 25 (1957): 59–85.

"Centre du Monde, Temple, Maison." In *Le Symbolisme Cosmique des Monuments Religieux*, ed. Guiseppe Tucci. Rome: Istituto Italiano per il Medio ed Estremo Oriente, 1957. Pp. 57-82.

"Manole et le Monastère d'Argeş." *Revue des Etudes Roumaines* 3–4 (1957): 7–28.

"Significations de la 'lumière intérieure.'" *Eranos-Jahbuch* 26 (1958): 189–242.

"Bi-Unité et Totalité dans la Pensée indienne." *Societas Academica Daco-Romana: Acta Philosophica et Theologica* 1 (1958): 1–7.

"Preistoria unui motiv folkloric românesc." *Buletinul Bibliotecii Române* 3 (1955/56): 41–54.

"Prestiges du mythe cosmogonique." *Diogène*, no. 23, 1958: 3–17.

"Prestigios del mito cosmogonico." *Diógenes* 6 (1958): 3–17.

"Scienza, idealismo e fenomeni paranormali." In E. de Martino, *Il Mondo magico*, 2d ed. Turin: Einaudi, 1958. Pp. 305–11.

"Religione dei Turco-Mongoli." *La Civiltā dell'Oriente* 3 (1958): 849–68.

"Mystique de la Lumière." *L'Age Nouveau*, November-December, 1958: 27–34.

"The Prestige of the Cosmogonic Myth." *Diogenes*, no. 23, 1958: 1–13. (Reprinted in *The Divinity School News* [University of Chicago], 26 [1959]: 1–12.)

"'Lupii' şi 'Lupoaica.'" *România*, February, 1959.

"Les Thèmes Initiatiques dans les Grandes Religions." *La Nouvelle Nouvelle Revue Française* 7 (1959): 390–407, 629–47.

"Der magische Flug." *Antaios* 1 (1959): 1–12.

"La *coincidentia oppositorum* et le mystère de la totalité." *Eranos-Jahrbuch* 27 (1959): 195–236.

"Les Daces et les loups." *Numen* 6 (1959): 15–31.

"Methodological Remarks on the Study of Religious Symbolism." In *The History of Religions: Essays in Methodology*, edited by Mircea Eliade and Joseph M. Kitagawa. Chicago: University of Chicago Press, 1959. Pp. 86–107.

"Structure et fonctions du mythe cosmogonique." In *La Naissance du Monde*. Paris: Edition du Seuil, 1959. Pp. 469–95.

"Etude comparative sur le 'Rope Trick.'" In *Akten des vierundzwanzigsten Internationalen Orientalistenkongress*, edited by Herbert Franke. Wiesbaden: Deutsche Morgenländishe, 1957. Pp. 562–64.

"The Yearning for Paradise in Primitive Tradition." (Reprinted from *Diogenes* 3 [1953] in *Daedalus* 88 [1959]: 255–67; in *Myth and Mythmaking*, edited by Henry A. Murray, New York: George Braziller, 1960 [pp. 61–75]; and in *The Making of Myth*, edited by Richard M. Ohmann. New York: G. P. Putnam's Sons, 1960 [pp. 84–98].)

"Le 'miracle de la corde' et la préhistoire du spectacle." *La Nouvelle Nouvelle Revue Française* 8 (1960): 682–93.

"Betrachtungen über religiöse Symbolik." *Antaios* 2 (1960): 1–12.

"Dimensions religieuses du Renouvellement cosmique." *Eranos-Jahrbuch* 28 (1960): 241–75.

"The Structure of Religious Symbolism." In *Proceedings of the IXth International Congress for the History of Religions*. Tokyo: Maruzen, 1960. Pp. 506–12.

"History and the Cyclical View of Time." *Perspectives* 5 (1960): 11–14.

"Spiritual Thread, sūtrātman, Catena aurea." Festgabe für Herman Lommel, edited by B. Schlerath and O. Harrassowitz. Wiesbaden, 1960. Pp. 47–56. (Reprinted in *The University of Chicago Committee on South Asian Studies*. Reprint Series, no. 9, 1960.)

"Les Américains en Océanie et le nudisme eschatologique." *La Nouvelle Revue Française* 8 (1960): 58–74.

"Alchemie und Zeitlichkeit." *Antaios* 2 (1960): 180–88.

"Encounters at Ascona." In *Spiritual Disciplines*, edited by Joseph Campbell. Bollingen Series XXX. New York: Pantheon Books, 1960. Pp. xvii–xxi.

"Structures and Changes in the History of Religion." In *City Invincible*. Chicago: University of Chicago Press, 1960. Pp. 351–66.

"Le symbolisme des ténèbres dans les religions archaïques." *Polarités du Symbole (Etudes Carmélitaines*, XXXIX), (1960): 15–28.

"Remarques sur le 'rope trick.'" In *Culture in History*, edited by Stanley Diamond. New York: Columbia University Press, 1960. Pp. 541–51.

"Divinità." *Enciclopedia Universale dell'Arte*. Rome: Istituto per la Collaborazione Culturale, 1960. Vol. 4, col. 361–366.

"Götter und Bilder." *Antaios* 2 (1961): 485–501.

"The Myths of the Modern World." *Jubilee* 8 (1961): 16–20.

"Un Nuevo humanismo." *La Gaceta*, April, 1961: 1, 6.

"Mythes et Symboles de la Corde." *Eranos-Jahrbuch* 29 (1961): 109–37.

"History of Religions and a New Humanism." *History of Religions* 1 (1961): 1–8. (Reprinted in *Criterion* 1 [1961]: 8–11.)

"Recent works on Shamanism. A review article." *History of Religions* 1 (1961): 152–86.

"Les Loups et les Daces, introduction à une histoire religieuse de la Dacie." *Revue des Etudes Roumaines* 7–8 (1961): 225–28.

"Die Amerikaner in Ozeanien und der eschatologische Nacktkult." *Antaios* 3 (1961): 201–14.

"Note pour un humanisme." *La Nouvelle Revue Française* 9 (1961): 872–78.

"Mythologies asiatiques et folklore sud-est européen: Le plongeon cosmogonique." *Revue de l'Histoire des Religions* 160 (1961): 157–212.

"Symbolika Środka. Studium religioznawcze." *Znak* 10 (1961): 1379–403.

"Le Créateur et son 'Ombre.'" *Eranos-Jahrbuch* 30 (1962): 211–39.

"Gedanken zu einem neuen Humanismus." *Antaios* 4 (1962): 113–19.

"Imágenes divinas y creacion artistica." *Philosophia* (Revista del Instituto de Filosofia, no. 25), (1962): 24–35.

"'Cargo-cults' and cosmic regeneration." In *Millennial Dreams in Action*, edited by Sylvia L. Thrupp. The Hague: Mouton, 1962. Pp. 139–43.

"Marginalien zum Wesen der Maske." *Antaios* 4 (1962): 396–404.

"Les élites modernes tentent de retrouver, par l'initiation, un monde perdu." *Arts*, December, 1962: 5–11.

"Repetizione della cosmogonia." In *Magia e Civiltà*, edited by E. de Martino. Milan: Garzanti Editore, 1962. Pp. 168–82.

"Survivances et camouflage des mythes." *Diogène*, no. 41, 1963: 3–27.

"Two spiritual traditions in Rumania." *Arena* 11 (1963): 15–25.

"Mythologies of Memory and Forgetting." *History of Religions* 2 (1963): 329–44.

"Mythologie de la mémoire et de l'oubli." *La Nouvelle Revue Française* 11 (1963): 597–620.
"La méthode de Roger Godel." In *Roger Godel, de l'humanisme à l'humain.* Paris: Les Belles Lettres, 1963. Pp. 99–105.
"The History of Religions in Retrospect: 1912–1962." *The Journal of Bible and Religion* 31 (1963): 98–109.
"Yoga and Modern Philosophy." *Journal of General Education* 15 (1963): 124–37.
"Maschera." *Enciclopedia Universale dell'Arte.* Rome, Istituto per la Collaborazione Culturale, 1963. Vol. 8, col. 877–82.
"Die Mythologie des Erinners und des Vergessens." *Antaios* 5 (1963): 28–48.
"Survivals and Camouflages of Myths." *Diogenes*, no. 41, 1963: 1–25.
"Beauty and Faith." In *Bridges of Human Understanding*, edited by John Nef. New York: University Publishers, 1964. Pp. 121–23.
"Mystery and Spiritual Regeneration in Extra-European Religions." In *Man and Transformation*, edited by Joseph Campbell. New York, Pantheon Books, 1964. Pp. 3–26.
"Die Suche nach den 'Ursprüngen der Religion.'" *Antaios* 6 (1964): 1–18.
"Introduction à l'étude des mythes." *Acta Philosophica et Theologica* 2 (1964): 145–59.
"Rosa del Conte: *Mihail Eminescu o dell'Assoluto.*" *Belfagor, Rassegna di varia umanità* 19 (1964): 367–71.
"Mythologie, Ontologie, Histoire." In *Festschrift für A. E. Jensen.* 2 vols. Munich, Klaus Renner, 1964. Vol. 1, pp. 123–33.
"The Quest for the 'Origins' of Religion." *History of Religions* 4 (1964): 154–69.
"Shamanism in Southeast Asia and Oceania." *International Journal of Parapsychology* 6 (1964): 329–61.
"Paradis et Utopie: Géographie mythique et eschatologie." *Eranos-Jahrbuch* 32 (1964): 211–34.
"Myth and Reality." In *Alienation: The Cultural Climate of Modern Man*, edited and with an introduction by Gerald Sykes. 2 vols. New York: George Braziller, 1964. Vol. 2, pp. 748–53.
"Sur la permanence du sacré dans l'art contemporain." *XXe siècle*, n.s., 26 (1964): 3–10.
"Los Sueños y las visiones de iniciacion entre los shamanes de Siberia." In *Los Sueños y las Sociedades Humanas*, edited by G. E. von Grunebaum. Buenos Aires, 1964. Pp. 417–30.
"The Oddest Graduate School in the U.S." *The University of Chicago Magazine* 57 (1965): 18–22.
"Archaic Myth and Historical Man." *McCormick Quarterly* (Special Supplement: *Myth and Modern Man)* 18 (1965): 23–36.
"Les mythes qui deviennent des idoles." *Janus* 5 (1965): 59–63.
"Notes sur le Journal d'Ernst Jünger." *Antaios* 6 (1965): 488–92.
"The Sacred and the Modern Artist." *Criterion* 4 (1965): 22–24.
"Crisis and Renewal in History of Religions." *History of Religions* 5 (1965): 1–17. (Reprinted in *New Theology No. 4*, edited by Martin E. Marty and Dean G. Peerman. New York: Macmillan, 1967. Pp. 19–38.)

"Mity a 'Mass-Media.'" *Współczesność* 8 (1965): 16–17.

"L'initiation et le monde moderne." In *Initiation*, edited by C. J. Bleeker. Leiden: E. J. Brill, 1965. Pp. 1–14.

"Notizen über das Heilige in der Modernen Kunst." *Antaios* 7 (1965): 305–9.

"L'orizzonte mitico della ballata di Mastro Manole." *Annali del Museo Pitré* 14–15 (1964): 80–94.

"In Memoriam: Paul Tillich." *Criterion* 5 (1966): 10–15.

"Paul Tillich and the History of Religions." In *The Future of Religions*, edited by Jerald C. Brauer. New York: Harper and Row, 1966. Pp. 31–36. (Revised text of article in *Criterion* 5 [1966].)

"Myths, Dreams and Mysteries." In *Myth and Symbol*, edited by F. W. Dillistone. London: Society for the Publication of Christian Knowledge, 1966. Pp. 35–50.

"Paradise and Utopia: Mythical Geography and Eschatology." In *Utopias and Utopian Thought*, edited by Frank E. Manuel. Boston: Houghton Mifflin, 1966. Pp. 260–80.

"Initiation Dreams and Visions among the Siberian Shamans." In *The Dream and Human Societies*, edited by G. E. von Grunebaum and Roger Caillois. Los Angeles and Berkeley: University of California Press, 1966. Pp. 331–40.

"W poszukiwaniu 'poczatków' religii." *Znak* 18 (1966): 899–913.

"Australian Religions, Part I: An Introduction." *History of Religions* 6 (1966): 108–34.

"Mitologias de la memoria y el olvido." *Estudios Orientales* 1 (1966): 3–23.

"Australian Religions, Part II; An Introduction." *History of Religions* 6 (1967): 208–35.

"Cosmogonic Myth and 'Sacred History.'" *Religious Studies* 2 (1967): 171–83.

"Australian Religions, Part III; Initiation Rites and Secret Cults." *History of Religions* 7 (1967): 61–90.

"Marc Chagall et l'amour du Cosmos." *XXe Siècle*, n.s., 29 (1967): 137–39.

"Rêves et vision initiatiques chez les chamans sibériens." In *Le rêve et les sociétés humaines*, edited by Roger Caillois and G. E. von Grunebaum. Paris: Gallimard, 1967. Pp. 315–23.

"Australian Religions, Part IV: The Medicine Men and Their Supernatural Models." *History of Religions* 7 (1967): 159–83.

"Significations du Mythe." In *Le Langage II*, edited by Societé de Philosophie de Langue Française. Geneva, 1966. Pp. 167–79.

"On Understanding Primitive Religions." In *Glaube Geist Geschichte*, Festschrift for Ernst Benz, edited by Gerhard Muller and Winfried Zeller. Leiden, E. J. Brill, 1967. Pp. 498–505.

"Briser le Toit de la Maison: Symbolisme Architectonique et Physiologie Subtile." In *Studies in Mysticism and Religion*, presented to Gershom G. Scholem, ed. E. E. Urbach, R. G. Zwi Werblowsky, Ch. Wirszubski. Jerusalem, Magnes Press, 1967. Pp. 131–39.

"Australian Religions, Part V: Death, Eschatology, and Some Conclusions." *History of Religions* 7 (1968): 244–68.

"Mythes de Combat et de Repos: Dyades et Polarités." *Eranos Jahrbuch* 36 (1968): 59–111.

"The Forge and the Crucible: A Postscript." *History of Religions* 8 (1968): 74–88.

"Notes on the Symbolism of the Arrow." In *Religions in Antiquity*, Essays in memory of Erwin Ramsdell Goodenough, edited by Jacob Neusner, Leiden: J. E. Brill, 1968. Pp. 463–75.

IV. MONOGRAPHS AND DISSERTATIONS ON MIRCEA ELIADE

Welbon, Guy Richard. "Mircea Eliade's Image of Man: An Anthropogeny by a Historian of Religions." M.A. thesis, Northwestern University, 1960.

Altizer, Thomas J. J. *Mircea Eliade and the Dialectic of the Sacred*. Philadelphia: The Westminster Press, 1963. 219 pp.

Duchêne, Henri. "Le Thème du Temps dans l'oeuvre de Mircea Eliade." Ph.D. dissertation, Université Catholique de Louvain, Faculty of Philosophy and Letters, 1965. 199 pp.

Saracino, Antoinetta. *Mircea Eliade, Novelle*. Ph.D. thesis, Università di Bari, Faculty of Letters, 1966. (Includes the Italian translation of *Nuvele* [Madrid, 1963].) 488 pp.

Critical Studies (with the exception of review articles)

Masui, Jacques. "Mythes et Symboles selon Mircea Eliade." *Les Cahiers du Sud*, no. 316 (1952): 478–90.

Revol, E. L. "Aproximación a la obra de Mircea Eliade." *La Torre* 1 (1953): 153–63.

Alvarez de Miranda, A. "Un tratado de Historia de las Religiones." *Cuadernos Hispanoamericanos*, no. 61 (1955): 109–12.

Frye, Northrop. "World Enough Without Time." *The Hudson Review* 12 (1959): 423–31.

Long, Charles. "Recent Developments in the History of Religions Field." *The Divinity School News* (University of Chicago), 26 (1959): 1–12.

Maguire, James J. "The New Look in Comparative Religion." *Perspectives* 5 (1960): 8–10.

Vázquez, Juan Adolfo. "Encuentro con Mircea Eliade." *La Gaceta*, June 26, 1960, p. 5.

Bharati, A. "Ueber Eliades Yogaanffassung." *Zeitschrift für Religions- und Geistesgeschichte* 12 (1960): 176–79.

Daniélou, Jean. "Témoignage sur Mircea Eliade." *Revue des Etudes Roumaines* 7–8 (1961): 217–18.

Pernet, Henry. "Rencontre avec Mircea Eliade." *Gazette de Lausanne*, September, 1961, p. 3.

Progoff, Ira. "Culture and Being: Mircea Eliade's Studies in Religion." *International Journal of Parapsychology* 3 (1961): 47–60.

Margul, Tadeusz. "Mircea Eliade jako teoretyk świetości i mitu." *Euhemer* 5 (1961): 36–52.

Altizer, Thomas J. J. "Mircea Eliade and the Recovery of the Sacred." *The Christian Scholar* 45 (1962): 267–89.

Mairet, Philip. "The Primordial Myths: A Note on the Works of Professor Mircea Eliade." *The Aryan Path* 34 (1963): 8–12.

Vázquez, Juan Adolfo. "Para una biobliografia de Mircea Eliade." *Universidad*, no. 59 (1964): 357–74.

Welbon, G. Richard. "Some Remarks on the Work of Mircea Eliade." *Acta Philosophica et Theologica* 2 (1964): 465–92.

Hof, Hans. "Religionsfenomelog med budskap: Mircea Eliade." *Vår Lösen*, June, 1965, pp. 251–56.

Hamilton, Kenneth. "Homo Religiosus and Historical Faith." *The Journal of Bible and Religion* 33 (1965): 213–22.

Kijowski, Andrzej. "Wizja ludzkości nieomylnej: Mircea Eliade, *Traité d'Histoire des Religions*." *Twórczość*, no. 10 (1965): 143–48.

Aner, Kerstin. "Mytens man." *Vår Lösen*, October, 1965, pp. 355–57.

"Myths for Moderns." *The Times Literary Supplement*, February 10, 1966, p. 102.

Luyster, Robert. "The Study of Myth: Two Approaches." *The Journal of Bible and Religion* 34 (1966): 235–43.

Wikander, Stig. "Mircea Eliade och den moderna religionsforskningen." *Svensk Missionstidskrift* 54 (1966): 217–24.

Ahlberg, Alf. "Mircea Eliade och de religiösa symbolerna." *Svenska Dagbladet*, September 21, 1966.

Ricketts, Mac Linscott. "Mircea Eliade and the Death of God." *Religion in Life*, Spring, 1967, pp. 40–52.

Penner, Hans H. "Bedeutung und Probleme der religiösen Symbolik bei Tillich und Eliade." *Antaois* 9 (1967): 127–43.

Ricketts, Mac Linscott. "Eliade and Altizer: Very Different Outlooks." *Christian Advocate*, October, 1967, pp. 11–12.

Hudson, Wilson M. "Eliade's Contributions to the Study of Myth." In *Tire Shrinker to Dragster*, edited by Texas Folklore Society. Austin, Texas: Encino Press, 1968. Pp. 218–41.

Rasmussen, David. "Mircea Eliade: Structural Hermeneutics and Philosophy." *Philosophy Today* 12 (1968): 138–146.

INDEX